# The End of Class Politics?

## *Class Voting in Comparative Context*

Edited by

GEOFFREY EVANS

OXFORD
UNIVERSITY PRESS

OXFORD
UNIVERSITY PRESS

Great Clarendon Street, Oxford OX2 6DP
Oxford University Press is a department of the University of Oxford.
It furthers the University's objective of excellence in research, scholarship, and education by publishing worldwide in

Oxford New York

Athens Auckland Bangkok Bogotá Buenos Aires Calcutta Cape Town Chennai Dar es Salaam Delhi Florence Hong Kong Istanbul Karachi Kuala Lumpur Madrid Melbourne Mexico City Mumbai Nairobi Paris São Paulo Singapore Taipei Tokyo Toronto Warsaw
with associated companies in Berlin Ibadan

Oxford is a registered trade mark of Oxford University Press in the UK and in certain other countries

Published in the United States by Oxford University Press Inc., New York



First published 1999 



British Library Cataloguing in Publication Data
Data available

Library of Congress Cataloging in Publication Data

The end of class politics? : class voting in comparative context / edited by Geoffrey Evans.
Includes bibliographical references.
1. Voting—History—20th century. 2. Social classes—Political aspects—History—20th century. I. Evans, Geoffrey.
JF1001.E528 1999 324.9182'1—dc21 99-19784

ISBN 0-19-828095-5
ISBN 0-19-829634-7 (Pbk.)

Typeset in Times by Best-set Typesetter Ltd., Hong Kong
Printed in Great Britain
on acid-free paper by
Biddles Ltd., Guildford and King's Lynn

# PREFACE

This book began as a panel on class and politics at the thirteenth World Congress of Sociology at Bielefeld in Germany in July 1994. At that meeting John Goldthorpe, Michael Hout, Paul Nieuwbeerta, and David Weakliem presented early versions of the papers that eventually became the chapters published here. The idea of a book certainly existed then, but its eventual fruition required further clarification and extension of both content and personnel. This was facilitated by the gathering together of many of the book's final contributors for a conference on 'The End of Class Politics?' at Nuffield College in February 1995 with funds generously provided by the Ford Foundation. Here the initial contributing authors were joined by new input from Kristen Ringdal and Stefan Svallfors, as well as further analyses from the initial group now joined by Anthony Heath. A special feature of this conference was the taped round-table session led by commentaries from John Goldthorpe, Michael Hout, Seymour Martin Lipset, and Peter Mair. After suitable editorial work these commentaries feature in Chapter 12 of this book.

Although the book was well under way after this meeting, there were important contributions still to be obtained. These arrived in the works by Petr Mateju and his co-authors and Walter Müller as well as in the addition of a chapter by Stephen Whitefield and myself on the emergence of class politics in Russia. These contributions helped broaden the focus from the well-trodden themes of class voting in Britain and the United States. This expansion of perspective not only mollified the (extremely helpful and supportive) reviewers for Oxford University Press but also facilitated the drawing of more robust conclusions about the conditional nature of trends in class voting and class politics—conclusions that form a key output of this work as a whole.

Other scholars have added to the debate and the work presented here, despite themselves not contributing written pieces: both Jan Jonsson in Bielefeld and Robert Erikson at the Nuffield meeting presented important papers and made valuable contributions to the discussions that followed. Terry Nichols Clark contributed an interesting if only electronic presence to the debate.

The resulting manuscript is a state-of-the-art analysis of the changing nature of class voting in advanced industrial societies. Considerable use is made of recent advances in loglinear and related modelling techniques that overcome many of the technical limitations that have characterized previous work on this fundamental issue in the political sociology of modern democracies. The use of these sophisticated analytic techniques owes a considerable debt to the robust critical environment provided by Research Committee 28 (stratification) of the International Sociological Association (ISA)—and many contributors are members of RC28. But the book also attempts to speak to an audience beyond the confines of social stratification and indeed of sociology more broadly construed. The study of political sociology forms part of political science and the aim here is to address the claims and assumptions of those many political scientists who have been concerned to understand politics not just in terms of the motives and activities of political actors and the institutions in which they take place, but with regard to the social contexts in which these occur. The book thus owes something to a body of work that has similarly straddled political sociology and political science—and which has likewise emerged from ISA meetings in 1970 and 1985. The ISA research committee on political sociology sponsored and provided the origins of influential works by Mark Franklin, Tom Mackie, Richard Rose, Henry Valen, and others. The present project has doubtless benefited from the efforts of these and other substantial contributors to our knowledge of the social bases of politics, although it should be clear to the reader that it disagrees on many points—theoretical, methodological, and substantive—with earlier research.

On a more personal front, various discussions, particularly those with Herbert Kitschelt—ever challenging and perceptive—on distinct but related topics, have likewise proved most helpful. John Goldthorpe displayed nerves of steel on the trip to Bielefeld and provided exemplary encouragement, not to say urgency, in his desire to ensure that the book emerged before too much time had passed.

# CONTENTS

# LIST OF TABLES

# LIST OF FIGURES

# LIST OF ABBREVIATIONS

| | |
|---|---|
| AFL–CIO | American Federation of Labor–Congress of Industrial Organizations |
| ALLBUS | Allgemeine Bevölkerungsumfrage der Sozialwissenschaft (General Social Survey for the Social Sciences) |
| ANES | American National Election Study |
| BES | British Election Surveys |
| BVA | Brule–Ville Associates |
| CBC | Centraal Bureau voor Statistiek |
| CCV | constant class voting |
| CDU | Christlich Demokratische Union |
| CNR | Czech National Council |
| DDA | Danish Data Archive |
| df | degrees of freedom |
| ESRC | Economic and Social Research Council |
| FDP | Freie Demokratische Partei |
| FS | Federal Assembly |
| GLIM | generalized linear interactive modelling program |
| GSS | General Social Survey |
| ICPSR | Inter-University Consortium for Political and Social Research |
| ILO | International Labour Office |
| INSEE | Institut National de la Statistique et des Études Économiques |
| ISA | International Sociological Association |
| ISCO | International Standard Classification of Occupations |
| ISSP | International Social Science Program |
| IVVM | Czech state-owned Institute for public opinion research |
| KCSM | Communist Party of Bohemia and Moravia |
| NORC | National Opinion Research Center |
| NSD | Norwegian Social Science Data Service |
| OLS | ordinary least squares |
| OPCS | Office of Population, Censuses, and Surveys |
| RC28 | Research Committee 28 |
| SCB | Statistika centralbyrån (Statistics Sweden) |
| SC&C | Czech privately owned public opinion and market research company |
| s.e. | standard error |

| | |
|---|---|
| SEG | socio-economic group |
| SEI | Swedish socio-economic classification |
| SEIU | Service Employees International Union |
| SOU | Sveriges Offentliga Utredningar (Swedish Public Commissions) |
| SPD | Sozialdemokratische Partei Deutschlands |
| SRC | Survey Research Center |
| SSDC | Social Science Data Archive |
| UNIDIFF | uniform difference model |
| WIIW | Institute for Comparative Economic Studies, Vienna |
| ZA | Zentral Archive |
| ZUMA | Zentrum für Umfragen, Methoden, und Analysen (Centre for Survey Research and Methodology) |
| ZUMABUS | ZUMA-Bevölkerungssurvey (Social Survey carried out by ZUMA) |

# LIST OF CONTRIBUTORS

Clem Brooks, Indiana University, Bloomington, Indiana, USA
Nan Dirk De Graaf, Department of Sociology, University of Nijmegen. Netherlands
Geoffrey Evans, Nuffield College, Oxford, England
John H. Goldthorpe, Nuffield College, Oxford, England
Anthony F. Heath, Nuffield College, Oxford, England
Kjell Hines, Department of Sociology and Political Science, Norwegian University of Science and Technology, Trondheim, Norway
Mike Hout, Survey Research Center, University of California, Berkeley, California, USA
Seymour Martin Lipset, The Institute of Public Policy, George Mason University, Fairfax, Virginia, USA
Peter Mair, Department of Politics, Rijksuniversiteit, Leiden, Netherlands
Jeff Manza, Pennsylvania State University, Pittsburgh, Pennsylvania, USA
Petr Mateju, Institute of Sociology, Academy of Sciences of the Czech Republic, Prague, Czech Republic
Walter Müller, University of Mannheim, Germany
Paul Nieuwbeerta, University of Utrecht, Utrecht, Netherlands
Blanka Rehakova, Institute of Sociology, Academy of Sciences of the Czech Republic, Prague, Czech Republic
Kristen Ringdal, Department of Sociology and Political Science, Norwegian University of Science and Technology, Dragvoll, Norway
Stefan Svallfors, Department of Sociology, Umea University, Sweden
David L. Weakliem, University of Connecticut, Storrs, Connecticut, USA
Stephen Whitefield, Pembroke College, Oxford, England

# 1

## Class Voting: From Premature Obituary to Reasoned Appraisal

GEOFFREY EVANS

### INTRODUCTION

The second half of the twentieth century has seen a prolonged debate over the importance of social class as a basis for political partisanship in advanced industrial societies. Much of the contribution to this debate has cast no little doubt on the significance of class voting and class politics. From being 'the motor of history', the basis of the 'democratic class struggle', class has for many become an outdated and increasingly irrelevant concept—more a part of 'folk memory' than a currently significant phenomenon. The arguments of postmodernists and disillusioned socialists have been combined with those of 'end of ideology' liberals and numerous empirical researchers to assert that class inequality has lost its political importance. Where it does survive, class politics has been redefined and reconstructed so that race, or gender, or 'new politics' issues replace the economic conflicts derived from class-based divisions of interests. Historically, the latter have formed the core of the left–right dimension of political competition in industrial societies. Now, in an age of 'postisms'—postmodernism, postindustrialism, poststructuralism, postmarxism, postfeminism, postmaterialism—class has apparently lost its salience. Depending on which authors one examines, different sources of interests have taken precedence, or the material inequalities associated with class are no longer central to politics, or 'voters have begun to choose'—in that their preferences are no longer structured sociologically—so that no less than 'the end of cleavage politics' is upon us.[1]

[1] The case for the decline of class is given in, for example, Clark and Lipset's 'Are Social Classes Dying?' (1991; see also Clark *et al.* 1993); a 'new politics' explanation of this change is presented succinctly in Lipset's *Political Man* (1981: 503–21) and in many of Inglehart's writings (e.g. Inglehart and Rabier 1986). Bauman's *Memories of Class* (1982) and Gorz's *Farewell to the Working Class* (1982) are examples of 'evidence-free' dismissals of class politics with more or less remorse at its demise. Franklin's *The Decline of Class Voting in Britain* (1985*a*) and Huckfeldt and Kohfeld's *Race and the*

While some class politics proselytizers have remained unmoved by these pronouncements,[2] it appears to have become commonplace to assume that the debate has been resolved, that class position—the 'old-fashioned' notion of class position derived from occupation and/or employment status—is no longer an important source of political preferences and is no longer consequential for political analysis. Increasingly, it would appear that the debate over the political consequences of class is becoming—even *has been*—resolved in favour of those who would declare it redundant—or at least in terminal decline.

Significantly, however, despite the considerable appeal that these pronouncements appear to have had, the empirical implications of these many examples of 'post-class' reasoning have not usually been subject to rigorous scrutiny; or even where there has been research purporting to do so, it is rather seriously flawed. This book is an attempt to address this important deficiency. It does so by presenting a state-of-the-art account of the changing nature of class voting in advanced industrial societies.[3] It combines broad-ranging comparative analysis with detailed country-specific studies and empirical tests of key theoretical and methodological explanations of changing levels of class voting. It concludes with commentaries from distinguished scholars from sociology and political science and a reconsideration of the implications for class politics of the changing nature of class structures.

Even as the finishing touches were being applied to this volume, the pressing need for such an enterprise was reiterated and illustrated with

*Decline of Class in American Politics* (1989) provide somewhat more empirical evidence for their claims. Kitschelt's analysis of *The Transformation of European Social Democracy* (1994) is explicit in its treatment of post-class party strategies. Eder's *The New Politics of Class* (1993) is a good example of an exercise in redefinition with no empirical basis, while in their portentous *The Death of Class*, Pakulski and Waters (1996) fare little better (on which, see Marshall 1997: 16–18). Rose and McAllister also make their 'end of class politics' agenda explicit in '*Voters Begin to Choose: From Closed-Class to Open Elections in Britain* (1986), while the idea of 'the end of cleavage politics' more generally, is most extensively advocated in Franklin *et al.*'s *Electoral Change* (1992).

[2] See, among others, Vanneman and Cannon's, *The American Perception of Class* (1987); Heath *et al.* (1985, 1991: 62–84); Evans (1993*a*); Evans *et al.* (1991, 1996); Goldthorpe's review of 'Class and politics in advanced industrial societies' (1996*a*); Marshall *et al.* 1988; Marshall (1997); Hout *et al.* (1993, 1995); Brooks and Manza (1997).

[3] The term class voting is used here to refer not just to the act of voting, but to intended vote and other expressions of party support. Even within this broad remit, the question of class and *politics* is of course being narrowed down to just one of its aspects—that is, the class basis of political preferences. Justification for this, limitations of space apart, lies in the considerable emphasis placed upon the supposed weakening of the class–vote link by those who have argued both for and against the decline of class politics.

some force when a major piece of research and argument by an eminent scholar appeared on the bookshelves. This substantial and far-reaching tome contained by chance an interesting entrée to the issues examined in the chapters that follow. Despite the book's many qualities, the main value of its author's observations on class voting and class politics is to provide a significant example of the general confusion and, arguably, ignorance that abounds with respect to the debates addressed here. For Ronald Inglehart (1997: 237):

> The shift towards postmodern values has brought a shift in the political agenda throughout advanced industrial society, moving it away from an emphasis on economic growth at any price towards increasing concern for its environmental costs. It has also brought a shift from political cleavages based on social class conflict toward cleavages based on cultural issues and quality of life concerns.

Unsurprisingly, it would appear, 'social class-based voting has declined markedly over the past 40 years' (1997: 254) as societies have moved from a modern to a postmodern political environment. His presentation (p. 255) of the by now *de rigueur* diagram based on Robert Alford's ubiquitous index showing class voting declining across the board to more or less insignificance would seem to clinch the issue (see also e.g. Inglehart 1984, 1990: chapter 8).

Despite the firm assuredness of these statements, Inglehart concedes that there 'has been extensive recent debate over whether social class voting has really been declining'. For him, however, opposition to his thesis would appear to rely on a misleading focus on 'selected periods for selected countries', or in the substitution of the 'theoretically clear and easy to operationalize' manual–nonmanual distinction using the 'simple and straightforward' Alford index by more complex measures of occupation accompanied by the use of logistic regression techniques. Particularly singled out in this respect are Hout, Brooks, and Manza (1993) for their 'questionable' interpretation of their logistic regression results. As an antidote to this apparent obfuscation, we are referred to an analysis using 'a massive database from 16 societies across four decades, and using more appropriate methodology' in which 'Nieuwbeerta and De Graaf (forthcoming) find a clear overall decline in class voting' (Inglehart 1997: 255–6).

This dismissal of the work of authors whose findings and interpretations run counter to Inglehart's ideas concerning the emergence of postmodern politics is perhaps understandable: no one likes seeing his or her cherished theories apparently threatened by inconvenient empirical findings. But the advertisement for at least part of *this* book contained in these excerpts (the forthcoming paper referred to by Inglehart is Nieuwbeerta and De Graaf's chapter in this volume) is merely a partial, in both senses, introduction to the complexities of class voting. As readers will see, Nieuwbeerta and De Graaf in fact use very much the same techniques—loglinear modelling and logistic regression—as do Hout, Manza, and Brooks in their latest analysis of these issues which also appears here, and as indeed do almost all of the authors in this volume. They will also see that the theoretical supremacy of the manual–nonmanual divide and the appealing simplicity of the Alford index are illusory. And even the apparently straightforward issue of 'when is a trend a trend'—rather than, for example, a discrete one-step change—is not as easy as Inglehart and others might believe.

The chapters that follow are not themselves constrained by any rigid orthodoxy, whether in terms of how class and vote (or proxies for vote) are measured, or the techniques of analysis used, or in the definition of what class voting is—and is not. Thus a simple class dealignment model is proposed and examined by some authors, whereas others examine patterns of realignment, and another models the structure of what is constant about class politics. Most authors assess the patterns of partisanship, but attention is also given by some to the class basis of nonvoting. One chapter examines class voting across many countries; most others tackle only one detailed case study. Some consider only class, while others examine class voting in a multivariate context. Most chapters look at the demographics of class politics, but a few examine also its attitudinal elements.

By the time this weight of evidence and debate has been considered, the reader will be forced to conclude that the thesis of a generalized decline in the class basis of voting in advanced industrial societies is, quite simply, wrong. On balance, indeed, it might well be more plausible to argue that class politics is actually increasing as the marketizing former-communist societies of Eastern Europe, many of whom are likely to be members of an expanded European Union in the not too distant future, display all of the signs of class-based political *polarization*. In short, the terms of the debate will have changed.

## SETTING THE CONTEXT

Before previewing what each of the chapters contributes to the aims of the book, it first makes sense to locate them within the debates on class voting and to clarify which assumptions are shared by the contributors and which form foci of dispute. This involves two elements: a brief summary of themes and issues that have emerged from research on class voting; and an introduction to the corresponding questions about method and measurement that underlie many of the substantive debates.

## Changing Class Voting?

It is not necessary to illustrate the history of research on class voting in any extended way because several useful reviews are already in circulation. Goldthorpe (1996*a*), Hout, Brooks, and Manza (1995), and Nieuwbeerta (1995) have between them supplied insightful and comprehensive examinations of various trends and issues in the area. Suffice to say, early studies in this genre found that in general 'lower-class' voters were more likely to vote for left-wing political parties than were those in 'higher' classes. Substantial cross-national differences were also discovered, with Scandinavia and Britain having the highest levels of class voting and the United States and Canada the lowest.[4] These ad hoc comparisons of different studies from different countries were inevitably rather restricted in their degree of comparability: in some cases, for example, income was used to measure social and economic position, whereas in others education or occupation was used. Even when researchers used the same type of measure, classifications often varied from the very detailed to the very crude.[5] Only since the 1970s have studies included comparable data, measures of class position, and measures of class voting from more than a handful of countries.[6]

The most noteworthy ancestor of the present work has to be Alford's (1963, 1967) early attempt at a systematic cross-national analysis. He examined trends in class voting in four Anglo-American democracies (Australia, Britain, Canada, and the United States) between 1936 and 1962, using a measure of social and economic position in which occupations were aggregated to form a dichotomous manual/nonmanual class division. This became standard practice in the cross-national and over time analyses that followed, and which usually concluded that class voting is in fact in decline: Lipset (1981: 505) presented evidence of a downward trend in Britain, Germany, and the United States between 1945 and 1980; Inglehart (1990: 260 and above) found further evidence of a continuing decline from the early 1980s onwards; Sainsbury (1987, 1990) found a decline in class voting

[4] Some of these studies were impressionistic (Sombart 1976/1906; Sorokin 1959/1927) or used aggregated ecological data (Tingsten 1937; Siegfried 1913), but by the 1950s nationally representative surveys of the electorate appeared in the United States (e.g. Campbell *et al.* 1960) and a range of other Western industrialized countries (Den Uyl 1951; Valen and Katz 1967; Alford 1963; MacRae 1967; Butler and Stokes 1974; Lipset and Zetterberg 1956). Nieuwbeerta's (1995) exhaustive review gives more details.

[5] In his comparison of Britain, France, and Italy, for example, Lipset (1960) did not present any standardized measure of class voting. Similar points apply to the studies collated by Rose and Urwin (1969) and Rose (1974*a*).

[6] See Books and Reynolds's (1975) review of research on a number of Western industrialized countries in the 1960s. Korpi (1983: 35) presents data showing differences across eighteen countries in the 1970s.

in the Scandinavian countries; while Lane and Ersson (1994: 94) found less class voting in nine Western industrialized nations in the 1970s and 1980s compared with the 1950s and 1960s and stronger levels of class voting in only two (France and Italy).[7]

On the basis of this sort of evidence, Clark and Lipset have argued that: 'Class analysis has grown increasingly inadequate in recent decades as traditional hierarchies have declined and new social differences have emerged'. (Clark and Lipset 1991: 397). They conclude that politics is now 'less organized by class and more by other loyalties' (Clark and Lipset 1991: 408). Moreover, this general position has been endorsed by an extensive cross-national study of electoral change and the decline of cleavage politics between the 1960s and the 1980s compiled by Mark Franklin, Tom Mackie, and Henry Valen (1992). This project modelled voting behaviour ('left' versus 'non-left') in no less than sixteen countries, including as explanatory variables social characteristics such as class (manual/non-manual), religion, trade union membership, sex, education, and issue/value orientations. No other study has employed such a wide range of comparative evidence with which to address questions raised in the sociology of politics. In his summary of the implications of the research reported in the book, Mark Franklin observes that 'almost all of the countries we have studied show a decline during our period in the ability of social cleavages to structure individual voting choice' (1992: 385; see also p. 387: figure 19.1).[8]

For many commentators, then, arguments about *whether* class voting has declined are no longer the issue: the question is *why* has the class basis of voting declined? Unsurprisingly, there has been a plethora of candidates for this role. From Goldthorpe (1996*a*) and Manza, Hout, and Brooks (1995), among others, we can discern five types of explanation for the decline of class voting in modern industrial societies:

1. In such societies social class has lost some or all of its importance as a determinant of life-chances and in consequence its influence as a source of divergent political interests. This has happened because of processes such as the 'embourgeoisement' of the working class, or the 'proletarianization' of white-collar work, and the presence of extensive intragenerational and intergenerational social mobility.

[7] See also, Andeweg (1982) on the Netherlands; Abramson *et al.* (1990) on the United States; Baker *et al.* (1981) on Germany; Franklin (1985*a*) and Kelley *et al.* (1985) on Britain; Listhaug (1989) on Norway; Kemp (1978) on Australia; Stephens (1981) on Sweden.

[8] Unfortunately, the failure to present suitable tests of the statistical significance of these over-time changes in explained variance makes an assessment of this claim rather difficult—notwithstanding the other limitations of the analysis, such as the use of OLS regression models with dichotomous dependent variables (see below).

2. New 'postindustrial' social cleavages are emerging and replacing class-based conflict. The significance of class position for voting behaviour has decreased as 'new' forms of social differentiation have become more important for political interests (gender, race, ethnicity, public and private production and consumption sectors, various 'identity groups', and so on).
3. Because of a general increase in levels of education and 'cognitive mobilization', identity-based responses to class-based divisions of interest are being replaced by the expression of preferences that reflect voters' increasing ability to make electoral decisions that are calculative and 'issue oriented' rather than driven by collective identities.
4. Values are becoming more important as a basis of party preference and cross-cutting the impact of social class. In particular, the increasing influence of postmaterial values has led to the traditional, class-based, left–right political continuum losing its importance for voting behaviour; the 'new left' draws its support from the middle classes thus weakening the class basis of left–right divisions.
5. Finally, since the manual working class has declined as a proportion of the electorate, left-wing parties have had to direct their programmes towards the concerns of the growing middle classes or face continued electoral defeat. They have therefore moderated the class character of their political appeals and weakened the class distinctiveness of the political choices facing the electorate.

Whatever their strengths and weaknesses—and there are many questions and doubts that remain unresolved in each case—all of these explanations tend to assume that the explanandum is unproblematic; that class voting has declined in a predictably general way; that there is indeed a widespread, secular decline in class-based political action which has then to be explained. But as readers will see, the findings contained in this book are directly at odds with the prevalence among both political scientists and sociologists of this generalized conception of the declining class basis of politics. The answer to the rhetorical question in the title of this book is a clear 'no', but the actual nature of changes in class voting and class politics is not easily summarized. It is, in truth, not a matter of being 'alive' or 'dead', as some of the discussants of its character have been apt to suggest. The question is whether, as advanced industrial societies have become increasingly *post*industrial, the pattern of class voting is *evolving* and how we might understand the form such evolution might be taking. The answer to that question will be strongly conditioned by the ways in which it is addressed: in other words, by issues of method and measurement. The empirical literature reviewed above, despite its apparent cumulative solidity, is characterized by shortcomings in both these respects.

## Method and Measurement

Detailed discussions of method and measurement are to be found in the chapters that follow, but some generic issues are usefully summarized here. Two areas are considered: operationalization and analysis. The main choices with respect to the former are considered and resolved in this section. Analytical issues are given an airing both now—at least for some relatively basic points—and in later chapters, where proponents of differing approaches consider their merits and shortcomings.

### *Operationalizing Class Position*

As readers will see, in this book a single interpretation of class structure has been adopted with little difference of opinion among the contributors. The measurement of class focuses almost exclusively on the notion of class position developed by John Goldthorpe and his colleagues, particularly Robert Erikson. My aim here is to explain why this choice was not contentious.

Class position is a much-abused construct. As we have observed, it often appears as a dichotomy of manual versus nonmanual workers. Sometimes allocation to classes is on the basis of subjective estimation and sometimes from some more or less rigorous interviewer classification. Sometimes, even when it is possible to measure class with greater discrimination, authors choose not to do so in order to facilitate cross-national comparison. Franklin, Mackie, and Valen's book referred to above is the clearest recent example of this practice. Not only class position, but all variables in their models—with the exception of the additional analyses contributed by some authors—are constrained to be a dichotomy.

The problem with the manual/nonmanual distinction, however, is that in pursuit of comparability it both impoverishes our measurement of class position and, by extension, obscures variations in the composition of the manual and nonmanual classes. Such changes in composition may in turn lead to spurious change in estimates of class voting. For example, if skilled manual workers are more conservative than unskilled manual workers and the number of skilled workers increases, the difference between manual and nonmanual workers will decline even if the relative political positions of skilled, unskilled, and nonmanual workers remain the same.[9]

Unsurprisingly, many sociologists have argued for the employment of a more detailed internationally comparable class schema in place of the

[9] The only way to completely eliminate the possibility of composition effects is to distinguish a very large number of occupational groups, which is not practical in most cases. We can at least assume, however, that composition effects will be less serious as the number of classes becomes greater, so going beyond the manual/nonmanual dichotomy will help to reduce them.

essentially atheoretical manual/nonmanual dichotomy. But the adoption of a more complex measure must be grounded in some conceptual distinction that is not simply an ad hoc augmentation of the two-class model in the hope of increasing predictive power. Otherwise, such a strategy can rightly be criticized for simply adding new distinctions that have no clear rationale in an attempt to save an inadequate theory from empirical refutation. In other words, the divisions between classes have to have some justification other than that they can predict things such as voting. Class divisions should be defined in terms of—and be shown to measure—a defensible concept of class position (see Evans 1998).

The Goldthorpe (or Erikson–Goldthorpe) class schema has exactly this characteristic. The schema was originally developed by John Goldthorpe and various colleagues (i.e. Goldthorpe 1980, 1987; Erikson, Goldthorpe, and Portocarrero 1979), and later elaborated by Erikson and Goldthorpe (1992*a*: 36–42; Goldthorpe 1997).[10] Versions of it have been widely used in comparative studies of intergenerational class mobility (see Ganzeboom *et al.* 1989, 1992; Erikson and Goldthorpe 1992*a*), and in those examining the relationship between class and voting behaviour.[11] The main classes identified by the schema are the petty bourgeoisie (small employers and self-employed), the service class—or salariat (professional and managerial groups, subdivided into 'higher' and 'lower'), the routine nonmanual class (typically lower grade clerical 'white-collar workers'), and the working class (subdivided into semi- and unskilled manual workers, skilled manual workers, and foremen and technicians). The schema can be used with a greater or lesser number of these distinctions depending on the needs of particular analyses and the information available to the researcher.[12] As each of the chapters using the schema presents information on the versions employed in their analyses, it is necessary at this point to elaborate only on the general conceptualization underlying the construction of the schema.

'The aim of the schema is to differentiate positions within *labour markets* and *production units* . . . . in terms of the *employment relations* that they

[10] Note that the Goldthorpe *class* schema is not to be confused with the Hope–Goldthorpe scale of the '*general desirability*' of occupations (Goldthorpe and Hope 1974).

[11] See, among others, Heath *et al.* (1985, 1991); Weakliem (1989, 1995*a*); Evans *et al.* (1991, 1996); Evans (1993*a*); Evans and Whitefield (1995*a*); De Graaf *et al.* (1995); Nieuwbeerta (1995); Ringdal and Hynes (1995). Goldthorpe and Marshall (1992) and Goldthorpe (1996*a*) provide more general reviews.

[12] The class schema is to be preferred to continuous prestige or status measures because it identifies more effectively particular category-based (i.e. farmers and other self-employed) and other non-linear sources of political orientations. It also allows more effective comparison of the sizes of different categories over time and cross-nationally.

entail' (Erikson and Goldthorpe 1992*a*: 37; emphasis in original). The notion of employment relations is represented in the first instance by the distinction between employers, the self-employed, and employees—a familiar set of class categories that reflects the origins of the schema in both Marxist and Weberian traditions of class analysis. More distinctive are the divisions made between classes *within* the category of employees: 'It is ... the distinction between employees involved in a *service relationship* with their employer and those whose employment relationships are essentially regulated by a *labour contract* that underlies the way in which, within our class schema, different employee classes have been delineated' (Erikson and Goldthorpe 1992*a*: 41–2; emphasis added).

Service relationships 'involve a longer-term and generally more diffuse exchange. Employees render service to their employing organization in return for "compensation" which takes the form not only of reward for work done, through a salary and various perquisites, but also comprises important *prospective* elements—for example, salary increments on an established scale, assurances of security both in employment and, through pensions rights, after retirement, and, above all, well-defined career opportunities.' Such employment relationships tend to evolve 'where it is required of employees that they *exercise delegated authority or specialised knowledge and expertise* in the interests of their employing organisation' (Erikson and Goldthorpe 1992*a*: 42; emphasis in original). The service relationship is contrasted with the labour contract typical of other wage-earning classes, notably of the working class. The labour contract entails 'a relatively short-term and specific exchange of money for effort. Employees supply more-or-less discrete amounts of labour, under the supervision of the employer or of the employer's agents, in return for wages which are calculated on a "piece" or time basis' (Erikson and Goldthorpe 1992*a*: 41–2).

Thus the mechanism of control by which loyalty is obtained from service-class employees is via advancement and perks—in particular, unless employees carry out their tasks adequately, they are unlikely to receive the long-term benefits of career advancement that characterize service-class employment. In contrast, working-class employees receive payment for work done over a shorter time-span and are closely supervised to make sure that they carry out that work. Service-class employees are controlled by the 'carrot' of long-term benefits, and workers by the 'stick' of close regulation and the labour contract. The main distinguishing characteristics of Goldthorpe's classes—their conditions of employment and payment, degree of occupational security, and promotion prospects—derive from these differing employment relations.[13]

[13] In earlier expositions of the schema, Goldthorpe (1980: 39, 1987: 40) referred to a somewhat more inclusive set of characteristics by which classes are differentiated. I focus here on Erikson and Goldthorpe's (1992*a*) and Goldthorpe's (1997) more recent elaborations of the core principles underlying the construction of the schema.

Goldthorpe (1997) further outlines why and how particular classes in the schema map onto the distribution of these employment relations or, more explicitly, *contracts* among workforces. The accuracy of the schema for operationalizing these conceptual distinctions underpinning its use has been empirically evaluated through the sort of validation programme that no other measure of class position has yet received (see Evans 1992, 1996, 1998; Evans and Mills 1998*a*, 1998*b*, 1999).[14] These tests show that, under a variety of conditions, position in the schema strongly predicts the theoretically defined aspects of employment relations identified in Erikson and Goldthorpe's writings; this applies whether examining all employees, or men and women separately, when using cross-national data, when controlling for influences on employment relations, and when using various aggregated versions of the schema.

When the schema is used to examine political behaviour, characteristics of the employment relationship are given explanatory primacy over factors such as income or social status (see Evans 1993*b*; Goldthorpe 1996*a*). As the employment relationship of the service class is relatively advantageous in terms of employment and payment conditions, occupational security, and promotion prospects, its members have a stake in preserving the status quo. This leads Goldthorpe (1982: 180) to expect that 'the service class . . . as it consolidates, will constitute an essentially conservative element within modern societies'. In contrast, the disadvantages of the labour contract can explain why the working class provides a basis of support for the redistributive programmes of the left.

### *Operationalizing Political Preference*

As well as a general agreement on the preferred way to measure class position, the following chapters also share—if not to the same degree—certain principles with respect to the measurement of partisanship. The treatment of political systems as left versus non-left is a feature of many influential works in political sociology. As we have seen, not only Alford's early study but also more contemporary projects such as that of Franklin, Mackie, and Valen (1992) display this proclivity. The main reason for the perpetuation of this questionable practice seems to be a desire to make the systematic

[14] The preferred procedure for allocating individuals to such positions within the schema involves using employment status information (i.e. self-employed, employee, management) and, for employees, information obtained from job descriptions concerning the employment contracts that are characteristic of different occupational categories. For this purpose, Goldthorpe and Heath (1992) provide a detailed listing of occupations and the classes they should be allocated to when using the latest British official classification of occupations. As will be seen, because of the practical problems in adapting and using this algorithm, some of the following chapters have adopted other strategies.

comparisons that are a key feature of the *Electoral Change* (ibid.) and similar projects. The problem is, of course, that the selective nature of what is being compared undermines any true comparability across systems. More importantly, it can undermine any attempt to assess over time trends or cross-national variability. The problem is analogous to that faced in the analysis of class position. Changes in the composition of party choice categories such as 'left' or 'non-left' may lead to spurious changes in estimates of class voting. For example, if 'the left' in a given country is constructed by aggregating communists, socialists, and social democrats, each of which has a different relationship to class position, any changes in the size of these parties over time will cause the class basis of the left and non-left to change even if the relative class support for communists, socialists, and social democrats remains the same.

The use of dichotomies to represent vote choices and social classes also precludes from observation any processes of class–party *realignment*. The concept of class *re*alignment in voting implies a change in the pattern of association between class and vote without any reduction in the overall strength of this association—that is, without class *de*alignment (or, of course, an increase in alignment). But this cannot be discerned if the distinction between realignment and dealigment is prevented by restricting the numbers of parties and classes to two in each case.

For example, in a two-by-two (manual/nonmanual by left/right), class–vote table an over-time switch by routine nonmanual workers from right-wing parties to left-wing parties would indicate class–party dealignment. On further examination, however, we might find that although routine nonmanual workers had changed their vote from right to left, their tendency to have an affinity to any one party remained unchanged. This would be evidence of an equivalently strong but different pattern of class voting. If we then expanded the number of parties considered, we might also observe that routine nonmanual workers now voted for just one 'left-wing' party whereas before their vote had been scattered among several 'right-wing' parties. In this case, we would be observing both class realignment and increased alignment. Exactly the same over-time change would be interpreted as evidence for dealignment, realignment, and increasing alignment as a function only of the specification of class and vote.

As will be seen in several of the empirical chapters and in the concluding commentaries and discussion, the issue of class–party realignment is central to an awareness of the continuing significance of the class basis of voting. In almost all of the chapters that follow, partisanship—whether measured as voting, intended vote, or party identity—is measured as more than just a dichotomy. The only chapter that deviates from this practice—on practical rather than principled grounds—is that by Nieuwbeerta and De Graaf.

## *Analysis*

Despite, or more likely because of, the high levels of technical expertise displayed by the contributors, there are many differences in analytic technique employed in the empirically focused chapters. Questions relating to statistical techniques are addressed in many of these chapters, but certain issues can usefully be summarized or at least signalled here. These can be divided into the reasonably well established and the still disputed.

In the first category we can place the decision to use logistic models to estimate the empirical relationship between classes and parties rather than more traditional indices of association such as that proposed by Robert Alford. The 'Alford index' is simply the difference between the percentage of manual workers that voted for left-wing political parties on the one hand and the percentage of nonmanual workers that voted for these parties on the other. With this and similar measures (i.e. Rose and McAllister's (1986: 37–9) index of determination), the measurement of the class–vote association is open to confounding by changes in the marginal distributions of the class-by-vote table deriving from changes in the class structure and in the general popularity of the parties. In other words, this type of index confounds differences in the marginal distributions of the variables with differences in the association it is supposed to measure. Exactly the same problem applies to the use of apparently more sophisticated linear (ordinary least squares) regression techniques. These indices are again not 'margin insensitive' (for further discussion, see Evans *et al.* 1991; Hout *et al.* 1995).[15]

In contrast, indices of relative class voting that are based on *odds ratios* measure the strength of the relationship between class and vote independently of the general popularity of political parties or changes in the size of classes. The use of logistic modelling techniques—adapted from research into social mobility (Hauser 1978; Erikson and Goldthorpe 1992*a*)—capitalizes on this basic feature of the odds ratio. So far, though, only a relatively limited number of class–vote studies have been

[15] Thus, as they are aware, the analyses reported in Franklin *et al.*'s book should preferably have used logistic rather than linear regression (Franklin *et al.* 1992: 435–6). As with the measurement limitations described above, the desire for cross-national consistency again appears to have led to the adoption of the lowest common denominator—although the authors of one or two country-specific chapters are clearly uncomfortable with this editorially imposed constraint and supplement it with their own more appropriate analysis (see e.g. the comments of Pappi and Mnich 1992: 191–2). The attempt to avoid the problems of bias in regression coefficients by emphasizing variance explained (Franklin *et al.* 1992: 436) not only fails to alleviate the technical and interpretative problems faced when using dichotomous dependent variables with linear regression models, but more than likely accentuates them (on which see King 1986, among others).

undertaken using these innovations: Heath *et al.* (1985, 1991), Weakliem (1989, 1995*a*), and Evans, Heath, and Payne (1991) modelled class voting in Britain and examined whether 'trendless fluctuation', a linear trend, or 'one-off' changes best captured the pattern of association in class voting over time; subsequent analyses tested for evidence of trends using 'uniform difference' models (Erikson and Goldthorpe 1992*a*; Xie 1992) in Britain, the United States, and Norway (Heath *et al.* 1995; Hout *et al.* 1995; and Ringdal and Hines 1995, respectively). The research reported here develops and consolidates this paradigm.

Less consensual is the extent to which models of class voting benefit from multivariate analysis. Readers versed in literature on voting which employs multivariate analysis will notice that in many of the following chapters there are relatively few independent variables—and in some cases (i.e. Chapter 3) just one: class position. Many familiar control variables—party identity, education, gender, political attitudes, left–right self-placement, for example—are not to be found. Are such models underspecified? I think not: although it is commonly assumed that 'multivariate is better', we often do not have a sufficient understanding of the relations between our independent variables, and between various independent variables and the dependent variable, to clearly understand what controlling for them implies. It makes little sense to include party identity or political attitudes in our models if such indicators of political orientation are part of what is to be explained. Class position is clearly distinct from the expression of political orientation, but party identity and the expression of attitudes on political issues are not. The effects of class position on voting can also be expected to be interpreted via experiences such as trade union membership. If controlling for union membership reduces the effect of class position on vote, it does not necessarily signify the weakness of class—if anything, it gives an insight into the mechanisms through which class position affects political orientation. Clearly, then, given that the choice of controls is not an exact science—and we do not usually have the benefits (or costs) of laboratory conditions in social research (cf. Lieberson 1985)—it is valuable to examine both multivariate and univariate models of the outcomes of social and political change. Also, of course, this book is particularly concerned with describing the relationship between class and vote over time. If changes in other variables, whether in their relations with class position or their relations with vote, have affected the strength and/or pattern of the class–vote relationship, then this should be observable without controlling for other variables. The *explanation* of such changes might benefit from a multivariate analysis, but their *consequences* should be apparent at the univariate level.

Finally, in the pages that follow there are questions of analytical method that are disputed even among the contributors to this volume who in other respects display marked agreement. In this category are differences in opinion over the emphasis put on more inductive versus more theory-driven approaches to data analysis. Examples of the former include *association models* (see Goodman 1987; Chapters 5 and 11 in this volume) while the latter appear here in the form of *topological models* (see Chapter 3). The relative appropriateness of these procedures depends to some extent on the degree to which expectations derived from theory can be assumed to be reliable and precise. On these issues, the reader is left to judge for his or herself. The main point to be kept in mind is whether or not the choice of these approaches itself affects the substantive conclusions reached by the authors. This possibility will be considered in the final section of the book.

## THE FOLLOWING CHAPTERS

The major part of this book features empirical studies that in combination provide both breadth and depth, ranging from an analysis of change over (up to) forty years across twenty countries, to detailed analyses of several important cases. The evidence is obtained mainly from surveys conducted as the basis of the election studies undertaken in each country or, as for example in Germany, a country's general social survey. Considerable use is made of recent advances in loglinear and related modelling techniques, but the issues raised in the empirical chapters are also discussed in a non-technical manner in the final section through a set of commentaries.

### *Class Voting in Advanced Industrial Societies*

We start with a remarkably wide-ranging analysis of Western democracies: Paul Nieuwbeerta and Nan Dirk De Graaf's 'Traditional Class Voting in Twenty Postwar Societies' is a major piece of work. It sets the agenda for many of the ensuing chapters by presenting a uniquely broad-ranging analysis on the basis of which it is argued that there has been a decline in levels of class voting in many, though not all, of these countries. It also addresses the implications of different ways of estimating the class–vote association and tests explanations of patterns of change that refer to national and over-time variations in the changing composition of classes. The scope of this work is such that it forms a reference point for many of the more focused chapters, some of which are not in agreement with Nieuwbeerta and De Graaf's findings. In a sense, then, this chapter provides at least an implicit 'target' for some of the case studies presented in Part II. Can the broad generalizations, bought at the cost of minimizing data-quality requirements and the measuring vote as a dichotomy, survive closer scrutiny?

This scrutiny takes place first in three traditionally important contexts among advanced industrial societies: Great Britain, the United States, and France. In 'Modelling the Pattern of Class Voting in British Elections, 1964–1992', John Goldthorpe takes a very different view from Nieuwbeerta and De Graaf. In his chapter the structure of association between classes and parties in Britain is examined over a thirty-year period using log-multiplicative and topological models. He argues that there is a substantial degree of stability in class–party associations over the period. The topological models show also that realignment has not occurred to any degree: the major changes over this period have been in the *overall* popularity of the main political parties. He also considers briefly the implications of the events surrounding the 1997 General Election for assessments of the future of class voting in Britain.

In 'Classes, Unions, and the Realignment of US Presidential Voting, 1952–1992', Michael Hout, Jeff Manza, and Clem Brooks argue that there has been significant *re*alignment, but not *de*alignment, in class voting in American post-war politics. Professionals and routine white-collar workers have shifted towards the Democrats, whereas the self-employed and managers have become more strongly Republican and class differences in non-voting have increased. Changes in the gender composition of classes, and in trade union involvement, explain some but not all of these changes. The authors focus instead on the role of political parties in producing realignment through their choice of policies and electoral strategies.

The first of the two chapters by David Weakliem and Anthony Heath is an ambitious attempt to conduct detailed analyses of change over three societies. 'The Secret Life of Class Voting: Britain, France, and the United States since the 1930s' introduces a range of evidence previously neglected in research into the social bases of electoral behaviour. By combining data from sources such as Gallup and the American General Social Survey, the authors' analysis extends back to a period before the standard election surveys, permitting better evaluation of claims about long-run trends and the potential to distinguish them more effectively from short-term fluctuations. Their most striking findings are the differences between the three nations: not only is there no convergence over the period in levels of class voting, but in some ways national differences increased. The idea that general social and economic trends drive changes in politics is unsupported. So too are simple models of the impact of ideological polarization between parties.

Walter Müller's exceptionally detailed study of the development of political cleavages over twenty or so years in the Federal German Republic combines class analysis with considerations of several competing perspectives on the character of the social bases of politics. He also formulates his own explicit hypotheses about the rise of the 'new politics' agenda—of particular importance in the German context—and its relation to differing class interests. Despite the complexity of the empirical analysis, which includes measures of education, gender, age cohort, union membership, and postmaterialism: '[T]he data argue for a quite astonishing constancy in the differences in party orientation among the antagonists of the classical class cleavage.' He also finds that the 'new politics' does appear to have a clear class basis, and one which is plausibly derived from interests linked to position in the class structure.

Two quite different contributions examine Scandinavia—generally considered the home of a highly developed form of class politics. Kristen Ringdal and Kjell Hines's 'Changes in Class Voting in Norway 1957–1989' examines trends in relative class voting in parliamentary elections over thirty years using an aggregation of four party groupings (Socialist Left, Labour, Centre, Conservative) to represent the main choices in the Norwegian multi-party system. As with several other chapters, these models are estimated both with and without controls for demographic variables. The main finding is a decline in class voting, especially in the traditional axis of class voting between the service and the working classes. Much of this decline appeared during a relatively short period of time in the 1960s. Ironically, the reason for this change appears to be the political success of class politics, in which universalistic welfare legislation—in part a response to the strength of the working-class movement—led to an erosion of middle-class opposition to social democracy.

The second of these Scandinavian excursions, 'The Class Politics of Swedish Welfare Policies' by Stefan Svallfors, pursues the implications of the practice of social democracy for social cleavages in more detail using extensive multivariate analyses. This chapter does not examine voting *per se*, but focuses on the relative importance of class as a basis of orientation towards several different aspects of the key policy programme divisions in Sweden—between state intervention and free market policies, between support for and opposition to welfare policies. He finds that other currently more fashionable sources of political orientation towards the state show no sign of under-cutting the continuing central importance of class position.

### *Post-communist Class Conflicts?*

Despite the various disagreements aired in this introduction with the authors of *Electoral Change*, Franklin, van der Eijk and Machie et al's very final observation is one with which concordance is assured: 'it may well turn out that in coming years the newly democratizing countries of Central

Europe will provide the best laboratories within which to further investigate the nature of the forces that govern electoral change' (van der Eijk *et al.* 1992: 431). Part III of the book presents evidence from this 'laboratory' with respect to the role of class in the politics of transition societies.

In contemporary Central and Eastern Europe, the debate about class politics takes on a very different form to that in the West: it concerns not whether class divisions have declined with the transition from industrialism to postindustrialism, but whether they have increased as the ex-communist countries—with their former ideology of classlessness—undergo the uneasy transition from command economy to free market democracy. Clearly, the very small amount of time which has elapsed since the commencement of Glasnost in the 1980s, the 'velvet revolutions' of 1989–90, or the break-up of the Soviet Union in 1991, would appear to militate against any marked changes in the social bases of politics. The patterns of evolution examined in such extensive detail and over a relatively lengthy extent of time in the Western democracies cannot be expected to occur in this context. Nevertheless, the dramatic changes of circumstance, opportunity, and the disruption of incomes, lifestyles, and futures in transition societies provide exactly the sort of impetus for the transformation of lines of division in political interests that may well render established ideas about the glacial character of social change inapplicable.

The significance of social class for voting behaviour—and politics more broadly conceived—in the relatively under-researched context of post-communism is addressed in two chapters. The first of these, 'The Politics of Interests and Class Realignment in the Czech Republic, 1992–1996' by Petr Mateju, Blanka Rehakova, and myself, studies a relatively 'Western' country, the Czech Republic, over a four-year period in which the costs of marketization would appear to have become increasingly apparent to the Czech electorate. The Evans/Whitefield chapter on 'The Emergence of Class Politics and Class Voting in Post-Communist Russia' moves eastward to a country whose post-communist experience has been very different from that of the relatively advantaged Czechs, and examines the emergence of class divisions in political preferences in Russia during the early and middle part of the decade. By examining the relationship between class position, economic perceptions, and orientations towards marketization over time, this study provides evidence of both the economic basis of class polarization and the role of an increasing understanding of the socially differentiated costs and benefits associated with market economies.

In both of these rather different post-communist contexts we find clear evidence of class-based political polarization along the 'classic' left–right axis. These analyses also suggest a different logic to the class–party relationship than that which has supposedly characterized class/party relations over time in the West: the pattern of influence in these Eastern European countries shows more evidence of being 'bottom-up' (from classes to political actors)—and reflecting a process in which voters are learning to relate their social position to their political interests—than 'top-down' (from political actors to classes).

## *Reappraisal, Commentary, and Conclusions*

In the final section we consider the strengths, weaknesses, and implications of the preceding contributions. As we have seen, differences in method and measurement are key factors in many of the disputes about class voting both here and in the literature more generally. In Chapter 11, attention is given to the role of differences in data sources and methods of data analysis in accounting for the divergent conclusions reached above in studies of the core nations. In 'Resolving Disputes about Class Voting in Britain and the United States: Definitions, Models, and Data' David Weakliem and Anthony Heath examine the methodological bases of the different findings reported in Chapters 3, 4, and 5 with respect to the two cases which have traditionally attracted most attention: Britain and the United States. Their aim is to resolve these contradictory conclusions through: first, a comparison of the findings obtained in Britain using the British Election Studies versus Gallup polls, and in the United States using the American National Election Studies, Gallup polls, and the General Social Survey; secondly, a comparison of the effects of differences in class coding; and thirdly, an assessment of the consequences of using differing statistical techniques. The effects of these sources of difference are interpreted in conjunction with an emphasis on their substantive implications.

The penultimate chapter is something rather different. The aim here is to complement the social scientific endeavour of the empirical studies with a more discursive and critical appraisal. These commentaries are presented by authors who have taken rather different positions in these debates. Thus one—Seymour Martin Lipset—having previously argued that in the postwar era class underpinned the divisions in the party systems of industrial societies, had by the 1980s accepted that this role was occupied by other social characteristics and value preferences. In a sense his observations mirror the orthodoxy against which this book takes issue. Peter Mair contributes a distinctive political science perspective, although certainly not one that is remote from the issue of stability and change in class politics. His collaborative study of electoral volatility from 1885–1985 in Western Europe contains an extensive analysis of the continuity of aggregate class cleavages as an aspect of party competition (Bartolini and Mair, 1990). Two other commentators, John Goldthorpe and Michael Hout, have argued explicitly, and independently of their contributions to the empirical research presented in this book, that class remains central to politics and many other areas of social activity. This eminent group of scholars thus contributes a range of sociological, historical, institutional, and technical expertise with which to assess the achievements of the empirical contributions to the book.

Finally, in the concluding chapter, I try to summarize the broad implications of the empirical analyses. It should be clear from this introduction that simple generalizations about the pattern of class politics, about the changing nature of class politics, and about the factors which lead to those changes, are not supported by the research presented here. This final consideration also highlights what the general reader should take away from the detailed and extensive empirical studies included in this book as well as, of course, pointing to the important questions that remain unanswered.

# PART I

## The Broad Comparative Picture

# 2

# Traditional Class Voting in Twenty Postwar Societies

PAUL NIEUWBEERTA AND NAN DIRK DE GRAAF

## INTRODUCTION

Many studies of stratification and politics have characterized elections in Western societies as the platform of 'the democratic class struggle' (Anderson and Davidson 1943; Lipset 1960; Korpi 1983; Przeworski and Sprague 1986). Early studies in this vein focused on differences in voting behaviour between manual and nonmanual classes. They showed that in all Western democratic countries, members of manual classes were more likely to vote for left-wing political parties than were members of nonmanual classes, but that the strength of the link between class and voting behaviour differed from country to country. More recently, it has been argued using this approach that in most countries in the postwar period class voting declined (Kemp 1978; Andeweg 1982; Korpi 1983: 35; Lipset 1981; Lane and Ersson 1994; Franklin 1985*b*; Dalton 1996; Inglehart 1990; Clark *et al.* 1993: 312). In response, however, scholars from rather different perspectives have argued that these trends arise from the failure to examine levels of class voting in an appropriate way (Korpi 1983; Heath *et al.* 1985; Hout *et al.* 1993; Goldthorpe 1996*a*).

First, it has been claimed that the traditionally used measure of class voting, that is, the Alford index, is sensitive to variation in the general popularity of political parties. Therefore, one should focus on levels of relative class voting instead of absolute class voting, and measure this by means of odds ratios, or log odds ratios instead. And secondly, it has been argued that earlier studies used class schemes too crude to take into account relevant developments in the class structure of these countries. A more detailed class scheme that takes into account the typical characteristics of a modern industrial society would be more appropriate.

The critique of traditional approaches to class voting has led to protracted debates in the literature between scholars advocating both standpoints (see e.g. Clark and Lipset 1991; Crewe 1986; Heath *et al.* 1985; Heath *et al.* 1991; Hout *et al.* 1993). In these debates, however, there has been no systematic comparison of the consequences of using different measures of class position and different ways of estimating the relationship between class and vote. In fact, until recently, the only studies of class voting using more complex methods and measures than the traditional approach have focused on trends in single countries, that is, Britain, France, Norway, and the United States (Evans *et al.* 1991, 1996; Heath *et al.* 1995; Ringdal and Hines 1995; Hout *et al.* 1995).

It is against this background that we will try to answer the following questions:

1. To what extent did levels of class voting differ across democratic industrialized countries in the postwar period?
2. To what extent was there a decline in levels of class voting in these countries over that period?

In doing so we endeavour to improve on previous studies in two ways: first by collating and analysing an extensive dataset from no less than twenty countries over a period (1945–90) of up to almost fifty years; secondly, by investigating whether the use of a more or less detailed class schema leads to different conclusions regarding differences and trends in class voting. More precisely, we want to know to what degree variation in manual/nonmanual class voting between countries and periods is the result of variations over time and across countries in the composition of manual and nonmanual classes. The answers to these questions will indicate to what extent conclusions derived from earlier, smaller-scale studies are robust. First, however, we elaborate on why a more detailed measure of class position has been advocated for the study of class voting and class politics.

## REFORMULATING THE CLASS BASIS OF TRADITIONAL LEFT–RIGHT VOTING

To understand why classes might vote differentially for left and right-wing parties is not difficult. In general, left-wing parties are in favour of the active redistribution of wealth by central government, whereas right-wing parties are not (Lipset 1981). They will thus be more likely to implement higher taxes, improve occupational security regulations, and endorse collectivist organizations such as labour unions, than will right-wing parties. Differences in the economic interests of classes therefore allow us to make predictions about the voting behaviour of class members. It has been argued, however, that the manual–nonmanual distinction fails to capture these divisions of interests adequately. According to the approach to measuring class position adopted by John Goldthorpe and his colleagues (see the introductory chapter to this volume), more distinctions are needed.

First, a major distinction between employer and employee classes should be recognized. Employer classes, that is, the petty bourgeoisie and farmers, can be expected to have the least left-wing voting behaviour of all classes. On the basis of their interests, employers are not in favour of wage regulations beneficial to the non-employer classes, and have a high degree of occupational security. Furthermore, to the extent that left-wing parties strive for greater equality, they might do so by levying higher taxes on inheritances. Since the petty bourgeoisie and farmers in particular are inclined to donate their property to their children, members of these classes can be assumed to be opposed to left-wing parties.

Within the different employee classes identified in the Goldthorpe class schema there are also significant differences in labour contracts and conditions of employment. Members of the service class enjoy conditions of employment which are decidedly advantaged relative to those of other grades of employees, especially when viewed in lifetime perspective. The service class, therefore, has a substantial stake in the status quo. Thus, the expectation must be that this class will constitute an essentially conservative element within modern societies (Goldthorpe 1982: 179–80), and that members of this class are likely to vote for a right-wing political party.

The manual classes (skilled, unskilled, and agricultural labourers) can be expected to be the most left-wing. Their members have least occupational security, lowest wages, and consequently the strongest incentives for collective action. Thus it is in their interest to vote for parties that are in favour of policies that are beneficial to them. Within the manual working classes, it might also be expected that unskilled workers are more likely to vote for left-wing parties than are skilled workers. In general, the employment conditions of the unskilled are poor compared to those of the skilled manual workers. Furthermore, the skilled manual workers have higher job security, and better chances of getting a job when they are unemployed. However, Evans (1992) failed to find clear differences between the employment relations of skilled workers and unskilled workers in Britain. If this also holds for other countries, the different classes of manual workers might in general display rather similar patterns of voting behaviour.

Special consideration also needs to be given to the voting behaviour of agricultural labourers. In principle, agricultural labourers are in the same position as skilled or unskilled labourers. Therefore, they are expected to have left-wing voting tendencies. However, many agricultural labourers are sons of farmers, and some know that they will inherit their father's farm in the near future. Agricultural labourers are thus a mixture of 'real' agricultural labourers and (future) farmers. Here we are applying the idea that voting behaviour is not only based on present interests, but also—and indeed more importantly (see Evans 1993*b*)—on future interests. Thus because it is in the interest of farmers' sons that the state does not restrict inheritance possibilities, and because farmers' sons are likely to vote according to their future interests, the voting behaviour of agricultural labourers can be expected to be somewhere between that of 'real' agricultural labourers and that of farmers.

Finally, the employment conditions of the routine nonmanual class lie between those of skilled manual workers and service-class workers (Evans 1992). The members of this class have levels of job security and wages that in general are higher than those of skilled manual class members, but lower than those of service-class members. Therefore, it can be anticipated that the voting patterns of the routine nonmanual class will be less left-wing than those of the skilled manual classes, and more left-wing than those of the service class.

## DATA AND ANALYSIS

Class–vote data were analysed from twenty countries over the period 1945–90. These twenty countries can be characterized as basically democratic over a substantial period of time (Lijphart 1984: 37). They include seventeen from Europe, two from North America (Canada and the United States), and Australia.

Two kinds of data are used. The first are *aggregated country data*, which include information about levels of class voting in each country for each available year since the end of the Second World War. These data were obtained from two sources: tables published in various articles and books, and tables calculated using data from national representative surveys. In total, there are 324 tables cross-classifying class (manual/nonmanual) by party voted for (left-wing/right-wing). Appendix A lists the sources of these tables.

The second kind of data are *individual-level data* obtained from national representative surveys of the twenty countries. These data derive from 75,783 male respondents aged 18 years or older from 113 surveys undertaken in sixteen countries and covering the period 1956–90 (for Greece, Luxembourg, Portugal, and Spain no useful individual-level datafiles were found). These 113 datasets have been extracted, made comparable, and collected in one large combined file (the 'International Stratification, Mobility, and Politics File'). For detailed information on this file, see the published codebook (Nieuwbeerta and Ganzeboom 1996) and the data references at the end of this chapter.

### Voting Behaviour

Voting preferences were measured in several ways: in some surveys respondents were asked to name the political party they would vote for if there were a national election tomorrow; in others they were asked to name the party they voted for at the most recent national election; in yet others they were asked which political party they preferred or identified with.[1]

In order to produce a classification of parties that would allow cross-country comparison, we followed Bartolini and Mair (1990) and Franklin and his colleagues (1992), and dichotomized the political parties into left-wing versus right-wing. This is arguably the most relevant distinction between political parties when investigating class-based voting. In deciding whether a specific party should be included in the left-wing block, we adopted the criteria proposed by Bartolini and Mair (1990: 42–3) and included all parties which were members of the Socialist International or the Communist Third International. Since, according to these criteria, hardly any left-wing voters would exist in the United States, for that country an exception was made, and the Democratic Party was defined as a left-wing party. In Appendix B we present a full list of the political parties classified as left-wing in all countries.

### Social Class

The manual versus nonmanual class distinction is traditionally used in research on the relationship between social class and voting behaviour. In this chapter we follow this tradition. We also use the seven-class version of Goldthorpe's class schema (Goldthorpe 1980), elaborated by Erikson, Goldthorpe, and Portocarrero (1979), and Erikson and Goldthorpe (1992*a*: 38–9). This produces the class categories presented in Table 2.1.

In order to obtain a comparable operationalization of class in all countries and years, the respondents were coded into Erikson–Goldthorpe classes on the basis of data on their occupation, self-employment, and supervisory status. First, the original occupation codes were recoded into the International Standard Classification of Occupation (ISCO) codes (ILO 1969); then these ISCO codes were translated into Erikson–Goldthorpe class positions through the Ganzeboom, Luijkx, and Treiman (1989) recoding scheme.

[1] The limitations introduced by such different measures of voting behaviour are appreciated. However, analyses using surveys containing only 'vote' and others using surveys containing only 'political preference', produced similar outcomes.

TABLE 2.1. *The Erikson–Goldthorpe class schema*

| Title | Description |
|---|---|
| Nonmanual classes | |
| Service class | Large proprietors; professionals, administrators, and managers; higher-grade technicians; supervisors of nonmanual workers |
| Routine nonmanual class | Routine nonmanual employees in administration and commerce; sales personnel; other rank-and-file service workers |
| Petty bourgeoisie | Small proprietors and artisans, with and without employees |
| Farmers | Farmers, smallholders and other self-employed workers in primary production |
| Manual classes | |
| Skilled workers | Lower-grade technicians; supervisors of manual workers; skilled manual workers |
| Nonskilled workers | Semi- and unskilled, nonagricultural manual workers |
| Agricultural labourers | Agricultural and other workers in primary production |

### *Manual/Nonmanual Class Voting*

The level of class voting in a country at a certain point in time can be operationalized in various ways. Traditionally, as already discussed, the *Alford index* has been used (Alford 1962, 1963). More recently, the log odds ratio has also been used as a measure of the strength of the class/vote relationship (Heath *et al.* 1985; Thomsen 1987; Manza *et al.* 1995). The log odds ratio is the natural logarithm of the odds ratio, where the odds ratio is the odds for manual workers of voting left-wing rather than right-wing divided by the odds for nonmanual workers of doing the same.[2] This log odds ratio can also be regarded as the log odds for manual workers of voting for a left-wing political party rather than a right-wing party minus the log odds for nonmanual workers of voting in this way. If voting behaviour is not dependent on class, the log odds ratio has the value of zero. We refer to the log odds ratio as the *Thomsen index* (Thomsen 1987). The Thomsen index is preferable to the Alford index as it is insensitive to changes in the general popularity of the political parties. However, in practice, for two-by-two class-voting tables, the differences between the Thomsen index and

[2] We prefer to use the log odds ratio over the odds ratio, since the latter does not adjust for floor effects. That is, if there is hardly a relationship between class and vote, a small change in the strength of that relationship results in a small alteration in the odds ratio, whereas if this relationship is strong, a small change results in a large alteration in this measure.

the Alford index should not be overstated. As Goodman (1975: 86) has implied, it is only when the distribution of the general popularity of political parties or the distribution of social classes is more skewed than 25:75 or 75:25, that the Alford and Thomsen indices might yield substantially different conclusions. In our datasets such distributions only occur in Canada and Ireland, where left-wing parties have less than 25 per cent of the votes.

### *Erikson–Goldthorpe Class Voting*

Log odds ratios can be applied to measure levels of class voting using the Erikson–Goldthorpe class schema. Here the advantages of log odds ratios are more apparent, since in this case the distribution of the classes and the voting behaviour are regularly more skewed than 25:75. Using our seven-class Erikson–Goldthorpe schema it takes six log odds ratios to measure all the differences in voting behaviour (left/right) between classes. However, as proposed by Hout, Brooks, and Manza (1995) the standard deviation of these log odds ratios—the *kappa index*—can be used as an overall measure of the level of Erikson–Goldthorpe class voting.

A drawback of the kappa index is that it does not take into account that in some classes there are more respondents than in others, and thus that some log odds ratios are more robust than others. Therefore, we also use the *delta index* measuring the overall level of class voting when using the seven class schema. This delta index is a parameter that results from specially designed loglinear models. These so-called 'uniform difference' models, developed by Erikson and Goldthorpe (1992*a*) and Xie (1992), provide a single parameter as a measure of the level of Erikson–Goldthorpe class voting for a country in a specific year. In these models it is assumed that differences between all classes in their voting behaviour, measured by log odds ratios, vary uniformly by a constant proportion across countries and years.[3] The models are fully equipped to examine the relationship between class and voting behaviour net of changes in the sizes of the classes and the popularity of the parties.

The general uniform difference model can be represented by the following equation:

[3] One could argue that our detailed class scheme also enables us to distinguish between class-specific processes of dealignment or realignment. For example, it is possible that the distance between the service class and the skilled manual class becomes smaller, while at the same time the distance between the service class and the farmers grows. In this study, however, we focus on the overall change in levels of class voting and leave class-specific dealignment and realignment processes for future research.

$$\log((\text{Left})/(1 - \text{Left})) =$$
$$\beta_{0jk} + \beta_{jk}*[\beta_1*(\text{Skilled manual class}) + \beta_2*(\text{Agricultural labourers}) +$$
$$\beta_3*(\text{Routine nonmanual class}) + \beta_4*(\text{Service class}) +$$
$$\beta_5*(\text{Petty Bourgeoisie}) + \beta_6*(\text{Farmer})]$$

where the variable for the voting behaviour of the respondents, Left, is coded (1) when respondents vote for a left-wing party and (0) when they vote for a right-wing party. The seven Erikson–Goldthorpe classes are represented by six dummy variables. The unskilled manual class is defined as the reference category. Consequently, the parameters $\beta_1$ to $\beta_6$ represent the average differences in voting behaviour, measured by log odds ratios, between the unskilled manual class and the other Erikson–Goldthorpe classes. According to the equation, the intercept, $\beta_{0jk}$ represents the log odds for unskilled manual workers of voting for a left-wing rather than a right-wing party. This intercept is allowed to vary over years ($j$) and countries ($k$) in order to control for the variations in the general popularity of left-wing parties in the various countries and years. This parameter, however, is of limited interest because our concern is with class differences in voting behaviour and not with the absolute popularity of left-wing and right-wing parties. Our main interest lies in the *delta indices*, that is, the $\beta_{jk}$ parameters of the model. Under the fitted model, the delta indices give a measure of the overall differences and changes in the strength of the relationship between class and voting behaviour. They therefore show in which direction and to what extent class differences in voting behaviour vary uniformly (i.e. by a constant proportion) across years ($j$) and countries ($k$). Thus, these delta indices can be regarded as the overall level of class voting in a specific year in a specific country.

## MANUAL/NONMANUAL CLASS VOTING

We start by computing both Alford and Thomsen indices for all years and countries where data is available in our aggregated country dataset. Although we regard the Thomsen indices as a better measure of class voting than the Alford index, it is of interest to examine to what extent use of one or other indices yields different results. We have already argued that in practice, for two-by-two class–vote tables, the advantages of the Thomsen index over the Alford index should not be overstated. This idea is confirmed by our analysis: the two indices produce very much the same conclusions: in the aggregated country dataset the Pearson correlation between the Alford and the Thomsen indices is 0.97.

### *Differences between Countries*

To examine the differences in class voting between countries—and in order not to be too dependent on single cross-tabulations and thus open to the influence of peculiarities in the data—we calculated the mean value of the Alford and Thomsen indices of each country for each of four periods. These mean values are given in Tables 2.2 and 2.3. Not surprisingly, when taking into account the high correlation between the values of the two indices, the rankings of the countries on both measures of class voting in all four periods are very similar.

The results of our analysis are thus consistent with the findings of previous studies that use only Alford indices. That is, there is a clear indication of substantial differences in levels of—both absolute and relative—manual/nonmanual class voting across democratic industrialized countries in the postwar period. The lowest levels of class voting are found in the United States and Canada. In these countries we find low positive Thomsen indices. This implies that manual workers are more left-wing than nonmanual workers, but the difference in voting behaviour between these classes—especially in Canada—is small. The Thomsen indices for these countries rarely exceed 0.5. Furthermore, France, Greece, Ireland, Italy, the Netherlands, Portugal, Spain, and Switzerland have somewhat higher, but still relatively low levels of class voting—the Thomsen indices are rarely larger than 1. Then follows a group of countries with intermediate levels of class voting: Australia, Austria, Belgium, Germany, and Luxembourg. In these countries the Thomsen indices have a value predominantly between 1 and 1.5. Finally, in some countries we find relatively high levels of class voting, in which the Thomsen indices are higher than 1.5. These are the four Scandinavian countries and Britain. In the Scandinavian countries the Thomsen indices are in some cases above 2.

### *Trends within Countries*

Our findings also show that a substantial decline in the levels of class voting occurred in most democratic countries in the postwar period. A first indication is provided by the higher indices for earlier periods than for more recent years. A second, more precise indication of the decline in levels of class voting in most countries is provided by the trend parameters in Tables 2.2 and 2.3. These trend parameters report the decline—or rise—in the level of class voting for each country measured by Alford indices and Thomsen indices. For every country, a linear regression analysis was performed on the indices with the exact year of observation as an independent variable. A decline in the level of class voting should be indicated by a negative trend-parameter. The reader should note, however, that we do

TABLE 2.2. *Levels of class voting (measured by Alford index) in twenty countries, 1945–1990 (aggregated country dataset)*

| Countries | Mean levels of class voting per period | | | | Linear trend (change over ten years) | | No. of cases | Range |
|---|---|---|---|---|---|---|---|---|
| | 1945–1960 | 1961–1970 | 1971–1980 | 1981–1990 | Parameter | s.e. | | |
| Australia | 32.9 | 29.3 | 27.8 | 19.4 | –4.2* | 0.7 | 17 | 1946–90 |
| Austria | — | 27.4 | 28.9 | 18.3 | –6.1* | 3.0 | 5 | 1968–89 |
| Belgium | — | 25.4 | 17.9 | 16.4 | –4.3* | 2.4 | 20 | 1968–90 |
| Britain | 37.3 | 38.3 | 24.3 | 23.4 | –5.9* | 1.2 | 30 | 1945–90 |
| Canada | 7.0 | 7.7 | — | 4.0 | –0.7 | 1.4 | 13 | 1945–84 |
| Denmark | 39.8 | 52.0 | 28.1 | 20.9 | –4.9* | 0.8 | 29 | 1945–90 |
| Finland | 48.4 | 50.2 | 36.9 | 35.7 | –6.1 | 4.6 | 5 | 1958–87 |
| France | 24.4 | 18.3 | 17.0 | 11.7 | –3.7* | 0.8 | 25 | 1947–90 |
| Germany | 36.0 | 24.8 | 14.9 | 13.4 | –7.0* | 1.0 | 25 | 1953–90 |
| Greece | — | — | 12.3 | 9.7 | 4.4 | 5.7 | 10 | 1980–89 |
| Ireland | — | 14.1 | 8.7 | 7.3 | –2.3 | 1.3 | 18 | 1969–90 |
| Italy | 26.6 | 14.5 | 17.8 | 13.1 | –4.3* | 1.2 | 20 | 1953–90 |
| Luxembourg | — | — | 24.8 | 18.8 | –3.8 | 4.1 | 17 | 1973–90 |
| Netherlands | 14.0 | 14.7 | 21.8 | 15.5 | –0.2 | 1.0 | 25 | 1950–90 |
| Norway | 52.5 | 32.0 | 33.8 | 20.5 | –9.1* | 1.5 | 11 | 1949–90 |
| Portugal | — | — | — | 14.9 | 5.9 | 6.0 | 5 | 1985–89 |
| Spain | — | — | 18.4 | 15.5 | –4.1 | 7.1 | 6 | 1979–89 |
| Sweden | 51.0 | 40.7 | 37.3 | 32.7 | –5.5* | 0.9 | 12 | 1946–88 |
| Switzerland | — | — | 17.6 | 12.8 | –3.8 | 4.4 | 4 | 1972–87 |
| United States | 16.2 | 7.7 | 10.9 | 8.1 | –2.8* | 1.0 | 27 | 1948–90 |
| Mean | 32.2 | 26.5 | 22.2 | 16.6 | | | | |
| Std. deviation | 14.9 | 14.2 | 8.6 | 7.8 | | | | |

*Notes*: * $p < 0.05$
The variable Year is centred around 1980.

TABLE 2.3. *Levels of class voting (measured by Thomsen index) in twenty countries, 1945–1990 (aggregated country dataset)*

| | Mean levels of class voting per period | | | | Linear trend (change over ten years) | | No. of cases | Range |
|---|---|---|---|---|---|---|---|---|
| | 1945–1960 | 1961–1970 | 1971–1980 | 1981–1990 | Parameter | s.e. | | |
| Australia | 1.38 | 1.22 | 1.16 | 0.80 | –0.18* | 0.03 | 17 | 1946–90 |
| Austria | — | 1.12 | 1.28 | 0.76 | –0.27* | 0.13 | 5 | 1968–89 |
| Belgium | — | 1.21 | 0.87 | 0.80 | –0.20* | 0.11 | 20 | 1968–90 |
| Britain | 1.64 | 1.67 | 1.07 | 0.90 | –0.22* | 0.03 | 30 | 1945–90 |
| Canada | 0.30 | 0.31 | — | 0.27 | –0.01 | 0.06 | 13 | 1945–84 |
| Denmark | 1.82 | 2.33 | 1.18 | 0.97 | –0.30* | 0.05 | 29 | 1945–90 |
| Finland | 2.17 | 2.24 | 1.60 | 1.52 | –0.30 | 0.21 | 5 | 1958–87 |
| France | 1.01 | 0.76 | 0.72 | 0.48 | –0.15* | 0.00 | 25 | 1947–90 |
| Germany | 1.55 | 1.06 | 0.61 | 0.55 | –0.31* | 0.04 | 25 | 1953–90 |
| Greece | — | — | 0.53 | 0.47 | 0.15 | 0.34 | 10 | 1980–89 |
| Ireland | — | 0.88 | 0.77 | 0.70 | –0.15 | 0.13 | 18 | 1969–90 |
| Italy | 1.13 | 0.66 | 0.73 | 0.53 | –0.19* | 0.05 | 20 | 1953–90 |
| Luxembourg | — | — | 1.10 | 0.86 | –0.14 | 0.19 | 17 | 1973–90 |
| Netherlands | 0.61 | 0.65 | 0.94 | 0.68 | –0.01 | 0.05 | 25 | 1950–90 |
| Norway | 2.39 | 1.38 | 1.43 | 0.84 | –0.44* | 0.06 | 11 | 1949–90 |
| Portugal | — | — | — | 0.62 | 0.27 | 0.72 | 5 | 1985–89 |
| Spain | — | — | 0.75 | 0.63 | –0.16 | 0.30 | 6 | 1979–89 |
| Sweden | 2.26 | 1.73 | 1.57 | 1.36 | –0.27* | 0.04 | 12 | 1946–88 |
| Switzerland | — | — | 0.82 | 0.80 | –0.07 | 0.25 | 4 | 1972–87 |
| United States | 0.67 | 0.36 | 0.46 | 0.34 | –0.12* | 0.05 | 27 | 1948–90 |
| Mean | 1.41 | 1.17 | 0.98 | 0.74 | | | | |
| Std. deviation | 0.66 | 0.59 | 0.33 | 0.30 | | | | |

*Notes*: * $p < 0.05$
The variable Year is centred around 1980.

not argue that a negative linear trend-parameter for a country-implies that trends in the level of class voting in that country are straightforwardly linear. The parameters are best regarded as a summary measure of the overall increase or decrease in class voting in a country, and not as the most detailed representation of country-specific developments in class voting over time. The latter would require a study beyond the scope of this chapter.

In Tables 2.2 and 2.3, negative trend-parameters are reported for eighteen out of the twenty countries for both indices. The only two countries with a positive (non-significant) trend-parameter are Greece and Portugal. However, for these two countries, data are only available over the periods 1980–90 and 1985–90, respectively. Of the eighteen slope-parameters that are negative in both tables, eleven are statistically significant at the 0.05 level. These are for Australia, Austria, Belgium, Britain, Denmark, France, Germany, Italy, Norway, Sweden, and the United States. The insignificant slope-parameters for Finland, Spain, and Switzerland might be a consequence of the limited number of surveys (i.e. years) for these countries. Thus, *in general*, our data lend support to the idea that levels of class voting in Western industrialized societies have declined over the postwar period. The only countries for which we do not find significant declines in their levels of class voting—and where we have data for a sufficient number of years to confidently detect significant trends—are Canada, Ireland, Luxembourg, and the Netherlands.

If we compare the trend-parameters for the Alford indices to those for the Thomsen indices, we find that the ranking of the countries is almost identical. The figures show that of all the countries featured in this study, Norway shows the strongest absolute decrease in manual/nonmanual class voting, followed by the other Scandinavian countries. In Germany and Britain substantial absolute decreases in the Thomsen indices are also found. In the other countries the decline in class voting is less marked, whereas in Canada and the United States hardly any trend emerges. Given the very low levels of class voting in even the earliest surveys in these two countries, a decline could hardly be expected.

## ERIKSON–GOLDTHORPE CLASS VOTING

### *Kappa Indices*

The next question concerns the extent to which the patterns of cross-national and over-time class voting are different when the more discriminating Erikson–Goldthorpe class schema is used.

As we have observed earlier, a variety of authors have posited that the decline in levels of manual/nonmanual class voting can, at least to some extent, be explained by changes in the composition of these two classes. Thus if, for example, the percentage of skilled workers within the manual class has grown and the percentage of unskilled workers has diminished—and skilled workers are less left-wing than unskilled workers—the manual class as a whole will be less left-wing and levels of manual/nonmanual class voting will be reduced. Analysis of levels of class voting using the Erikson–Goldthorpe schema—which controls for changes in the composition of manual and nonmanual classes—might therefore show a different picture.

Table 2.4 presents the mean log odds ratios of differences in voting behaviour between Erikson–Goldthorpe classes for sixteen countries across four periods. These were calculated from the individual-level data. In this table, classes are ordered from the generally most left-wing class, the unskilled manual workers, to the typically least left-wing class, the farmers. When calculating the log odds ratios, the unskilled manual class was chosen as the reference category. Consequently, the calculated log odds ratios represent the difference in voting behaviour between the unskilled manual class and the other classes. Kappa indices (the standard deviations over the displayed log odds ratios) are also presented (in Table 2.5) as a measure of the overall level of Erikson–Goldthorpe class voting in each period in each country.

The measures of Erikson–Goldthorpe class voting in Tables 2.4 and 2.5 reveal very much the same picture as that observed when using a manual/nonmanual class distinction. Again, the differences in voting behaviour between the classes vary substantially from country to country. Furthermore, the ranking of the countries with respect to levels of class voting is similar to the ranking for manual/nonmanual class voting.[4] For example, in Norway during the 1971–80 period, the difference between the most left-wing class and the most right-wing class, that is, between the unskilled manual workers and the farmers, is 2.75, while in the United States for the same period, the difference between these classes is only 0.97. Moreover, in each of the four periods the countries from the continent of North America (Canada and the United States) have the lowest kappa indices, while Britain and the Scandinavian countries have the highest.

To investigate whether levels of Erikson–Goldthorpe class voting have declined over the postwar period we examine the linear trend-parameters for the kappa indices that are given in Table 2.5. These figures show negative trend-parameters for all countries under investigation, except

[4] We also compared all Erikson–Goldthorpe class voting outcomes with Alford and Thomsen indices based solely on our individual-level dataset. This resulted in the same conclusions.

TABLE 2.4. *Difference in voting behaviour (in log odds ratios) between the unskilled manual class and the other Erikson–Goldthorpe classes in sixteen countries, 1956–1990 (individual dataset)*

| Countries | | Unskilled manual (ref.) | Skilled manual | Agricultural labourers | Routine nonmanual | Service class | Petty bourgeoisie | Farmers |
|---|---|---|---|---|---|---|---|---|
| Australia | 1961–70 | 0 | 0.04 | 0.34 | 0.89 | 1.37 | 0.97 | 2.27 |
| | 1971–80 | 0 | –0.02 | 0.14 | 0.83 | 1.42 | 1.14 | 2.75 |
| | 1981–90 | 0 | 0.22 | 0.81 | 0.68 | 1.03 | 1.15 | 2.39 |
| Austria | 1971–80 | 0 | –0.03 | 1.86 | 1.31 | 0.97 | 2.09 | 3.13 |
| | 1981–90 | 0 | 0.05 | 1.09 | 0.19 | 0.59 | 1.63 | 3.29 |
| Belgium* | 1971–80 | 0 | –0.39 | — | 0.93 | 1.11 | 1.47 | 1.69 |
| Britain | 1961–70 | 0 | –0.09 | 0.41 | 1.05 | 1.77 | 1.82 | 2.43 |
| | 1971–80 | 0 | 0.03 | 1.40 | 1.03 | 1.45 | 2.05 | 3.18 |
| | 1981–90 | 0 | 0.14 | 0.48 | 1.05 | 1.40 | 1.23 | 2.06 |
| Canada | 1981–90 | 0 | –0.02 | –0.38 | 0.10 | 0.38 | 1.07 | –0.40 |
| Denmark* | 1971–80 | 0 | –0.05 | — | 0.99 | 1.78 | 2.42 | 4.19 |
| | 1981–90 | 0 | –0.41 | — | 0.89 | 2.37 | 3.63 | 3.30 |
| Finland | 1971–80 | 0 | –0.13 | 0.23 | 0.87 | 1.72 | 1.78 | 3.28 |
| France | 1971–80 | 0 | 0.39 | 0.64 | 0.55 | 1.16 | 1.79 | 2.05 |
| Germany | 1961–70 | 0 | 0.07 | 0.44 | 0.42 | 0.70 | 1.39 | 3.93 |
| | 1971–80 | 0 | –0.17 | 0.59 | 0.51 | 0.61 | 1.86 | 2.73 |
| | 1981–90 | 0 | 0.05 | 0.73 | 0.61 | 0.72 | 1.57 | 1.98 |

| Ireland | 1981–90 | 0 | 0.09 | 0.07 | –0.20 | 0.94 | 2.24 | 2.30 |
|---|---|---|---|---|---|---|---|---|
| Italy | 1961–70 | 0 | 0.25 | 0.74 | 1.06 | 1.67 | 0.86 | 0.94 |
| | 1971–80 | 0 | 0.25 | 1.04 | 1.18 | 0.91 | 0.88 | 1.86 |
| | 1981–90 | 0 | 0.17 | 0.11 | 0.46 | 0.63 | 1.04 | 1.01 |
| Netherlands | 1961–70 | 0 | 0.25 | 0.61 | 0.78 | 1.20 | 1.33 | 2.71 |
| | 1971–80 | 0 | 0.01 | 1.04 | 0.69 | 1.00 | 1.65 | 2.82 |
| | 1981–90 | 0 | 0.15 | 0.62 | 0.67 | 0.87 | 1.20 | 2.04 |
| Norway | 1961–70 | 0 | –0.07 | 1.31 | 0.71 | 2.14 | 1.19 | 2.40 |
| | 1971–80 | 0 | 0.23 | 0.04 | 0.85 | 1.68 | 1.28 | 2.75 |
| | 1981–90 | 0 | –0.09 | 0.22 | 0.65 | 1.11 | 0.62 | 1.25 |
| Sweden | 1971–80 | 0 | –0.52 | 1.07 | 0.92 | 1.37 | 1.93 | 3.56 |
| | 1981–90 | 0 | –0.13 | 1.30 | 0.81 | 0.80 | 1.39 | 2.48 |
| Switzerland | 1971–80 | 0 | 0.24 | — | 0.68 | 1.44 | 1.57 | 2.69 |
| United States | 1956–60 | 0 | –0.12 | –0.75 | 0.26 | 0.63 | –0.01 | 0.21 |
| | 1961–70 | 0 | 0.32 | 0.43 | 0.31 | 0.50 | 0.53 | 0.62 |
| | 1971–80 | 0 | 0.26 | 0.08 | 0.50 | 0.77 | 0.37 | 0.97 |
| | 1981–90 | 0 | 0.30 | 0.87 | 0.40 | 0.69 | 0.77 | 0.22 |
| All data | 1945–90 | 0 | 0.06 | 0.56 | 0.66 | 1.00 | 1.13 | 1.77 |

*Note*: * Figures for Belgium and Denmark are incomplete, because in these countries agricultural labourers are classified as unskilled manual workers.

TABLE 2.5. *Levels of class voting (measured by kappa index) in twenty countries 1956–1990 (individual dataset)*

| Countries | Mean levels of class voting per period | | | Linear trend (change over ten years) | | No. of cases | Range |
|---|---|---|---|---|---|---|---|
| | 1961–1970 | 1971–1980 | 1981–1990 | Parameter | s.e. | | |
| Australia | 0.81 | 1.00 | 0.78 | –0.04 | 0.07 | 9 | 1965–90 |
| Austria | — | 1.14 | 1.18 | 0.24 | 0.22 | 4 | 1974–89 |
| Belgium | — | 0.83 | — | — | — | 1 | 1975 |
| Britain | 0.99 | 1.12 | 0.74 | –0.15* | 0.06 | 12 | 1964–90 |
| Canada | — | — | 0.50 | — | — | 1 | 1984 |
| Denmark | — | 1.62 | 1.71 | –0.34 | 0.38 | 6 | 1971–81 |
| Finland | — | 1.23 | — | –0.77 | — | 2 | 1972–75 |
| France | — | 0.76 | — | — | — | 1 | 1978 |
| Germany | 1.37 | 1.05 | 0.73 | –0.41* | 0.08 | 13 | 1969–90 |
| Ireland | — | — | 1.08 | –0.62 | — | 2 | 1989–90 |
| Italy | 0.55 | 0.61 | 0.42 | –0.08 | 0.08 | 3 | 1968–85 |
| Netherlands | 0.90 | 0.98 | 0.68 | –0.11 | 0.07 | 14 | 1970–90 |
| Norway | 0.96 | 1.01 | 0.52 | –0.25* | 0.07 | 7 | 1965–90 |
| Sweden | — | 1.33 | 0.89 | –0.24 | — | 2 | 1972–90 |
| Switzerland | — | 1.00 | — | –0.15 | — | 2 | 1972–76 |
| United States | 0.20 | 0.35 | 0.32 | –0.04 | 0.04 | 24 | 1956–90 |
| Mean | 0.83 | 1.00 | 0.80 | | | | |
| Std. deviation | 0.34 | 0.30 | 0.37 | | | | |

*Notes*: * $p < 0.05$
The variable Year is centred around 1980.

Austria. Thus, we might conclude that in most countries levels of Erikson–Goldthorpe class voting have declined. However, only in Germany, Britain, and Norway do these trend-parameters differ significantly from zero. That most trend-parameters are not statistically significantly different from zero might again be due to the fact that for the pertinent countries only a limited number of datasets were available. Only in the case of the United States and the Netherlands, that is, countries where we have data for more than ten years, can we be reasonably certain that no systematic decline in Erikson–Goldthorpe class voting has occurred.

## *Delta Indices*

As pointed out already, when using log odds ratios (and kappa indices) it is important to remember that the ratios are based on different numbers of respondents and that estimates of log odds ratios vary in their reliability. When describing the levels of Erikson–Goldthorpe class voting in the countries during the period 1956–1990, therefore, we also use delta indices.

These indices ($\beta_{jk}$ parameters) result from applying the uniform difference models to the individual-level data.

To test statistically whether the overall levels of class voting differed significantly across countries and whether significant trends had occurred within these countries, variations of the uniform difference models were applied. After carefully testing a variety of nested models (see Nieuwbeerta 1995: chapter 6), we employed the country-difference and country-specific linear trend model, assuming that in each country a different linear trend has occurred in levels of class voting ($\beta_{jk} = \beta_{0k} + \beta_{1k}$* Year). Alternative models allowing for non-linear trends did not result in a substantial improvement on our linear trend model.

### *The General Pattern of Class Voting*

The parameter estimates of the country-difference and country-specific linear trend model are presented in Table 2.6. In the note to this table, the estimates of the $\beta_1$ to $\beta_6$ parameters for the model are presented. These represent the general pattern of association between the Erikson–Goldthorpe classes and vote. The estimates of the β parameters indicate that the difference between the unskilled manual class and the skilled manual class is 0.07, while between the unskilled manual class and the farmers it is 1.88. The pattern of class voting obtained from the estimated β parameters is—as could be expected—almost identical to that found in the last row of Table 2.4 where we calculated log odds ratios on class-voting tables based on our total dataset.

### *Differences between Countries*

The levels of class voting in countries are represented by the country-parameters, that is, the $\beta_{0k}$ parameters. These parameters are presented in the main part of Table 2.6. Because in the model the variable Year was linearly transformed by subtracting 1980 from its original value, the estimates of the country-parameters represent the differences in the levels of class voting between countries in 1980. In Norway, for example, all log odds ratios are 1.21 times the general level. Hence, in 1980 the log odds ratio indicating differences in voting behaviour between the unskilled manual workers and the service class is $1.21 * 1.02 = 1.24$, while the parameters for the United States imply that all log odds ratios in the United States are 0.42 times smaller than the general level. The parameters also allow us to compare countries with each other. For example, in Norway all log odds ratios are 1.21/0.42, or 2.9 times, larger than in the United States.

TABLE 2.6. *Country differences and trends models*

| Countries | Model 1 country differences and general linear trends | | | | Model 2 country differences and country-specific linear trends | | | |
|---|---|---|---|---|---|---|---|---|
| | Intercept (Class voting in 1980) | | Trend (change over ten years) | | Intercept (Class voting in 1980) | | Trend (change over ten years) | |
| | Parameter ($\delta_{0k}$) | s.e. | Parameter ($\delta_1$) | s.e. | Parameter ($\delta_{0k}$) | s.e. | Parameter ($\delta_1$) | s.e. |
| All countries | — | — | –0.14* | 0.02 | — | — | — | — |
| Australia | 1.16* | 0.13 | — | — | 1.15* | 0.13 | –0.16* | 0.05 |
| Austria | 1.35* | 0.17 | — | — | 1.37* | 0.17 | –0.22 | 0.15 |
| Belgium | 1.28* | 0.26 | — | — | 1.35* | 0.26 | — | — |
| Britain | 1.43* | 0.13 | — | — | 1.45* | 0.13 | –0.25* | 0.05 |
| Canada | 0.01* | 0.18 | — | — | –0.00 | 0.18 | — | — |
| Denmark | 1.75* | 0.15 | — | — | 1.64* | 0.18 | –0.40 | 0.24 |
| Finland | 1.71* | 0.20 | — | — | 0.80 | 0.67 | –1.59 | 1.05 |
| France | 0.97* | 0.15 | — | — | 0.96* | 0.16 | — | — |
| Germany | 0.97* | 0.13 | — | — | 0.97* | 0.13 | –0.19* | 0.07 |
| Ireland | 1.25* | 0.23 | — | — | 4.68 | 3.50 | –3.77 | 3.69 |
| Italy | 0.59* | 0.14 | — | — | 0.63* | 0.14 | –0.02 | 0.08 |
| Netherlands | 1.04* | 0.13 | — | — | 1.04* | 0.13 | –0.21* | 0.06 |
| Norway | 1.22* | 0.14 | — | — | 1.21* | 0.14 | –0.41* | 0.06 |
| Sweden | 1.53* | 0.22 | — | — | 1.50* | 0.22 | –0.45* | 0.20 |
| Switzerland | 1.30* | 0.19 | — | — | 1.37 | 0.21 | 0.04 | 0.26 |
| United States | 0.35* | 0.13 | — | — | 0.42* | 0.13 | 0.01 | 0.03 |

*Notes*: * $p < 0.05$

The variable Year was centred around 1980.

For both Models 1 and 2 the parameter estimates for the general pattern of class voting are: Unskilled manual class (–): 0; Skilled manual class ($\beta_1$): 0.07; Agricultural labourers ($\beta_2$): 0.58; Routine nonmanual class ($\beta_3$): 0.66; Service class ($\beta_4$); 1.02; Petty bourgeoisie ($\beta_5$); 1.21; Farmers ($\beta_6$): 1.88.

The country-parameters indicate that in 1980 levels of class voting differed substantively from country to country.[5] Denmark, Sweden, and Britain had the highest levels, followed by Austria, Switzerland, Belgium, Norway, and Australia. Countries with relatively low levels of class voting are the Netherlands, Germany, France, Finland, and Italy. The two countries with the lowest levels are the United States and Canada. Thus again it can be concluded that the ranking of the countries when measured by the Erikson–Goldthorpe class schema is fairly similar to the ranking obtained when using the traditional manual and nonmanual class schema.

## *Trends*

The trend-parameters of the country-difference and country-specific linear trends model make it possible to check whether or not trends differ from country to country. These country-specific trend-parameters, the $\beta_{1k}$ parameters, represent the linear trends in class voting within countries. The value of the estimated trend-parameters represents the magnitude of the general linear trend in levels of class voting within the countries. For example, for Norway this parameter takes the negative value –0.41 (standard error (s.e.) 0.06), which implies a decline in the association between class and vote at the rate of 41 percentage points per decade.

Table 2.6 shows that in eleven out of the thirteen countries the country-specific trend-parameter has a negative value. Switzerland and the United States have positive trend-parameters, but the standard errors of these are so large that no definite conclusions concerning an increase in class voting can be drawn. Of the negative trend-parameters, six are statistically significant: for Australia, Britain, Germany, the Netherlands, Norway, and Sweden. The strongest declines (ignoring Ireland where our two surveys are too close together in time to interpret trends) are found in Finland, Norway, and Denmark.

To examine whether the trends in class voting, when measured by the Erikson–Goldthorpe class schema, are comparable to the trends in class voting measured by the manual/nonmanual class scheme, we can compare the linear trend-parameters in Table 2.6 with the linear trend-parameters concerning manual/nonmanual class voting presented in Tables 2.2 and 2.3. This comparison shows that in all countries, except Switzerland and the United States, a declining trend is found in both the manual/nonmanual and Erikson–Goldthorpe schema-based estimates of class voting. Furthermore, in general, the larger the decline in manual/nonmanual class voting, the larger is the decline in Erikson–Goldthorpe class voting. (This is

[5] The counter-intuitive country-parameters for Finland and Ireland are a result of the use of only two datasets collected at rather similar time points.

illustrated by the positive correlations between the trend-parameters from Table 2.3 and Table 2.6 (Pearson correlation: 0.48, N = 11, p = 0.134; leaving Finland and Ireland aside), and between the entries of Table 2.4 and Table 2.6 (0.67, N = 11, p = 0.024).) Thus although it is theoretically preferable to measure class voting using Erikson–Goldthorpe classes and log odds ratios, descriptions of the levels of class voting using more or less discriminating class schemas in general result in the same ranking of the countries with respect to levels of class voting and the amount of change observed in those levels.

## SIMULATIONS: EXPLAINING DIFFERENCE BETWEEN COUNTRIES AND CHANGES OVER TIME

### *Explaining Differences between Countries*

Finally, we examine the extent to which variation in manual/nonmanual class voting can be explained by variation in the composition of the manual and nonmanual classes. Therefore, we again analyse our dataset on individual respondents from sixteen countries over the years 1956–90. The most obvious way to examine the link between the class compositions and the level of class voting in a country would be to link directly a single measure of a country's class composition with a single measure of class voting in that country. However, because differences might exist in the composition of both the manual and the nonmanual classes, and since within the manual and nonmanual classes more than two classes can be distinguished, no single measure of a country's class composition is applicable. For this reason, following Heath and his colleagues (1985: 36) when they analysed the effects of changing class structures on election results, we will do some simulations. These simulations take two consecutive steps.

As a first step, we constructed two-by-two class-voting tables and calculated the Thomsen indices for each year, assuming constant voting behaviour for the Erikson–Goldthorpe classes across countries and time. To do this we had to decide what measure of the voting behaviour of the Erikson–Goldthorpe classes to choose as a baseline. To avoid dependence upon incidental changes we decided not to choose the voting behaviour of a single country in a specific period but rather the average voting behaviour of the Erikson–Goldthorpe classes over all countries and years (see the bottom row of Table 2.4). The closer the Thomsen indices obtained in this first step are to the observed Thomsen indices, the more the varying composition of the Erikson–Goldthorpe classes can be held responsible for differences in class voting between countries.

These outcomes, however, do not tell us about the relative amount of variation that can be explained by differences in class composition and in the voting behaviour of Erikson–Goldthorpe classes. Therefore, as a second step, we examine the extent to which variation in the voting behaviour of the Erikson–Goldthorpe classes, controlling for variation in the composition of these classes, is responsible for variation in manual/nonmanual class voting. To do this, we calculated Thomsen indices under the assumption of constant sub-class distributions over countries and time, but varying the voting behaviour of the Erikson–Goldthorpe sub-classes. As a baseline we chose the mean class distribution over all years and countries. The closer the Thomsen indices obtained in this second step are to the observed Thomsen indices, the more the variation in voting behaviour of the Erikson–Goldthorpe classes can explain variation in levels of class voting. Furthermore, if the Thomsen indices obtained in this second step are closer to the observed Thomsen indices than the Thomsen indices obtained in the first step, then the between-country variation in the composition of the manual and nonmanual classes explains less between-country variation in class voting, than does the between-country variation in the voting behaviour of these sub-classes.

In order not to be too dependent on individual datasets and possible error in them, we present in Table 2.7 the results of the two simulation steps and the observed values of the Thomsen indices for each country in three periods: 1961–70, 1971–80, and 1981–90. For these three periods we find that the mean of the Thomsen indices obtained under the assumption that voting behaviour was constant across the countries (and where the Erikson–Goldthorpe class distribution was allowed to vary) has a small level of variation across countries. The mean of the Thomsen indices obtained when assuming the class distribution to be constant across countries (and the voting behaviour of the classes to differ) shows more variation across countries. More importantly, the Thomsen indices of the various countries, predicted under the assumption of constant class distribution, very much resemble the observed Thomsen indices, whereas the Thomsen indices predicted under the assumption of constant voting behaviour do so to a much smaller extent. In other words, it seems that differences between countries in the observed Thomsen indices can be explained to a much smaller extent by differences in the composition of manual and nonmanual classes than by differences in the voting behaviour of sub-classes.

To quantify the relative contribution of these two explanations in accounting for variations in class voting, we estimated parameters of a simple linear regression model in which we took, for each period separately, the observed Thomsen indices as the dependent variable, and the Thomsen indices obtained in the first and second step as explanatory variables:

TABLE 2.7. *Observed and simulated levels of class voting (measured by Thomsen index) per period in sixteen countries, 1961–1990*

| Countries | 1961–1970 | | | 1971–1980 | | | 1981–1990 | | |
|---|---|---|---|---|---|---|---|---|---|
| | Observed | Simulated | | Observed | Simulated | | Observed | Simulated | |
| | | Vote constant | Class constant | | Vote constant | Class constant | | Vote constant | Class constant |
| Australia | 1.34 | 1.01 | 1.44 | 1.37 | 0.97 | 1.41 | 0.87 | 0.93 | 1.17 |
| Austria | — | — | — | 1.55 | 1.10 | 1.52 | 0.94 | 0.98 | 1.13 |
| Belgium | — | — | — | 1.30 | — | — | — | — | — |
| Britain | 1.66 | 0.93 | 1.79 | 1.39 | 0.94 | 1.63 | 1.28 | 0.95 | 1.47 |
| Canada | — | — | — | — | — | — | 0.84 | 1.04 | 0.14 |
| Denmark | — | — | — | 2.11 | 1.09 | — | 2.11 | 0.95 | 2.11 |
| Finland | — | — | — | 2.22 | 1.17 | 1.99 | — | — | — |
| France | — | — | — | 0.96 | 1.01 | 1.24 | — | — | — |
| Germany | 0.84 | 0.96 | 1.18 | 0.92 | 0.90 | 1.16 | 0.74 | 0.91 | 0.99 |
| Ireland | — | — | — | — | — | — | 1.18 | 1.15 | 0.88 |
| Italy | 0.73 | 0.82 | 1.19 | 0.85 | 0.95 | 1.12 | 0.58 | 0.91 | 0.71 |
| Netherlands | 1.04 | 0.94 | 1.33 | 0.99 | 0.92 | 1.24 | 0.78 | 0.90 | 1.07 |
| Norway | 1.85 | 1.10 | 1.77 | 1.69 | 1.06 | 1.74 | 1.08 | 0.98 | 1.05 |
| Sweden | — | — | — | 1.81 | 1.01 | 1.76 | 0.98 | 0.95 | 1.16 |
| Switzerland | — | — | — | 1.25 | 1.00 | 1.47 | — | — | — |
| United States | 0.83 | 1.00 | 0.97 | 0.56 | 0.95 | 0.69 | 0.43 | 0.95 | 0.41 |
| Mean | 1.18 | 0.97 | 1.38 | 1.36 | 1.01 | 1.41 | 0.98 | 0.97 | 0.93 |
| Std. deviation | 0.40 | 0.10 | 0.28 | 0.47 | 0.10 | 0.33 | 0.41 | 0.00 | 0.35 |

Observed Thomsen index =
$\beta_0 + \beta_1$*(Thomsen index: Vote constant)
$+ \beta_2$*(Thomsen index: Class constant).

The standardized parameter estimates $\beta_1$ and $\beta_2$ then represent the relative effects of differences in class composition and of differences in voting behaviour on the differences in class voting between the countries. It is to be noted that these two effects together explain all variation in levels of class voting between countries. Therefore, it holds that the variation in the observed Thomsen indices between countries can for $(\beta_1/(\beta_1 + \beta_2))*100$ per cent be explained by variation in class composition, and for $(\beta_2/(\beta_1 + \beta_2)) * 100$ per cent by variation in voting behaviour of the sub-classes.

Analyses for the three periods demonstrate that in the period 1961–70 a proportion of 0.315/(0.315 + 0.845), or 27 per cent of the variation in class voting, was due to variation in class composition between the countries. For the period 1971–80 this was 0.240/(0.240 + 0.800), or 23 per cent, and for the most recent period 0.438/(0.438 + 0.925), or 32 per cent.[6] Conversely, in the three subsequent periods about 73 per cent, 77 per cent, and 68 per cent of the variation in class voting between the countries can be explained by variation in the voting behaviour of the Erikson–Goldthorpe classes between these countries.

Thus, the conclusion is that on average about a quarter of the total variation in levels of manual/nonmanual class voting between countries can be explained by cross-national variation in the composition of manual and nonmanual classes. The remaining three-quarters can be explained by differences between countries in the voting behaviour of the sub-classes of the manual and nonmanual class. Thus, the claim by scholars such as Goldthorpe (1996*a*) and Hout, Brooks, and Manza (1995), that country differences in levels of manual and nonmanual class voting are to some extent the result of variations in the class composition of manual and nonmanual classes, seems to be correct.

## *Explaining Changes Over Time*

We next investigated the extent to which changes in the composition of the manual and nonmanual classes are responsible for the observed decline in class voting within most countries, when employing the manual/nonmanual distinction. For this purpose we applied similar analyses to those used for investigating differences between countries. The difference is that we now assume, not that voting behaviour and class distributions are constant over time and countries, but that voting behav-

[6] All unstandardized effect parameters differ significantly from zero at the 0.05 level.

iour and the Erikson–Goldthorpe class distribution are constant over time within countries. In doing so, we avoid confounding the effects of between-country and over-time variation in class composition.

As a first step, Thomsen indices of each year were calculated while assuming constant voting behaviour over time (not over countries) for the seven Erikson–Goldthorpe categories. In order not to be dependent upon incidental changes, we chose the average voting behaviour for each class in each country as a baseline. As a second step, we calculated Thomsen indices under the assumptions of varying voting behaviour but constant class distributions over time. The average voting behaviour within each country was chosen as a baseline.

If changes in the composition of the Erikson–Goldthorpe classes are to a substantial extent responsible for changes in class voting within countries, we would expect the Thomsen indices obtained in the first step to be closer to the observed Thomsen indices than the Thomsen indices obtained in the second step. We find, however, that there is hardly any over-time variation in the Thomsen indices from the first step within countries, whereas we find much over-time variation in Thomsen indices from the second step. This suggests that most of the over-time variation in observed levels of class voting is the result of changes in the voting behaviour of the Erikson–Goldthorpe classes, and only to a small extent, if at all, of changes in the composition of the manual and nonmanual classes.

We can again quantify the extent to which the observed over-time variation in levels of manual/nonmanual class voting can be explained by variation in class composition or by variation in the voting behaviour of the Erikson–Goldthorpe classes. We take the observed Thomsen indices as the dependent variable, for each country separately, and the Thomsen indices obtained in the first and second step as explanatory variables.[7] In the nine countries where we have data from more than two points in time, we find that changes in class composition to some extent explain changes in levels of manual/nonmanual class voting: in Australia the over-time variation in the composition of the manual and nonmanual classes explains 12 per cent of the over-time variation in the levels of class voting. In Austria it explains 31 per cent of the variation; in Britain 17 per cent; in Denmark 52 per cent; in Germany 18 per cent; in Italy 41 per cent; in the Netherlands 20 per cent; in Norway 3 per cent; and in the United States 5 per cent. Thus we can conclude that on average about a fifth of the changes in levels of manual/nonmanual class voting within countries can be explained by changes in the composition of those classes. The remaining four-fifths of the over-time variation in levels of manual/nonmanual class voting within

[7] In all countries, except Australia and Italy, the unstandardized effects differ significantly from zero at the 0.05 level. In Austria the estimated effect of 'Thomsen index: vote constant' is insignificant. In Italy both effect estimates are insignificant.

countries is due to changes in the voting behaviour of the sub-classes of the manual and nonmanual classes.

## CONCLUSIONS

Many scholars have argued that the strength of the relationship between class and voting behaviour differs between countries and that in many countries the strength of that relationship declined over the postwar period. These conclusions are particularly characteristic of research that applies measures of absolute class voting and uses a dichotomous manual/nonmanual class scheme. It has been claimed in response, however, that the use of measures of relative class voting and distinguishing between more detailed classes would lead to different conclusions.

In this chapter the tenability of these revisionist claims has been tested using a wide-ranging data set. The main finding is that the various measures of class voting yielded the same conclusions with respect to the class–vote ranking of countries. Furthermore, we could not detect major differences between measures in the rate of decline of class voting. The results indicate that substantial differences in levels of relative class voting existed between democratic industrialized countries in the postwar period. The Scandinavian countries and Britain had the highest levels of class voting, and the United States and Canada the lowest. Not unexpectedly, in the latter two countries we detected little evidence of a decline in class voting, probably because of the low level of class voting which already existed at the start of the postwar period. Similar conclusions apply, although less strongly, to Ireland, Switzerland, and the Netherlands. On the other hand, our analysis showed unequivocally that in countries where class voting was rather strong after the Second World War, there were substantial declines in levels of class voting. In most of these countries, the fluctuations in class voting can in our view be regarded as part of an overall declining trend, and not as trendless fluctuations. These results, however, do not imply that revisionist claims about the impact of changes in class composition were wrong. Simulations indicate that variations of composition within the manual and nonmanual classes are, although to a small extent, responsible for cross-national and over-time differences in levels of class voting.

Some might argue that in this chapter we have not fully utilized the possibilities offered by revisionist arguments. To begin with, we were dealing with a question that pertains only to the overall levels of class voting in countries. Thus we did not examine the voting behaviour of these detailed classes separately, nor did we investigate the specific trends in the voting behaviour of these different classes. Such class-specific trends are of interest, since—as suggested, for example, for Britain by Heath *et al.* (1991)

and Evans, Heath, and Payne (1991)—some classes might have started to vote less according to their class interest, while others might have kept the same voting pattern or even started to vote more according to their interests. These separate class-specific trends cannot always be detected fully when investigating the overall levels of class voting. Therefore, in future studies, the focus should not be restricted to overall levels of class voting, but should also be concerned with class-specific voting behaviour.

Another relevant issue is whether the Erikson–Goldthorpe class schema is precise enough to take into account important institutional changes in postindustrial societies. There are indications that the Erikson–Goldthorpe class categories are not detailed enough to tap relevant changes over time. It has been suggested, for example, that intra-class variations in voting behaviour—especially in the service class—are more marked than inter-class variations (Butler and Savage 1995; De Graaf and Steijn 1997). The service class has also grown in size and some authors (e.g. Inglehart 1990; Kriesi 1989) propose that within this class there is a substantial sub-class of 'cultural and social' specialists. This sub-class, which is characteristic of postindustrial society, has a left-wing rather than a right-wing political preference. In the Netherlands, members of this sub-class are among the strongest supporters of left-wing parties (De Graaf and Steijn 1997) rather than providing a *conservative* element within modern society (Goldthorpe 1982: 100).

Is class the only traditional cleavage that is in decline? Franklin *et al.* (1992), Inglehart (1990), and De Graaf (1996) suggest that there is also a decline in religious voting. Inglehart's explanation is most explicit: he claims that due to increasing affluence the classic left–right issues are in decline and higher levels of education are responsible for a secularization trend and less traditional voting. If transitions in religious and class cleavages are indeed connected, it might be worthwhile to study these simultaneously (see Need 1997; and Walter Müller in this volume)—especially as in most European countries religious cleavages are more important for political behaviour than class cleavages.

It might also be worthwhile to distinguish between the different types of political parties that compete with each other, rather than just the left–right distinction operationalized here. This would make it possible to find out whether substantial changes in the voting patterns of social classes have occurred within left-wing or right-wing political blocks. For example, it is possible that in a country where we did not find a systematic decline in class voting, the manual workers are just as likely to vote for left-wing parties as before, but are less apt to vote for extreme left-wing parties, choosing instead more moderate left-wing parties. Evans, Heath, and Payne (1991; Heath *et al.* 1995) have already applied more detailed party classifications when investigating trends in Britain, while Hout, Brooks, and Manza (1995) have done likewise for the United States and Ringdal and Hines (1995) for Norway. Also, of course, the other chapters in this volume present for some countries the most extensive set of analyses yet undertaken of class voting in the context of more detailed party choices. At present, however, it is not possible to model comparative trends for many countries *simultaneously* when distinguishing between several political parties. We believe therefore that the comparative analysis of traditional left/right class voting presented here is a major step forward.

# APPENDIX A
## Aggregated Country Data

The aggregated country data analysed in this chapter—324 tables cross-classifying class (manual/nonmanual) by party voted for (left-wing/right-wing) from twenty countries in the period 1945–90, were collected from two types of sources: tables published in various articles and books, and tables calculated with the individual-level data (see data references and Nieuwbeerta and Ganzeboom 1996).

The tables published in articles and books come from the following sources: Australia: Alford (1963); Baxter *et al.* (1991); McAllister (personal communication 1992); Rose (1974*a*). Austria: Rose and Urwin (1969); Crewe and Denver (1985); Lijphart (1971); Lane and Ersson (1994). Belgium: Frognier (1975); Lijphart (1971); Rose (1980). Britain: Alford (1963); Heath *et al.* (1985, 1991); NORC (1948); Rose and McAllister (1986). Canada: Alford (1963); Rose (1974*a*, 1980). Denmark: Andersen (1984); Lane and Ersson (1994); Rose (1980); Sainsbury (1990). Finland: Allardt and Littunen (1964); Allardt and Wesolowski (1978); Berglund (1988); Matheson (1979); Rose and Urwin (1969); Rose (1974*a*). France: Converse and Pierce (1986); Dalton (1996); Dalton *et al.* (1984); MacRae (1967). Germany: Dalton (1996); Forschungsgruppe Wahlen (1990); De Jong (1956); Lijphart (1971); Rose and Urwin (1969). Ireland: Crewe and Denver (1985); Laver *et al.* (1987); Rose (1974*a*). Italy: Allum (1979); Crewe and Denver (1985); Lijphart (1971); Lipset (1981); Rose (1974*a*); Von Beyme (1985); Rose and Urwin (1969). Netherlands: Lijphart (1968). Norway: Listhaug (1989); Valen (personal communication 1992). Portugal: Lane and Ersson (1994). Spain: Gunther *et al.* (1986); Rose (1980). Sweden: Holmberg (1991); Stephens (1981). Switzerland: Kerr (1987); Lane and Ersson (1994); Rose (1980). United States: Alford (1963); Abramson *et al.* (1990).

# APPENDIX B
## Left-Wing Political Parties

| | |
|---|---|
| Australia | Australian Labor Party (0101); Communist Party (0110); Democratic Labor Party (0121); Queensland Labor Party (0122). |
| Austria | Socialists (0201); Communist Party (0205); Democratic Progressive Party (0212). |
| Belgium | Belgian Socialist Party (0303); Communist Party (0310); Walloon Workers' Party (0317); Labour Party (0324); Flemish Socialist Party (0330). |
| Britain | Labour Party (2406); Communist Party (2410); Social Democratic and Labour Party (2418); Social Democratic Party (2420). |
| Canada | Communist Party–Labour Progressive Party (0406); New Democratic Party (0408). |
| Denmark | Social Democrats (0504); Communist Party (0509); Socialist People's Party (0516); Left Socialist Party (0518). |
| Finland | Social Democrats (0601); Finnish People's Democratic Union (0613); Social Democratic League of Workers and Smallholders (0615); Democratic Alternative (0622). |
| France | Socialist Party (0701); Communist Party (0709); other extreme left (0718); Unified Socialist Party (0719); other left (0727). |
| Germany | Social Democrats (0802); Communist Party (0828); Action for Democratic Progress (0850). |
| Greece | Communist Party of Greece (0904); United Democratic Left (0925); Communist Party of Greece (0935); Pan-Hellenic Socialist Movement (0937); Greek left (0945). |
| Ireland | Irish Labour Party (1108); Communists (1109); National Progressive Democrats (1118); Workers' Party (1119); Socialist Labour Party (1121); Democratic Socialist Party (1123). |
| Italy | Socialist Party (1303); Communist Party (1311); Social Democrats (1323); United Socialist Party (1331); Manifesto/Party of Proletarian Unity for Communism (1332); Proletarian Democracy (1337). |
| Luxembourg | Social Democratic Party (1502); Communist Party (1507); Social Democratic Party (1519); Independent Socialists (1521). |
| Netherlands | Communist Party (1710); Labour Party (1723); Pacifist Socialist Party (1727); Democratic Socialists '70 (1730). |
| Norway | Labour Party (1904); Communist Party (1909); Socialist People's Party (1914). |
| Portugal | Communist Party (2002); Socialist Party (2004); Democratic Movement (2005); Movement of the Socialist Left (2006); Popular Democratic Union (2007); Revolutionary Socialist |

| | |
|---|---|
| | Party (2012); Union of the Socialist and Democratic Left (2013); Socialist Unity Party (2015). |
| Spain | Socialist Party (2101); Communist Party (2102); Popular Socialist Party (2132); Spanish Labour Party (2133). |
| Sweden | Social Democrats (2205); Communist Party (2210). |
| Switzerland | Social Democrats (2305); Communist Party (2309); Autonomous Socialist Party (2317). |
| United States | Democratic Party (2501); Socialist Labor Party (2515); Socialist Party (2517); Communist Party (2521). |

*Note*: The numbers in parentheses refer to the numbers of the chapters and parties in Mackie and Rose (1991).

# APPENDIX C
## Data References


| | |
|---|---|
| DDA:081 | E. Allardt and H. Uusitalo, *Scandinavian Welfare Survey, 1972.* |
| ESRC:1577 | S. Bernard, S. Delruelle *et al.*, *Belgian Citizen in the Political System, 1975.* |
| ESRC:1987 | J. Capdevielle, E. Dupoirier, G. Grunberg, E. Schweisguth, and C. Ysmal, *French National Election Study, 1978.* |
| ICPSR:7004 | D. Butler and D. E. Stokes, *Political Change in Britain, 1969–1970.* |
| ICPSR:7098 | H.-D. Klingemann and F. U. Pappi, *German Pre- and Post-Election Study, 1969.* |
| ICPSR:7108 | M. Kaase, U. Schleth, W. Adrian, M. Berger, and R. Wildenmann, *German Election Study: August–September 1969.* |
| ICPSR:7214 | A. Campbell, P. Converse *et al.*, *American National Election Study, 1956.* |
| ICPSR:7215 | A. Campbell, P. Converse *et al.*, *American National Election Study, 1958.* |
| ICPSR:7216 | A. Campbell, P. Converse *et al.*, *American National Election Study, 1960.* |
| ICPSR:7235 | SRC (Survey Research Center, *American National Election Study, 1964*). |
| ICPSR:7250 | D. Butler and D. E. Stokes, *Political Change in Britain, 1963–1970.* |
| ICPSR:7256 | H. Valen, *Norwegian Election Study, 1965.* |
| ICPSR:7259 | SRC (Survey Research Center), *American National Election Study, 1966.* |
| ICPSR:7261 | F. M. Heunks, M. K. Jennings, W. E. Miller, P. C. Stouthard, and J. Thomassen, *Dutch Election Study, 1970–1973.* |
| ICPSR:7281 | SRC (Survey Research Center), *American National Election Study, 1968.* |
| ICPSR:7282 | D. Aitkin, M. Kahan, and D. E. Stokes, *Australian National Political Attitudes, 1967.* |
| ICPSR:7298 | CPS (Center for Political Studies), *American National Election Study, 1970.* |
| ICPSR:7342 | H. Kerr, D. Sidjanski, and G. Schmidtchen, *Swiss Voting Study, 1972.* |
| ICPSR:7768 | S. Verba, N. H. Nie, and J.-O. Kim, *Political Participation and Equality in Seven Nations, 1966–1971.* |
| ICPSR:7777 | S. H. Barnes and M. Kaase *et al.*, *Political Action: An Eight Nation Study, 1973–1976.* |
| ICPSR:7870 | I. Crewe, B. Sarlvik, and J. Alt, *British Election Study: October 1974, Cross-Section.* |

| | |
|---|---|
| ICPSR:7953 | S. H. Barnes, *Italian Mass Election Survey, 1968.* |
| ICPSR:8196 | I. Crewe, B. Sarlvik, and D. Robertson, *British Election Study: May 1979, Cross-Section.* |
| ICPSR:8409 | A. F. Heath, R. M. Jowell, J. K. Curtice, and E. J. Field, *British Election Study: June 1983.* |
| ICPSR:8544 | R. D. Lambert, S. D. Brown, J. E. Curtis, B. J. Kay, and J. M. Wilson, *Canadian National Election Study, 1984.* |
| ICPSR:8909 | International Social Science Program (ISSP), *International Social Science Program: Role of Government, 1985–1986.* |
| ICPSR:8946 | O. Borre *et al.*, *Danish Election Studies Continuity File, 1971–1981.* |
| ICPSR:9205 | International Social Science Program (ISSP), *International Social Science Program: Social Networks and Support Systems, 1986.* |
| ICPSR:9383 | International Social Science Program (ISSP), *International Social Science Program: Social Inequality, 1987.* |
| ICPSR:9505 | J. A. Davis and T. W. Smith, *General Social Survey Cumulative File, 1972–1991.* |
| NSD:NOR77e | H. Valen, *Norwegian Election Study, 1977.* |
| NSD:NOR81e | H. Valen, *Norwegian Election Study, 1981.* |
| NSD:NOR85e | H. Valen, *Norwegian Election Study, 1985.* |
| NSD:NOR89e | H. Valen, *Norwegian Election Study, 1989.* |
| NSD:NOR90e | H. Valen, *Norwegian Election Study, 1990.* |
| NYM:BRI87e | A. F. Heath *et al.*, *British Election Study: 1987.* |
| NYM:ITA85 | Department of Social Policy, University of Trento, Department of Educational Science, University of Bologna, and Department of Human Science, University of Trieste, *Survey of Social Mobility and Education Italy, 1985.* |
| NYM:NET87 | P. L. J. Hermkens and P. J. van Wijngaarden, *Criteria for Justification of Income Differences, Netherlands 1987.* |
| NYM:NET89 | K. Arts, E. Hollander, K. Renckstorf, and P. Verschuren, *Media-Equipment, Media-Exposure and Media-Use in the Netherlands, 1989.* |
| NYM:SWE90 | S. Svallfors, *Attitudes to Inequality, 1990.* |
| SSDA:423 | J. L. Kelley, R. G. Cushing, and B. Headey, *Australian National Social Science Survey, 1984.* |
| SSDA:445 | I. McAllister and A. Mughan, *Australian Election Survey, 1987.* |
| SSDA:570 | I. McAllister, R. Jones, E. Papodalis, and D. Gow, *Australian Election Survey, 1990.* |
| SSDA:7 | L. Broom, F. L. Jones, and J. Zubrzycki, *Social Stratification in Australia, 1965.* |
| SSDA:8 | L. Broom, P. Duncan-Jones, F. L. Jones, P. McDonnel, and T. Williams, *Social Mobility in Australia Project, 1973.* |
| SSDA:9 | D. Aitkin, *MacQuarie University Australian Political Attitudes Survey, 1979.* |
| STEIN:P0328 | Centraal Bureau voor Statistiek (CBS), *Life Situation Survey, Netherlands 1977.* |

| | |
|---|---|
| STEIN:P0350 | Werkgroep Nationaal Kiezersonderzoek, *Dutch Parliamentary Election Study, 1981*. |
| STEIN:P0353 | Werkgroep Nationaal Kiezersonderzoek, *Dutch Parliamentary Election Study, 1972*. |
| STEIN:P0354 | Werkgroep Nationaal Kiezersonderzoek, *Dutch Parliamentary Election Study, 1977*. |
| STEIN:P0633 | Werkgroep Nationaal Kiezersonderzoek, *Dutch Parliamentary Election Study, 1982*. |
| STEIN:P0653 | P. L. J. Hermkens and P. J. van Wijngaarden, *Criteria for Justification of Income Differences, Netherlands 1976*. |
| STEIN:P0866 | C. Van der Eijk, G. A. Irwin, and B. Niemoeller, *Dutch Parliamentary Elections Study, 1986*. |
| STEIN:P1012 | A. J. A. Felling, J. Peters, and O. Schreuder, *Social Relevance of Religion in the Netherlands, 1985*. |
| STEIN:P1100 | A. Felling, J. Peters, and O. Schreuder, *Social Relevance of Religion in the Netherlands, 1990*. |
| ZA:1188 | K. R. Allerbeck, M. Kaase, H.-D. Klingemann, P. C. Stouthard, F. J. Heunks, J. J. A. Thomassen, J. W. van Deth, S. H. Barnes, B. G. Farah, R. Inglehart, and M. K. Jennings, *Political Action II, 1979–1980*. |
| ZA:1233 | ZUMA (Zentrum für Umfragen, Methoden, und Analysen, *ZUMA-Standard Demographie (Zeitreihe), Germany 1976–1980*. |
| ZA:1700 | International Social Science Program (ISSP), *International Social Science Program: Family and Changing Sex Roles, 1988*. |
| ZA:1795 | K. R. Allerbeck, M. R. Lepsius, K. U. Mayer, W. Müller, K.-D. Opp, F. U. Pappi, E. K. Schreuch, and R. Ziegler, *Allgemeine Bevolkerungsumfrage der Sozialwissenschaften Allbus Kumulierter Datensatz, 1980–1988*. |
| ZA:1800 | ZUMA (Zentrum für Umfragen, Methoden, und Analysen, *German Social Survey (Allbus), 1990*. |
| ZA:1840 | International Social Science Program (ISSP), *International Social Science Program: Work Orientations, 1989*. |
| ZA:1950 | International Social Science Program (ISSP), *International Social Science Program: Role of Government II, 1990*. |

*Data Archives*

| | |
|---|---|
| DDA | Danish Data Archive, Odense, Denmark. |
| ESRC | Economic and Social Research Council Data Archive, Essex, United Kingdom. |
| ICPSR | Inter-University Consortium for Political and Social Research, Ann Arbor, USA. |
| NSD | Norwegian Social Science Data Service, Bergen, Norway. |

| | |
|---|---|
| NYM | Department of Sociology, University of Nijmegen, Nijmegen, The Netherlands. |
| SSDA | Social Science Data Archive, Canberra, Australia. |
| STEIN | Steinmetz Archive, Amsterdam, The Netherlands. |
| ZA | Zentral Archive, Köln, Germany. |

# PART II

## Case Studies of Western Democracies

# 3

## Modelling the Pattern of Class Voting in British Elections, 1964–1992

JOHN H. GOLDTHORPE

### INTRODUCTION

The relationship between class and party within modern democracies is a matter of protracted debate (Manza *et al.* 1995; Goldthorpe 1996*a*). Over the course of the debate, the techniques that have been applied in analysing data on class and party support have steadily developed. The general direction taken by this development—close parallels can be found in other areas of sociological research—has been from a reliance on entirely ad hoc indices through to the application of formal statistical models of increasing analytic power. The present chapter is intended to contribute to this process.

At the centre of the debate is the question of whether, as the economic development of modern societies proceeds, the association between class and party support shows a steady and general decline. Consequently, the typical form of the data analysed has been a series of class-by-party (i.e. party preference or reported vote) tables, extending over a period of years or a number of national elections. Attempts to establish trends in class voting on the basis of such data were initially made by the use of the Alford Index (Alford 1962, 1963), and further indices, some improving on Alford (e.g. Thomsen 1987), others not (e.g. Rose and McAllister 1986; Dunleavy 1987), were subsequently proposed and implemented.

However, a significant advance was made by Heath, Jowell, and Curtice (1985) who organized data from successive British Election Surveys (BES)

An earlier version of this paper was presented to the meeting of the ISA Research Committee on Social Stratification and Mobility, held in conjunction with the World Congress of Sociology, Bielefeld, Germany, in 1994. I am grateful to Clem Brooks, David Cox, Robert Erikson, David Firth, Garret Fitzmaurice, Anthony Heath, Hiroshi Ishida, and Clive Payne for critical comments on this version and for help in the present revision. I am also indebted to Anthony Heath for providing me with data from the British General Election Surveys.

into a *three-way* table of class ($C$) by party ($P$) *by* election ($E$), and then applied the simple loglinear model

$$\log F_{ijk} = \mu + \lambda_i^{C} + \lambda_j^{P} + \lambda_k^{E} + \lambda_{ik}^{CE} + \lambda_{jk}^{PE} + \lambda_{ij}^{CP} \qquad (3.1)$$

where $F_{ijk}$ is the expected frequency in the *ijk*th cell of the three-way table. The model thus proposes 'constant class voting' in that no term is included for the possible three-way interaction $\lambda_{ijk}^{CPE}$ which would allow the level of class–party association to differ across elections. In other words, the model of equation (3.1) requires that all corresponding odds ratios defining the pattern of association between class and party remain identical from one election to another.

This new approach had two major advantages over the use of indices. First, it opened up the possibility of subjecting hypotheses on the class–party relationship to formal test. Secondly, and still more importantly, while the Alford and other indices could be applied only to two-by-two class-by-party tables—which can be shown to be conceptually quite inadequate (see Goldthorpe 1996*a*; cf. also Whitten and Palmer 1996)—modelling methods were subject to no such limitation. Heath and his associates worked with a five-class version of the schema proposed by Goldthorpe (1987) and with three party categories, Conservative, Labour, and Liberals (i.e. the 'old' Liberals, the Alliance, or the Liberal Democrats, according to period).[1]

In the British case, the constant class voting (CCV) model proved in fact to give a rather close fit to data for elections from 1964 to 1983, thus undermining widely canvassed notions of progressive 'class dealignment' in party support (e.g. Butler and Kavanagh 1980; Sarlvik and Crewe 1983; Robertson 1984; Franklin, 1985*a*; Kelley *et al.* 1985). And, more recently, Heath and his associates have shown that a similar result is obtained if the elections of 1987 and 1992 are also included in the series (Heath *et al.* 1991; Evans *et al.* 1991, 1996; Heath *et al.* 1994).

Further, though, in this later work, greater recognition has been given to the fact that the CCV model is in fact a rather crude one, which, even while providing a close reproduction of the data overall, might still fail to

[1] Another crucial advantage that the modelling approach has over all indices proposed, except for that of Thomsen, is that it enables the association between class and vote to be treated *net* of effects deriving from the marginal distributions of the class-by-party table. The obvious 'margin-insensitive' measure of association to adopt is the odds ratio. The Thomsen index is simply the single odds ratio calculable from a two-by-two class-by-party table, expressed in log form. Odds ratios are, however, the basic elements of loglinear models, and such models can be used to test hypotheses relating to the entire set of odds ratios implicit in contingency tables of any form or dimension. It is easy to show how indices that are not 'margin-insensitive' can lead to misleading conclusions, especially regarding *changes* in the class–vote association, on account of the confounding of effects that they entail.

detect minor changes in the class–vote association—including ones that could represent a steady, even if slight, reduction in its strength.[2] In order then to test for such a possibility, the CCV model has been supplemented by one of a more refined, logmultiplicative character, initially proposed by Erikson and Goldthorpe (1992*a*; cf. also Xie 1992) in the context of social mobility research. This 'uniform difference' (UNIDIFF) model may, as applied to three-way class, party, and election tables, be written as

$$\log F_{ijk} = \mu + \lambda_i^{C} + \lambda_j^{P} + \lambda_k^{E} + \lambda_{ik}^{CE} + \lambda_{jk}^{PE} + \beta_k X_{ij} \qquad (3.2)$$

where $X_{ij}$ represents the *general pattern* of the class–vote association over elections—to be derived initially from the $\lambda_{ij}^{CP}$ term in the CCV model (3.1)—and $\beta_k$ represents the *relative strength* of this association that is *specific* to the *k*th election.

By way of illustration, Table 3.1 shows the result of fitting both the CCV and UNIDIFF models to the British data for the entire period 1964 to 1992, and Figure 3.1 plots the β parameters estimated under the UNIDIFF model. In this analysis the full version of the Goldthorpe (1987) class schema is used, thus giving a seven (classes) by three (parties) by nine (elections) array.[3] Three main conclusions can be drawn from the results presented.

1. As already noted, the CCV model fits rather well. Although the p value indicates a statistically significant degree of deviation, this is of no great magnitude: the model accounts for almost 95 per cent of the total class–vote association and misclassifies only a little over 3 per cent of all individual cases.
2. The UNIDIFF model does give a significant improvement in fit over the CCV model—a reduction in $G^2$ of 27.4 is achieved for the 8 degrees

[2] It is ironic that while the initial work of Heath *et al.* attracted a good deal of criticism (e.g. Crewe 1986; Dunleavy 1987), this was largely ill-informed and quite failed to identify the 'global' nature of the CCV model as, potentially, the most serious limitation of their analyses at this stage of their development.

[3] An account of the theoretical basis of the class schema is given in Erikson and Goldthorpe (1992*a*: ch. 2). In the tables used here—and subsequently in the paper—the class position of respondents is determined by 'head of household's' class. Thus, a married woman is usually allocated to the same class as her husband. This practice is followed in preference to an 'individual' approach since the latter tends to produce a lower association between class and party preference (Erikson and Goldthorpe 1992*b*). However, it appears (Heath *et al.* 1995) that the results of analyses of class voting carried out on the basis of the BES dataset are little affected by this choice of the unit of class composition. On the party axis, it would in principle be desirable also to add a category of 'non-voter', since non-voting may itself constitute an important aspect of the class–party relationship as, for example, in the USA (Hout *et al.* 1995). However, in the British case, it appears that non-voting has rather little connection with class position (Swaddle and Heath 1989).

TABLE 3.1. *Results of fitting the CCV and UNIDIFF models to seven-by-three class-by-party tables for nine British elections, 1964–1992*

| Model | $G^2$ | df | p | $rG^2$ | Δ |
|---|---|---|---|---|---|
| Conditional independence | 2,524.6 | 108 | 0.00 | — | 16.8 |
| CCV | 134.0 | 96 | 0.01 | 94.7 | 3.2 |
| UNIDIFF | 106.6 | 88 | 0.09 | 95.8 | 2.8 |
| (N = 16,866) | | | | | |

β parameters for each election under UNIDIFF model (average = 0)

| 1964 | 1966 | 1970 | 1974[a] | 1974[b] | 1979 | 1983 | 1987 | 1992 |
|---|---|---|---|---|---|---|---|---|
| 0.24 | 0.11 | –0.17 | 0.02 | 0.06 | –0.14 | 0.02 | –0.13 | 0.01 |

*Notes*: [a] February election.
[b] October election.

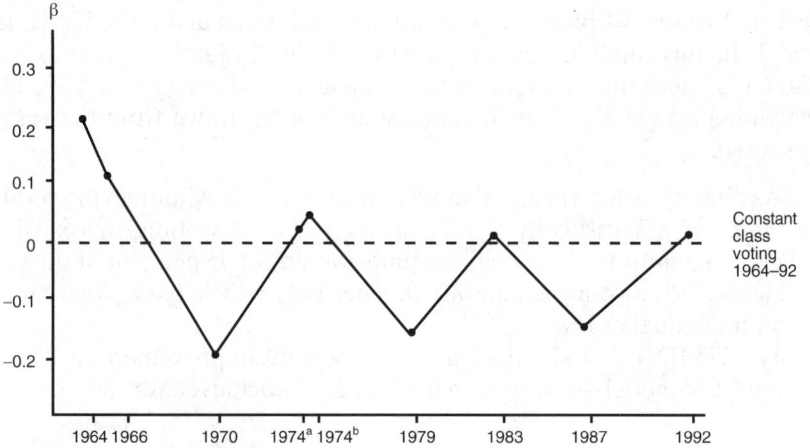


FIG. 3.1. β parameters for each election under the UNIDIFF model (average = 0)

*Notes*: [a] February election.
[b] October election.

of freedom (df) lost—although the change in the other statistics of fit is small. That is to say, it is suggested that some real, but rather slight, changes have occurred across elections in the strength of the class–vote association.

3. However, the β parameters from the UNIDIFF model reveal that these changes do not take the form of a monotonically decreasing trend—as claims of 'class dealignment' in voting would imply. A decline in class voting is indicated from 1964 to 1970 but afterwards

there is merely fluctuation. Class voting in 1992—as also in 1983—was in fact at the average level for the whole period covered.

Finally in this connection it has to be noted that Fitzmaurice (1995) has raised the issue of probable overdispersion in large-scale datasets such as that provided by the BES: that is, the presence of more variability in the data than is predicted by the assumed sampling model. When a correction for overdispersion proposed by Fitzmaurice is applied to the analyses shown in Table 3.1, it is no longer possible to reject the CCV model by conventional standards ($p > 0.05$), even though the UNIDIFF model still gives a significant improvement in fit.

These findings, taken overall, are of obvious importance. They correct those of earlier studies that lacked statistical and conceptual refinement and in this way call into question the conventional wisdom regarding the weakening influence of class in British electoral politics.[4] At the same time, they carry implications for party electoral strategies that seem not always to have been fully appreciated. However, they remain in one major respect incomplete. They tell one about the trend—or rather the absence thereof—in the net association between class and party support but they do not say anything about the actual *pattern* on which this support is produced and, it would seem, reproduced, with a notable degree of temporal stability. The primary aim of the present paper, then, is to extend the statistical modelling of class voting in the British case in order to make good this shortcoming and, on this basis, to add something further to the debate on class and party from a rather novel perspective.

## A TOPOLOGICAL MODEL FOR THE PATTERN OF CLASS VOTING

A type of loglinear model does in fact exist which appears well suited to the purpose in hand. This is what has been described by Hauser (1979) as a 'structural' model and by Hout (1983)—as applied in the analysis of social mobility tables—as a 'topological' model. The basic idea of such a model is to reproduce the data of a two-way contingency table by allocating each of its internal cells to a number of subsets, and then requiring that

[4] Weakliem and Heath (Chapter 5, this volume) show that if use is made of more extensive Gallup poll data—which, it should be recognized, are by no means of the same quality as those of the BES—then the period of decline in class voting can be seen as extending from 1945 to 1970. However, these same data also indicate that class voting in 1935 was much lower than in 1945, so that the overall trend over the last sixty years is a curvilinear one—that is to say, still inconsistent with a thesis of progressive decline.

all cells placed in the same subset show the same level of association or 'interaction'.

Formally, such a model, for a class-by-party table, could be written as

$$\log F_{ij} = \mu + \lambda_i^{C} + \lambda_j^{P} + \lambda_{a(ij)}^{L} \tag{3.3}$$

where the $\lambda_{a(ij)}^{L}$ term refers to the particular subset—and thus level of interaction—to which the *ij*th cell of the table is allocated.

From the foregoing, it may be understood that simply to devise a statistically acceptable topological model need not prove difficult: the number of subsets of cells, or levels of interaction, deemed to be present in the table can simply be increased, and particular cells shifted between them, until a good fit to the data is achieved. However, if a model is to be of some substantive value, it is important that the number of levels should be kept small and, further, that the allocation of cells to levels should be carried out according to some explicit rationale.

In the case of a class-by-party table there is, fortunately, one rather obvious starting-point for designing a topological model in a fairly parsimonious and intelligible way: namely, the well-established idea of 'natural' class parties. Drawing on this idea, one may envisage a model in which the number of levels pertaining to the strength of the association between class and vote is limited to just three:

1. a positive level for cells in the table referring to class–party pairs where the party can be regarded as the natural one for members of the class to support—that is, a party for which they have a distinctive propensity to vote on account of class interests, ideologies, identities, and so on;
2. conversely, a negative level, for cells in the table referring to class–party pairs where the party can be regarded as an 'unnatural' one for members of the class to support—that is, a party for which they have a distinctive propensity not to vote;
3. a neutral level, for cells in the table referring to class–party pairs where the party can be regarded as neither a natural nor an 'unnatural' one for members of the class—that is, a party which they have no particular propensity either to support or to shun.

If, then, it is supposed that each class should have a natural party but may be either negative or neutral towards other parties, a three-level design for seven-by-three class-by-party tables of the kind previously analysed may be suggested along the lines shown in Table 3.2. The propositions embodied in this design are not, it should be said, ones rigorously derived from pre-existing theory, since no theory of the class–vote relationship has so far been elaborated to an extent that would allow for such a derivation.

TABLE 3.2. *Design for the allocation of cells of the seven-by-three class-by-party table to three levels of interaction: positive, negative, and neutral*

| Class | | Conservative | Labour | Liberal |
|---|---|---|---|---|
| I | Service class or salariat, higher | + | − | 0 |
| II | Service class or salariat, lower | + | 0 | 0 |
| III | Routine nonmanual workers | + | 0 | 0 |
| IV | Petty bourgeoisie | + | − | − |
| V | Supervisors of manual workers and technicians | 0 | + | 0 |
| VI | Skilled mannual workers | − | + | − |
| VII | Nonskilled manual workers | − | + | − |

The design is, however, influenced by the results of recent work (see especially Evans 1993*b*; Clifford and Heath 1993; Weakliem and Heath 1994; De Graaf *et al.* 1995) that has begun to investigate, both empirically and theoretically, how features of the class positions distinguished by the schema are actually linked to the political attitudes and preferences of individuals holding these positions (or having been mobile between them). Moreover, a good part of what is claimed should not be found surprising from any standpoint. The Conservative and Labour parties are seen as having their main sources of support in two different areas of the class structure—broadly speaking, in the nonmanual and manual classes, respectively—while the Liberals are without a clear class base. In more detail, the higher and lower divisions of the salariat or service class, classes I and II, the routine nonmanual class, class III, and the petty bourgeoisie, class IV, are each given the Conservative Party as their natural party, while the natural party of both the skilled and the nonskilled divisions of the working class, classes VI and VII, and also of supervisors of manual workers and lower technicians, class V, is taken to be Labour.

In so far as the design of the model does run counter to certain notions that have been at least implicit in previous studies of class voting, it is in regard to 'unnatural' and neutral pairings. What is in effect claimed is that differences in class interests, ideologies, and identities do here find expression in political preferences and partisanship *within* both the nonmanual and the manual 'blocs'. Thus, in the former case, class IV, the petty bourgeoisie of small proprietors and self-employed workers, is seen as the class whose members will be most unequivocally positive towards key right-wing policies of low, and less progressive, taxation, downward pressure on social welfare expenditure, and labour-market deregulation: hence, a negative orientation is indicated to both Labour and the Liberals. However, for the other nonmanual classes the situation is not quite so clear-cut.

Although those at higher income levels, in class I especially, will stand to benefit substantially from right-wing fiscal policies, classes I, II, and III alike are primarily employee classes with therefore some employee interests in labour markets; and further, members of classes II and III, as well as being less able to afford private welfare services, are also more likely than members of class I to be dependent on the state welfare sector for employment opportunities. While, then, class I is represented as having a negative propensity to vote Labour but as being neutral in relation to the Liberals, classes II and III are seen as being neutral towards both the Liberals *and* Labour.

Somewhat analogously within the manual bloc, class V, that of manual foremen and lower-level technicians, is treated as having a neutral voting propensity towards both the Conservatives and the Liberals, whereas classes VI and VII are seen as negative to both. The consideration here is that members of class V tend not only to have higher incomes than rank-and-file manual wage-workers but, more importantly, better economic *prospects* in terms of continuity of employment, pay increases, and eventual promotion into the salariat. Note, however, that the class schema provides little basis for differentiating voting propensities as between classes VI and VII, the skilled and non-skilled divisions of the working class, and that no such differentiation is in fact made in Table 3.2—contrary to the frequent claims of political pundits that skilled workers have shown a clearly stronger propensity to vote Conservative.

The general implication of the model devised for seven-by-three class-by-party tables is then that while the manual/nonmanual division is of evident importance in shaping the pattern of class-voting propensities, to rely *merely* on such a dichotomy—as other analyses of class voting have often done—is unacceptably crude; and, further, that such crudity is only compounded where parties are likewise forced into a twofold division, that is, of 'left' and 'non-left'.

One other preliminary point should be made here concerning the voting propensities indicated in Table 3.2. These are *not* to be understood as referring to the simple probabilities of individuals voting, or not voting, for particular parties. As will be shown later, it is possible, once the model proposed is estimated, for these propensities to be given a precise interpretation in terms of odds ratios. But, for the present, they might best be regarded as referring to the voting propensities of collectivities of class members *considered as such and relative to those of other class collectivities*. It is evident from equation (3.3) that the actual number occurring in any cell of the class-by-party table—that is, the actual number of individuals in class *i* voting for party *j*—is not determined by these propensities alone but also by other terms in the model (to be discussed further below) that pertain, on the one hand, to the relative sizes of classes and, on the other, to the relative attractiveness of parties *considered apart from* all propensities for class voting.

## THE MODEL APPLIED

The model that has been proposed for the pattern of class voting in Britain exploits the idea of natural class parties in a fairly simple and straightforward manner. But the question remains, of course, of how well it is able to reproduce the relevant data. Moreover, since the main purpose of developing the model is to elucidate the pattern of class voting that appears to have *persisted* over a series of elections, attention must centre not on the fit of the model to class-by-party tables taken election by election but rather on its performance when applied *simultaneously* to such tables for *all* elections in the series—that is, for all nine elections from 1964 to 1992. As thus applied, the model may be written as

$$\log F_{ijk} = \mu + \lambda_i^{C} + \lambda_j^{P} + \lambda_k^{E} + \lambda_{ik}^{CE} + \lambda_{jk}^{PE} + \lambda_{a(ij)}^{L} \tag{3.4}$$

where $L = 3$ and the allocation of cells to these levels, for all elections alike, is as indicated in Table 3.2.

The results of fitting the model in this way are reported in the second row of the upper panel of Table 3.3. As comparison with Table 3.1 will reveal, the data are not now as well reproduced as by the CCV model—which is indeed only to be expected. The CCV model is an 'all-interactions' model: that is, it allows each cell in the class-by-party table to take its own level of interaction (though this must, of course, remain constant across elections). However, the very point of a topological model is to restrict levels of interaction—as in the present case to just three. In other words, as applied across elections in the form of equation (3.4), the model not only requires constant class voting but, further, that this constancy should follow a fairly elementary pattern.[5]

The relevant question is, therefore, whether the loss in fit that occurs in moving from the CCV to the topological model is compensated for by the greater interpretability that the latter affords. In fact, although the difference in fit is statistically significant, it is still quite small. As can also be

[5] Another way of putting this is to say that the odds ratios expressing the net association between class and vote are much restricted in the values they can take. In fact, with only three levels of interaction, the maximum number of different odds ratios is thirteen. David Firth has provided the following general formula for this maximum $R$, where $k$ is the number of interaction levels: $R_k = 1 + \frac{1}{2}k(k-1)[2(k-1) + (k-2)(k-3)]$. On the relationship between interaction levels and odds ratios under the topological model, see below.

TABLE 3.3. *Results of fitting two versions of the topological model of class voting to seven-by-three class-by-party tables for nine British elections, 1964–1992*

| Model | $G^2$ | df | p | $rG^2$ | Δ |
|---|---|---|---|---|---|
| Conditional independence | 2,524.6 | 108 | 0.00 | — | 16.8 |
| Topological (3-level) | 175.3 | 106 | 0.00 | 93.1 | 3.6 |
| Topological (4-level) | 163.9 | 105 | 0.00 | 93.5 | 3.6 |
| (N = 16,866) | | | | | |

Parameters, in log-additive form, for positive and negative voting (neutral = 0)

| 3-level model | | 4-level model | |
|---|---|---|---|
| positive | 0.42 | positive (Con.) | 0.30 |
| negative | −0.63 | positive (Lab.) | 0.06 |
| | | negative | −0.58 |

seen from comparison with Table 3.1, the total class–vote association accounted for (reduction in $G^2$) falls only from 94.7 to 93.1 per cent, while the proportion of cases misclassified (Δ) increases from 3.2 to 3.6 per cent. There would thus seem to be reasonable grounds for preferring the topological model.[6]

One could, of course, go on to inspect residuals under the model and, in the light of this, seek a still better fitting version by reallocating cells. However, in proceeding thus, the dangers of ad hoc over-fitting are evident enough.[7] The alternative way to improve fit is by increasing the number of interaction levels distinguished, although, as earlier noted,

[6] No more than this is claimed—except that in the acceptance or rejection of statistical models in sociological analysis, judgement is *always* likely to be involved. In comment on this paper in its earlier version, Ringdal and Hines (1995: 380) express concern that the topological model does not fit the data well enough—that is, by conventional criteria. Others, who believe that the *bic* statistic (Raftery 1986) provides the basis for a 'consistent model selection procedure' with large-scale datasets, have argued that the topological model is clearly to be preferred since it returns a *bic* of −856.4 as against one of −800.4 for the CCV model. However, the first view seems to overlook the very point of developing a topological model—that is, to bring out the basic *pattern* of the large constancy in class voting that the fit of the CCV model indicates; while the second neglects powerful criticisms of the *bic* statistic that have recently been made (Cox, 1995; Weakliem 1999).

[7] Most of the larger residuals under the topological model occur in cells that relate to voting for the Liberals. This may not be thought surprising in that one is in fact dealing here (as noted earlier in the text) with a succession of three somewhat different parties—as well as with generally quite small cell counts. A rather better fitting model could, for example, be obtained if one were to allow the petty bourgeoisie to be neutral towards the Liberals up to the advent of the Alliance and negative only thereafter. Such a 'class realignment' may sound quite plausible but the evidence is scarcely sufficient to be sure that it really did occur.

this will only be helpful substantively if a clear rationale for the different levels is preserved. One rather obvious possibility for consideration in this respect is that levels of class voting may vary by party. It has, after all, often been suggested that while Labour is in its very nature a 'class' party, the Conservative Party is not. Investigation of this possibility did in fact reveal a four-level development of the model that improves significantly on the original version, even if by no very great extent. In this case *two* positive levels of class voting are posed: one for members of classes I, II, III, and IV voting for the Conservatives as their natural party, and the other for members of classes V, VI, and VII voting thus for Labour—but with no differentiation by party being made in the case of the supposed negative level.[8] In other words, the positive cells in the first column of Table 3.2 are allowed to take a different level of interaction from the positive cells in the second column.

The fit of this four-level version of the model is shown in the third row of the upper panel of Table 3.3. As can be seen, $G^2$ is reduced by 11.4 for the one degree of freedom lost, although there is little change in the total association accounted for or in the proportion of cases misclassified. Whether or not the four- or the three-level version should be accepted could then be debated. With the danger of over-fitting in mind, the simpler one might be preferred.[9] However, for present purposes at least, it is not apparent that a choice needs to be made and, in the following, results from both versions of the model will be presented and discussed.

The parameters for class-voting propensities that are estimated are given in the lower panel of Table 3.3. It should be noted that these parameters are in log-additive form and are obtained via the GLIM program (Francis *et al.* 1993). With this program, the constraints imposed in the estimation procedure entail setting the parameter for a reference category at zero and estimating other parameters in the set relative to zero. In the present case, it would seem an obvious move to let neutral class voting be the reference category—that is, take the zero parameter—with the expectation that the parameter (or parameters) for positive class voting will then prove to have a positive value and the parameter for negative class voting, a negative value. However, it must be emphasized that interpretation has at all times to centre on the relativities of the parameters and that the zero

[8] A further six-level model, allowing for differentiation in the strength of negative voting propensities as against the Conservatives, Labour, and the Liberals, gave no significant improvement in fit.

[9] Those who retain faith in *bic* may wish to know that, as against the *bic* value of –856.4 reported above for the three-level model, the four-level model returns a *bic* of –858.1. However, after the adjustment for overdispersion proposed by Fitzmaurice (1995, and see text above), *bic* values move in favour, in a similarly marginal way, of the three-level model.

value applying in the neutral cells is not to be understood in any absolute way—for example, as implying that in these cells *no* association between class and vote exists.[10]

What, then, can be learnt from the parameters reported about the pattern of class voting that has largely persisted in British elections over recent decades? To begin with, it may be observed that all parameters take their expected sign. Under the three-level version of the model, the salient point, then, is that negative class voting appears as clearly stronger than positive class voting—in the sense of being at a level further removed from that which applies where class 'neutrality' is supposed. The positive class voting parameter of 0.42 can be interpreted to mean that individuals are one-and-a-half times more likely ($e^{0.42} = 1.52$) to vote for the natural party of their class than they are to vote for a party towards which they are deemed to be neutral. But the negative class voting parameter of –0.63 indicates that, by this same standard of comparison, individuals are only half ($e^{-0.63} = 0.53$) as likely to vote for parties treated under the model as being 'unnatural' ones for their class. Some support might thus be seen here for the view, from time to time advanced by political commentators, that members of the electorate are more inclined to vote *against* particular parties than for them.

However, under the four-level version of the model, this view would seem in need of qualification. What is now indicated is that natural class voting by members of the manual classes for Labour is in fact at a higher level than that of the nonmanual classes for the Conservatives. The former is at one-and-four-fifths times the neutral level ($e^{0.60} = 1.82$), but the latter at only one-and-a-third times ($e^{0.30} = 1.35$), with the strength of negative voting relative to the neutral level being little changed. In other words, relatively weak positive class voting appears as confined to the nonmanual–Conservative connection, while the stronger manual–Labour connection serves to confirm that Labour is indeed more distinctively a class party.

As well as allowing propensities for positive and negative class voting to be thus quantified, the parameters reported also enable one readily to calculate *all* rates of relative class voting, as measured by odds ratios (cf. Heath *et al.* 1985), that are implicit in class-by-party tables under the two versions of the model. In illustrating this, it will be useful to refer to Table 3.4, which is simply Table 3.2 with estimated positive and negative voting parameters for each version of the model substituted for plus and minus signs.

[10] The strength of the association between class and vote in the neutral cells, relative to that existing in the positive and negative cells, would of course be likely to change with any change in the design of the model: that is, with any reallocation of class–party pairs among the levels of interaction distinguished.

TABLE 3.4. *Interaction parameters in cells of the seven-by-three class-by-party table following design of Table 3.2 for three- and four-level versions of the topological model (upper and lower figures, respectively)*

| Class | | Conservative | Labour | Liberal |
|---|---|---|---|---|
| I | Service class or salariat, higher | 0.42<br>0.30 | –0.63<br>–0.58 | 0<br>0 |
| II | Service class or salariat, lower | 0.42<br>0.30 | 0<br>0 | 0<br>0 |
| III | Routine nonmanual workers | 0.42<br>0.30 | 0<br>0 | 0<br>0 |
| IV | Petty bourgeoisie | 0.42<br>0.30 | –0.63<br>–0.58 | –0.63<br>–0.58 |
| V | Supervisors of manual workers and technicians | 0<br>0 | 0.42<br>0.60 | 0<br>0 |
| VI | Skilled manual workers | –0.63<br>–0.58 | 0.42<br>0.60 | –0.63<br>–0.58 |
| VII | Nonskilled manual workers | –0.63<br>–0.58 | 0.42<br>0.60 | –0.63<br>–0.58 |

If $i, i'$ are two classes and $j, j'$ two parties, it can be shown (cf. Goldthorpe 1987: 119), using the notation of (3.3) above, that

$$e^{(L_{ij} - L_{ij'}) - (L_{i'j} - L_{i'j'})} = \frac{F_{ij}/F_{ij'}}{F_{i'j}/F_{i'j'}}$$

Suppose then one wishes to obtain, under, say, the three-level version of the model, the odds of members of class I or of class IV, the higher salariat or the petty bourgeoisie, voting Conservative rather than Labour relative to those of members of class VI or class VII, the two divisions of the working class, voting Conservative rather than Labour. One takes from Table 3.4 ((0.43 – (–0.64)) – ((–0.64) – 0.43)) which, exponentiated, gives an odds ratio of

$$\frac{1.54/0.53}{0.53/1.54} = 8.56$$

Or, alternatively, working with the four-level version, one would in this way arrive at an odds ratio of 7.94.

Odds of this magnitude serve to show the strength that, in some instances, the class–party association as here modelled may attain over the series of elections covered. Further, though, one may also proceed as above in order to underline the point raised earlier concerning the importance of the differences in voting propensities that occur *within* the manual and, especially, the nonmanual bloc. Thus, for example, it can be similarly calculated from Table 3.4 that the odds for a member of class I voting Conservative rather than Labour are one-and-four-fifths times those for a member of class II or of class III ($e^{0.63} = 1.88$ and $e^{0.58} = 1.79$ under the three- and four-level versions of the model, respectively); or, again, that the odds of a member of class II or of class III voting Conservative rather than Liberal are only half those for a member of class IV ($e^{-0.63} = 0.53$ and $e^{-0.58} = 0.56$, respectively).

The point of chief importance thus brought out is the following. Although differences of the kind illustrated can in no way be regarded as negligible, they are of course entirely left out of account where class voting is treated on the basis simply of class and party dichotomies. The results here presented suggest that this practice may easily lead both to an underestimation of the degree of class voting and further—as a result of shifting compositional effects within very broad class categories that are politically too heterogeneous—to a misjudgement of any trend over time that class voting may display.

## VARIATION WITHIN THE PATTERN OF CLASS VOTING OVER TIME

As was earlier emphasized, the primary objective in developing the topological model is to elucidate the pattern of class-voting in Britain that appears to have persisted, little altered, since at least the 1960s. If, however, one believes that some, albeit minor, change in this pattern has at times occurred, it is of additional interest to enquire what happens if the model is applied to the class-by-party tables for successive elections in such a way that variation in the strength of the class-voting propensities that it identifies can be shown up. This can be done by retaining the *design* of the model, in its three- and four-level versions, while, however, relaxing the requirement that the differing propensities should take the same parameter across all elections alike. The model thus becomes

$$\log F_{ijk} = \mu + \lambda_i^{C} + \lambda_j^{P} + \lambda_k^{E} + \lambda_{ik}^{CE} + \lambda_{jk}^{PE} + \lambda_{a(ij)k}^{L} \qquad (3.5)$$

where L = 3 or 4.

The pattern of class voting, one might say, is now required to be only *qualitatively*, not quantitatively, the same from election to election; or, more figuratively, the contours of class voting have still to run on the same lines in all cases but the actual 'heights' and 'depths' can change.[11]

[11] It may be noted that it is an advantage of the topological model over the CCV model that a modification on these lines can be made. If a further term were included in (3.1), allowing the pattern of class voting to vary by election—that is, the term $\lambda_{ijk}^{CPE}$—then the model would become saturated. With the topological model,

TABLE 3.5. *Results of fitting two versions of the topological model of class voting to seven-by-three class-by-party tables for nine British elections, 1964–1992, with variation allowed in the strength of class-voting propensities from election to election*

| Model | $G^2$ | df | p | $rG^2$ | Δ |
|---|---|---|---|---|---|
| Conditional independence | 2,524.6 | 108 | 0.00 | — | 16.8 |
| Topological (Three-level) | 136.9 | 90 | 0.00 | 94.6 | 3.1 |
| Topological (Four-level) | 109.4 | 81 | 0.02 | 95.7 | 2.9 |

*Notes*: N = 16,866.

The results of applying the model in this way are reported in Table 3.5. As comparison with Table 3.3 will show, the data are now *prima facie* better reproduced, although there are grounds for querying this claim, especially with the four-level version,[12] and the improvement in fit achieved is in any event slight. If, however, the results are accepted as they stand, then the parameters for class voting estimated separately for each of the nine elections represented are of obvious interest. These parameters are plotted in Figures 3.2 and 3.3 for the three- and four-level versions of the model respectively.

It must in this regard again be stressed that the setting of the parameter for neutral class voting at zero, with other parameters then being expressed relative to this level, is no more than a useful presentational device, and that interpretation should always be concerned with the differences between parameters—or the distances between their graphs—rather than with their absolute values. (For example, no inference should be made from Figures 3.2 and 3.3 that the level of neutral class voting itself remained unchanged over the period covered; it is simply that, as the data are presented here, such a shift in relativities would be shown in changing parameters for positive and negative class voting.)

From results under the three-level version of the model, the main conclusions to be drawn might then be put as follows. First, while, as earlier noted, negative class voting is generally stronger than positive class voting, in the sense of being further removed from the neutral level, it also appears, by this same standard, to be the more subject to fluctuation. Secondly, if Figure 3.2 is compared with Figure 3.1, the indication is that in

however, this difficulty does not arise since the term for the class–vote association is 'vectorized'.

[12] In the three-level case, the model of equation (3.5) returns a *bic* of –739.1, as against –856.4 for the equation of model (3.4), and the corresponding *bics* in the four-level case are –679.1 as against –858.1. With the Fitzmaurice adjustment for overdispersion, these deteriorating *bic* values are confirmed and, more tellingly, in the four-level case the improvement in fit made by the model of equation (3.5) over that of model (3.4) is barely significant at the conventional 0.05 per cent level.

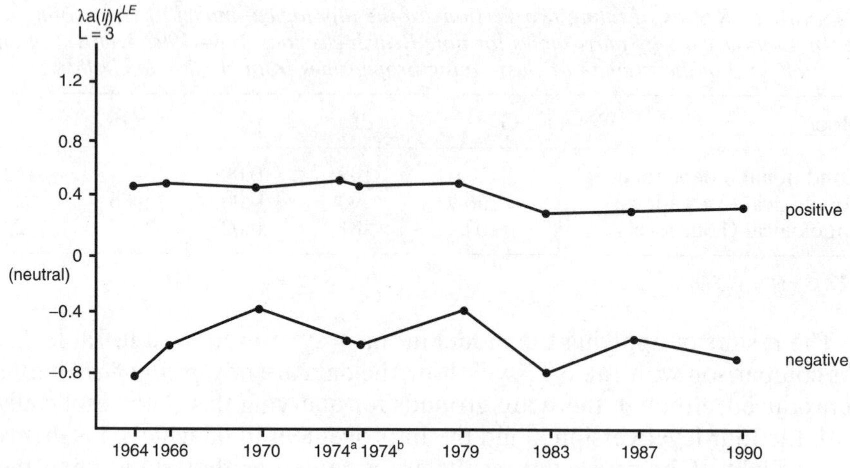


FIG. 3.2. Parameters for positive and negative class voting

*Notes*: [a] February election.
[b] October election.

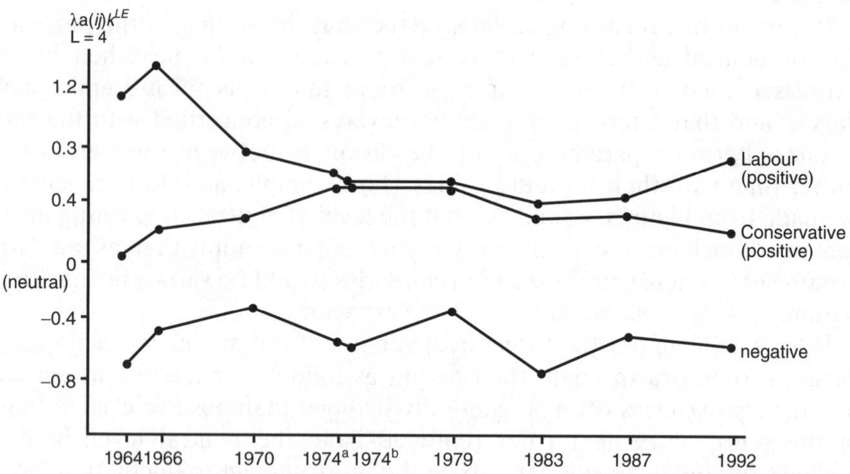


FIG. 3.3. Parameters for Labour and Conservative positive and negative class voting

*Notes*: [a] February election.
[b] October election.

those elections where class voting was at a relatively low level overall—that is, the elections of 1970, 1979, and 1987—it was a decline in negative class voting that was the key factor. That is to say, at these elections members of different classes tended, for whatever reasons, to vote for parties 'unnatural' for them with a propensity closer than at other elections to that with which they voted for parties towards which the model treats them as neutral. It is of interest that in their report on the 1970 election, when class voting reached its lowest level in the period covered, Butler and Pinto-Duschinsky (1971: 346) should remark on an 'unprecedented volatility' in public opinion which pointed, in their view, to 'a lack of conviction or enthusiasm among a substantial proportion of voters'. They also note poll results indicating that many Labour 'identifiers' were intending to vote Conservative, and that a low proportion of all voters 'cared very much' about which party would win.[13]

Results under the (perhaps less acceptable) four-level version of the model also suggest an elaboration of an earlier finding. The relative weakness of positive class voting in the nonmanual–Conservative, as compared with the manual–Labour, connection now appears as chiefly a phenomenon of the earlier elections covered, though again evident to some extent in 1992.[14] From the 1974 elections through to that of 1987, members of Classes I, II, III, and IV show in fact little less propensity to vote for the Conservatives as their natural party (relative always to the neutral level) than do members of Classes V, VI, and VII to vote for Labour. Thus, the idea that Labour is 'inherently' more of a class party than the Conservatives may not, after all, be so secure.

Finally, though, even if the model of equation (3.5) is preferred to that of equation (3.4) in which constancy of class voting is imposed, it should still be noted that the graphs of Figures 3.2 and 3.3 do not show any clear tendency to converge. If class voting were in secular decline, such a tendency ought to be apparent, with the prospective meeting point of the graphs being that at which no class–party association of any kind remains. In fact, looking across the nine elections represented, one must conclude

[13] It might be thought that the greater fluctuation evident in negative class voting simply reflects smaller counts in the relevant cells of the class-by-vote tables. However, negative class-voting parameters are no less convincing as compared to their standard errors than are positive class-voting parameters. The relative importance of fluctuation in negative class voting can further be indicated by fitting a modified form of the model of equation (3.5) in which variation across elections is allowed *only for* such voting—that is, positive class voting remains constrained—as in the equation of model (3.4)—to be at a constant level. The $G^2$ returned increases only from 136.7 to 145.0 for 8 df saved in the three-level case, and from 109.4 to 134.2 for 16 df saved in the four-level case.

[14] It will be noted that for 1964 positive class voting for the Conservatives stands in fact at zero. In other words, what the model suggests is that at this election the propensity of members of the nonmanual classes in general to vote Conservative was itself at the neutral level—that is, it was no greater than the propensity of members of class I to vote for the Liberals, of members of classes II and III to vote for the Liberals or for Labour, and so on. This result might, however, be regarded as providing further grounds for doubt about the model of equation (3.5) in its four-level version.

from these graphs that class-voting propensities appear no more likely to converge as to move in the same, or even in divergent, directions.

## FURTHER IMPLICATIONS

So far, and for good reasons, discussion has concentrated on the two central features of the topological model: that is, the allocation of the cells of the class-by-party table to different levels of interaction—as represented by the $\lambda_{a(ij)}{}^{L}$ term in equation (3.4)—and the parameters correspondingly estimated. However (and staying now with the model as in this equation), there are two other terms, $\lambda_{ik}{}^{CE}$ and $\lambda_{jk}{}^{PE}$, that also merit some attention.

The $\lambda_{ik}{}^{CE}$ term yields a set of parameters which, so to speak, run across the rows of the class-by-party table and which may be taken as referring to the net effect on the count in any cell of the table of the relative sizes of different classes from election to election. In a class-by-party table, one would suppose that the direction of causation is from class to vote—that is, that the former is the independent, and the latter the dependent variable. Thus, the relative sizes of classes are to be seen as determined exogeneously to any model of the association between class and party support. This being so, interest in the parameters estimated for the $\lambda_{ik}{}^{CE}$ term must chiefly lie in the way in which they can serve as a check on the realism of the topological model, and especially the allocation of cells under the $\lambda_{a(ij)}{}^{L}$ term. That is to say, it is desirable that these parameters should tell essentially the same story about the relative sizes of classes, and changes therein, as do the row marginal distributions of class-by-party tables for successive elections. Otherwise, it could be feared that a mis-specified design of the pattern of class voting was giving an acceptable fit only by dint of the 'distortion' of other effects (on the 'malleability' of topological models, cf. Macdonald 1981, 1994, though these papers neglect the possibility of checks of the kind introduced here).

Inspection of the parameters in question, whether under the three- or four-level version of the model, is in fact reassuring in this regard. In essentially the same way as the row marginal distributions, these parameters point to a process of class structural change in which the salient features are, on the one hand, a steady growth in the proportion of the electorate found in class I, the higher salariat, and, on the other hand, a steady decline in the proportion found in classes VI and VII, the skilled and nonskilled divisions of the working class. The implication of the model must then of course be that these changes are ones seriously detrimental to Labour's electoral chances. The two classes that have Labour as their natural party and are negative towards the Conservatives are in contraction, while the main offsetting tendency is the expansion of a class that has the Conservatives as its natural party and is negative towards Labour.[15]

The set of parameters for the $\lambda_{jk}^{PE}$ term can be interpreted in an analogous way to those for $\lambda_{ik}^{CE}$. These are parameters that run down the columns of the class-by-party table and can be taken as referring to the net effect on the count in any cell of the table of the relative attractiveness of different parties from election to election: or, that is, to this effect considered net of the effects of relative class size ($\lambda_{ik}^{CE}$) and of the specified pattern of class voting ($\lambda_{a(ij)}^{L}$). However, while it is again relevant to ascertain that the $\lambda_{jk}^{PE}$ parameters are of a plausible kind, it is here also the case that, if the topological model of equation (3.4) is acceptable, these parameters can provide substantive insights that are not otherwise so readily gained.

In Figure 3.4 the $\lambda_{jk}^{PE}$ parameters are used to show how, under this model, the Conservative and Labour parties appear to fare across elec-

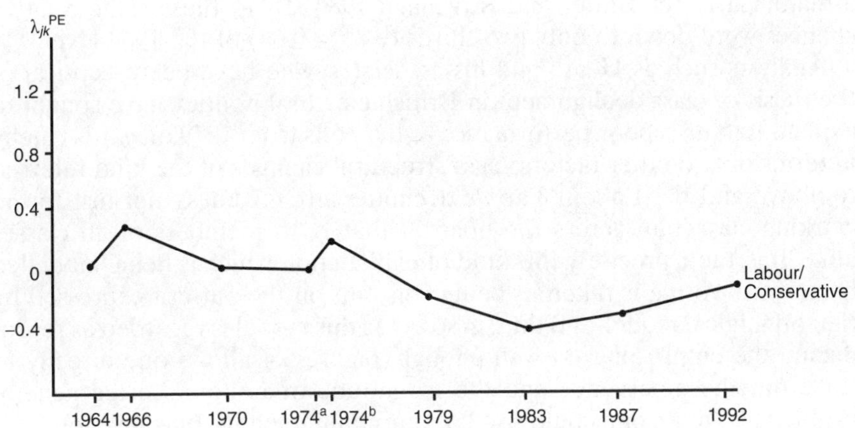


FIG. 3.4. Parameters for relative 'non-class' appeal of Labour versus Conservtives (1964 = 0)

*Notes*: [a] February election.
[b] October election.

[15] The results referred to in this paragraph are available on request. As acknowledged in the text, the modelling exercise undertaken is itself validated by, rather than being necessary for, the achievement of these results. It is none the less important to reaffirm their significance, especially as a corrective to the argument that it is working-class *defection* that has constituted Labour's major electoral problem. Thus, for example, Butler and Kavanagh write (1992: 276), apropos the 1992 election (and problems generally posed for parties of the centre-left by current economic and social changes) that 'Labour still failed to capture even half of the working class vote'. For this statement to be true, some very broad 'market research' definition of the working

tions in what might be described as their relative 'non-class' appeal. This appeal could lie in the image of being a 'national' rather than a 'class' party, in perceived greater competence in government, in actually greater competence in fighting elections, or, in principle, in anything else that is unrelated to class and class voting. In the figure, the parameters are estimated under the three-level version of the model—but those under the four-level version are virtually identical—and the election of 1964 is taken as the reference point. Positive values indicate a relative advantage to Labour, negative values to the Conservatives. The movement of the graph from 0 in 1964 to 0.25 in 1966 can then be taken to mean that, net of all effects of class size and of class-voting propensities, the chances of a voter in 1966 supporting Labour rather than the Conservatives were almost one-and-a-third times ($e^{0.25} = 1.28$) greater than the chances in 1964. Or, to take a contrasting instance, the fall of the graph to –0.42 in 1983 indicates that at this election—when Labour was burdened by a disastrous manifesto, a weak and divided leadership, and one of the most inept campaigns ever run by a major party (cf. Butler and Kavanagh 1984: 274)—these same relative chances were down to only two-thirds ($e^{-0.42} = 0.66$) of the 1964 level.[16]

Analysts such as Heath and his associates, who have been sceptical of the thesis of class dealignment in British electoral politics, have sought to explain Labour's poor performance at the polls from 1979 onwards chiefly in terms of two other factors: class structural changes of the kind referred to above and the Labour Party's declining attractiveness, not just to the working class, but 'across the board'—that is, to members of all classes alike. It is, then, precisely this kind of explanation which is being modelled here. Class voting is taken as being constant on the pattern expressed by the topological model, and thus, in so far as this model is regarded as reproducing the empirical data well enough, Figure 3.4 allows one directly to trace out the emergence and the magnitude of Labour's more general problem. Overall, one could say, Labour maintained its 1964 level of 'non-class' appeal as against the Conservatives until the elections of 1974 but its position then rapidly fell away to the nadir of 1983, from which only about a three-quarters recovery to the 1964 standard had been achieved

class must be adopted which lumps together socially—and politically—quite heterogeneous groupings. The 1992 class-by-party table used in the present analyses shows that in fact 58 per cent of members of classes VI and VII together—i.e. of all manual wage-workers—supported Labour. But what is far more disturbing is that if the working class is understood so as to comprise self-employed artisans, foremen, technicians, and so on, then the fact that is of prime electoral importance, namely, its decline in size, rather than in political solidarity, can only be obscured.

16 Analogous graphs to that of Figure 3.4 can of course be drawn under the model setting the 'non-class' appeal of Labour against the Liberals and of the Conservatives against the Liberals. These graphs are available on request.

by the election of 1992. And it should of course be further recognized that since class structural change continues to work strongly against Labour, election victory for the party in 1997 must, all else being equal, imply its achievement of a level of 'non-class' appeal *substantially above* that which sufficed thirty years before.[17]

## CONCLUSIONS

Using a relatively refined class schema and appropriate statistical techniques, it can be shown that over a quarter of a century the net association between class and vote in British elections did not progressively weaken but in fact remained rather little changed. The primary concern of the present paper has then been to model the actual pattern of association between class and party support that underlies this temporal stability. A topological model of a parsimonious, three-level design, derived from the idea of natural class parties, has been shown to reproduce seven-by-three class-by-party tables for nine elections rather satisfactorily; and a four-level version of the model offers a yet closer fit to the data. The propositions directly expressed by the model, as regards natural or 'unnatural' class parties or instances where neutral class voting may be supposed, are in themselves fairly commonplace. But from the application of the model in its two versions, several results of interest are obtained.

Negative class voting, for example, turns out to be generally stronger, or further from the neutral level, than is positive class voting, although results under the four-level version of the model suggest that this may be largely the outcome of a relative weakness in the propensity of members of non-manual classes to vote for the Conservatives, rather than of members of the manual classes to vote for Labour, as their natural party. Again, the relative rates of class voting—for every combination of class and party—

[17] As indicated in the text, exactly the same conclusions would follow from $\lambda_{jk}^{PE}$ parameters estimated from the four-level version of the model; and, it may be added, no significantly different interpretation would follow from parameters estimated under the model as elaborated in equation (3.5) so as to allow for temporal variation in class voting—if taken in its three-level version. However, when, in the four-level version, variation is allowed for in positive class voting for the Conservatives and for Labour considered separately, another story is suggested, at least for the period from 1964 to 1970. It is in the 1964 election (rather than that of 1983) that Labour's 'non-class' appeal, relative to that of the Conservatives, now appears at its lowest level, so that Labour's success in 1964—as also in 1966—has to be seen (cf. Figure 3.3) as due to its vast superiority over the Conservatives in actually mobilizing its 'class' constituency (cf. n. 14). Again, though, the question arises of whether the degree of plausibility of this alternative account strengthens or, rather, further weakens the grounds for favouring this version of the model.

that are readily calculable under the model reveal (with whichever version) quite marked differences in the propensities of members of the four nonmanual classes distinguished to vote Conservative as opposed to either Labour or Liberal. This result serves to confirm the inadequacies of the unfortunately still common practice of treating the issue of class voting on the basis simply of manual/nonmanual class, and left/non-left party, dichotomies.

If the model is modified so that voting propensities may vary by election, it is further found that the level of negative class voting fluctuates more widely, relative to the neutral level, than does positive voting; and, in turn, that such shifts in the strength of class voting overall as can be detected in the course of recent decades chiefly reflect variation in voters' propensities *not* to vote for particular parties. It further appears from the four-level version of the model—though doubts may be entertained over whether this should be favoured—that from the 1974 elections up to 1987 at least, the Conservatives take on the character of a 'class' party to much the same degree as Labour.

Finally, apart from parameters relating to the pattern of class voting, two other sets that can be estimated under the topological model have been examined: those that can be understood as indicating, from election to election, the relative size effects of classes and the relative attractiveness of parties considered net of all effects of class voting. These parameters tell reassuringly plausible stories and are together informative about the sources of Labour's failing election fortunes since the 1970s and the nature and magnitude of task of restoring them.

Other than where the model, in the form of equation (3.5), specifically allows for variation in the strength of class-voting propensities, all results reported do of course rest on the supposition that class voting in Britain has remained quite constant across General Elections from 1964 to 1992. This would, at least if taken *sensu stricto*, appear a rather unlikely proposition, and the graph of Figure 3.1 indicates the extent to which it could be regarded as mistaken.[18] It is, however, the very purpose of models to simplify reality somewhat in the interests of better understanding it. What emerges from the application of the model here proposed is that in the period in question the degree of stability present in the level and pattern of class voting has indeed been one of the dominant features of the

[18] It may be added here that if the topological model in either its three- or four-level version is supplemented by the UNIDIFF model (appropriately modified for use with a topological rather than an 'all-interactions' model), the $\beta$ parameters returned follow very closely those, given in Table 3.1 and plotted in Figure 3.1, under the CCV model as supplemented by UNIDIFF. The improvement in fit achieved is also very similar: $G^2$ falls by 27.8 for the 8 df lost with the three-level version, and by 28.5 with the four-level version, as against the reported fall of 27.4 with the CCV model.

class–party relationship in British electoral politics—together with the changing class structural context and, since the 1970s, Labour's deficit, relative to the Conservatives, in 'non-class' appeal. In comparison, such shifts as can be shown up in the net association of class and vote have, on any reckoning, to be treated as being of a minor, if not negligible, order of importance, and one that then appears strangely incommensurate with the attention that many prominent academic analysts and political commentators have chosen to bestow upon them.

## POSTSCRIPT: THE GENERAL ELECTION OF 1997

Before this collection went to press, preliminary data became available from the British Election Survey of 1997. These data are subject to final cleaning and checking, and further investigation will need to be made into the causes, and possible consequences, of the unusually low response rate for the survey of only 63 per cent. All results of analyses made at this stage must therefore be regarded as subject to revision. However, with this proviso, a brief postscript might be added along the following lines.

First, so far as Labour's success in 1997 is concerned, it is evident that this was overwhelmingly the result of a very marked increase in its 'non-class' appeal relative to that of the other parties; or, in other words, of the extent to which, relative to them, it gained support 'across the board' from members of all classes alike. If the three-level version of the topological model of class voting—that is, model (3.4)—is applied to the BES dataset with the preliminary 1997 results included, then the extended version of the graph of Figure 3.4, showing Labour's 'non-class' appeal relative to that of the Conservatives, rises sharply between 1992 and 1997, and in fact to a substantially higher point than for any other of the elections covered.

Secondly, there are clear indications also that between 1992 and 1997 class voting declined somewhat. With the new dataset, the model of constant class voting—model (3.1)—still accounts for well over 90 per cent of the total class–vote association; but application of the UNIDIFF model shows that the extension of the graph of parameters in Figure 3.1 moves downwards to a level for the 1997 election that is in fact below that for 1970. Application of the three-level topological model with its parameters being allowed to vary over elections—model (3.5)—further reveals that in 1997, as in 1970, and in 1979 and 1987 when class voting also declined, this shift was chiefly linked to weakening propensities for 'negative' voting. Examination of residuals under model (3.4) suggests in this regard two tendencies of particular interest—which must of course be understood net of the overall movement towards Labour. First, members of class I, the higher salariat, showed a greater propensity to vote Labour relative to voting

Liberal (though not Conservative); and secondly, members of class VII, nonskilled manual workers, showed a greater propensity to vote Conservative or Liberal relative to voting Labour. It might also be said that, for 1997, model (3.4) would have fitted the data better had members of class III, routine nonmanual employees, been regarded (in the same way as members of class V) as 'positive' towards Labour rather than 'neutral', and 'neutral' rather than 'positive' towards the Conservatives.

This decline in class voting to a lower level than that found in any other election since 1970—and, quite possibly, since the 1930s—would appear open to two different interpretations. One would be that it represents the start of a new era in British electoral politics in which the diminished importance of class as a basis of party support—for so long asserted—is at last empirically demonstrable. However, if such an interpretation is to be pursued, it would then seem necessary for at least the immediate explanation of the change to be given in political rather than sociological terms: most obviously, that is, in terms of Mr Blair's repositioning of his party towards the centre and the concerted efforts made by 'New Labour' to appeal to 'middle-class' voters. To seek to account for the fall in the level of class voting between 1992 and 1997 as the result of class decomposition, increased class mobility, reduced class inequalities in living standards, and so on would scarcely be plausible.

The alternative interpretation is a far less portentous one. It would be that the decline in class voting between 1992 and 1997 is simply another 'leg' in the zigzag pattern that is evident in this regard at least from 1970 onwards (cf. Figure 3.1), and that there is no particular reason for expecting class voting to remain in future at or below the 1997 level rather than again increasing. In this case, fluctuating levels of class voting would be seen as reflecting a variety of influences of a more or less transient character that are unlikely to have much lasting effect on the underlying pattern of association between class membership and party affiliation.

Which of these two interpretations has the more merit will only be ascertained through the study of electoral behaviour in the twenty-first century.

# 4

# Classes, Unions, and the Realignment of US Presidential Voting, 1952–1992

MICHAEL HOUT, JEFF MANZA, AND CLEM BROOKS

## INTRODUCTION

American presidential elections since the 1960s have offered ample material for political scientists and political sociologists who have contended that the stable class politics of industrial capitalism is giving way to a new, 'postmaterial' politics (e.g. Inglehart 1977, 1990; Lipset 1981; Clark and Lipset 1991; Abramson and Inglehart 1995). They point to newer cleavages based on gender, identity, and 'postmaterialist' values which—they argue—have taken on more electoral importance. In a world of new political movements and politicians standing for office who are completely outside traditional party systems, claims of class dealignment ring true. Others—most of whom are represented in this volume—have countered that conclusions of 'dealignment' do not square with the empirical evidence and/or exaggerate the significance of these developments. The rise of one set of cleavages does not imply the fall of others. Instead of class dealignment, defenders of class analysis argue that the association between class and vote is merely subject to patterns of 'trendless fluctuation' (Heath *et al.* 1985, 1991) or class realignment (Hout *et al.* 1995). In related work we have reviewed the literature on class voting in Western Europe, North America, and Australia (Manza *et al.* 1995) and mined the long time-series on the United States for evidence (Hout *et al.* 1995; Brooks and Manza 1997). In this chapter we summarize our main results and show how the demise of the labour movement in the United States intersects with those trends. In particular, we show that the

This is a substantially revised version of a paper we first gave at the conference on The End of Class Politics?, Nuffield College, Oxford, 14 February 1995. We thank Geoff Evans, Peter Mair, Paul Nieuwbeerta, and Stefan Svallfors for their comments on that original draft. We also thank the Survey Research Center and Committee on Research at the University of California, Berkeley, for financial support.

decline of union membership harmed the Democratic Party and probably removed an important working-class voice from presidential politics. But the effect of union membership turns out to be independent of class *per se*. The realignment of class voting in the United States is independent of these union-based trends.

## CLASS VOTING AND CLASS POLITICS

Interest in class voting goes back to the dawn of contemporary understandings of class in the nineteenth century. The roots of contemporary debates are planted in data, however, not in class theory. The national election surveys that accumulated in many countries since the 1960s yielded a harvest of class-voting studies over lengthy time-series, and most findings through the early 1970s suggested that class had a strong—if variable—influence on voting behaviour (Lipset 1981 (1st edn. 1960); Alford 1963; Lipset and Rokkan 1967; Rose 1974*a*). Lipset and Rokkan's influential theoretical synthesis argued that two revolutions, the National Revolution and the Industrial Revolution, initiated everywhere processes of social differentiation and conflict. The two revolutions produced four basic sets of cleavages: (1) church(es) versus the state, (2) dominant versus subject cultures, (3) agriculture versus manufacturing, and (4) employers and workers (1967: 14). The precise political articulation of these cleavages varied from country to country, depending on geopolitical structures and the timing of political and economic development, but all countries were subject to the same basic pattern. Further industrialization led to the decline of most types of social cleavage other than class, magnifying the importance of the democratic class struggle.

In many Western European countries and Australia the cleavage structure was 'frozen' in an institutional structure dominated by class-based parties (Lipset and Rokkan 1967; also Rose and Urwin 1970; Bartolini and Mair 1990). Where this occurred, it is appropriate to talk of a 'class politics' (Mair 1993 and this volume). But even in places like the United States where class-based parties have not emerged, the long-run pattern of class voting calls for our attention. In particular, as our analysis of the US case has shown, the absence of a 'class politics' actually raises a new possibility of class realignment. In the United States, classes have shifted their allegiance from one party to another, while parties have sought to revise their traditional appeals in order to attract voters from classes that may be 'available'. In many ways it is a two-sided dance in which both partners try to lead.

This process has been explicit in the elections of 1992 and 1996. Mr Clinton dropped the Democrats' familiar appeals to 'working people' in favour of direct calls to 'the middle class'. It is well known that many blue-collar workers identify with the middle class (Halle 1984). Mr Clinton appealed to them and to insecure white-collar workers in 1992 with proposals to reform health care and welfare, and in 1996 with promises to defend middle-class entitlements like old-age pensions and health care (Social Security and Medicaid), and pledges to subsidize higher education by giving tax credits to students' parents.

Unions used to be the agents that bound the working class to the Democrats in the United States. The Democratic Party gave the unions an important voice in the selection of candidates from 1936 to 1968. In exchange, the unions delivered their share of the working-class vote to the Democrats. That tie was effectively broken by electoral reforms in the 1970s. The demise of unions' political brokerage was hastened by a crisis in public trust of unions and the trend away from union membership. Scandals rocked organized labour in the 1960s and 1970s, eroding public trust (Lipset and Schneider 1983) and making identification with unions more of a liability than an asset for a politician. All the while firms were leaving states with long union traditions and moving to 'right-to-work' states that promised to block union organizing. At the same time, the National Labor Relations Board made it harder for workers to organize new union locals (Fischer *et al.* 1996: ch. 6).

Some of these shifts in presidential politics may have encouraged rising class voting on the right. Republican candidates promised to cut government spending and regulation in ways designed to appeal to managers and entrepreneurs. The emphasis on 'taming the unions' presumably has a constituency among those who oppose unions in the workplace.

Our analysis of class voting in the United States distinguishes between what we term 'traditional' and 'total' class voting and develops statistical models appropriate to each (Hout *et al.* 1995). Traditional models of class voting hinge on the theoretical assumption that there should be a close correspondence between the working class and parties of the left and between the middle class and parties of the centre or right. This assumption can be embedded in models of class voting that identify the 'natural' party of a given class (Rose and McAllister 1986; Weakliem 1995*a*), or models that array classes and parties as ordered points on latent continua and examine the degree to which the latent variables are associated (Chapter 5, this volume). Whatever its particular form, the traditional assumption is, however, only appropriate to understanding the historically significant but specific pattern of the relationship between classes and parties that has tended to characterize capitalist democracies in the twentieth century.

Class voting need not be limited to the combinations embedded in the traditional conception. First, class affects turnout as well as partisan choice

(Verba *et al.* 1978). This class skew in participation is likely to have important consequences for the party system and public policy (Burnham 1982; Piven and Cloward 1986). Yet analyses of class voting in the United States almost never simultaneously consider voting and nonvoting (Weakliem and Heath (Chapter 5) and Hout *et al.* (1995) provide exceptions). Secondly, even within the ambit of partisan choice, traditional alliances need not be the only class differences we consider. In other words, total class voting—the sum of all class differences in voting behaviour—is more inclusive than 'traditional' class voting. Traditional class voting, while clearly important to the study of class voting, is a specific configuration in the comparative and historical alignment of classes and parties, but not the *only* way in which classes can differ at the polls. Traditional class voting contributes to total class voting, but the patterns of voting and partisanship can and do shift. Shifts in traditional class voting patterns are typically interpreted as *dealignment* (i.e. as confirmation of the declining importance of class for voting behaviour). Our 'total' class-voting approach allowed us to see that while the traditional linkages between classes and parties have undergone *realignment*, the effect of class location on voting behaviour remains significant.

Our distinction between traditional and total class voting is related to Mair's distinction between 'class politics' and 'class voting' in this volume. According to Mair, class voting signifies a tendency for classes to ally themselves with different parties in a given election; class politics requires that the coalitions persist over several elections and become institutionalized. Total class voting as we have defined it here requires only class voting. Discussions of the decline of traditional class voting implicitly assume—but do not demonstrate—an erosion of class politics.

The concept of traditional class voting is deeply rooted in the literature. It is unavoidable when class is conceived or operationalized as a dichotomy. A multi-class approach implied by contemporary theories of class and stratification invites the distinction between total and traditional class voting as does the simultaneous consideration of several voting outcomes (including nonvoting). In our analysis of class voting in the United States since the Second World War we specify statistical models predicated on both conceptions, show how models predicated on the total class-voting conception fit the data better, and conclude that the data contradict the thesis of declining political significance of class.

Our previous work addressed the realignment of class *voting* in the United States. Here we begin to examine class politics by piecing together the demise of the unions and the rise of the white-collar Democrat. We follow the same statistical strategy that we used before. We use a multivariate statistical model to assess the total effect of class in each Presidential election since 1948. Then we add union membership to that model to ascertain how much of the effect of class was once attributable to unions and how much is now attributable to unions. After considering several functional forms, we conclude that union membership has an independent effect on voting. The trends in class voting have emerged independent of the demise of American labour unions. The decline in union membership has cost the Democrats an important constituency, but it has not interacted with the class realignment in any obvious way.

## DATA AND METHODS

The data come from the American National Election Study (ANES)—a time-series that stretches back to the presidential election of 1952. The 1952 ANES included a question about voting in the 1948 election. We used the retrospective voting item before (Hout *et al.* 1995), but do not do so here because there is no corresponding retrospective question about union membership. The ANES is a stratified random sample of voting-age Americans, with the sample size varying from approximately 1,200 to 2,500 respondents in a given year.

The dependent variable in our analyses is self-reported vote for president. Self-reports exaggerate turnout but reproduce the partisan split well in each election (e.g. Abramson *et al.* 1994).

We measure the effect of elections using dummy variables. We use two strategies to assess changes in the effects of other variables. The first is to test for the statistical interaction between the election dummy variables and each of the socio-demographic variables in our model. The other is to test for the interaction between a linear time variate and each of the socio-demographic variables. We prefer the simpler linear change specification whenever it fits the data acceptably well, but we are not inclined to extrapolate the trends beyond the observed time-series.

We use one class scheme in all elections. It is the six-class scheme we devised for our previous analyses of voting in US presidential elections (Hout *et al.* 1995). To the familiar five-class version of the Erikson–Goldthorpe (1992*a*) scheme used by many contributors to this volume, we add a distinction between managers and professionals among the so-called 'salariat.' Thus, our class categories are: (1) professional (including self-employed), (2) manager, (3) nonmanagerial white-collar employee,[1] (4) self-employed (except professional), (5) skilled blue collar,

[1] This class is mostly composed of clerical and sales workers. In the United States, this class is sometimes called 'pink collar' because the majority of clerical, sales, and white-collar service workers are women. Workers in this category are also distinct

and (6) less skilled blue collar. The key variables are self-employment (yes or no) and occupation.

We use a combination of graphical displays and logistic regression methods to analyse the ANES data. In our logistic regressions, we combine data on all elections into a single dataset and estimate the main effects of election, class, gender, age, region, and race. The general form of the logistic regression equation is:

$$\begin{aligned} y_i &= \ln(p_i/(1-p_i)) \\ &= \beta_0 + \sum_{j=1}^{11} \beta_j T_{ij} + \sum_{j=12}^{16} \beta_j X_{i(j-11)} + \sum_{j=17}^{P} \beta_j Z_{i(j-16)} \end{aligned} \tag{4.1}$$

where $y_i$ is the log odds on person i voting for the Democratic candidate in an election, $T_{ij}$ ($t = 1, \ldots, 11$) is a dummy variable for election, $X_{i(j-11)}$ ($J = 12, \ldots, 16$) is a dummy variable for class, and $Z_{i(j-16)}$ ($J = 17, \ldots, P$) represents the other variables in the model. We then selectively introduce interaction effects—especially those involving time—and keep only the significant ones.

## THE REALIGNMENT OF CLASS VOTING

The traditional pattern of class voting held in the US presidential elections of 1948 up until 1960.[2] With the exception of the self-employed, middle-class voters supported the Republican candidates and working-class voters supported the Democrats. The self-employed split evenly between the two parties. After 1964 professionals shifted rapidly towards the Democrats; routine white-collar workers followed at a slower pace. At about the same time, the self-employed and skilled blue-collar workers shifted in the Republican direction. The self-employed had split between Democrats and Republicans; they became strong Republicans. The skilled blue-collar workers had been strong Democrats; they began to split their votes and were actually strong Republicans in 1988.

from other white-collar employees because they tend to be paid hourly wages instead of a salary. They are also more unionized than other white-collar classes. In recent years union organizers have targeted this class with success; the number of union members in this fast-growing class has increased while the number of union members in blue-collar occupations has fallen. In 1995 the American Federation of Labor–Congress of Industrial Organizations (AFL–CIO) elected John Sweeney president. Mr Sweeney was president of the Service Employees International Union (SEIU)—the largest union for workers in this class—prior to winning the AFL–CIO presidency.

[2] The 1948 data are from the retrospective reports of respondents to the 1952 ANES.

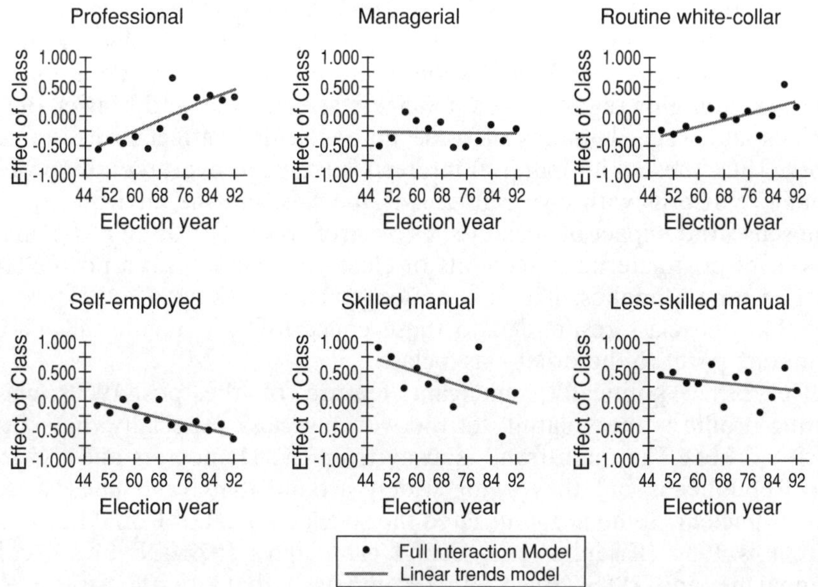


FIG. 4.1. Total effect of class on partisan choice by year, class, and model: United States, 1948–1992

*Note*: Total effect controls for gender, race, region, age, education, and significant trends in their effects, but not for union membership.

Managers and less-skilled blue-collar workers showed no significant trend, although the lower working-class vote became more volatile after 1960.

We summarize these results in two forms in Figure 4.1 (from Hout *et al.* 1995: fig. 2). The data in the figure are coefficients from two logistic regression models. The simpler model fits a linear trend that varies by class to the voting time-series; the coefficients are connected by the straight lines in each panel of the figure. The more complicated model allows each class parameter to take its best-fitting value in each election; the coefficients are shown as dots in the figure. The simpler linear interaction model is preferred for these data, even though the dots spread around the lines.[3]

The most important feature of these trends is the bifurcation of the 'salariat'. Managers and professionals have followed different political paths since the 1960s. Managers' interests cling closely to the low-tax, deregulation agenda of the Republican Party. Professionals have less of a

[3] The likelihood ratio test (the difference between −2 log-likelihood for the full interaction and linear change models) is 45 with 61 degrees of freedom (with a *bic* value of −501).

stake in those policies for several reasons. Although their incomes have been as high as managers' in recent years and were actually slightly higher in the 1970s (Levy 1995), professionals are not as worried about government spending or regulation as managers are (Brooks and Manza 1997). Strikes and wage demands of trade unions seldom affect professionals' work. Thus, these mild material interests have been overtaken by professionals' concerns with civil rights, civil liberties, and the environment. In one sense, the impact of social issues on professionals' voting is a point in favour of postmaterialist accounts of electoral change. But a postmaterialist argument implies that class no longer correlates with vote. Here we see that one class responded to these concerns by switching allegiance from one party to the other—as a class.

The other politically significant feature of the post-1960s class-voting profile is the volatility of the working class, especially the skilled craft workers. The main trend is away from the Democrats and towards the Republicans, but they swing widely around that trend line. Exactly why is unclear. Some accounts cited the special appeal of Ronald Reagan. But it is 1956 (Eisenhower's second campaign), 1972 (Nixon's second campaign), and 1988 (Bush's first campaign) that are the strong Republican showings among skilled blue-collar workers. Two of these are reelection bids. Skilled workers also strongly backed the incumbent—Carter—in 1980. But it is more than an attraction to the incumbent as neither Johnson in 1964 nor Reagan in 1984 did better than the trend would suggest.

Elections are interactions between candidates and voters. To parse the realignment of classes it will be necessary to find changes in the appeals of candidates as well as in the responses of voters. Another strategy is to focus on the voters, however, and to find changes in the institutional links between individuals and parties. One of the most important of these institutions is the labour movement. So we turn to a discussion of trade union politics.

## UNIONS AND REALIGNMENT

The dealignment of blue-collar voters corresponds to their falling union membership—from 66 per cent of skilled blue-collar men in the 1950s to 30 per cent in the early 1990s. The rates were lower but the drop as steep among less-skilled and female blue-collar workers. Meanwhile union membership among professionals increased from 5 per cent in 1956 to 15 per cent in the 1980s and early 1990s. The number of routine white-collar workers belonging to unions increased from the 1960s, but the rate of unionization did not increase for this rapidly growing class. Managers and

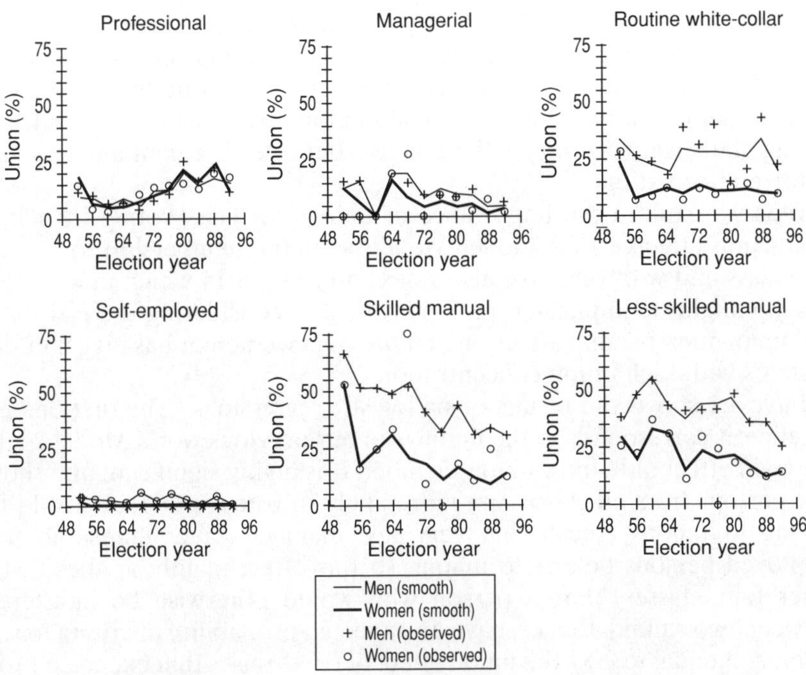


FIG. 4.2. Union membership by time, class, and gender: United States, 1952–1992

the self-employed have never been union members in significant numbers. We depict these trends in Figure 4.2. The symbols show the observed percentages (circles for women, plus signs for men). We also smoothed the time-series using a loglinear model that excluded the four way interaction among class, gender, union, and election year. The lines connect the percentages expected under the model of no four-way interaction.

To assess whether the demise of this important working-class institution affected class voting, we proceed by adding union membership to our model. What would constitute evidence of a union effect? A necessary but insufficient piece of evidence is a significant main effect of being a union member, that is, evidence that union members are more likely to vote Democrat than other members of the same class. To say that unions affected class voting we would have to see one of two other possible outcomes. Either class differences in voting patterns among union members would have to be significantly weaker than overall class differences or trends within combinations of class and union membership/nonmembership would have to be insignificant. The first would be the strongest evidence that the demise of unions explains the realignment of class voting. If union members share a strong partisan attachment in all years, but there are fewer union members in recent years, then the volatility of blue-collar voters would be explained by the lack of institutional representation for them. The second kind of evidence—no trends in voting for people who have the same combination of class and union membership—is a fully satisfying statistical account of the change, but one that contains less substantive information.

Thus we explore the importance of unions for class voting by adding interaction effects to the model. We allow union membership to interact with class and with time. We also assess other ways in which union membership might be implicated in class voting by considering the possibility that union membership affects men more than women or has bigger effects in states with high union concentration.

Table 4.1 shows the results of six logistic regressions.[4] The first one is a baseline; it corresponds to the findings in our previous work. Model 2 adds the main effect of being a union member. It is highly significant and shows that persons from all classes are more likely to vote for Democrats if they belong to unions (recall that very few managers and almost no self-employed persons belong to unions, so this effect mainly applies to the other four classes). For a person who would otherwise be indifferent between two candidates (i.e. have an expected probability of voting for the Democrat equal to 0.5), the union effect of 0.691 raises that expected probability to 0.67. Thus, on average at least, union membership makes a substantial difference for a person's vote.

The simplicity of the main effect is appealing, but it assumes that union membership affects blue-collar workers no more or less than white-collar workers, men no more or less than women, and all elections to the same extent. We introduce four interaction effects to test whether the union effect really is so pervasive and unchanging. We begin with class. Model 3 introduces five dummy variables for the full interaction between class and union membership; it is not significant. The coefficients suggest that perhaps less-skilled blue-collar workers are *less* affected by union membership than are white-collar workers and skilled blue-collar workers. Model 4 pairs the interaction between class and union membership to the contrast between unskilled blue-collar workers and everyone else; it is statistically significant by the usual criterion, but *bic* implies that it is weak evidence of a difference. If we were to take the point-estimate at face value, we would conclude that union membership increases the log odds on voting for Democrats by 0.78 for most classes but only by (0.78 – 0.32 = ) 0.46 among less-skilled blue-collar workers.

[4] In addition to the variables listed in Table 4.1, each regression includes the main effect of election year, gender, race, region, and interactions between election year and region and election year and race. Each also includes a set of dummy variables that capture deviations from linearity in the trend in the skilled blue-collar workers' voting.

TABLE 4.1. *Estimates of the effects of class and union membership on presidential voting: United States, 1952–1992*

| | Model | | | | | |
|---|---|---|---|---|---|---|
| Category | 1 | 2 | 3 | 4 | 5 | 6 |
| Class: main effect | | | | | | |
| Professional | –0.410 | –0.365 | –0.308 | –0.354 | –0.361 | –0.364 |
| Managerial | 0.000 | 0 | 0.000 | 0.000 | 0.000 | 0.000 |
| Routine white-collar | –0.029 | –0.066 | –0.008 | –0.060 | –0.060 | –0.072 |
| Self-employed | 0.249 | 0.319 | 0.378 | 0.330 | 0.322 | 0.331 |
| Skilled blue-collar | 1.186 | 0.873 | 0.845 | 0.840 | 0.847 | 0.833 |
| Less-skilled blue-collar | 0.790 | 0.585 | 0.737 | 0.695 | 0.568 | 0.559 |
| Class: linear trend | | | | | | |
| Professional | 0.118 | 0.104 | 0.100 | 0.102 | 0.103 | 0.103 |
| Managerial | — | — | — | — | — | — |
| Routine white-collar | 0.055 | 0.049 | 0.045 | 0.048 | 0.048 | 0.047 |
| Self-employed | –0.044 | –0.049 | –0.053 | –0.050 | –0.050 | –0.051 |
| Skilled blue-collar | –0.056 | –0.040 | –0.039 | –0.039 | –0.049 | –0.046 |
| Less-skilled blue-collar | –0.014 | –0.008 | –0.016 | –0.013 | 0.010 | 0.010 |
| Union | | 0.691 | 1.066 | 0.783 | 0.705 | 0.668 |
| Union by Class | | | | | | |
| Professional | | | –0.358 | — | — | — |
| Managerial | | | — | — | — | — |
| Routine white-collar | | | –0.359 | — | — | — |
| Self-employed | | | –0.487 | — | — | — |
| Skilled blue-collar | | | –0.222 | — | — | — |
| Less-skilled blue-collar | | | –0.602 | –0.319 | 0.152 | 0.159 |
| Union by Class: linear trend | | | | | | |
| Professional | | | | | 0.001 | 0.013 |
| Managerial | | | | | — | — |
| Routine white-collar | | | | | 0.004 | 0.022 |
| Self-employed | | | | | — | — |
| Skilled blue-collar | | | | | 0.041 | 0.033 |
| Less-skilled blue-collar | | | | | –0.068 | –0.066 |
| Union by Region: Midwest | | | | | | 0.262 |
| Union by Gender: Women | | | | | | –0.321 |
| –2 log-likelihood | 9,382.61 | 9,283.61 | 9,277.02 | 9,279.12 | 9,274.09 | 9,266.12 |
| Degrees of freedom | 7,532 | 7,531 | 7,526 | 7,530 | 7,526 | 7,524 |
| Change in –2 log-likelihood | 1,129.65 | 99.01 | 6.59 | 4.49 | 5.03 | 7.97 |
| Change in degrees of freedom | 74 | 1 | 5 | 1 | 4 | 2 |
| *Bic* | –57,930 | –58,020 | –57,982 | –58,015 | –57,984 | –57,975 |

*Note*: — indicates that the category is either a reference category or is set equal to zero for another reason.

More important than the universality of the effect of union membership is its ability to explain the trend in class realignment. As we noted above, it could be said to do so if the net effect of class goes to zero once the effect(s) of union membership is (are) removed. The first six rows of Table 4.1 make clear that this form of explaining away the realignment does not apply. The second way would be if the changes in voting were to disappear once we control for union membership. To see if that form of explanation holds, we have to compare the linear trends for each class effect with the interaction between that effect and union membership. Model 5 makes this test possible. If the two interaction effects are nearly zero or of equal or nearly equal magnitude but opposite sign, then unionization is implicated as a source of the trends. The loss of union representation explains a portion of the trend for skilled blue-collar workers but for no other class. The class-by-time linear interaction effect for skilled blue-collar workers is –0.049; the union-by-class-by-time linear interaction effect is 0.041. Thus nearly all of the linear part of the trend in the effect of being a skilled-blue collar worker is restricted to un-unionized skilled workers. Recall, however, that there is a substantial nonlinear class-by-time interaction for this class only. So even for unionized skilled blue-collar workers there is some trend in partisan choice.[5]

Finally we add two more interaction effects to the model. From model 6 we see some evidence that unions have bigger effects on their members in the Midwest (we actually began the analysis with a full set of regions and then trimmed back to this one contrast) and do not affect female members as much as they affect male members. These effects are statistically significant at the conventional level but the *bic* value indicates that the evidence is none the less weak. The gender effect is particularly important if it is reliable because it indicates that unions affect women's votes only about half as much as they affect men's votes.

## CONCLUSIONS

Class voting in the United States underwent a historic realignment in the 1960s and 1970s. The new alignment persists into the 1990s. Structural changes in the social bases of American politics—the emergence of postindustrial class structure, the increase in women's labour force participation, and the demise of unions—exist alongside this class realignment and contribute to American voting behaviour, but they do not account for the realignment itself.

Unions play a significant role in American politics. Union membership boosts the propensity to vote Democrat by approximately 19 percentage points among men in unions and 13 percentage points among women in unions. There is weak evidence that unions may increase Democratic

[5] The evidence for this effect appears to be very weak in Table 4.1; the likelihood ratio test is barely greater than its degrees of freedom. However, nearly all of the difference between the log-likelihoods for model 4 and model 5 is owing to the effect among skilled blue-collar workers.

voting among their members by an additional 5 percentage points in the Midwest. Yet these differences exist beside class differences in voting patterns. Neither the differences among classes nor the difference between union members and other employees is reducible to the other kind of difference. The class differences among nonmembers of unions are nearly as large as the total class differences (ignoring union membership).

The demise of unions has cost Democrats an important constituency—compounding the loss they would have suffered as the class structure shifted away from blue-collar labour. In that sense it was imperative that the Democrats pick up new constituencies which they found among professionals and routine white-collar workers.

If structural factors like gender, unions, and sector do not explain the change in class voting, what does? To understand the changing class coalitions of postwar American politics, analysts will need to turn to the other approaches—the investigation of party strategies and class-specific changes in public opinion. The Democratic and Republican parties themselves have changed their appeals. Since the late 1960s, the Republicans have frequently played on skilled workers' economic self-interest to lure their votes. They have met with varying degrees of success. These appeals have lost them some support among routine white-collar workers and professionals. Explicit appeals by Democrats and 'new Democrats' have shored up that latent support. In recent presidential campaigns, the Democrats have explicitly invoked the 'middle class' as their primary electoral target. Further research, perhaps combining qualitative and quantitative research on the bases of party appeals, is called for to explore these possibilities (for the few existing efforts to explore the party coalitions, see Stanley *et al.* 1986 and Carmines and Stanley 1992).

Research on the class effects of changes in public opinion are also appropriate. In our own earlier work (Brooks and Manza 1997), we have found that the increased salience of liberal attitudes on social issues explains much of the shift of professionals towards the Democratic Party. Others have explored the increased salience of racial divisions in dividing the US working class since the mid-1960s (Huckfeldt and Kohfeld 1989; Edsall 1991). Other studies focusing on attitudes may continue to reveal class-specific differences which can help account for class realignment.

In rejecting classical sociological accounts of the realignment of American class politics, the conclusions of the present chapter are not completely negative. First, our multi-class approach revealed the pattern of class realignment we now take as the object to be explained. Secondly, these general findings suggest that the likely social bases of the class coalitions have undergone significant change. Finally, by ruling out major structural explanations for these shifts, we have advanced the state of the debate. Our findings here may be contrasted with those for other capitalist democracies where distinct social bases of political change still appear to hold (Heath *et al.* 1985, 1991). In the US case, most of the action now appears to be taking place away from the classic sources of voting behaviour emphasized in the political sociological tradition.

# 5

# The Secret Life of Class Voting: Britain, France, and the United States since the 1930s

DAVID L. WEAKLIEM AND ANTHONY F. HEATH

## INTRODUCTION

A central tenet of many otherwise diverse analyses of modern politics is that the influence of social class on political behaviour is declining. This important empirical claim, however, is based on surprisingly limited data. Most research has used standard academic surveys, especially the British Election Surveys and the American National Election Studies, which go back no further than the 1950s or 1960s. As a result, we know a good deal about class voting in recent years, but much less about the 1950s and before—the period when the impact of class is supposed to have been at its peak. Hence, conclusions about long-run trends in class voting do not rest on a solid foundation. In addition, nearly all discussion of class and political behaviour focuses on party choice and ignores the relationship between class and turnout. Since a substantial fraction of the eligible population does not vote, an analysis of the general political importance of class must take account of nonvoting as well as party choice. Finally, most work has not clearly distinguished between simple changes in class polarization and more complex realignment. If there is a general convergence or divergence of the voting patterns in all classes, it is possible to speak of a simple decrease or increase in the influence of class on vote. However, there might instead be changes in the relative political positions of the classes, with differences between some classes or parties decreasing and others increasing. In this case, one might say that certain class alignments had become less important.

A version of this paper was presented at the thirteenth World Congress of Sociology, July 1994. Data were obtained from the ESRC Data Archive, the Roper Center for Public Opinion Research, and the CIDSP Banque de Données Socio-Politiques. We thank Jane Roberts and Fern Bennett for responding promptly to numerous requests for additional datasets. Bruno Cautres, Maurice Garnier, Barb Halpenny, Marilyn Potter, and Paul Weakliem also provided help in obtaining or processing the data. We also thank Nuffield College for financial support.

This, however, is not the same as saying that class in general has become less important.

While changes in general class voting, changes in class influences on turnout, and changes in class alignments might occur simultaneously, they are conceptually distinct, and different theories have distinct implications about the type of change that might occur. Most empirical work, however, has been based on dichotomous contrasts between manual and nonmanual workers and between left and right parties. This approach makes it impossible to distinguish between different types of change: for example, a decline in the differences between manual and nonmanual workers might reflect a general decline in class polarization, but it could also reflect the convergence of lower nonmanual workers with the manual working class predicted by classical Marxist theory. Without a more detailed categorization of class, it would be impossible to say which process was occurring.

In this chapter, we compile data on class and vote in Britain and the United States since the 1930s and in France since the 1940s, using the most detailed categorizations of class and party that the original sources permit. Given the presence of sampling error in all survey data, there is obviously some value in presenting any new information about class and vote. In addition, our series begins before the standard election surveys, permitting better evaluation of claims about long-run trends and enabling us to distinguish them from short-term fluctuations in class voting. Finally, the use of more detailed information on class and party allows us to test hypotheses about class voting that cannot be evaluated using a dichotomous categorization.

## THEORY AND HYPOTHESES

### *General Changes*

Several authors have suggested that social divisions other than class have become more important in modern societies, so that class has been driven into the background. Inglehart (1990) argues that, as people's material standard of living improves, they shift their attention away from economic issues and towards social and cultural issues that are largely independent of class. Consequently long-term economic growth produces a long-term decline in class voting. Others suggest that class is becoming less important because diversity within classes is growing. Lash and Urry (1987; see also Dunleavy and Husbands 1985), for example, argue that classes are increasingly divided by skill, region, specific branch of industry, and other factors. Hence, even if people continue to vote according to their economic interests, these interests are less closely tied to class.

Despite the differences between these accounts, all imply that general class voting will decline fairly steadily in all industrialized nations. Since the long-term social changes that they focus on are highly correlated, it is not possible to choose among these accounts using these data. Rather, they can be treated as a group, and contrasted with accounts that do not predict steady declines in class voting.

One alternative accepts the idea that prosperity shifts attention away from class-related issues, but focuses on short-term change (Converse 1958). Inglehart (1990) assumes that desires are fixed, so economic growth leads to increasing satisfaction with material standards of living. If, however, expectations change with experience, the level of material well-being will be less important than recent changes. Class voting would then be expected to fall in periods of relatively rapid improvement in living standards, such as the 1950s and 1960s, and rise in periods of economic decline such as the mid-1970s. If popular expectations gradually adjust to the actual standard of living, however, there would be no long-term trend in class voting.

More generally, class voting might be lower when economic issues are overshadowed by other issues that are not closely linked to class. Although measures of the relative importance of different issues are not generally available, it is possible to examine the effects of one important special case, major war. Many observers suggested that threats to national survival and common experience of hardship promote solidarity across classes (Campbell *et al.* 1960: 361). Even where a war is politically divisive, as with the Korean and Vietnam wars, the divisions will not usually be closely connected to class. Converse (1958) found some evidence that class voting was lower during wartime in the United States, but there seem to have been no subsequent investigations.

Another approach focuses on changes in the political options offered by parties. If the parties offer clear ideological alternatives, voters will be able to make a choice based on their class interests, and class voting will be strong. If the ideological differences between parties are smaller or less clear, however, voters will not be able to make a choice based on class interests. Voting will be based primarily on idiosyncratic personal preferences, and class will have little influence. Converse (1958) suggests that class voting fell in the United States between the 1940s and 1950s because the ideological differences between the Democrats and Republicans declined. Vanneman and Cannon (1987) offer a similar explanation of national differences in class voting—in their view, Americans do not vote on the basis of class because the political parties do not give them the opportunity of doing so. Most scholars appear to think that there has been some long-term tendency to ideological convergence in most countries, but also a good deal of short-term change. Thus, this account can be empirically distinguished from accounts that focus on general social changes as the major force driving class voting.

### *Class and Turnout*

Turnout is almost always lower in the working class than in the middle class. Like class voting, however, the strength of the relationship varies among nations (Lipset 1981). Comparative research suggests that the influence of class on party choice is unusually small in the United States but that the influence of class on turnout is unusually large. Verba and Nie (1972; see also Verba *et al.* 1978) suggest that these two facts are linked. One possible explanation is that the decision to vote can be influenced by party positions: if no party appeals to their class interests, working-class people may not vote at all. Hence the lack of strong ideological differences between the parties in the United States may produce low class voting and large class differences in turnout (Vanneman and Cannon 1987; Verba *et al.* 1978: 308). Similarly, Przeworski and Sprague (1986: 61–4) suggest that when parties of the left pursue 'supraclass strategies', some workers will respond by abstaining. Verba, Nie, and Kim (1978: 308–9) suggest another explanation for a connection between class differences in turnout and class voting, focusing on organization. People in the working class generally have less political knowledge and interest and are less likely to see voting as an obligation of citizenship. Hence, working-class turnout may be sensitive to the strength of party, union, or community organizations (see also Lipset 1981: 203–4). Workers will vote in large numbers only where such organizations are active. Where they are weak, workers will be unlikely to vote in any case, and parties will have little incentive to appeal to their interests. The two accounts suggest different causal orders, but both imply that low levels of class voting will be associated with large class differences in turnout.

While Verba, Nie, and Kim (1978) focus on comparisons among nations, the same arguments can be applied within nations to predict an inverse relationship between class voting and class differences in turnout over time. That is, a weakening of the link between left parties and working-class interests would be associated with a relative increase in working-class abstention. This view does not necessarily imply that there will be any trend in either class voting or turnout differentials. Verba, Nie, and Kim (1978: 308–9), however, make a stronger argument suggesting that there will be a long-term trend in both relationships. Like authors such as Inglehart (1990) and Rose and McAllister (1986) they hold that there is a general shift towards individualism in modern societies. Like those authors, they see a general decline in class voting as one result of this change, but they also suggest that individualism will tend to magnify class differences in turnout. That is, those members of the working class who once voted for left parties because of class loyalty or ties to union organizations will be less likely to vote at all as these collective attachments weaken.[1]

An alternative view of the relationship between class and turnout is that it is explained by psychological factors such as differences in information and political efficacy (Wolfinger and Rosenstone 1980). These ultimately depend on class differences in factors such as education, exposure to the mass media, and child-rearing practices. This view suggests that class differences in turnout will show little changes in the short term, and any change will be unrelated to change in class voting. Over the long term, they would be expected to decline as the result of growing exposure to the mass media and narrowing educational differences between classes.

## *Theories of Class Realignment*

Although support for the left is almost always higher among manual workers than among nonmanual workers, it is possible to make finer distinctions within each group. Differences between specific types of nonmanual workers are often large; business owners and managers are generally more conservative than professionals, who are in turn usually more conservative than routine white-collar workers (Heath and Savage 1995). Given sufficient data, even finer divisions could be made among detailed occupations: Ladd and Lipset (1975: 55–92), for example, find substantial political differences among university professors in different disciplines. Differences among manual workers are generally smaller, but skilled workers and manual foremen are usually more conservative than unskilled workers (Heath *et al.* 1985: 13–27).

Hence, different categorizations of class will necessarily produce different estimates of the effect of class on vote at any given time. As long as changes in class voting take the form of a uniform convergence or divergence of classes, however, conclusions about *change* will not be greatly affected by the definition of class. Conclusions will depend on the categorization only if there is realignment, that is, changes in the relative

[1] Implicit in these views is the assumption that turnout is more variable in the working class than it is in the middle class. If working-class people alternated between voting for left parties and abstaining, increases in class voting would be associated with declines in class differences in turnout. However, if similar processes operated within the middle class, with middle-class people alternating between voting for parties of the right and abstaining, increases in class voting would be associated with increases in turnout differentials. While there have been few discussions of this point, Lipset (1981: 211–15) does offer some evidence that turnout is more variable in the working class: he ascribes this to the existence of 'cross-pressures' that inhibit working-class participation.

political position of different classes. For example, suppose that there are three 'true' class categories containing equal numbers of voters. At time 1, support for the left is 70 per cent in group A, 60 per cent in group B, and 30 per cent in group C. At time 2, it is 70 per cent in group A, 40 per cent in B, and 30 per cent in C. If A and B were combined into a single category, support for the left would fall from 65 to 55 per cent between times 1 and 2. Since support for the left would remain at 30 per cent in group C, class voting would appear to fall. If, however, B and C were combined into one group, class voting would appear to rise: support for the left would remain at 70 per cent in group A and fall from 45 per cent to 35 per cent in the combined groups B and C.

Consequently, using a more detailed categorization reduces the possibility of gross distortions that exists with a dichotomy. In addition, several distinct theories of class and politics suggest roughly similar distinctions among groups, although they imply different relative shifts by those groups. The most important distinctions are among nonmanual workers, where Marxist, Weberian, and empiricist accounts all suggest a need to distinguish between routine white-collar workers, owners and managers, and professionals. There is less agreement, however, about changes in the political alignments of these groups. Although there are many conceivable alternatives, three have received clear theoretical expression. They can be given the labels of 'nonmanual proletarianization', 'manual embourgeoisement', and 'new politics'.

Most socialists, including Marx, considered at least some nonmanual workers to be a part of the working class. According to Marx (1967/1894) 'the commercial worker . . . belongs to the better-paid class of wage workers—to those whose labour is classed as skilled and stands above average labour', but 'with few exceptions, [their] labour-power . . . is devaluated with the progress of capitalist production'. Socialists have traditionally believed that lower-level nonmanual workers might begin by identifying with capital, but that the realities of their situation would cure them of this 'false consciousness' (Lockwood 1958: 13–14). That is, they would shift away from capital and towards the working class. Obviously neither manual nor white-collar workers have shown the steady growth of class consciousness predicted by nineteenth-century socialists. However, given the growth of white-collar unionization over the last few decades, the idea that the voting patterns of lower white-collar workers are coming to resemble those of the manual working class cannot be dismissed.

An alternative which may be called 'manual embourgeoisement' holds that the traditional manual working class is becoming less politically distinctive (Goldthorpe *et al.* 1968). That is, the differences between manual and nonmanual workers decline more than the differences among the various nonmanual groups. In the 1950s, it was often argued that the working class was being absorbed into a large middle class (Mayer 1956; Abrams *et al.* 1960). Like the traditional Marxist analysis, this view implies a convergence of manual and lower nonmanual workers. As Mayer (1956: 78) points out, however, it differs from the traditional Marxist view in suggesting that it is the manual workers who change: 'the "proletarian" wage-earners are becoming homogeneous with the white-collar workers and are joining the middle class'. A variant on this view that has become popular in recent years is that manual workers have been absorbed into what Dahrendorf (1988: 153–4) calls the 'majority class', and that the major political division is between this class and an underclass including the unemployed and marginal low-paid manual workers.

Finally, the 'new politics' analysis suggests a more complex set of political shifts. Some nonmanual groups, especially professionals, are usually to the left of manual workers on cultural and social issues. According to observers such as Lipset (1981) and Inglehart (1990), the importance of these issues is increasing, producing a new class division that partly counteracts the traditional alignment. The new alignment, however, is not exactly opposite to the traditional alignment, as farmers and small businessmen tend to be conservative on both economic and non-economic issues. Hence, this model suggests a convergence of the new middle class—especially professionals, but to some extent managers and routine nonmanual workers as well—with the working class, and a divergence between the old and new middle classes.

The new politics hypothesis can be put in a stronger or weaker form. The weaker form is simply that the new alignment will grow over time. The stronger hypothesis is that the growth of the new alignment will be accompanied by the decline of the traditional class alignment. That is, the new alignment will not just coexist with the traditional alignment, but will tend to replace it. This stronger hypothesis has been advocated most clearly by Inglehart (1990) on the grounds that political alignments are based on mutually exclusive 'value orientations'.

The hypotheses discussed in this section are summarized in Table 5.1, along with references to the sources from which they are derived.

## DATA

We have constructed tables of class by vote for all British general elections from 1935 to 1992 (with the exception of 1950), all American presidential elections from 1936 to 1992, and all French legislative elections from November 1946 to 1993. Our choice of nations is governed mainly by the fact that these three nations have the longest histories of systematic opinion polling, but they nevertheless offer an interesting contrast.

TABLE 5.1. *Hypotheses on changes in class voting*

| Hypothesis | | Principal sources |
|---|---|---|
| A | General Class Voting | |
| A1 | Long-term decline in all nations | Inglehart (1990); Lipset (1981) |
| A2 | Varies inversely with recent prosperity | Converse (1958) |
| A3 | Lower in wartime | Converse (1958) |
| A4 | Varies directly with ideological differences between parties | Converse (1958) |
| B | Class Voting and Differences in Turnout | |
| B1 | Inverse relationship between class voting and class differences in turnout | Verba, Nie, and Kim (1978); Vanneman and Cannon (1987) |
| B2 | B1 plus long-term increase in class differences in turnout | Verba, Nie, and Kim (1978) |
| B3 | Long-term decline in class differences in turnout | Not explicit in any source; inspired by Wolfinger and Rosenstone (1980) |
| C | Changes in Class Alignments | |
| C1 | 'Proletarianization': Convergence of manual working class and lower white-collar workers | Marx (1967/1894) |
| C2 | 'New Politics': professionals versus old middle class and manual workers | Inglehart (1990); Lipset (1981) |
| C3 | 'Embourgeoisement': manual working class becomes less distinct | Mayer (1956); Dahrendorf (1988) |

International comparisons indicate that class is an unusually strong influence on political choice in Britain and an unusually weak one in the United States (Alford 1963). Both nations, however, share a tradition of relatively equal competition between two ideologically moderate parties. French politics were highly polarized ideologically for most of the period because of the large Communist movement, but there is no consensus about how strongly class has affected political behaviour. According to the figures in Clark and Lipset (1991; see also Dalton 1994), the association of class and vote has been rather weak historically in France and has declined since the 1950s. Lewis-Beck (1984: 436), however, holds that the association has been 'essentially stable' since the 1950s, while Frears (1991: 134) states that 'voting is much more polarised by social class in France than it used to be'.

Because we are interested in nonvoting as well as in party choice we use data on voting in actual elections, not party identification or hypothetical votes 'if an election were held today'. The one exception is that we use a British survey of hypothetical voting intentions in 1943. Because of the Second World War, no general election was held in Britain between 1935 and 1945. This period is of great interest for this analysis, however, since Labour recovered from crushing defeats in 1931 and 1935 to win its first parliamentary majority in 1945. The 1943 data, although they must be treated with care, will consequently provide some evidence about the development of class polarization before Labour's victory.[2]

We consider legislative elections in France because the presidential system was not established until the 1960s and because the party affiliations of the major presidential candidates have not always been clear.[3] In the United States, we focus on presidential elections because regional differences in party ideologies were very large at least through the 1950s. In much of the country, congressional elections were not seriously contested, and in contested elections, Democratic candidates were not necessarily to the left of Republican candidates. It is only in presidential elections that the Democrats can be consistently regarded as the 'left' party.

In the United States, we concentrate on the two major parties, since none of the significant third parties endured for more than one election. In Britain, Social Democrats are included with the Liberals in 1983 and 1987, producing a three-party classification into Conservatives, Labour, and Liberals.[4] In France, we classified the parties into three groups: Communists; other left (mainly Socialists, but also including Ecologists, the PSU, and several small groups); and centre/right. Because French conservative parties have been short-lived and frequently divided by personalities rather than ideology, it is impossible to make further distinctions within the centre/right group. Converse and Dupeux (1966/1962) found that French voters themselves had difficulty drawing clear distinctions between the centre and right parties. The broad left versus right distinction, however, is widely recognized by the French public (Michelat 1993).

The main data sources were the Gallup polls in Britain; Gallup polls (1936–92) and the General Social Survey (GSS) in the United States; and Gallup (1946–78), SOFRES (1973–86), and Brule–Ville Associates

[2] The 1935 data also require special treatment, since Labour and Liberal votes were originally combined into one category. It is possible to estimate the proportion of Liberal and Labour votes in each class by means of the EM algorithm, a well-known method of dealing with incomplete or missing data (Chow 1983: 268–71; Dempster *et al.* 1977). The Liberal vote in this election was small enough so that different assumptions about its composition have little effect on the overall estimates of class voting. Still, results that are strongly dependent on this single election must be regarded with caution.

[3] For example, in 1969, most of the Socialist party refused to support the official candidate of the party, so the non-Communist left vote was scattered over a variety of candidates in the first round. As a result of this split, there was no true left candidate in the second round.

[4] Northern Ireland, which has a distinct party system, was not included in the original surveys.

(1981–8) polls in France. More detail on data sources is given in the Appendix at the end of this chapter. The original data were not available for a few elections in Britain and France, so in these cases the tables were taken from published sources which did not include information on non-voting.

Most of the original surveys used fairly broad occupational categories. In addition, comparisons over time require the use of the same class schema throughout. Consequently, our classifications use only the distinctions that are common to all surveys for that nation. They are nevertheless more detailed than the traditional manual/nonmanual distinction. Four classes can be distinguished in Britain: proprietors and executives, professionals, white collar, and manual. Five classes can be distinguished in France: farmers and farm labourers, professionals and managers, small proprietors, white collar, and manual. Six classes can be distinguished in the United States: farmers and farm labourers, professionals, managers and proprietors, white collar, skilled manual, and semi- and unskilled manual.[5]

These class divisions are not based on any particular theory of stratification. It would certainly be desirable to have more detailed information on employment status and occupation, but the classifications are adequate for testing the hypotheses outlined above. None of these hypotheses is closely tied to a specific definition of class boundaries. For example, the general idea of a leftward shift of some professionals has been suggested from a variety of different viewpoints, and there is considerable disagreement about exactly which groups are involved (Brint 1984). If we find that professionals, taken as a whole, do shift to the left relative to other classes, it would then be interesting to look at more detailed data in order to describe the shift more precisely. However, if political changes among professionals as a whole parallel those among other occupational groups, there will be little point in pursuing more specific versions of the 'new politics' thesis. Similarly, traditional Marxists would not all agree on exactly which white-collar workers are becoming proletarianized. Nevertheless, virtually all would agree that the leading candidates for proletarianization are found mostly in routine or lower-level positions rather than managerial or professional jobs. Thus, all traditional Marxist accounts would agree that 'routine' white-collar workers should, on the average, move to the left relative to managers and professionals. They would suggest, however, that more theoretically informed ways of drawing a boundary between classes would reveal even sharper differences in the trends. In summary, the hypotheses discussed above are least common denominators that can be tested using the class schemas available in the original surveys. Using other

[5] In Britain, farm owners are counted as proprietors and farm labourers as manual workers. The very few large proprietors in France are combined with professionals and managers.

definitions of class, the results reported here might be amplified, but it is very unlikely that they would be reversed.

It is possible to check the estimates of class voting derived from these data against estimates derived from other sources. In Chapter 11, we systematically compare the estimates of class voting from the Gallup data to those from the American National Election Studies (ANES) and British Election Surveys (BES), and find that the differences are no larger than could be expected to occur by chance. For a shorter period, 1964–70, a third source is available in Britain, the National Opinion Poll, and estimates from this source also track the Gallup estimates closely.

Our analysis of the relationship between class and party does not control for other possible influences on voting. We do not attempt to control for political opinions and attitudes towards the candidates and parties because these are best regarded as intervening variables. The relationship between class and party choice is at least partly an indirect one operating through attitudes. While distinguishing between direct and indirect effects would be interesting, the total effects are meaningful in their own right. Because of data limitations, we are unable to control for other structural influences on vote; some of the surveys contained additional information, but race (in the United States) and sex were the only variables that were recorded for the whole period.[6] While the inclusion of other structural variables would be desirable, since class is clearly not the only influence on vote, their exclusion is not very damaging in practice. Including control variables would change the estimated effects of class only to the extent that the additional variables had a strong influence on vote and a high correlation with class. In the United States, race is strongly correlated with both vote and class. For this reason, and because blacks have always shown low levels of class voting in the United States, we restrict the analysis to whites. The other demographic variables that generally have a strong relationship to vote are religion and region, which are not highly correlated with class.

Moreover, for the purpose of studying *change*, a bias in the estimates resulting from the exclusion of controls is not necessarily cause for concern. What matters is whether the bias changes over time. The effect of including control variables can be evaluated with the General Social Survey data from 1972–92 and with the British election survey data for 1964–92.[7] In the case of the GSS, adding controls for sex, region (South versus non-South), religion (Protestant, Catholic, Jewish, other, or none), and age (linear and quadratic terms) increased the estimated effect of class by about 20 per cent. However, this increase was very similar in all

[6] Because we found no large or consistent differences in class voting among men and women, we combine both in the analysis.

[7] Details of this analysis are available from the authors on request.

elections, so that conclusions about temporal change in class voting were unaffected. Even when the effects of the control variables were allowed to change from election to election, the resulting estimates of class voting remained quite similar to the original ones: the correlation of the estimates was 0.92, and the differences were not statistically significant using the test proposed by Clogg, Petkova, and Haritou (1995).[8] The 1972–92 period covered by the GSS saw substantial changes in the effect of some of the controls, especially sex and region, and relatively small changes in class voting. Hence, the effect of including controls would probably be even smaller in the earlier part of the period (see also Hout *et al.* 1995). In the case of Britain the effects were trivial: adding controls for sex, region, religion, and age reduced the estimated effect of class by 2 per cent.[9]

## METHODS

Much empirical work on class voting relies on the 'Alford index', defined as the percentage of manual voters supporting the left minus the percentage of nonmanual voters supporting the left. However, while the simplicity of the Alford index makes it useful for descriptive purposes, its reliance on dichotomies of class and party makes it unsuitable for more rigorous analysis (Korpi 1972). The most widely accepted alternative measures of class voting involve loglinear and related models, which can be applied to tables of any dimension and consequently eliminate the need to dichotomize classes and parties. A major difficulty with standard loglinear models, however, is that they use many parameters to model the association between variables, making the results difficult to interpret. Hence, it is desirable to employ models that impose some structure on the association between class and party. The logmultiplicative 'association models' developed by Goodman (1987; 1991) provide a useful alternative to conventional loglinear models.

Intuitively, association models can be thought of as assigning scores to the categories on one or more numerical scales. Formally, the one-dimensional association model for a three-way table of election by class by party can be written:

$$\log(n_{ijk}) = \log(N) + c_{ik} + p_{jk} + \phi_k \gamma_{ik} \tau_{jk} \qquad (5.1)$$

[8] More precisely, the hypothesis that one set of estimates was a constant multiple of the other could not be rejected.

[9] Adding housing tenure as a control variable in Britain leads to a substantial reduction in the size of the class coefficient, but housing status is largely a consequence of class position. Like political opinions, housing tenure is best regarded as an intervening variable between class and vote.

where the subscripts $i$, $j$, and $k$ refer to class, party, and election, respectively. N is the total sample size, $c_{ik}$ represents the proportion of the sample in class $i$ at time $k$, and $p_{jk}$ represents the proportion of the sample in party $j$ at time $k$. The association between class and party is modelled by the product of the class scores $\gamma$, the party scores $\tau$, and a measure of the strength of association $\phi$.[10] When the class and party scores in the association model are constrained to be equal in all elections, changes in the relationship between class and party depend entirely on changes in the $\phi$ parameters. These $\phi$ parameters provide a simple measure of the strength of class voting that can be used in place of the Alford index. The model displayed above involves only one 'dimension', or set of class and party scores. Whether a one-dimensional model will fit a given dataset is an empirical question, and we will later consider models with multiple dimensions.

An important feature of the model is that the total support for each party in each election, represented by $p_{jk}$, is completely distinct from the association between class and vote, represented by $\phi_k\gamma_{ik}\tau_{jk}$. The $p_{jk}$ parameters thus reflect the combined effect of all factors that affect the popularity of the parties across all classes, such as personal qualities of the candidates, general economic conditions, or foreign policy. Hence, there is no need to control for such factors explicitly.

In the association model the scores are usually estimated from the data rather than chosen by the investigator. This procedure is appropriate when expectations derived from theory are not very precise. For example, most observers would expect the voting patterns of routine nonmanual workers to fall somewhere in between those of manual workers and managers and proprietors. Expectations about exactly where they would fall, however, are much vaguer. Different theories of the relationship between class and vote provide no guidance on whether routine nonmanual workers will be exactly in the middle or closer to one of the other classes. In this situation, it is reasonable to let the data decide the exact scores, as long as the general pattern is consistent with expectations.

In comparing models for categorical data, differences in the likelihood-ratio statistic ($L^2$) or Pearson chi-square statistic ($\chi^2$) can be used to test hypotheses about the parameters. The overall fit of a model is sometimes judged by a comparison with the saturated model—that is, the model that achieves a perfect fit by including one parameter for each cell. Although we will use the usual tests for comparing models, comparisons with the saturated model must be treated with caution. Our goal is not to explain

[10] Because there are no natural scales for the class and party scores, they are usually standardized to have mean 0 and variance 1.0. Standardizing them in other ways would simply change $\phi$ by some constant multiple, and would not affect any of the comparisons over time.

all of the variation in the association between class and party, but to examine the main trends over time and to test several major hypotheses about these trends. For these purposes, the differences among models are of more interest than the fit of any individual model. In order to account for all variation, it would be necessary to include numerous parameters relating to specific elections.[11] Our main focus will therefore be on the extent of improvement from baseline models rather than on comparisons with the saturated model.

## ANALYSIS

### *General Class Voting*

We begin with an analysis of general class voting. As noted above, if we constrain the class and party scores to be constant, the $\phi$ parameters in the association model provide a simple measure of the strength of class voting.

TABLE 5.2. *Fits of one-dimensional models of class voting (excluding nonvoters) in Britain, France, and the United States*

| Country | $L^2$ | $\chi^2$ | df | Index of Dissimilarity | $L^2$/df |
|---|---|---|---|---|---|
| Britain | | | | | |
| 1. No association | 5,447.7 | 5,275.6 | 90 | 0.1496 | 60.53 |
| 2. Constant $\phi$ | 333.0 | 330.3 | 86 | 0.0271 | 3.87 |
| 3. $\phi$ changes | 181.0 | 178.9 | 72 | 0.0160 | 2.51 |
| N = 47,565 | | | | | |
| France | | | | | |
| 1. No association | 2,716.4 | 2,630.9 | 144 | 0.1112 | 18.86 |
| 2. Constant $\phi$ | 371.9 | 365.8 | 139 | 0.0386 | 2.68 |
| 3. $\phi$ changes | 300.0 | 294.4 | 127 | 0.0319 | 2.36 |
| N = 31,397 | | | | | |
| United States | | | | | |
| 1. No association | 1,886.2 | 1,863.6 | 95 | 0.0649 | 19.85 |
| 2. Constant $\phi$ | 360.7 | 360.5 | 90 | 0.0258 | 4.01 |
| 3. $\phi$ changes | 225.8 | 224.6 | 76 | 0.0185 | 2.97 |
| N = 75,531 | | | | | |

[11] For example, a party might make a relatively successful bid for farmers' votes in one election. To model this occurrence, it would be necessary to include a dummy variable for the combination of farmers and that party in that election. Such an effect, even if statistically significant, would be of little interest in terms of general trends in class voting.

If changes in class voting take the form of realignment, rather than simple convergence or divergence, it will be necessary to allow changes in the $\gamma$ or $\tau$ parameters, or to add additional dimensions. These more complex models will be considered later, when we consider hypotheses about realignment. However, it is useful to begin with simple one-dimensional models in order to obtain an overview of the long-run trends in class polarization. While there is no guarantee that they will capture all changes in the association between class and party, they provide a parsimonious measure of general class voting.[12]

Table 5.2 shows the fits of one-dimensional association models with constant class and party scores in France, Britain, and the United States. To facilitate comparison with other work on change in class voting, these models are based only on voters. In all three nations, a one-dimensional model accounts for most of the association between class and party, although the unexplained residual is statistically significant. The standardized class and party scores in each country are shown in Table 5.3. The class scores show the expected division between a left based in the working class and a right based in the middle class. The French Communist vote is concentrated in the working class, while the Socialists have more cross-class appeal.[13] In terms of class composition, the British Liberals are considerably closer to the Conservatives than to Labour. Although the differences between class schemas mean that precise comparisons among nations are not possible, the index of dissimilarity from the model of no association can be used as a rough measure of the overall strength of the relationship between class and party. By this measure, class voting is strongest in Britain, somewhat weaker in France, and considerably weaker in the United States.

The changes in $\phi$ are highly significant in all nations; the smallest change is 71.9 with twelve degrees of freedom in France. Figure 5.1 displays the estimates of $\phi$ by election for the three nations. The changes are substan-

[12] Estimates of change in general class voting can also be obtained from the 'log-multiplicative layer effects' or 'uniform difference' model developed by Xie (1992) and Erikson and Goldthorpe (1992*a*). The estimates of class voting derived from this model are almost identical to those based on the one-dimensional association model, except for a scaling factor. Comparing the index of dissimilarity across elections also produces very similar estimates of change in class voting.

[13] Since none of the third parties in the United States endured for more than one election, they cannot be included in an analysis of change. However, their estimated positions given these class scores may be of interest. The 1968 George Wallace vote was more heavily working class than either the Democratic or Republican vote. Thurmond and Henry Wallace in 1948 and Anderson in 1980 were supported mainly by middle-class voters; their estimated party scores are similar to the Republican score. In 1992, Perot drew fairly evenly from all classes, and his party score is almost exactly midway between the Democratic and Republican scores.

TABLE 5.3. *Estimated class and party scores from one-dimensional association models*

| Britain | All | Voters only | France | All | Voters only | United States | All | Voters only |
|---|---|---|---|---|---|---|---|---|
| Business | 1.025 | 1.032 | Farm | 0.967 | 0.891 | Farm | 0.008 | 0.168 |
| Professional | 0.683 | 0.665 | Manager/professional | 0.527 | 0.502 | Business | 1.114 | 1.353 |
| Nonmanual | –0.148 | –0.131 | Small proprietor | 0.796 | 0.905 | Professional | 1.182 | 0.834 |
| Manual | –1.562 | –1.565 | Nonmanual | –0.637 | –0.661 | Nonmanual | 0.191 | 0.145 |
| | | | Manual | –1.653 | –1.638 | Skilled manual | –0.937 | –0.882 |
| | | | | | | Other manual | –1.559 | –1.618 |
| Conservative | 1.229 | 0.968 | Centre and right | 1.297 | 1.181 | Republican | 1.247 | 1.000 |
| Liberal | 0.629 | 0.404 | Socialist | 0.097 | 0.078 | Democratic | –0.050 | –1.000 |
| Labour | –1.293 | –1.372 | Communist | –1.374 | –1.260 | Nonvoter | –1.198 | |
| Nonvoter | –0.603 | | Nonvoter | –0.026 | | | | |

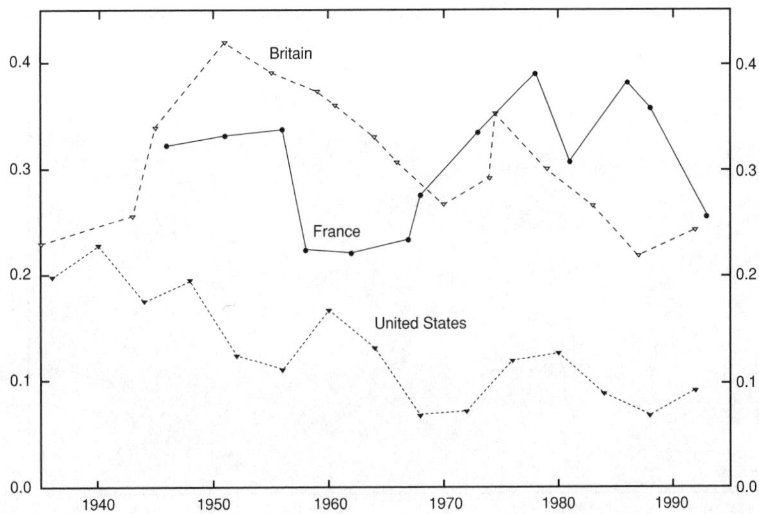


FIG. 5.1. Estimates of class voting from association model, France, Britain and United States

tial: in the United States, $\phi$ is almost three times as large in the 1930s as in the 1970s and 1980s; in Britain and France, the largest values of $\phi$ are about twice the size of the smallest ones. It is also clear from Figure 5.1 that the patterns of change in class voting are very different in the three nations. In the United States, there is an approximately linear decline from the 1930s to the 1990s. In Britain, there is a clear non-linear pattern: an increase from 1935 until 1951, and a decrease of similar magnitude since that time. The estimated levels of class voting are almost identical in 1935 and 1992. In France, there is no obvious trend in either direction.

It is instructive to compare these results to those obtained using the Alford index. Figure 5.2 shows values of the index for the three nations. Following the usual custom, farmers are excluded and left voting is defined as support for the Democrats in the United States, Labour in Britain, and the Communists and Socialists in France. Over the short term, the Alford index and $\phi$ estimates of class voting track each other fairly closely, but there is substantial divergence over the long term. The Alford indexes show a substantial decline in class voting in all three nations. In fact, tests for linear trends fail to reject the hypothesis that the trend is the same in all three nations. Thus, the Alford index and association model correspond closely in the United States, but diverge in Britain and France.

The major reason for the difference in results appears to be the use of a manual/nonmanual dichotomy in the Alford index. Given the substantial differences in voting patterns among various types of nonmanual

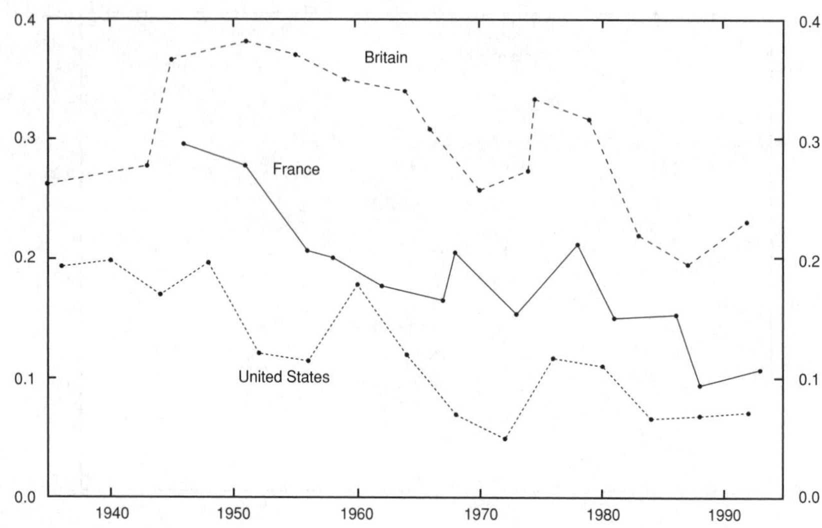


FIG. 5.2. Alford Indexes of class voting, France, Britain, and United States

workers, an increase in the number of the more moderate types relative to the more conservative types means that nonmanual workers as a whole will move to the centre, producing an apparent decline in class voting. The most conservative group of nonmanual workers in France, small proprietors, have become considerably less numerous over the last fifty years. In the British sample, routine white-collar workers increased relative to the more conservative professional and business groups between the 1930s and 1950s, largely masking the increase in class voting that the association model shows in that period. The change in France certainly reflects a real change in the class structure. It would be accurate to say that the political impact of class has declined in France in the sense that the more politically extreme groups have become less numerous. This process, however, does not necessarily mean that class has become less important at the level of the individual voter, as most theoretical accounts suppose. In Britain, it is not clear how much of the change in the sample reflects real change in the class structure and how much reflects change in sampling procedures. The fact that there are large political differences among nonmanual groups means that any estimates of class voting that rely on a manual/nonmanual dichotomy will be sensitive to any changes in the relative size of different nonmanual groups, regardless of their source. Hence, evidence of a general decline in class voting based on contrasts between manual and nonmanual workers, such as that presented by Lipset (1981) and Inglehart (1990), must be regarded with caution.

## *Explaining Change in General Class Voting*

The hypotheses listed in Table 5.1 can be tested by treating the estimate of class voting as the dependent variable in a regression model.[14] The relationship between $\phi$ and the independent variables will not necessarily be linear; in fact, since there is a strong expectation that $\phi$ will not fall below zero, one would expect the independent variables to have less effect at low levels of $\phi$. After some experimentation, we chose the square root of $\phi$ as the dependent variable. In all analyses, we include dummy variables for the intercept in each nation as a control. Parameter estimates from several models are shown in Table 5.4. The hypothesis that class voting will show a similar long-term decline in all nations can be tested by regressing the estimates of $\phi$ on a time trend.[15] The trend is negative and significant in the United States, negative but non-significant in Britain, and positive and significant in France. The hypothesis that the trend is the same in all nations can be rejected using an F-test ($F_{2,36} = 4.441$ $p = 0.0189$). Hence, we include separate national trends in class voting in the more elaborate models. We constrain the effects of the other variables to be the same in all nations, since there is no theoretical rationale for allowing them to differ.

'Prosperity' might be understood in many ways. We focus on real income, the unemployment rate, and inflation as the most important components (see the Appendix for sources). Estimates from a regression including the logarithm of average real wages of employed workers, the unemployment rate, and the changes in unemployment, real wages, and prices over the last three years are shown in the second column of Table 5.4. Overall, the addition of the economic variables does not produce a significant improvement in fit ($F_{5,31} = 1.64, p = 0.179$). The *t*-ratios of unemployment and the three-year change in real wages are near zero. However, the estimated effects of real income, inflation, and the three-year change in unemployment have the expected signs and approach statistical significance. Thus, the results give some support to the hypothesis that class voting varies inversely with prosperity.

Given the general upward trend in real wages, the estimated effect of real wages must be interpreted in conjunction with the estimated national time-trend terms. For example, in France, if the logarithm of real wages increases by 0.0567 per year—that is, if the rate of growth is 5.6 per cent—the effect will be to reduce class voting by $0.1482 \times 0.0567 = 0.00841$, exactly

[14] Since the precision of the estimates of $\phi$ differs from one election to the next, mainly because of differences in sample size, we perform a weighted least squares analysis with weights based on the standard errors estimated in the association model. We exclude the French election of 1946 entirely because of missing data for some of the economic variables.

[15] Similar results are obtained if real GNP per capita is used instead of a time trend.

TABLE 5.4. *Models predicting the level of class voting, all nations combined*

| Independent variables | Model | | | |
|---|---|---|---|---|
| | (1) | (2) | (3) | (4) |
| Time trend: France | 0.364 | 0.841[a] | 0.916[b] | 0.955[a] |
| | (0.211) | (0.465) | (0.435) | (0.483) |
| Time trend: Britain | –0.132 | 0.090 | 0.097 | 0.091 |
| | (0.089) | (0.246) | (0.229) | (0.264) |
| Time trend: United States | –0.278[c] | –0.131 | –0.113 | –0.118 |
| | (0.070) | (0.178) | (0.166) | (0.180) |
| Real wages | | –0.148 | –0.171[a] | –0.182 |
| | | (0.106) | (0.099) | (0.115) |
| Unemployment | | 0.098 | 0.247 | –0.259 |
| | | (0.264) | (0.254) | (0.271) |
| Inflation | | 0.168[a] | 0.159[a] | 0.167 |
| | | (0.097) | (0.090) | (0.102) |
| Change in real wages | | 0.028 | 0.120 | 0.133 |
| | | (0.237) | (0.224) | (0.240) |
| Change in unemployment | | 0.486 | 0.428 | 0.451 |
| | | (0.378) | (0.353) | (0.379) |
| War | | | –0.438[b] | –0.445[b] |
| | | | (0.184) | (0.193) |
| Ideological difference | | | | 0.005 |
| | | | | (0.073) |
| Degrees of freedom | 36 | 31 | 30 | 28 |

*Note*: Standard errors in parentheses. Coefficients and standard errors for time trends, unemployment, change in unemployment, and ideological differences are multiplied by 100. Dummy variables for nation are included in all models, and a dummy variable for cases with missing values on the ideological difference variable is included in model 4.

Statistical significance of parameter estimates: [a] 10 per cent; [b] 5 per cent; [c] 1 per cent.

balancing out the estimated annual trend. Thus, class voting is predicted to increase if real wages increase by less than 5.6 per cent, and to decline if real wages increase by more than that amount. In Britain, class voting is predicted to decline when real wages increase at a rate of more than 0.6 per cent a year; in the United States, when they increase at more than –0.6 per cent a year. Inflation and change in unemployment have the expected effects—class voting tends to be greater when prices and unemployment are increasing. There is no evidence, however, that the actual rate of unemployment has any effect. If unemployment and the three-year change in real wages are dropped from the model, the *t*-ratios for the remaining economic variables increase slightly, and inflation becomes significant at the 5 per cent level.

Considering the small sample size, these results provide some support for the idea that class voting is inversely related to prosperity. Differences in economic conditions, however, do not account for the national differences in the long-term trend of class voting. Controlling for the economic variables in model 2, the differences between the national time trends are still statistically significant ($F_{2,31} = 3.97, p = 0.029$), and are only slightly smaller than they were in the first model. That is, differences in economic conditions cannot explain why the general trend of class voting differs among the nations.

In model 3, a dummy variable for wartime is added to the economic variables. War years are considered to be 1943 and 1945 in Britain, 1940, 1944, 1952, 1968, and 1972 in the United States, and 1956, 1958, and 1962 in France.[16] There is room for disagreement about the classification of certain years, but results are similar regardless of the exact specification of the variable. The war variable has a statistically significant negative effect, which is robust under reasonable changes of specification such as dropping the less significant economic variables. The widespread idea that war reduces the political influence of class divisions thus appears to be correct. More generally, the result indicates that the influence of other issues can reduce class voting. With the present data, it is not possible to determine if this effect applies in less extreme cases—for example, whether class voting varies according to the prominence of economic issues relative to foreign policy or social issues, as suggested by Converse (1958). The significant effect of war, however, at least indicates that this idea is worth pursuing.

The idea that ideological differences between parties influence class voting is tested in model 4. The measure of ideological difference is based on responses to questions in the ANES (1962 and 1960–92) and BES (1964–92) on whether respondents thought there were any important differences between the parties. Since omitting cases with missing data on this variable would reduce the sample substantially, we include a dummy variable for cases with missing values as suggested by Maddala (1977). Surprisingly, the ideological difference variable has no effect. That is, there is no sign that class voting is higher when most voters say that there is a real difference between the parties than when most voters say that they are essentially the same.

When an effect that is clearly expected is not observed, one must ask whether the negative result reflects poor measurement of the independent variable. In the present case, the most likely problem is that the differences that voters have in mind when answering the question might not involve class-related issues. That is, perceived overall differences might not be closely correlated with perceived differences on class-related issues. To evaluate this possibility, we performed a supplementary analysis using

[16] Although the United States was not at war in 1940, the war in Europe was generally regarded as the dominant political issue in the election.

individual-level data in the ANES and BES. Class voting was significantly higher among those who perceived a real difference between the parties, as one would expect if the differences involved class-related issues (see also Campbell *et al.* 1960). Moreover, the ANES contains questions on perceived party positions on two economic issues, government provision of health insurance and programmes to provide jobs, during the 1970s and 1980s. As perceived overall party differences increased in the 1980s, perceived differences on these issues increased as well, mainly because Republicans were seen as becoming more conservative. Hence, there is no reason to think the ideological difference variable is driven mainly by issues unrelated to class. Rather, it is necessary to consider the possibility that changes in party ideology, at least over the short term, have relatively little influence on class voting. This result can be understood by recalling that Campbell *et al.* (1960) found that many voters did not have a clear idea of where parties stood on specific issues, but merely had a general sense that different parties were oriented to different groups. Once established, these perceptions seem to be resistant to change. The idea that voters respond relatively quickly to ideological shifts may understate the importance of this less sophisticated level of ideology.

### *Class Voting and Nonvoting*

We next extend the analysis to include nonvoting. Table 5.5 shows fit statistics from several association models when nonvoters are included. Model 3 makes the differences between all political options rise or fall together. In effect, it holds that when class voting increases, the differences between voters and nonvoters increase as well. Model 4 is of most interest for present purposes, since it imposes no restrictions on the 'party' (including nonvoter) scores at each election. Compared to model 3, the improvement in $L^2$ is statistically significant in all nations, although by far the largest in the United States.

To evaluate the hypotheses on nonvoting given in Table 5.1, it is necessary to examine the parameter estimates from model 4. Recall that the party scores represent class composition relative to nonvoters, with larger scores representing a more heavily middle-class group of voters. Verba, Nie, and Kim (1978: 307) suggest that middle-class participation is 'natural', while working-class participation varies according to the degree of '*explicit* contestation on the basis of social class' (emphasis in original). In terms of the model, this means that there should be less variation in the right-party score than in the left-party score. In the extreme case where the score for the right party is constant while the score for the left party varies, there will be a perfect inverse relationship between changes in class voting and changes in class differences in turnout.

TABLE 5.5. *Fits of one-dimensional models of class voting (including nonvoters) in Britain, France, and the United States*

| Country | $L^2$ | $\chi^2$ | df | Index of Dissimilarity | $L^2$/df |
|---|---|---|---|---|---|
| Britain | | | | | |
| 1. No association | 5,677.0 | 5,574.0 | 123 | 0.1412 | 46.15 |
| 2. Constant $\phi$ | 423.4 | 419.2 | 118 | 0.0285 | 3.59 |
| 3. $\phi$ changes | 274.2 | 270.9 | 105 | 0.0197 | 2.61 |
| 4. Party scores change | 233.1 | 233.4 | 80 | 0.0166 | 2.91 |
| N = 47,565 | | | | | |
| France | | | | | |
| 1. No association | 2,995.6 | 2,917.8 | 200 | 0.1078 | 14.98 |
| 2. Constant $\phi$ | 546.3 | 542.2 | 194 | 0.0419 | 2.82 |
| 3. $\phi$ changes | 473.9 | 469.8 | 182 | 0.0373 | 2.60 |
| 4. Party scores change | 415.4 | 416.9 | 160 | 0.0359 | 2.60 |
| N = 37,064 | | | | | |
| United States | | | | | |
| 1. No association | 4,681.6 | 4,588.1 | 190 | 0.0863 | 24.64 |
| 2. Constant $\phi$ | 673.0 | 676.4 | 184 | 0.0292 | 3.66 |
| 3. $\phi$ changes | 587.1 | 589.4 | 170 | 0.0257 | 3.45 |
| 4. Party scores change | 443.5 | 439.5 | 156 | 0.0217 | 2.84 |
| N = 97,811 | | | | | |

The conventional view, on the other hand, suggests that, over the short term, there will be little change in the class composition of voters relative to nonvoters. For this to be the case, left- and right-party scores would have to have similar variances and a negative correlation. Over the long run, a decline in the differences between voters and nonvoters would imply a decline in the scores of both left and right parties. If the variances of the left- and right-party scores are similar, but the correlation is zero or positive, fluctuations in class voting and class differences in turnout will be unrelated.

These differences can be understood in terms of the movement of individuals among voting for the left, voting for the right, and abstaining. Suppose that some working-class individuals shift from voting left to voting right. Other things equal, the left-party score will increase, because the middle class makes up a larger share of the remaining left voters, and the right-party score will decrease. On the other hand, suppose that some working-class individuals shift from voting left to not voting at all. In that case, the left-party score will increase, but the right-party score will not change. Thus, the analysis of Verba, Nie, and Kim (1978) focuses upon shifts between left voting and nonvoting in the working class, while the conventional view focuses upon shifts between left voting and right voting, and

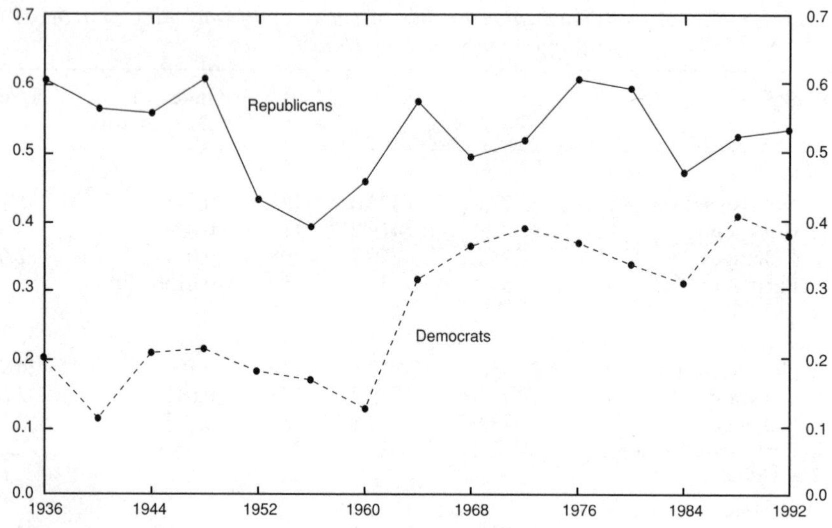


FIG. 5.3. Class composition of voters relative to nonvoters, United States

assumes that the class differences between voters and nonvoters are fixed in the short term.

Class scores from association models including nonvoters are shown in Table 5.3. Figure 5.3 shows party scores by election in the United States. The Republican score shows no clear trend, and relatively little fluctuation. In fact, using the standard errors estimated in model 4, the variation in the Republican scores is barely significant ($x^2 = 25.8$ with 14 df, $p = 0.027$). Excluding the 1952 and 1956 elections, when the middle-class character of the Republican vote was less pronounced than usual, the remaining variation is no longer significant ($x^2 = 11.2$ with 12 df). The Democratic score, in contrast, shows much more variation and a clear trend. Over the whole period, therefore, Democratic voters have become more middle class relative to nonvoters, while Republicans have remained unchanged. Putting these two facts together, class differences between the two major parties have decreased while class differences between major party voters and nonvoters have increased, as Verba, Nie, and Kim (1978: 309) predict.

Party scores for France are shown in Figure 5.4.[17] The pattern is quite

[17] The 1956 and 1981 elections are excluded because no information on nonvoters is available.

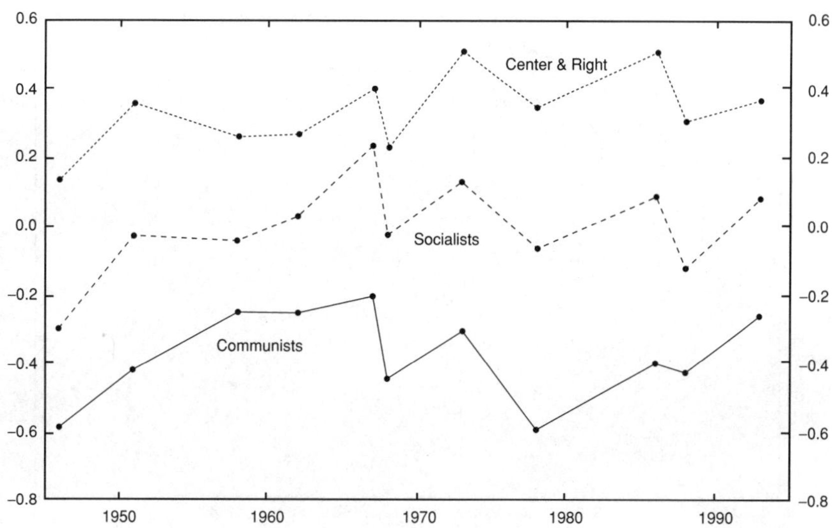


FIG. 5.4. Class composition of voters relative to nonvoters, France

different from that found in the United States. All parties show similar amounts of variation. Scores for the right parties have tended to increase over time, but scores for the Communists and Socialists show no statistically significant trend. Verba, Nie, and Kim's (1978) account therefore does not fit the French situation well. However, a model in which class differences between voters and nonvoters remain constant does not fit well either, since the party scores show a positive correlation. For example, all three party scores were larger in 1992 than in 1988, indicating that the supporters of all parties were somewhat more middle class relative to nonvoters in 1992 than they had been in 1988. The consequence is that class differences in turnout show a good deal of short-term fluctuation, but no connection to changes in class voting and little trend, although there may be a slight increase over time.

Party scores for Britain are shown in Figure 5.5. For simplicity, only the Labour and Conservative party scores are shown.[18] Contrary to what the Verba, Nie, and Kim (1978) model predicts, Conservative scores show somewhat more variation than Labour scores. Over the whole period, Labour scores show a U-shaped pattern, first falling and then rising,

[18] Since the Liberal vote was quite small in most of the period, there is substantial error in the estimates of the Liberal Party scores. The 1951 election is excluded entirely because no information on nonvoters is available.

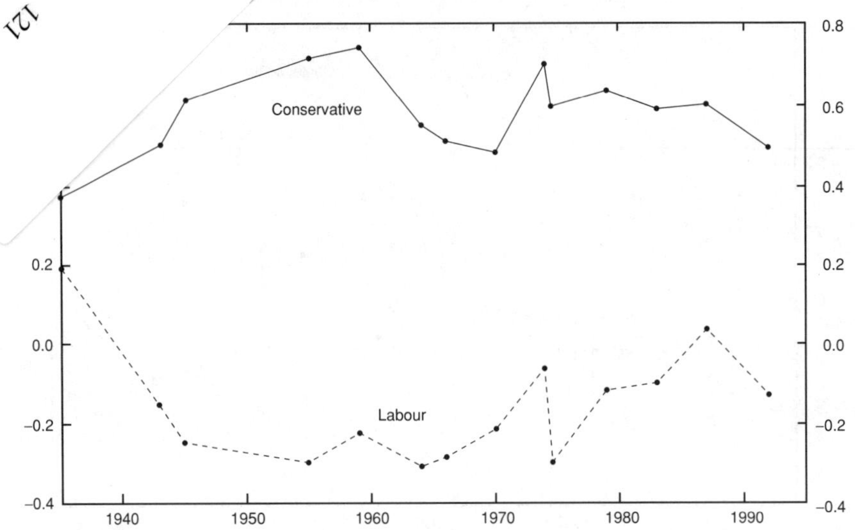


FIG. 5.5. Class composition of voters relative to nonvoters, Britain

while the Conservative scores show an inverted-U shape. Thus, the class differences between nonvoters and voters as a whole show little or no long-term trend. Both Labour and Conservative scores show a similar amount of variation, and the overall correlation between them is essentially zero. Consequently, class differences in turnout are largely constant over the period, and any variation is unrelated to changes in class voting.

One other important point revealed by the figures is that the relative class composition of voters and nonvoters differs among the nations. In Britain, the negative scores for Labour indicate that Labour voters are more heavily working class than are nonvoters (with the exception of 1987). In France, Socialist voters and nonvoters are quite similar in class terms, while Communist voters are much more heavily working class than either. In the United States, on the other hand, both major parties have positive scores, meaning that voters for both parties are more middle class than are nonvoters. Thus, the unusually strong relationship between class and political participation in the United States found by Verba, Nie, and Kim (1978) and Vanneman and Cannon (1987) is confirmed here. Moreover, this difference between the United States and the other nations has become larger over time. While the use of different class schemas in the three nations makes precise comparisons impossible, a rough idea of the magnitude of the change can be obtained by calculating the difference between the percentages of nonvoters among manual and nonmanual workers. In the United States, this 'Alford index' for nonvoting ranged from +5 to +12 between 1936 and 1960 and from +16 to +20 between 1964 and 1992. In both Britain and France, it has fluctuated around +5 and shown no apparent trend. Thus, the national differences in the relationship between class and turnout have grown dramatically since the 1960s.

In conclusion, the hypothesis of an inverse relationship between changes in class voting and class differences in turnout is supported for the United States, but not for the other two nations. There also are no common long-term trends in the relationship between class and turnout. The widening class differences implied by Verba, Nie, and Kim (1978) have occurred only in the United States, while the narrowing suggested by the conventional view has not occurred in any of the nations. The interpretation of these results will be discussed further in the Conclusions.

### *Change in Class Positions*

The models considered up to this point do not allow for realignment in the sense of changes in the relative political positions of particular classes. It seems likely that there is some short-term realignment because of factors specific to each election. The more theoretically interesting possibility, however, is that there are long-term shifts in political alignments. The hypotheses discussed above—white-collar proletarianization, working-class embourgeoisement, and new politics—all suggest a long-term shift in class alignments. The association model may be extended to include additional row and column scores representing these hypotheses.

The extended model is:

$$\log(n_{ijk}) = \log(\mathrm{N}) + c_{ik} + p_{jk} + \phi_{k1}\gamma_{i1}\tau_{j1} + \phi_2\gamma_{i2}\tau_{j2} + \beta t\tau_{i2}\tau_{j2} \qquad (5.2)$$

The $c$ and $p$ terms are defined as in model (5.1), while $t$ is time in years. The hypotheses about realignment imply fairly specific changes in class and party positions, so the row ($\gamma_{i2}$) and column ($\tau_{j2}$) scores for the additional dimensions are fixed in advance rather than estimated from the data. Moreover, because the hypotheses under consideration all focus on long-term change, the strength of the additional dimensions is constrained to change as a linear function of time. In addition, to facilitate comparison with the previous results on general class voting, the class and party scores from the one-dimensional model are taken as fixed in model 2. Hence, only the $c, p, \phi$, and $\beta$ parameters are freely estimated in this model.

The class and party scores implied by the hypotheses discussed above are displayed in Table 5.6. There is room for disagreement about several of the decisions. but we have found little difference in the results when the doubtful cases are scored differently. The hypothesis of white-collar proletarianization suggests that lower nonmanual workers will move to the

TABLE 5.6. *Class and party scores implied by hypotheses of realignment*

| Country | Nonmanual proletarianization | Manual embourgeoisement | New politics |
|---|---|---|---|
| Britain | | | |
| Professionals | 0 | 0 | 1 |
| Proprietors and executives | 0 | 0 | –0.5 |
| Nonmanual | 1 | 0 | 0 |
| Manual | 0 | 1 | –1 |
| Labour | 1 | –1 | 1 |
| Liberal | –1 | 1 | 1 |
| Conservative | –1 | 1 | –1 |
| France | | | |
| Farmers and farm labourers | 0 | 0 | –1 |
| Professionals, large business | 0 | 0 | 0.5 |
| Small proprietors | 0 | 0 | –1 |
| Nonmanual | 1 | 0 | 0 |
| Manual | 0 | 1 | –1 |
| Communist | 1 | –1 | –1 |
| Left | 1 | –1 | 1 |
| Centre and right | –1 | 1 | –1 |
| United States | | | |
| Farmers and farm labourers | 0 | 0 | –1 |
| Professionals | 0 | 0 | 1 |
| Managers and proprietors | 0 | 0 | –0.5 |
| Nonmanual | 1 | 0 | 0 |
| Skilled manual | 0 | 1 | –1 |
| Semi- and unskilled manual | 0 | 0.5 | –1 |
| Democratic | 1 | –1 | 1 |
| Republican | –1 | 1 | –1 |

left. That is, it effectively identifies lower nonmanual workers as a special case. For the party scores, we take the conventional contrast used in works such as Lipset (1981), where the Democrats, Labour, and the Communists and Socialists are counted as 'left' parties.

The hypothesis of working-class embourgeoisement implies that manual workers will turn away from their traditional parties as a consequence of their incorporation in the general culture. It makes no predictions about changes within the nonmanual group. Hence, the class scores in Britain and France involve a simple contrast between manual workers and all others. In the United States, however, the distinction between skilled and unskilled must also be considered. To the extent that the embourgeoisement account focuses on factors such as exposure to the mass media, there is no reason to distinguish between skilled and unskilled workers. Observers like Dahrendorf (1988), however, suggest that a marginal group of underemployed unskilled workers remains apart from the rest of society. While this marginal group would be almost entirely composed of unskilled manual workers, a significant number of semi- and unskilled manual workers would not normally be considered marginal. Hence, less skilled manual workers are given an intermediate score in the United States.

The new politics hypothesis is more complex, since it cannot be reduced to a contrast between one class and all others. Proponents of the hypothesis have clearly suggested that professionals are on the left and manual workers, farmers, and the petty bourgeoisie are on the right of a new political alignment (Inglehart 1990; Lipset 1981). Lower-level nonmanual workers have received less attention, but it seems reasonable to assume that the same factors that apply to professionals also apply to them, but more weakly. Hence, they are given a neutral score. The business classes are the most difficult to place. Inglehart (1990: 164, 319) finds that the self-employed are strongly materialist, but that managers and executives tend to be postmaterialist. This is to be expected given that managers tend to be well educated and to come from affluent backgrounds, conditions that Inglehart (1990) sees as the sources of postmaterial values. Bell (1976: 77–8), however, suggests that the 'corporate class' is divided in complex ways on cultural issues, but on average is more conservative than professionals. On balance, it appears that managers and executives should be regarded as neutral and proprietors as conservative on the new politics dimension. In the United States, the business group combines managers and proprietors, and consequently is given a moderately conservative score on the new politics dimension. In France, managers in large businesses are combined with professionals, and this group is consequently given a moderately leftist score. The petty bourgeoisie is separately distinguished in France. and is given a strongly conservative score. Turning to the parties, Labour and the Liberals are given the same scores in Britain. While Labour is clearly to the left of the Liberals on economic issues, there are few clear differences on the social issues that are relevant to the new politics hypothesis. In France, both the right parties and the Communists are counted as 'conservative' for the purposes of this hypothesis. The Communists have generally been rather conservative on social and environmental issues, and their authoritarianism is also incompatible with the stress on individual autonomy that Inglehart (1990) sees as central to the new politics.

In France and the United States, it is also necessary to consider the possibility that farmers are a special case. It has long been noted that farmers are politically volatile, and sometimes go against the general voting trends (Lipset 1960). In both the United States and France, farmers appear to have moved to the right relative to other groups in the period under consideration. Given the changes in the economic and social position of farmers, this shift is understandable apart from any of the hypotheses discussed above. Hence, any results which depend strongly on the inclusion of farmers must be regarded as suspect. Models for the United States and France will therefore be estimated twice, once including all classes and once excluding farmers.

The signs of the scores are chosen so that the expected trends are positive for each hypothesis. While the $\phi_2$ parameters are necessary in order to estimate the trends accurately, they are of no particular theoretical interest. Hence, only the trend terms are discussed below. To simplify interpretation, we begin by considering each hypothesis separately.

The parameter estimates and *t*-ratios for the trends implied by each hypothesis are shown in Table 5.7. The trend term implied by the hypothesis of nonmanual proletarianization is not significant in Britain or the United States. In France, the trend term is positive and significant when all classes are included, but drops to almost zero when farmers are excluded. The trend implied by the hypothesis of embourgeoisement is positive and significant in Britain. In France, it is positive and significant when all classes are included, but becomes non-significant when farmers are excluded. In the United States, on the other hand, it is significant only when farmers are excluded. Finally, the trend implied by the new politics hypothesis is positive and significant in Britain and the United States. In France, it is positive and significant when farmers are included, but drops to near zero when they are excluded. In the United States, in contrast, the parameter estimate falls by only about 20 per cent when farmers are excluded.

Given the lack of evidence for the nonmanual proletarianization hypothesis in any of the three nations, it can be dropped from further consideration. Because there is some overlap between the implications of embourgeoisement and new politics hypotheses, it is useful to consider them together. Hence, the second panel shows estimates when both trend terms are included at once. In France, both estimates are again strongly affected by the exclusion of farmers, dropping to very near zero. In the United States, the trend implied by the new politics analysis remains significant, while the trend implied by the embourgeoisement hypothesis is no longer significant. Finally, in Britain, both the embourgeoisement and new politics trends remain positive and significant.

France thus presents the simplest picture: the only long-term realignment that is visible is the rightward shift of farmers mentioned above. In

TABLE 5.7. *Estimated trends in additional class alignments in Britain, France, and the United States*

| Trends | Britain | France | United States |
|---|---|---|---|
| 1. Trends entered separately | | | |
| Proletarianization | | | |
| All voters | 0.168 | 0.275[a] | –0.031 |
| | (1.70) | (2.17) | (–0.51) |
| Non-Farm | | 0.006 | –0.081 |
| | | (0.05) | (–1.31) |
| Embourgeoisement | | | |
| All voters | 0.536[b] | 0.500[b] | 0.073 |
| | (2.61) | (2.72) | (0.73) |
| Non-farm | | 0.149 | 0.229[a] |
| | | (0.75) | (2.18) |
| New politics | | | |
| All voters | 0.257[c] | 0.245[a] | 0.269[c] |
| | (3.78) | (2.21) | (5.77) |
| Non-farm | | 0.054 | 0.221[c] |
| | | (0.45) | (4.31) |
| 2. Trends entered together | | | |
| Embourgeoisement | | | |
| All voters | 0.625[b] | 0.255 | –0.094 |
| | (3.03) | (1.12) | (0.90) |
| Non-farm | | 0.086 | 0.047 |
| | | (0.32) | (0.40) |
| New politics | | | |
| All voters | 0.274[c] | 0.157 | 0.288[c] |
| | (4.03) | (1.15) | (5.95) |
| Non-farm | | 0.019 | 0.212[c] |
| | | (0.12) | (3.74) |

*Notes*: *t*-ratios in parentheses.
Statistical significance of parameter estimates: [a] 5 per cent; [b] 1 per cent; [c] 0.1 per cent.

the United States, there is strong evidence of the type of realignment predicted by new politics accounts. Britain shows the most complex pattern, with evidence in favour of the new politics hypothesis and somewhat weaker evidence of a political 'embourgeoisement' of manual workers.

The embourgeoisement hypothesis implies a trend away from Labour and towards the Conservatives and Liberals. Closer examination of the data, however, suggested that the change left unexplained when the new politics term was included was primarily a shift of manual workers towards the Liberals. Including a dummy variable and trend term for manual Liberals produces a significantly better fit than including the embourgeoisement trend. When both are included, the manual Liberal trend remains significant and the embourgeoisement trend becomes negative and non-significant. Thus, the evidence for the embourgeoisement hypothesis becomes much weaker on closer examination.[19] The estimate for the new politics trend, in contrast, is quite robust and remains significant under all reasonable specifications.

Thus, the 'new politics' analysis receives clear support in Britain and the United States, but not in France. This is not to say that the British or American results are positive proof of this analysis since there is no evidence on the reasons for the shifts. If the new politics analysis is not accepted, however, there is still evidence of realignment that requires an alternative explanation.

Up to this point, only the weaker version of the new politics hypothesis has been considered. The stronger version (Inglehart 1990) is that there is an inverse relationship between the strength of the traditional and 'new politics' alignments: that to the extent that people are driven by the social and cultural values that are thought to explain the new class alignment, they are not driven by the economic interests that are thought to explain the traditional one. To test this account, it is necessary to consider models in which the strength of association on both parameters for both the 'traditional' and the 'new politics' dimension are allowed to vary freely from election to election.

Figures 5.6 and 5.7 show the estimates of the strength of traditional and new politics dimensions in Britain and the United States. The increasing trend in the new politics dimension is visible in both nations, but the smallest values seem to occur in the 1950s rather than at the beginning of the period. In the United States, a quadratic trend model predicts the values of $\phi$ significantly better than a linear trend, and indicates a decline from the 1930s to the 1950s. In Britain, the changes are less regular, but apart from 1935, the three lowest values of $\phi$ are found in 1955, 1959, and 1964. If the 'new politics' interpretation of the second dimension is accepted, these facts suggest that the idea of a gradual growth of a politics of cultural and social alignments is questionable. Rather, it appears that the strength of this alignment may rise and fall over time, and that it was at a low point in the 1950s.

The decline in 'traditional' class voting is still visible in the United States, but is less pronounced than in Figure 5.1. In fact, there seems to have been no clear change since the 1950s. That is, the decline in class voting visible in Figure 5.1 occurs partly because of the rise of the offsetting new

[19] Although the manual Liberal trend is a *post hoc* construction, it can be given a reasonable interpretation in terms of the seats contested by the Liberals. Until the 1970s, the Liberals left many constituencies uncontested, and these generally included a disproportionate number of heavily working-class constituencies. Thus, working-class opportunities to vote Liberal may have increased over the period.

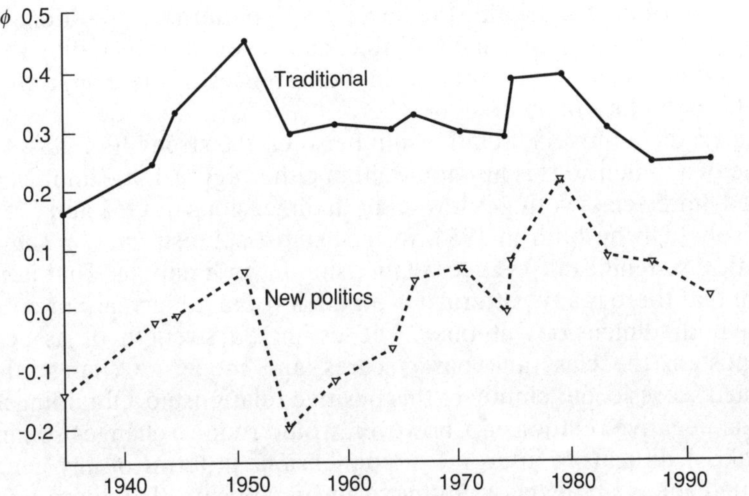


FIG. 5.6. Class voting along traditional and new politics dimensions, Britain

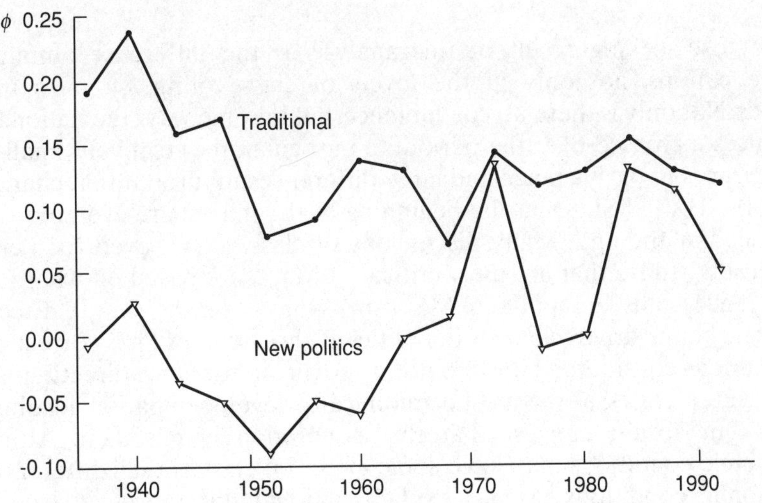


FIG. 5.7. Class voting along traditional and new politics dimensions, United States

politics division. In Britain, the inverted-U pattern in traditional class voting is weakened, but remains visible. Thus, even after including the new politics dimension, significant national differences in the course of traditional class voting remain.

The predicted inverse relationship between the strength of class voting on the two dimensions is not apparent in either figure. For example, in the United States, class voting is low on both dimensions in 1952 and 1956 and relatively high on both in 1984. In fact, statistical tests show a slight but statistically significant positive relationship in both nations. That is, to the extent that there is any pattern, it is for class voting to increase or decrease along both dimensions at once. The estimated strength of association depends on the class and party scores, and moderate changes in the assigned scores could eliminate this positive relationship. Obtaining a substantial negative relationship, however, would require changes so large as to make it difficult to interpret the dimensions in terms of any generally accepted ideas about class voting. Thus, it appears that there are two largely independent dimensions of class voting in Britain and the United States. The idea that they are in a competitive relationship, as argued by Inglehart (1990) and assumed in many other discussions, receives no support from these data.

## CONCLUSIONS

The most striking result of this analysis is the difference among the three nations, not only in the levels of class voting, but also in the trends. Not only is there no convergence, but in some ways the national differences increased over the period. In particular, the relatively small class differences in party choice and large differences in turnout that characterized the United States at the beginning of the period are even more pronounced at the end. Many discussions of class voting, even (or perhaps especially) those that are most critical of Marx, are based on what Lipset (1981: 504) calls 'an apolitical Marxism'—that is, on the idea that technological change drives changes in politics. If this assumption is correct, all of the nations considered here should be moving in the same direction—with the United States, as the most economically developed nation, leading the way. Our results suggest that the assumption is mistaken. Although economic conditions may have some effect on class voting, differences in economic conditions do not explain national differences in trends of class voting.

Several authors, notably Przeworski and Sprague (1986: 5–8) have criticized the idea of class voting as a simple reflection of economic interests and have argued that more attention must be paid to political and historical factors. The existence of significant national differences in trends is evidence in favour of this general position. However, Przeworski and Sprague's (1986) focus on party ideology as the primary explanation of variation in class voting is not supported in this analysis. Perceived differences between the parties showed no relationship to class voting in Britain and the United States. Given the difficulty of measuring party ideology, it would be unwarranted to conclude that it has no effect. It is clear, however, that ideological change cannot be the main explanation of variations in class voting: in Britain, class voting reached its peak in the 1950s, when virtually all observers thought that ideological differences between the parties were at a low point.

These negative results suggest that attention should be focused on another level of ideology. Parkin (1971: 90) suggests that 'a kind of fatalistic pessimism' tends to follow from the conditions of working-class life. If this attitude prevails, the programmes offered by reformist parties may be dismissed as mere rhetoric, or as attractive but unrealistic ideas. Similarly, McKenzie and Silver (1968) note that working-class conservatives often characterize reformers as well-intentioned but incompetent. This suggests that changes in the perception of the relative effectiveness of the parties, and of government action generally, may influence changes in class voting. In general, class voting might be expected to be higher when confidence in the possibilities of government action is greater. In this interpretation, the relatively low levels of class voting in Britain in 1935 may reflect a lack of confidence in government action following the failure of both Labour and Conservative governments to reduce unemployment, and the increase through the 1950s may reflect increased confidence owing to the successful management of the wartime and postwar economy. While this account cannot be tested with the present data, it offers some promise of explaining the changes in class voting seen in these data. Accounts based on changes in overt party ideology, on the other hand, seem much less promising given the observed patterns.

Two other national differences need to be explained. First, the inverse correlation between class voting and class differences in turnout suggested by Verba, Nie, and Kim (1978) appears to hold only in the United States, and only the United States shows a long-term trend in turnout differences. One possible explanation is that the strength of the trade-off between class voting and class differences in turnout is itself a function of working-class turnout. In the United States, working-class turnout in national elections probably never exceeded 50 per cent during this period. If the habit of voting is not firmly established, turnout may be sensitive to short-term changes in party policies, candidates, and organization. On the other hand, once the habit of voting has been established, it may be transmitted through the family and informal social pressures. As a result, even if working-class political organization has declined in Britain and France, as some observers suggest, these informal pressures may be strong enough to keep working-class participation from declining. Like Verba, Nie, and Kim's (1978) model, this account assumes that working-class turnout will be low in the absence of explicit organization and contestation on the basis of class. It differs, however, in holding that continuous organization is not necessary: once a tradition of participation has been established, it can endure even if organization declines. This account cannot be evaluated with these data, but is testable in principle.

Secondly, while the changes in class voting predicted by the postmaterialist account were clearly visible in the United States and Britain, they were not found in France. There the postmaterialist account is valid in the sense that there are two class-related dimensions in both voting and attitudes (Weakliem 1991; Grunberg and Schweisguth 1993). There is no evidence, however, that their relative importance is changing. This difference may reflect the fact that disputes over social and cultural issues, centring on the role of the church, have long been prominent in French politics. In the United States and Britain, there are periods for which one could plausibly argue that economic issues were overwhelmingly dominant, and all other concerns were of minor importance, but it would be much more difficult to make this case for France. Even in the United States and Britain, there are some hints that the idea of the rise of a new alignment is too simple. In Figures 5.5 and 5.6, the minimum values for the 'post-material' alignment occurred not in the 1930s, but in the 1960s. This fact lends some support to Brand's (1990) view that there are 'waves of cultural criticism', rising and falling over a period of several decades. This hypothesis is difficult to test given the lack of survey data before the 1930s, but it is certainly plausible. In the first half of the century, there were several major political movements, including temperance and women's suffrage, which appeared to draw more support from parts of the middle class than from the working class. Thus, the extent to which the 'new politics' represents a genuinely new trend, rather than part of a cycle, is an open question.

Finally, our results suggest that the influence of class on mass political behaviour was never as strong as is often assumed. In Britain, traditionally supposed to be strongly divided by class, class voting was not substantially higher before the 1950s than it has been in recent years. On the other hand, class influences have not declined as much as is commonly believed. Even in the United States, class is politically significant as a strong and probably increasing influence on turnout. Rather than supposing that there was a rise and fall of class politics, we should begin from the assumption that class is an enduring, but rarely or never a dominating, influence on political behaviour. To do otherwise is to mistake changes in the popularity of sociological theories, particularly Marxism, for real changes in society.

# APPENDIX

This appendix discusses the major issues involved in constructing the datasets. More details are available from the authors on request.

## *Sources*

In the United States, Gallup polls are used from 1936 to 1972, the General Social Survey from 1972 to 1992. In Britain, Gallup surveys are used throughout. In France, Gallup surveys are used in 1946–68 and 1978; SOFRES surveys in 1973, 1978, 1981, and 1988, and Brule–Ville Associates (BVA) surveys in 1986, 1988, 1993. Where we had surveys of the same election from different sources, we kept them separate in order to avoid possible distortions resulting from differences in marginal proportions. For example, there are two tables for 1988 in France, one from the BVA survey, the other from the SOFRES survey. Our models assume that all parameters pertaining to class voting are the same in all surveys involving the same election, but that parameters involving the marginal proportions may differ. Whenever possible, we obtained tables from the original datafile. In several cases, however, the original file was unavailable, and we used published tables as a substitute. Gallup surveys of the French elections of 1956, 1958, 1968, 1978 are reported in the journal *Sondages* (various issues), while data from a SOFRES survey of the 1981 election are reported in Lancelot and Lancelot (1983).[20] In Britain, data from Gallup surveys of the 1945 election are reported in Durant (1945) and data from 1951 in Bonham (1952).

The Gallup polls in the United States used quota samples until about 1950, when they switched to probability samples. The British and French Gallup polls seem to have used quota samples throughout, while the SOFRES surveys used probability samples. It is not clear what sampling method was used for the BVA polls. There is, however, no reason to think that the sampling technique should affect estimates of class voting.[21] Moreover, when surveys using different techniques were available for the same election (1948 in the United States, 1978 and 1986 in France), the estimates of class voting were similar in both.

## *Occupational Coding*

The French surveys all use a standard occupational classification developed by INSEE. In the United States the Gallup organization changed its occupational classification system several times between the 1930s and early 1950s. We there-

[20] In 1958, 1968, and 1978, we also have original data from other surveys.

[21] Sample weights were provided in some of the surveys. For the sake of consistency, we use unweighted frequencies throughout.

fore combined some categories into the standard classes based on their titles and marginal distributions. For the GSS data, we combined the census occupation codes to conform to the Gallup classifications, relying on our judgement in doubtful cases. For the 1936, 1940, 1948, and 1972 elections, we have a sample for both the old and the new classification systems. The differences in the estimates of class voting under the two classifications are small except in 1940, and even in this year both of the estimates are well above the average for the whole period. Thus, changes in classification systems do not seem to have a substantial effect on the estimates of class voting. The British classification system also changed slightly in the early years, although it remains constant after 1955. For example, the documentation for the 1945 data refers to 'salaried clerical' workers, while later documentation refers simply to 'clerical', suggesting that the category was broadened to include clerical workers on hourly wages. Thus, some of the estimated changes in class voting in Britain through the 1950s may be artefacts of changes in occupational classification, but we have conducted several checks suggesting that any such effects are small.

There has been considerable debate on whether people should be assigned to classes based on their own occupation, the 'head of household's' occupation, or some combination of the two. For this analysis, however, we are forced to use whatever approach is found in the original sources. The French data use the head of household's occupation. The American data use respondent's occupation until 1952 and head of household's occupation beginning in 1956.[22] The British surveys report only respondent's occupation until 1970 and only the head of household's occupation beginning in 1974. In those surveys where both head's and respondent's occupation are available, we have found that the choice makes very little difference in estimates of the strength of class voting. Comparisons of the two methods using British Election Surveys shows that the trends over time are almost identical (Heath *et al.* 1995).

## *Nonvoting*

Identification of nonvoters is easiest in the United States, where all of the data are obtained from post-election surveys. The British data for 1959–87 are mainly post-election surveys, but include some pre-election surveys. The pre-election surveys contain questions on the probability of voting, and we define nonvoters as all those who say it is possible or likely that they will not vote. We have found no significant differences in the estimated relation of class to nonvoting in the pre-election and post-election data. The French data on nonvoting are the most problematic; in the 1950s and 1960s, the post-election surveys do not always distinguish between nonvoters and refusals to answer and the pre-election surveys do not always distinguish between those who were undecided and those who did not expect to

[22] 'Head's' occupation was not regularly asked until 1952. We use it in preference to using respondent's own occupation throughout because head's occupation leaves fewer missing values, resulting in more precise parameter estimates.

vote. The surveys from the 1970s and 1980s, however, do make these distinctions, so the data on nonvoting are more reliable in recent years.

### *Retrospective Data*

The British and French data are obtained mainly from election surveys. There were, however, a few elections (1935 and 1955 in Britain and 1946 and 1956 in France) for which no contemporary survey was available and retrospective data from the following election survey were used. Much of the data in the United States is taken from surveys conducted some time after the most recent election. With the Gallup data, generally we were able to use surveys completed within a year of the election, but the GSS necessarily has a longer delay; for example, people were asked about their vote in the 1972 election in 1973–6. We have compared contemporary and retrospective data in elections for which both were available, and have not found significant differences in the estimates of class voting: even after delays of as much as five years. There are sometimes changes in the recollection of vote, such as an increased tendency to recall voting for the winner, but they appear to affect all classes equally. Estimates of class differentials in turnout also appear to be unaffected.

### *Economic Conditions*

Data are taken from Mitchell (1992, 1993), supplemented by the United Nations Statistical Division (1992), and the International Labour Office (1994). These sources contain more details on original sources and definitions. Three-year changes in prices, unemployment, and real wages were chosen because they generally produced the best fit. The average real wage of employed workers is used as a measure of prosperity in preference to real GDP per capita because it is less influenced by changes in labour force participation and the age structure of the population.

### *Ideological Differences*

No measure is available for France. In the United States, the question is 'Do you think there are any important differences in what the Republicans and Democrats stand for?', with a choice of 'yes' or 'no'. In Britain, the question is 'Considering everything the Conservative and Labour Parties stand for, would you say that there is a great difference between them, some difference, or not much difference?' Our measure was the difference between the proportions of 'yes' and 'no' in the United States, and 'great difference' and 'not much difference' in Britain. Alternative measures such as the ratio of positive to negative answers produced very similar results.

# 6

# Class Cleavages in Party Preferences in Germany—Old and New

WALTER MÜLLER

## THE DEBATE ABOUT THE DECLINE OF CLASS VOTING IN GERMANY

The Federal Republic of Germany has inherited a twofold cleavage structure in voting patterns from the Kaiserreich and the Weimar Republic: a class cleavage and a religious cleavage. The class cleavage—as anywhere—derives from the opposing economic interests which, since industrialization, mainly separate workers from owners of various kinds of capital. The religious cleavage is historically based on the nineteenth century's *Kulturkampf* between Catholics and Protestants. After the Second World War the earlier *confessional* cleavage between Protestants and Catholics was transformed into a *religious* cleavage separating those allied to either the Catholic or Protestant Church and those having no religious affiliation (Pappi 1985; Schmitt 1988).

Since the first postwar elections in 1949 both cleavages have come into play most clearly in the selective alliance of specific population groups with either the CDU or the SPD: membership in either church and religious practice is related to voting for the CDU rather than the SPD. As for the class cleavage, the core class support for the SPD comes from the working

This chapter is an extended and revised version of 'Klassenstruktur und Parteiensystem. Zum Wandel der Klassenspaltung im Wahlverhalten', which appeared in *Kölner Zeitschrift für Soziologie und Sozialpsychologie* 50 (1) 1998. For their critical discussion and stimulating suggestions, I would like to thank Johannes Berger, Geoff Evans, Peter Flora, John H. Goldthorpe, Ronald Inglehart, Ulrich Kohler, Hanspeter Kriesi, Max Kaase, Karl Ulrich Mayer, Colin Mills, Rüdiger Schmitt-Beck, Susanne Steinmann, and the fellows of the 1996/7 NIAS Nucleus, Stratification in Eastern and Western Europe in the 1960s, including Tom DiPrete, Robert Erikson, Harry Ganzeboom, Paul M. de Graaf, Ruud Luijkx, Peter Robert, Michael Tahlin, Don Treiman, and Wout Ultee. I am particularly obliged to Stefanie Neurauter and Gunnar Otte for their efficient support during the preparation of the data and the statistical analyses, Gretchen Wiesehan for professional language editing of the manuscript, and Beate Rossi for careful secretarial assistance.

class, in particular workers organized in one of the trade unions. The core classes voting for the CDU are the so-called *old* middle classes: landowners and farmers, owners of financial and industrial capital, and the nonagricultural petty bourgeoisie. Since the religious and the class cleavages are overlaid, there have always been substantial cross-pressures between religious *values* and economic *interests*. This particularly holds for the working class. The cross-pressures partly explain why the division between the working class and other classes in terms of voting has never been particularly strong in postwar Germany. Even less clear are the party orientations of the *new* middle classes. They are located in an ambivalent position in the class structure, and their party orientation is equally ambivalent. The literature, however, describes them as closer to the CDU than to the SPD, although it is generally assumed that at the end of the 1960s and in the 1970s (in the years of the CDU/SPD coalition government and of the Brandt and Schmidt governments) the new middle classes moved somewhat away from the CDU towards the SPD (Pappi 1979, 1986; Berger *et al.* 1983).

The literature on the development of the class cleavage in Germany echoes Clark's and Lipset's (1991; Clark *et al.* 1993) claims that the cleavage structures have weakened. Several general trends in the development of modern societies are supposed to contribute to declining class cleavages. The most general assumption is that all kinds of membership in large categorical social groupings are becoming less relevant for social orientations and behaviour as modernization progresses. With continued social differentiation, the number of groups individuals belong to multiplies. The intersection of a plurality of 'social circles' strengthens the consciousness of individuality and leads to increasing cross-pressures. The likelihood that a dominant group membership determines individual attitudes and behaviour is therefore expected to decline (Schnell and Kohler 1995).

Among a number of more specific arguments advanced to explain declining associations between class positions and voting patterns are the following: increasing incomes and other resources are assumed to free people from the (economic) constraints of life and to increase their range of options. As a consequence, behaviour is expected to depend less on membership in a broad social class, and more on specific situational conditions. In the words of Beck (1983), society has moved to a stage 'Jenseits von Stand und Klasse' ('beyond status and class'). Therefore, loyalty to class-linked parties is expected to become weaker. And with claims that class-bound milieux of social interaction have more or less disappeared (Mooser 1983), it is assumed that there are fewer incentives to follow class-directed voting norms of one's social milieu and lower costs of deviating from them.

Furthermore, as individuals become more resourceful in terms of education, they will decreasingly follow voting norms existing in groups they belong to. The 'wählerische Wähler' (Bürklin 1994) will instead decide as a rational actor consciously evaluating what can be expected from the various parties in a given context. He or she votes on the basis of specific issues and according to his or her perception of candidates' and parties' competence to handle the issues, maximizing in this way the utility to be expected from the vote (Downs 1957; Dalton and Rohrschneider 1990; Weßels 1994; Fuchs and Kühnel 1994).

In line with arguments that the binding power of associational memberships has generally declined (Streeck 1987), it is also argued that intermediary (interest) organizations lose their abilities to unite their members on a party line. In particular, unionism is assumed to be of declining importance in affecting political orientation. Instead individuals associate with issue-specific social movements, whose links to parties are relatively weak. These developments are considered to contribute to fluctuating votes, as does the increased role of the mass media in setting the political agenda and taking the place of group opinion leaders in transporting political issues to the public (Schmitt-Beck and Schrott 1994).

Finally, the 'silent revolution' (Inglehart 1971) is seen as a major force responsible for the decline in class voting. The growing replacement of materialist, often class-based value orientations by postmaterialist preferences not only weakens the old cleavages. It also constitutes a new 'new politics' dimension, which along with the class cleavage affects voting preferences and partly replaces the old cleavages. It is explicitly stressed that 'this new dimension is not primarily based on homogenous social groups with well-defined social or economic interests. Instead, it rests on individual preferences that may have been moulded through quite diverse processes' (Poguntke 1993: 181). In *Alternative Politics*, Poguntke concludes that postindustrial politics are characterized by the emergence of a new kind of citizenry, who no longer need a strong party organization in order to defend their interests because they possess educational and other resources. Green parties or other parties of alternative politics can be seen as 'trend-setters' in the direction of a 'party of individual participation'. 'Whereas, in earlier historical periods, parties were based on specific social groups with particular interests, the "individualistic society" seems to allow for more variation' (Poguntke 1993: 184).

Empirical studies evaluating these claims come to different conclusions regarding the development of the religious and class cleavages for Germany. As for the religious cleavage, secularization seems to have only a limited impact. Fewer people are church members and fewer attend religious services, and this compositional change affects voter turnout. But several studies agree that it is only the prevalence of church membership and religious practice in the population which has changed, *not* the *effects* of membership or practice (Pappi 1977, 1979, 1985; Schmitt 1988; Pappi and Mnich 1992; Müller 1993; Emmert and Roth 1995). For the class cleavage, on the other hand, there is widespread agreement in the literature that not only have significant compositional changes in the class structure occurred, but also that class membership affects party vote less strongly. There is, however, disagreement concerning the extent of the decline. Beck (1983) sees class effects declining to the point of irrelevance of class structures. Strong declines are also diagnosed by Hildebrandt and Dalton (1977) and Schnell and Kohler (1995). The majority of studies, however, consider the changes to be much less dramatic (Pappi 1979; Klingemann 1984; Bürklin 1988; Pappi 1990; Pappi and Mnich 1992; Müller 1993; Emmert and Roth 1995).

The present chapter attempts an empirical evaluation of these claims using a database that is much larger and allows more refined differentiation than those used previously. It also addresses an issue that has been neglected so far: an analysis of the party orientations of the growing middle classes. On the one hand, it discusses changes in the class structure which may affect class voting, in particular the growth and changing composition of the service class; on the other, it takes into account the changing party structure, in particular the emergence and establishment of the Green Party. The chapter examines the extent to which voting patterns for this party can be understood as class-based and the extent to which a decline in the class cleavage in voting preferences for either the CDU or the SPD is paralleled by new class-based voting for the Greens. The chapter refers only to the developments in West Germany since the historical conditions for class-based voting in East Germany are so different that they need separate studies (see e.g. Pappi 1994; Schultze 1991*b*).

## CHANGING CLASS STRUCTURE AND CHANGING PARTY STRUCTURE

Lipset and Rokkan (1967) elaborate the historical roots of the cleavages in the voting patterns of European societies and discuss the mechanisms through which they can be expected to change or remain the same. The basic assumption is that the social and economic characteristics of class positions condition specific interests, which are shared by individuals holding these positions. Class organizations help to articulate and accumulate these interests. Political elites and parties compete in the market for votes by adopting particular political packages and programmes that represent and defend these interests. The relationship between class location and party vote is thus highly mediated and historically contingent. However, if in the market for votes a package is offered which is congenial to the interests of voters in specific class positions, it is likely that class-based voting patterns will emerge. In order to understand changes in the association between class and vote, one must pay attention to changes both in the class structure and in the constellation of parties and the policy packages they offer.

In Germany, the structure of classes has dramatically changed since the establishment of the party system after the Second World War. In 1950 almost one-quarter of voters made their living in agriculture (most of them farmers and their family members), 10 per cent were self-employed outside agriculture, close to 50 per cent were workers, and about 20 per cent were nonmanual employees. Since then the core classes of CDU and SPD voters—the petty bourgeoisie and the working class—have become much smaller. The ambivalent new middle classes have more than doubled and are now by far the largest segment of the population. It can be assumed that these changes in the class structure have had implications not only for the 'demography of voters'. They will have exercised considerable pressure on the parties to adapt their ideological and programmatic rhetoric as well as their policies in order to attract new types of voters. The major parties on the two sides of the class divide basically had the same problem: the core groups of their voters were declining in size. Although this merits a much more detailed treatment, it can be said that the two parties opted for similar solutions. Both struggled to catch as much as they could from the growing piece of the cake while trying not to lose their traditional sources of support. Both wanted to be *Volksparteien*, and as a consequence their political packages became somewhat blurred. Therefore the holding power of the traditional affiliations is assumed to have declined and the traditional class cleavage in party preferences and voting will have become less marked.

The most important qualification to be added to this account is the following: the adaptation of the SPD to the changing class structure was—and possibly had to be—much more far-reaching than that of the CDU. From their historical legacy, the new middle classes in Germany—the *Angestellte and Beamte* or the *Bildungsbürgertum*—were rather conservative. At best they held liberal economic convictions. They thus stood rather close to the CDU. As will be outlined further below, the SPD changed its programmatic outlook much more with the explicit aim of appealing to the new middle classes.

The dominant view among German electoral sociologists is that the changing voting pattern of the new middle classes is not primarily related to the characteristics of their class position, but has rather been a consequence of the growth of postmaterialist value orientations, to be found particularly among the highly educated members of the birth cohorts born and raised under conditions of economic well-being in the postwar years.

The SPD catered to the 'new politics' preferences of these voters, but in so doing accepted the costs of a dualism between the old and the new left and the tensions of accommodating followers who vote for the party for different reasons. In the aftermath of the emergence of the Green Party in the 1980s, the political orientations of the middle classes became even more fragmented, as their votes are now distributed among four main parties: CDU, SPD, FDP, and the Greens. Indeed, recent studies have repeatedly shown that the typical Green voters share the same characteristics as the new SPD voters: they were born after the Second World War, are highly educated, hold postmaterialist values, and work in middle-class jobs (Veen 1984; Müller-Rommel 1993; Raschke and Schmitt-Beck 1994).

### *The Need for a More Adequate Class Conceptualization*

These views play down the class (interest) aspect in explaining voting preferences and emphasize new values instead. Value orientations, not class or other social conditions, are seen as affecting preferences. I question these interpretations and suggest that class might appear to have lost its power to explain voting preferences because most studies have used inadequate conceptualizations and operationalizations of class. This is especially true for the representation of the new middle classes in voting studies. Particularly in earlier studies they are treated as a fairly undifferentiated category (Pappi 1973, 1986; Emmert and Roth 1995). At best, two groups of middle classes (lower and upper) are distinguished, quite often without any theoretical rationale (Schultze 1991*a*; Berger *et al.* 1983, 1986). However, the new middle classes are a heterogeneous category composed of subgroups so different from one another that no homogeneous party orientation can be expected. The claim of the present chapter is that by using a theoretically more refined class schema some of the recent changes in voting patterns can be shown to be class-based. To some extent this has already been substantiated in a study by Pappi (1990), who used a class schema which partly resembles the schema proposed here.

In common with most other chapters, I use a version of the Erikson–Goldthorpe class schema. In addition to the distinctions between classes elaborated in Chapter 1, however, I distinguish between different segments of the service class (see also Chapter 4). The question of interest is whether the service class is homogeneous enough to produce a similar political stance among its members and whether their class interests are indeed conservative as Goldthorpe (1982: 180) has argued.

Service-class employees exercise either delegated authority or specialized knowledge and expertise. They have either managerial or professionalized work roles. However, the two conditions leading to a service relationship are quite different in nature. The exercise of delegated authority is typical of employees in administrative hierarchies who run an organization, make administrative decisions, command and survey the work of others. The exercise of specialized knowledge and expertise is typical of professional services. From the different nature of these roles one would expect different implications for the interests of the holders of the different positions and, in consequence, for their political orientations. Goldthorpe (1997) argues exclusively from the perspective of the rational employer and underlines the common elements in the agency problem of the employers which lead them to establish service-relationship contracts. There are, however, important differences between the administrative–managerial and the expert–professional group when looked at from the employee's perspective. These differences mainly have to do with participation in organizational power versus defence of professional autonomy against organizational authority.

For the 'delegated authority' group—managers and other administrators—the employment situation is defined by the sharing of power within the command structure of the employing organization. This should imply a high level of loyalty towards the employer or the employing organization. Managers and administrators are directly concerned with the preservation of the organization to which they belong. Their position is often such that their own personal success is closely tied to the success of the organization. The organization and its future is central to their orientation.

The 'professional group', on the contrary, will have at least one further point of reference: its professional community. Professionals generally legitimate their claims for high levels of autonomy with reference to professional norms and the exercise of professional competence. A primary orientation towards the employing organization seems therefore less likely. Among the professionals, a further distinction can be made between (technical) experts and the social and cultural services (medical services, education, social work, various services related to cultural activities in the arts, the media, and so on). For the latter, the organizational orientation is weakened by an additional element: the exchange with clients and the norms of care for them puts members of this group in a position where they are likely to be responsive to social rather than organizational concerns. Among the service class I therefore distinguish three groups, according to the relationship to organizational power and the kind of tasks performed: the *administrative*, the *expert*, and the *social* (*and cultural*) *services*.

Related distinctions have been proposed by several other authors, generally based on different theoretical concerns or introduced on an *ad hoc* basis (see e.g. Wright 1985; Kriesi 1989, Esping-Andersen 1993; Heath and

Savage 1995, Hout *et al.* 1995; De Graaf and Steijn 1997; Brooks and Manza 1997). The present analysis owes most to Kriesi's (1989) study of the Netherlands, where he finds the social and cultural specialists to be particularly active in the new social movements. In a class-theoretical perspective, however, one must determine whether these distinctions constitute different classes themselves or whether they have to be better conceived in terms of occupational (or other) differentiation within the service class. This is not a question which can easily be resolved. Even if the conditions which constitute the service relationship (exercise of delegated authority versus exercise of expert knowledge) differ considerably, one has to acknowledge that the three different segments share other important characteristics of the employment relationship of the service class. Following Goldthorpe, one possibility is to understand the differentiation within the service class in terms of occupational situs, by which he refers 'to "the functional context" of an occupation or groups of occupations, which may exert an influence on the lifestyles and patterns of action of their incumbents, independently of that of the class, or status positions that they simultaneously hold' (Goldthorpe 1995: 328). As Heath and Savage (1995) argue, decisions about the class-theoretical interpretation must be based on considerations of the structural location of a position. Important aspects involve the similarity in labour market chances, patterns of intergenerational and worklife mobility, as well as patterns of social networking through marriage and friendship. Such studies are lacking for Germany; thus for the time being the class-theoretical interpretation must remain open. Nevertheless, whether understood as separate classes or segments within the service class, the political stance of the service class and its homogeneity remains an important issue, to which I now turn.

### *Hypotheses about Class-Based Party Preferences within the Service Class*

Several hypotheses can be formulated concerning the political preferences and party affinities of the three segments distinguished within the service class. These hypotheses concern three aspects: the position of these groups (1) with respect to the *classical class cleavage* in party preferences; (2) with respect to the '*new politics*'; and (3) with respect to *changes in party* preferences over time.

1. Relating to the *classical class cleavage*, the administrative service class should be most closely associated with the party that represents the side of capital in the traditional class cleavage, while the expert and the social service segment should tend towards the other side. The *raison d'être* of the administrative service class is to exercise delegated authority and power in the interest of the employer and with a view to realizing the aims of the employing organization. The loyal exercise of this role, which is the

basis of the privileged position of their members, should lead them to identify with the perspective of the employers and to form interest coalitions with them. Their political orientations can therefore be expected to be rather close to those of owners and top management, particularly in private industry. The group of experts and social service professionals has much less reason to adopt such an orientation; on the contrary, they should see themselves rather on the opposite side, not primarily for material reasons like the classical wage labourer, but in rejecting subordination under organizational dominance and to defend their autonomy, which constitutes the base of their professional identity (Abbott 1988). Owing to their clientele orientation, the motives of autonomy and resistance against authority should be most pronounced among social service professionals. In addition, social service professionals should favour egalitarian values, again in response to their frequent exchange with clients and in consonance with the norms of care they share. In sum, in the voting alternative between the CDU and the SPD, which marks the tension of the classical class cleavage, the administrative service class should be close to the CDU, while, for the experts and even more for the social service professionals, we should expect a closer affinity with the SPD. The social service professionals' solidarity with the party of the workers, however, is based on different reasons and has different aims than those of the working class itself.

2. In Germany, the programme of the so-called *'new politics'* has been formulated most explicitly by the Green Party. It is important to note that their program is not limited to environmental issues. The core elements of the Green political credo and—at least the symbolic—practice of Green policy are the safeguard of individual autonomy and the emphasis on grassroots participation, mistrust of the iron cage, and the fight against all forms of bureaucratic control. The Green programme advocates citizens' rights and decentralized decision-making in all social, economic, and political areas. Concrete examples can be found in policies concerning immigration, political asylum, the Third World, and women's rights. These policies are manifested in dramatic political protests such as opposition to large-scale technical projects or to the population census in the 1980s, which was portrayed as a dangerous instrument of political control over free citizens. There is a striking correspondence between the emphasis on professional independence and professionals' desire for autonomy and self-determination, and the ideological rhetoric of the Greens. An interest-based link thus exists between the class characteristics of the two segments of the professional service class—the experts and the social and cultural service professionals—and party preferences for the Greens. The administrative service class, on the other hand, can be expected rather to distance itself from such a programme. In sum, we can expect that the three segments of the service class differ in their stance towards the Green Party

along the same lines as they differ towards the parties of the traditional class cleavage. The differences among them in Green preferences should be even larger, because the Green programme is more focused on the specific conflicting interests between the service class segments than is the classical left–right cleavage.

3. As to *changes across time in class-related party preferences*, here the task of formulating precise hypotheses and specifying the mechanisms assumed to be at work is extremely difficult. One would have to consider at least three aspects at the same time: (*a*) on the demand side, changes in the conditions for the formulation of class-based interests among voters; (*b*) on the supply side, changes in the party programmes and concrete policies; and (*c*) changes in the processes that mediate between parties and voters. I certainly cannot do justice to the full complexity of this task. The model I use is extremely simplified, and the historical circumstances are taken into account only in a very crude way. I will neglect almost entirely the mediating processes, and I will proceed with strong simplifying assumptions, both concerning voters' demands and the supply of party programmes.

Concerning voters' demands, I begin with the assumption that no major change occurred with respect to the constellation of interests associated with class positions, that is, that there is basically no change in the conditions associated with the class position that would lead class members to change their party preference. This is a strong null hypothesis which can be tested against the empirical evidence. It may be that this assumption will have to be revised if the supply factors, when explicitly taken into account, cannot satisfactorily explain the changes I observe.

Concerning supply, I consider only major changes in the programmatic stance of the parties of the classical class cleavage and changes in the structure of the party system connected with the emergence of stable new parties. The most significant change in the programmatic stance of the main parties concerns the adoption of the 'new politics' issues. The CDU has not adopted the 'new politics' issues in clearly recognizable ways. The position of the CDU has also remained more or less constant with respect to other issues relevant to the class cleavage in the post-Second World War decades. There has been no major change in this party's political orientation. The programmatic outlook of the SPD has changed to a larger extent. With its Godesberg programme, the party gave up Marxist ideology, and since the mid-1960s, under Brandt's leadership, has incorporated positions of the new left to some extent (Müller-Rommel 1990; Kitschelt 1994). Both moves, the latter more than the former, can be seen as a partial acceptance of 'new politics' issues. The most significant change in the party system is the emergence and the consolidation of the Green Party, which participated in national elections for the first time in 1980.

As rough as this sketch is, what expectations can we derive from it concerning changes in the party preferences of various classes? I begin with the three segments of the service class. The administrative service class can be expected to show a stable affinity towards the CDU, as the CDU is posited to be the preferred party of this class and has not changed its position with respect to the classical class cleavage or new politics issues. The expert and social service segments, however, can be expected to move even further away from the CDU towards the SPD and the Greens, as the SPD becomes more responsive to the specific interests of these classes and the Greens emerge with a programme that is particularly proximate to them. Now, what about the antagonists in the classical class cleavage: the working class and the petty bourgeoisie? As the SPD gives up a narrow working-class identity, one might expect the working-class affiliation with the SPD to weaken and the petty bourgeoisie's distance from the SPD to shrink somewhat. However, such changes should be rather limited. There is no obvious alternative party to which working-class members could turn, nor is there any apparent reason why the petty bourgeoisie should turn away from the CDU. As the new politics issues do not respond to a particular demand of these classes, they will not be dealt with here. I also refrain from formulating hypotheses for the routine nonmanual class, as its position in the class structure is too undetermined.

In developing the hypotheses in this section I have adopted a class-based interpretation of party preferences, given the offer of a specific party programme. This touches upon the serious problem of the causal interpretation of the association between class position and party preference that needs to be addressed briefly. As recent controversies have underlined, the class-based interpretation presupposes that it is indeed class position that conditions the vote for a specific party and not some individual characteristics existing independently of and possibly even preceding class position, such as individual competencies, political attitudes, or value preferences (see Butler and Savage 1995). In particular, having a job in one of the administrative, expert, or social service segments of the service class is probably at least in part a matter of individual choice and of occupational self-selection (Bagguley 1995). Education is particularly pertinent here. People choose their educational specialization in view of their occupational future and—when they have appropriate qualifications—can orientate themselves towards either a managerial or a professional career. Education also conditions the development of a reflective and critical stance towards politics, for example, through enhanced political interests, ideological conceptualizations of political action (Klingemann 1979), postmaterialist values (Inglehart 1971), and the readiness to participate in non-conventional political action (Barnes and Kaase 1979). One has to be aware of the possibility that to a greater or lesser extent the varying party preferences of members of different classes, notably in the various segments of the service class, are a spurious consequence of education, value orientations, and other experiences and preferences of individuals rather than a pure result of their class position. This argument has been made with no lack of clarity or determination by Inglehart (1990) and underlined by Scarbrough (1995): 'The rise of Postmaterialism and its subsequent penetration of technocratic and professional élites has been a major factor behind the emergence of the new class' (Inglehart 1990: 332). The only way to rule out such alternative interpretations is to control explicitly for the respective factors in the analyses and to examine whether class effects remain in spite of such controls.

In sum, a study of changes in the class cleavages in voting preferences is a matter of considerable complexity. In addition to the issue as to whether the traditional class cleavage in political voting preferences has declined, a proper assessment of the class–vote link involves taking into account the rapid expansion of the service class, the growth of specific types of jobs within the service class, and their links to the potential development of *new* class-based cleavages. The examination of changing alignments with respect to the traditional class parties must therefore be supplemented with an analysis of the class bases of the vote for the new Green Party, and we must carefully attempt to separate the class effects on voting from those of individual characteristics which may be correlated with class, but are theoretically distinct from class.

## DESIGN, DATA, AND VARIABLES

### *Design of the Study*

Ideally the study of these issues would involve longitudinal data covering attitudes of individuals, their value priorities, their careers in the class structure, and their voting preferences over a long period of time. I do not have such a database. The analyses will rely on cross-sectional surveys regularly replicated between 1976 and 1994. I cannot follow individuals across time, but I will attempt to control for individual characteristics and conditions of life which may be responsible for 'spurious' effects of class. The more such factors are controlled for, the less class will appear to influence voting preferences, but also the more conservative a test of the continued relevance of class will become. The data available allow us to control for the following variables.

- *Religion.* In particular because the association between religion and class has changed in postwar Germany, it is advisable to control for church affiliation and religious practice, which have proved to be the best indicators of the religious cleavage.

- *Gender*. As the association between class and gender changes and men and women have different party preferences, it is similarly important to control for gender.
- *Employment status*. This rather heterogeneous variable is used to control for specific conditions that may affect party orientation among different categories of voters who are not employed (the unemployed, students, pensioners, and other persons not in the labour force). With the status of students and pensioners, we also touch upon specific conditions of life at particular stages of the life-cycle and thus partly control for age-related factors in party preferences.
- *Education*. In the present analysis I understand education mainly as a broad indicator of the climate of political socialization in higher education, which—partly connected to the 1968 movement—has moved in a more left-wing and Green direction in the postwar decades. Controlling for education should 'purify' the effects of class position from these and other correlated educational elements mentioned above.
- *Union membership*. The reasons for considering the role of union membership are different from those for the variables discussed so far. It is not included in order to 'purify' class effects from those of other factors. The intention rather is to show how class effects are mediated through becoming a member of a collective that organizes class interests and to what extent changes in the class cleavage of party vote may be due to the changing role of membership in class organizations.
- *Postmaterialism*. This is the only attitudinal variable measured regularly in the series of surveys I will use. Controlling for it is important in verifying whether particular party preferences are class-based or value-driven.

Besides paying regard to the decisive control factors, an important aspect of the study design relates to the dimension of time in which change is studied. I will consider change in time with respect to the period and the cohort dimension, but will not deal with the *age* dimension. Theory and evidence of earlier research in the German case make a cohort interpretation of age-correlated differences in party preferences more convincing than regarding them as a true consequence of ageing (Lepsius 1973; Pappi 1990). In addition, by controlling for employment status, in particular the status of persons in education and in retirement, some of the potentially most relevant age-related life-stage effects are explicitly taken into account.

The period dimension of time can only be observed for 1976–94, the years in which the data I will use were collected. Unfortunately, this is a rather short time-span. Nevertheless, if there is a continuous decline in the class cleavage in party preferences and if this decline occurs according to a period-model of change, this trend should be observable during these years. But if—compared for instance to the 1950s—a period-related decline only occurred during the 1960s and early 1970s, I will not be able to observe this period change with the data used. I will return to the respective implications of the design in the concluding section of the chapter.

The *cohort* dimension of time can be observed for a much longer length of time. But how can we define cohorts in a way that makes sense theoretically, and why is it important to control for cohort effects? With a cohort interpretation of party preferences one usually assumes that cohort differences result from early political socialization and experiences (some years before and around the time when people begin to participate in political elections). Cohorts should then be defined in line with the particular historical circumstances that could have influenced the formation of party preferences. As many factors affect political socialization and early political experiences, divisions between cohorts can only be drawn with regard to major political events and eras. For Germany I consider one such division particularly significant: the one separating voters born before and after the outbreak of the Second World War in 1939. It represents the main 'watershed' in the political experience of the cohorts of voters observed in the present study. Those born before 1939 experienced the Third Reich (or at least a part of it), the Second World War, and the postwar collapse in the years of their political socialization. The oldest among them also experienced the instability of the Weimar Republic, a time marked by economic crises and strong class and other political conflicts. Those born in 1939 and later may have some personal recollection of the final years of the war and the difficult time immediately following it, but most of them became aware of politics within the democratic order of the German Federal Republic, the *Wirtschaftswunder*, and the enormous improvement in living conditions in the postwar decades. Only the youngest respondents may be more strongly hit by the return of unemployment than they are impressed by the high standard of living and social security achieved.

The distinction between those born before and after the war is thus conceived as the main dividing line. However, in order to test for the relevance of this distinction and to control for birth cohort differences in more refined ways, ten-year birth cohorts will also be used. These cohorts are formed going backwards and forwards from the 1938/9 split. The more detailed cohort definition will consist of those born 1909–18, 1919–28, 1929–38, 1939–48, 1949–58, 1959–68, and 1969–76.

Cohort effects on party preferences must be examined in two ways. First, the control of cohort membership as a main effect is crucial for a valid test of class effects on party preferences. From much research we know that it is mainly the younger cohorts who support new politics and in particular the Green parties. This is partly on account of the fact that members of the postwar cohorts hold increasingly postmaterialist values (see e.g. Inglehart 1971; Scarbrough 1995). As jobs in the expert and social service segment of the service class became available mainly for younger cohorts, the affinity of these classes to the new politics could be spurious. Controlling for cohort membership is therefore an important step in ensuring that measured class effects are real class effects.

Secondly, the strength of class effects may vary with cohort membership. The posited changes in the association between class position and party preferences discussed above may indeed occur through weaker or stronger bonds in successive cohorts between a specific class location and particular preferences for specific parties. Social service professionals, for instance, who enter political life at a time when there is a party responsive to the interests of this class will develop a closer affiliation with this party than class members in older cohorts who did not have this option. Even if the option becomes available later, voters may not turn away (immediately) from the political affiliations established in an earlier, different political context. In an election at a given point in time, cohort differences within classes may therefore exist and reflect the legacy of political history. Such differences should show up in the analysis when we specify an interaction between cohort membership and class position.

## *Data*

The data used in this chapter are from surveys taken at more or less regular intervals in the years 1976–94. They derive from ten replications of the ZUMABUS (1976) and the ALLBUS surveys (1980, 1982, 1984, 1986, 1988, 1990, 1991, 1992, 1994). These surveys have been integrated into a large merged datafile, in which the survey years represent the period variable. For the reasons just mentioned it would have been preferable to include data for earlier years in order to extend the observations further into the past. However, comparability of measurement would have been lower, in particular for the construction of the class schema, which is crucial for the arguments in this chapter. The surveys used are all very similarly designed representative random samples of the adult German population and refer (with the exception of non-random unit non-response) to the population of all individuals entitled to participate in political elections in the respective survey year. They also measure the variables used in a highly comparable way and they are surveys of the best quality available in Germany. The data used constitute an exceptionally large (N = 26,165) and comparable base which allows stable estimates of the factors affecting party preferences and how they have changed in recent decades.

It is important to stress, however, that the data used in this chapter do not derive from election studies. The data for the dependent variable (vote intention) have been collected at different points in time from parliamentary elections; they derive from a question asking which party the respondent would vote for 'if elections took place next Sunday'. This approach has advantages and disadvantages. Responses are not affected by electoral campaigns and are probably less dependent on particular politicized issues and the characteristics of party candidates. Therefore, in contrast to data deriving from election studies, the measures used here are most likely to relate to underlying long-term affinities (commitment, sympathy, identification) with given parties. The data are thus more appropriate for capturing long-term political orientation rather than actual voting behaviour. The pattern of responses may also show less fluctuation over time than do data collected in proximity to elections.

### *Variable Definitions and Distributions*

Most of the variables used in the analyses derive from common operationalizations of concepts referring to individuals' social structural locations and do not need explicit explanation. Their definitions can be seen in Tables 6.1 to 6.3 and the notes to these tables. The central variable used in the analysis is respondents' social class. As discussed above, it is defined as a modified version of the Erikson–Goldthorpe class schema: the service classes I and II are at first combined and then divided into the following three segments: the *experts* include all professional and semi-professional occupations in engineering, technology, natural, and economic sciences. The social (and cultural) services include professional and semi-professional occupations rendering services mainly in the various domains of education, health, and social work. This category also includes services in the media, the arts, and other domains of public culture. For brevity they are labelled social services. The administrative services (and management) include all other occupations coded into the service classes I and II. Most respondents assigned to this category do work related to management, administration, and control in the public and private sector or render services mainly to private and public organizations as lawyers and business consultants. The other categories of the class schema can be seen from panel A of Table 6.1. Because preliminary analyses showed no substantial differences in party preferences between skilled and unskilled workers, these two groups have been combined for all analyses.[1]

The various panels of Table 6.1 show the distributions of most of the variables in the data used in the analyses and indicate how the distributions change across the survey years or combined survey years. From panel A of Table 6.1 we see that the proportion of voters in the service classes I and II increases (from 29 per cent to 35 per cent). This growth is due exclusively to employees employed in expert and social services. The proportion of manual workers, mainly unskilled manual workers, declines slightly. Consistent with general trends in educational participation, I find a greater number of voters with higher education, defined as having obtained the *Abitur* certificate or some tertiary education degree. The slightly larger proportion of pensioners in the most recent samples is consistent with the trend towards earlier retirement and general 'ageing of the population'. The fluctuations in the figures for students result from variations in measurement precision across surveys.[2] Consistent with the general process of secularization, membership of the Protestant Church generally declines and the proportion of respondents who are not church members increases. Among members of both churches the proportion of those regularly practising also clearly declines. Among the variables used, vote intention shows the largest volatility from survey to survey. The data series on vote intention, however, clearly shows the emergence of the Green Party in 1980 and its subsequent stabilization. The share of Green votes is slightly overestimated.

Table 6.1 (panels A and F) also shows that the proportions of missing data are quite large for social class and vote intention. The exceptionally high proportion of missing data for social class in 1976 is owing to the fact that in this year one of the proxy variables used to assess class (if the respondent was not employed) was not measured. For vote intention the proportions of missing data have increased in more recent years. This is true for respondents who say they would not vote as well as for those who refuse to indicate their preferred party. In order to adjust for this trend, missing data on vote intention will constitute one response option explicitly taken into account in the multinomial regression models with which

[1] Class positions were assigned according to respondents' current job if they were employed at the time of the interview. For those not employed, the assignment of a class position was attempted by using a succession of proxies: respondent's last occupation; spouse's occupation; and respondent's father (for those who were still in education). Even using these proxies it was impossible to assign a class position to quite a large number of respondents, mostly because their job information was not sufficiently detailed for reliable coding.

[2] In some of the surveys used there is no direct information on whether someone is a student. In these cases this variable had to be derived from other information contained in the surveys.

TABLE 6.1. *Variable distributions in surveys aggregated in four survey periods (per cent)*

| Variable (N) | | 1976 (2,036) | 1980–84 (8,950) | 1986–90 (9,198) | 1991–94 (5,981) | Per cent (N) (26,165) |
|---|---|---|---|---|---|---|
| A Social class | | | | | | |
| I/IIa | Administration | 17 | 13 | 14 | 15 | 14 (3,208) |
| I/IIe | Experts | 4 | 8 | 10 | 9 | 8 (1,960) |
| I/IIs | Social services | 8 | 8 | 10 | 11 | 9 (2,133) |
| IIIab | Routine nonmanual | 17 | 18 | 18 | 15 | 17 (4,010) |
| IVabc | Petty bourgeoisie | 9 | 9 | 8 | 8 | 8 (1,922) |
| V | Foremen, technicans | 9 | 8 | 8 | 9 | 8 (1,935) |
| VI | Skilled workers | 17 | 18 | 17 | 17 | 17 (3,942) |
| VIIab | Unskilled workers | 18 | 19 | 16 | 16 | 17 (4,003) |
| | Missing data | 29 | 8 | 11 | 13 | 12 (3,052) |
| B Union membership | | | | | | |
| | Non-member | 87 | 88 | 88 | 86 | 87 (22,740) |
| | Member | 13 | 13 | 12 | 14 | 13 (3,312) |
| | Missing data | 0 | 0 | 1 | 0 | 0 (113) |
| C Education | | | | | | |
| | Below *Abitur* level | 84 | 84 | 80 | 80 | 82 (21,141) |
| | *Abitur* or higher | 16 | 16 | 20 | 20 | 18 (4,717) |
| | Missing data | 2 | 2 | 1 | 1 | 1 (307) |
| D Labour force participation | | | | | | |
| | Employed | 51 | 49 | 50 | 53 | 51 (13,176) |
| | Unemployed | 1 | 3 | 3 | 3 | 3 (669) |
| | Student | 7 | 4 | 2 | 5 | 4 (1,052) |
| | Retired | 19 | 20 | 19 | 23 | 20 (5,300) |
| | Other not employed | 23 | 23 | 26 | 17 | 23 (5,903) |
| | Missing data | 0 | 0 | 0 | 1 | 0 (65) |

| E | | | | | |
|---|---|---|---|---|---|
| Religion | | | | | |
| Catholic, high church attendance | 31 | 30 | 26 | 25 | 28 (7,151) |
| Catholic, low church attendance | 12 | 13 | 16 | 17 | 15 (3,883) |
| Protestant, high church attendance | 24 | 22 | 19 | 19 | 20 (5,286) |
| Protestant, low church attendance | 26 | 28 | 29 | 27 | 28 (7,178) |
| Not church member | 8 | 8 | 10 | 12 | 10 (2,451) |
| Missing data | 0 | 1 | 2 | 1 | 1 (216) |

F Vote intention by survey year

| | 1976 | 1980 | 1982 | 1984 | 1986 | 1988 | 1990 | 1991 | 1992 | 1994 | Per cent (N) |
|---|---|---|---|---|---|---|---|---|---|---|---|
| CDU | 47 | 38 | 46 | 41 | 36 | 34 | 34 | 31 | 26 | 31 | 37 (7,775) |
| SPD | 41 | 41 | 27 | 38 | 40 | 42 | 40 | 43 | 36 | 35 | 38 (8,023) |
| FDP | 11 | 11 | 11 | 5 | 7 | 6 | 9 | 11 | 8 | 8 | 9 (1,809) |
| Grüne | 0 | 6 | 8 | 10 | 9 | 8 | 9 | 8 | 11 | 13 | 8 (1,734) |
| NPD, Rep | 1 | 0 | 0 | 0 | 0 | 1 | 1 | 1 | 6 | 3 | 1 (253) |
| Other | 1 | 0 | 1 | 1 | 1 | 2 | 2 | 0 | 1 | 2 | 1 (234) |
| Non-voters | 0 | 4 | 7 | 6 | 7 | 8 | 4 | 6 | 10 | 8 | 6 (1,264) |
| missing | 12 | 17 | 16 | 19 | 23 | 26 | 15 | 20 | 24 | 21 | 19 (5,073) |
| % | 100 | 100 | 100 | 100 | 100 | 100 | 100 | 100 | 100 | 100 | 100 (26,165) |
| N | (2,036) | (2,955) | (2,991) | (3,004) | (3,095) | (3,052) | (3,051) | (1,477) | (2,315) | (2,189) | |

*Note*: Percentages for missing data relate to N, as given in first row; other percentages relate to N minus missing data.

party preferences are studied below. In order not to lose respondents with missing data on social class, a missing data dummy variable was created and included in all multivariate analyses.

## PATTERNS OF PARTY PREFERENCE OVER TIME AND ACROSS COHORTS

I begin the presentation of empirical results with a brief discussion of Table 6.2, which shows the distributions of party preferences among the social classes for the pre-war and postwar cohorts. From the marginal distributions we learn that voters born before the Second World War have a much higher preference for the CDU than those born thereafter. The postwar cohorts intend to vote for the Greens in much greater numbers than the pre-war cohorts. They also show a slight preference for the SPD. The table also shows major changes between the cohorts in the voting preferences of the different social classes. Among the voters born before the Second World War, members of all social classes except workers give the largest share of their votes to the CDU. Of those born later, the voters of all classes except the petty bourgeoisie and the administrative services prefer the SPD to the CDU. The most severe losses for the CDU have occurred among the experts and the social services. From the members of these expanding classes born after the war, the CDU receives less than half the proportion of votes it received from voters born before the war. Among the postwar members of these classes, the Greens appear to be on equal footing with the CDU. In fact, they receive almost one in four votes.

We thus find quite substantial differences in voting intentions between voters born before and after the Second World War. The voting preferences also seem to have changed quite dramatically among voters from different social classes. However, the differences in party preferences between the very broad cohort aggregates in Table 6.2 may derive from many factors along which the cohort aggregates differ. To mention only the most obvious compositional differences, the postwar cohorts include a larger proportion of respondents from the more recent surveys; more of their members are highly educated, more have no religious affiliation, and fewer are already in retirement than is true for the pre-war cohorts. Such differences can only be controlled through adequate multivariate models, on which I will focus for the remainder of the chapter.

### *In Search of a Model for Party Preferences in Germany*

In these analyses I proceed in a series of steps in which I model the choice of a party as an outcome dependent on the factors discussed above. In

TABLE 6.2. *Distribution of vote intention by cohort and social class (per cent)*

| | Pre-war cohorts (1908–38) | CDU | SPD | FDP | GREEN | NDP/REP | Other | Nonvoters | Missing | (N) |
|---|---|---|---|---|---|---|---|---|---|---|
| I/IIa | Administration | 55 | 26 | 14 | 3 | 1 | 1 | 22 | | (1,200) |
| I/IIe | Experts | 55 | 24 | 15 | 5 | 1 | 0 | 21 | | (561) |
| I/IIs | Social services | 48 | 31 | 13 | 7 | 0 | 1 | 20 | | (704) |
| IIIab | Routine nonmanual | 49 | 38 | 9 | 3 | 0 | 1 | 23 | | (1,342) |
| IVab | Petty bourgeoisie | 69 | 17 | 10 | 2 | 1 | 0 | 25 | | (979) |
| V | Foremen, technicians | 44 | 47 | 6 | 2 | 1 | 0 | 22 | | (812) |
| VI/VII | Workers | 42 | 50 | 5 | 1 | 1 | 1 | 24 | | (3,842) |
| | Missing data | 50 | 36 | 9 | 3 | 1 | 1 | 26 | | (1,064) |
| | | 49 | 38 | 9 | 3 | 1 | 1 | 23 | | 100 |
| | (N) | (3,949) | (3,088) | (694) | (215) | (72) | (43) | (2,452) | | (10,513) |
| | Postwar cohorts (1939–76) | | | | | | | | | |
| I/IIa | Administration | 40 | 35 | 11 | 10 | 1 | 1 | 23 | | (1,354) |
| I/IIe | Experts | 24 | 37 | 13 | 22 | 0 | 3 | 24 | | (1,017) |
| I/IIs | Social services | 20 | 43 | 12 | 23 | 0 | 2 | 24 | | (998) |
| IIIab | Routine nonmanual | 32 | 44 | 9 | 13 | 2 | 1 | 29 | | (1,724) |
| IVab | Petty bourgeoisie | 46 | 25 | 12 | 13 | 3 | 1 | 26 | | (594) |
| V | Foremen, technicians | 31 | 44 | 7 | 14 | 2 | 2 | 26 | | (729) |
| VI/VII | Workers | 27 | 50 | 6 | 12 | 3 | 1 | 29 | | (2,559) |
| | Missing data | 27 | 39 | 8 | 22 | 1 | 2 | 30 | | (973) |
| | | 30 | 42 | 9 | 15 | 2 | 2 | 27 | | 100 |
| | (N) | (2,980) | (4,184) | (921) | (1,516) | (172) | (175) | (3,627) | | (13,575) |

*Note*: Percentages for missing data relate to N, as given in last column; other percentage relate to N minus missing data.

order to elaborate more clearly the varying significance of these factors for the choice between specific party alternatives, I first study choices between various groups of two parties contrasted with each other. For these analyses I apply binomial logistic regression models. For selected models I then use multinomial logistic regression in order to study preferences among the full set of party alternatives.

Table 6.3 gives an overview of results from a series of logistic regression models that test the potential of the various socio-structural factors to explain voter preferences. These models represent the choices between different sets of two parties contrasted with each other. The table shows the values of the degrees of freedom and deviance explained, measured in terms of the log-likelihood $G^2$. For each of these contrasts, the table includes four blocks of models. Model 1 is considered as a baseline in reference to which all other models are then evaluated. This baseline model includes all variables as main effects. It assumes that changes in voting preferences across time only occur as shifts through the main effects of periods (*P*) and cohorts (*C*). For all substantive variables constant effects across all dimensions of time are assumed.

The last row of Table 6.3 gives the Pseudo-$R^2$ measures ($P^2$) for this baseline model B1. They can be understood as estimates of the extent to which party preferences are predictable from the set of social structural variables included in the model. As can be seen from the varying size of $P^2$, the complete set of variables differs considerably in the power to explain the choices between the various party alternatives. For the CDU versus SPD alternative—that is, the major contenders in the market for votes and the traditional opponents in both the religious and the class cleavage—this measure is 13.3 per cent. This is substantially larger than the proportion found in earlier research using slightly different measures.[3] Against the standard of the CDU/SPD contrast, the results for the FDP and the Greens differ markedly. FDP voters do not seem to differ much from those of the CDU or the SPD in terms of their social characteristics.[4] In contrast, Green voters differ strongly from those of both parties of the traditional cleavage structure. The contrast between Green voters and CDU voters is particularly marked. The $P^2$ for the CDU/Green contrast is more than twice as large as for the CDU/SPD contrast.

Model 2.1–2.12 of the second block in Table 6.3 give a summary

[3] Schnell and Kohler (1995: 646) report $P^2$ values of about 10 per cent or lower for the period investigated here; the results given by Emmert and Roth (1995: 142–8), who additionally include several attitudinal variables in their models, lead one to conclude that their data and classifications—if analysed in comparable ways—would produce $P^2$ values even smaller than those obtained by Schnell and Kohler.

[4] Analyses not presented here show that the $P^2$ for the contrast of the SPD versus the FDP is similar in size to the contrast between the CDU and the FDP.

TABLE 6.3. *$G^2$ values for various logistic models of voting preference*

| | | Model to which compared | df | $df_{Green}$ | Party contrasts | | | |
|---|---|---|---|---|---|---|---|---|
| | | | | | CDU/SPD (N = 14,593) $G^2$ | CDU/GREEN (N = 8,079) $G^2$ | SPD/GREEN (N = 8,531) $G^2$ | CDU/FDP (N = 8,798) $G^2$ |
| 1 | Bl = M L S P C R U K E | | 34 | 33 | 2,691.4 | 2,489.6 | 1,268.9 | 728.1 |
| 2.1 | Bl – M | 1 | –2 | –2 | –44.1 | –6.1 | –31.4 | –3.5 |
| 2.2 | Bl – L | 1 | –4 | –4 | –20.7 | –22.0 | –8.5 | –4.8 |
| 2.3 | Bl – S | 1 | –1 | –1 | –33.7 | –21.2 | –1.3 | –16.2 |
| 2.4 | Bl – P | 1 | –9 | –8 | –156.7 | –35.0 | –110.5 | –99.1 |
| 2.5 | Bl – C | 1 | –6 | –6 | –168.7 | –603.8 | –345.0 | –29.3 |
| 2.6 | Bl – R | 1 | –4 | –4 | –1,110.3 | –475 | –75.1 | –311.8 |
| 2.7 | Bl – E | 1 | –1 | –1 | –0.9 | –71.4 | –65.7 | –51.5 |
| 2.8 | Bl – U | 1 | –1 | –1 | –379.4 | –53.9 | –6.5 | –10.2 |
| 2.9 | Bl – K | 1 | –6 | –6 | –368.1 | –90.2 | –60.5 | –22.6 |
| 2.10 | Bl – (K + U) | 1 | –7 | –7 | –908.4 | –159.0 | –70.4 | –30.6 |
| 2.11 | Bl – (E + K + U) | 1 | –8 | –8 | –927.5 | –322.2 | –254.1 | –144.8 |
| 2.12 | Bl – (E + K + U + R) | 1 | –12 | –12 | –2,095.8 | –851.5 | –348.4 | –481.9 |
| 3.1 | Bl + P′K | 1 | 6 | 6 | 4.3 | 3.1 | 1.4 | 6.7 |
| 3.2 | Bl + $PK_{I/IIe}$ | 1 | 9 | 8 | 7.9 | 2.9 | 8.3 | 5.5 |
| 3.3 | Bl + $PK_{I/IIs}$ | 1 | 9 | 8 | 11.3 | 10.6 | 16.6 | 11.5 |
| 3.4 | Bl + $PK_{I/IIa}$ | 1 | 9 | 8 | 7.8 | 5.8 | 3.1 | 8.3 |
| 3.5 | Bl + $PK_{IIIab}$ | 1 | 9 | 8 | 6.8 | 8.6 | 6.4 | 7.3 |
| 3.6 | Bl + $PK_{IVIabc}$ | 1 | 9 | 8 | 16.2 | 1.9 | 6.6 | 7.9 |
| 3.7 | Bl + $Pk_v$ | 1 | 9 | 8 | 4.2 | 5.0 | 4.6 | 10.3 |

TABLE 6.3. *Continued*

| | Model to which compared | df | $df_{Green}$ | Party contrasts | | | |
|---|---|---|---|---|---|---|---|
| | | | | CDU/SPD (N = 14,593) $G^2$ | CDU/GREEN (N = 8,079) $G^2$ | SPD/GREEN (N = 8,531) $G^2$ | CDU/FDP (N = 8,798) $G^2$ |
| 4.1 Bl + CE + CU + CK | 1 | 42 | 42 | 133.3 | 58.0 | 75.0 | 38.8 |
| 4.2 Bl + C′E + C′U + C′K | 1 | 7 | 7 | 91.2 | 14.0 | 26.7 | 10.8 |
| 4.3 Bl + C′E + C′U + $C'K_{nw/w}$ | 1 | 3 | 3 | 83.8 | 10.7 | 22.4 | 2.1 |
| 4.4 Bl + CE + CU + CK +P′K | 4.1 | 6 | 6 | 1.4 | 5.3 | 3.5 | 6.8 |
| 4.5 Bl +C′E + C′U + C′K + P′K | 4.2 | 6 | 6 | 2.6 | 3.0 | 1.3 | 6.4 |
| 4.6 Bl + C′E + C′U + $C'K_{nw/w}$ + P′K | 4.3 | 6 | 6 | 3.0 | 3.3 | 1.6 | 7.0 |
| $P^2$ in model 1 (Bl) | | | | 13.3 | 30.1 | 15.0 | 8.4 |

*Notes*: Variable definitions

M Missing data.
L Labour Force Participation: employed/unemployed/students/retired/others not in labour force.
S Sex: female/male.
C Cohorts: 1909–18/1919–28/1929–38/1939–48/1949–58/1958–68/1969–76.
C′ Cohorts: 1909–38/1939–76.
P Period: survey years 1976/1980/1982/1984/1986/1988/1990/1991/1992/1994.
P′ linear trend for period (P′ = survey year—1976); P′K: each class dummy is interacted with P′
E Education: below *Abitur* level/*Abitur* or higher.
R Religion: not church member/Catholic, high church attendance/Catholic, low church attendance/Protestant, high church attendance/Protestant, low church attendance.
U Union membership: not member/member.
K Class VI, VIIab/V/IVab/IIIab/I,II adm./I,II exp./I,II soc.
$K_{I/IIe}$ Dummy variable for class I/II experts; P $K_{I/IIe}$: interaction of class I/II experts with all survey year dummies.
$K_{nw/w}$ Dummy variable contrasting non-working class (I–IVab) versus working class (V–VIIab).

overview of the relative importance of the various factors affecting the choice between sets of two parties contrasted with each other. They show how much the deviance ($G^2$) declines if one or several variables are excluded from the set of variables contained in the baseline model. With only a few exceptions,[5] all variables contribute significantly to explaining party choice in all contrasts. For most variables, however, the unique contribution of each single variable is generally small. This is particularly true for missing data, labour force participation, gender, and—surprisingly—also survey year. For education, union membership, and social class the unique contribution tends to be small because these variables overlap in explaining party choice. A more adequate measure of the impact of class and related factors is therefore given by the combined effects of class (*K*) and union membership (*U*) or by the combined effect of $K + U + E$ (education). The strongest effects result from cohort membership, religion, and the combined effect of class-related variables. The impact of these variables, however, varies for different party contrasts. Class and union membership most strongly affect the choice between the CDU and the SPD and somewhat less the choice between the CDU and the Greens. Religion plays a major role in all the contrasts in which the CDU is involved. Cohort membership is the strongest single variable in all the contrasts involving the Greens. Finally, education, in particular when combined with the class-related variables, is relatively important in the contrasts which involve either the FDP or the Greens. Education thus seems to be important if either of the two parties of the traditional (FDP) or the new (Greens) liberalism is involved.

Regarding the two time-related variables—survey period (*P*) and cohort (*C*)—party choice varies more by cohort than by survey year, an exception being the CDU/FDP contrast. With respect to this contrast, inspection of the parameter estimates shows that the relatively strong variation between surveys taken at different points in time results mainly from the fact that in 1982 the FDP switched from a coalition with the SPD to one with the CDU. This year marked the end of the era of Willy Brandt and Helmut Schmidt and inaugurated the chancellorship of Helmut Kohl. But beside this fact, the rather small single contribution of *P* (survey year) to the $G^2$ value of the baseline model already indicates that, once other variables are controlled for, variation in voting preferences across the ten surveys from 1976 to 1994 is very small compared to the variation related to the theoretically interesting variables in the study.

The impression of a very high stability of the patterns of relations assumed in the baseline model is reinforced by the results presented in

[5] The exceptions are education in the CDU/SPD contrast, gender in the SPD/Green contrast, and labour force participation and missing data in the CDU/FDP contrast.

blocks 3 and 4 of Table 6.3. The models in these blocks show how much deviance explained ($G^2$) improves if one takes into account the possibility that the effects of various factors may have changed over time or across cohorts. In block 3 the effects of class positions are assumed to vary across our ten surveys from 1976 to 1994. Variation is assumed to occur in two different ways. In model 3.1, I assume linear trends. Each of the five class dummy variables (indicating membership in one of the classes outside the working class, i.e. I/IIe, I/IIs, I/IIa, IIIab, IVabc) is multiplied by an indicator measuring the difference between the survey year and 1976. For none of the contrasts did this produce a significant improvement in explained deviance. In models 3.2 to 3.7, I interact successively one of the class variables with dummy variables for each of the survey years, 1980–1994. Of twenty-four of these tests, only two (more or less) meet the 5 per cent significance criterion. The conclusion from both attempts to identify systematic changes in class effects in the sequence of the various surveys taken over our observation period of almost twenty years is thus negative.[6]

From these analyses we can therefore already reach one major conclusion: we do not find any evidence of a trend or of any other significant variation in the pattern of class voting in the series of our ten surveys taken between 1976 and 1994. As the $G^2$ values for the main effect of $P$ show (model 2.4), there is some variation in the *general attraction* the various parties held for the public during these two decades. But these fluctuations are generally small compared to the constant impact of religion and the class-related variables. The volatility in party preferences between survey years that we see in Table 6.1 thus has nothing to do with changes in class-specific party preferences across the survey years.[7] But is there change in class effects across cohorts?

In block 4, I test in various ways for differences in effects between cohorts. In model 4.1, I interact education, union membership, and the five dummy variables for the non-working classes with the ten-year birth cohorts. In model 4.2, I contrast the effects of the same variables for the aggregated pre-war/postwar cohort split indicated by $C'$. In model 4.3, the same cohort split $C'$ is used, but for the class variable I only distinguish between working class and non-working class. Compare now the results of these models and consider the degrees of freedom they use. For the

[6] One might argue that the control of cohort membership explains away the potential variation of class effects in the period-dimension of time. Therefore I have replicated the analysis of block 3 using models which do not include the main effect of cohort membership. Results from these analyses are almost identical to those presented in Table 6.3.

[7] The significant main effects for $P$, however, also imply that the variability over survey years in the proportion of votes for the various parties that we observe in Table 6.1 cannot be (fully) explained by the changing composition of the voters captured by the other variables in the baseline model.

CDU/FDP contrast none of these models produces a significant improvement in fit. For all other contrasts it can be argued that the most parsimonious model 4.3 catches most of the systematic variation in the class effects across cohorts. Although the more detailed models also produce significant improvements in fit if compared to the baseline model (at least for the CDU/SPD and the SPD/Green contrasts), the improvements compared to model 4.3 are below the usual margins of statistical significance. But as model 4.1 includes a large number of additional parameters, it is possible that some of these parameters are statistically and substantially significant even if the model as a whole does not seem to be an improvement over its more parsimonious alternative. We can thus summarize that for all choices except for the CDU/FDP contrast, class effects change across cohorts. Judged on the basis of deviance explained, the change seems to occur mainly between persons born before and after the Second World War and between voters who belong to the working class and those who do not. Below I will examine in more detail whether such a simplified account is acceptable.

In models 4.4–4.6, I have added the variables indicating changes of class effects across survey years (defined as in model 3.1) to the models in 4.1–4.3. In none do I find any indication of a systematic change in class effects tied to the survey years. I have also carried out a number of additional analyses testing for changing effects of religion and gender and of gender interacted with class across periods and cohorts. None of these tests revealed any additional systematic variation in the data.

What we find, then, is a remarkable stability in the main effects of most variables throughout the almost twenty years surveyed here. For all contrasts, we find variation in party preferences across survey years and cohorts, but generally only in terms of the main effects of these variables. The main cohort effects are particularly strong in contrasts involving the Greens. Only for three variables do we find their effects differ across cohorts: education, union membership, and social class.

In the next section I discuss the parameter estimates for the various party contrasts. They show how the characteristics of voters influence their party preferences and in what way these influences change over time. As a general overview, I start with a discussion of the estimates of model 4.3. Later, in order to obtain a more detailed representation of the changes of class effects, I will also show results based on models 4.1 and 4.2.

### *Constancy and Changes in Party Preferences*

Table 6.4 shows the effects on one of the party contrasts in each column. The effects result from a multinomial regression model specified

TABLE 6.4. *Effects on voting preference (and z values) from multinomial regression model 4.3*

| | Party contrasts | | | |
|---|---|---|---|---|
| | CDU/SPD | CDU/GREEN | SPD/GREEN | CDU/FDP |
| Main effects | | | | |
| Gender: male | 1.27 (*5.51*) | 1.39 (*4.85*) | 1.10 (*1.43*) | 1.24 (*3.30*) |
| Employment: employed | 1.00 | 1.00 | 1.00 | 1.00 |
| Student | $1.25^{-1}$ (*1.96*) | $1.45^{-1}$ (*2.77*) | $1.16^{-1}$ (*1.24*) | 1.34 (*1.69*) |
| Retired | $1.12^{-1}$ (*1.54*) | $1.28^{-1}$ (*1.33*) | $1.15^{-1}$ (*0.74*) | 1.22 (*1.74*) |
| Unemployed | $1.29^{-1}$ (*2.11*) | $2.00^{-1}$ (*4.38*) | $1.54^{-1}$ (*3.08*) | 1.05 (*0.23*) |
| Other not employed | $1.15^{-1}$ (*2.71*) | $1.25^{-1}$ (*2.77*) | $1.09^{-1}$ (*1.12*) | 1.01 (*0.12*) |
| Religion: not church member | 1.00 | 1.00 | 1.00 | 1.00 |
| Catholics, high church attendance | 5.35 (*22.46*) | 9.39 (*20.95*) | 1.76 (*5.67*) | 3.89 (*12.8*) |
| Catholics, low church attendance | 1.79 (*7.31*) | 2.91 (*10.05*) | 1.62 (*5.08*) | 1.51 (*3.86*) |
| Protestants, high church attendance | 2.00 (*9.02*) | 4.71 (*13.88*) | 2.36 (*8.42*) | 1.65 (*4.53*) |
| Protestants, low church attendance | 1.30 (*3.46*) | 2.36 (*8.89*) | 1.83 (*7.18*) | 1.20 (*1.71*) |
| Cohort 1909–18 | 1.00 | 1.00 | 1.00 | 1.00 |
| Cohort 1919–28 | $1.08^{-1}$ (*1.01*) | $1.35^{-1}$ (*1.25*) | $1.26^{-1}$ (*0.95*) | $1.15^{-1}$ (*1.11*) |
| Cohort 1929–38 | $1.22^{-1}$ (*2.38*) | $2.81^{-1}$ (*4.00*) | $2.31^{-1}$ (*3.22*) | $1.36^{-1}$ (*2.24*) |
| Cohort 1939–48 | $1.58^{-1}$ (*4.70*) | $4.01^{-1}$ (*4.98*) | $2.54^{-1}$ (*3.33*) | $1.58^{-1}$ (*2.99*) |
| Cohort 1949–58 | $2.34^{-1}$ (*8.54*) | $11.41^{-1}$ (*8.82*) | $4.87^{-1}$ (*5.73*) | $1.63^{-1}$ (*3.12*) |
| Cohort 1959–68 | $2.28^{-1}$ (*7.59*) | $18.73^{-1}$ (*10.04*) | $8.23^{-1}$ (*7.53*) | $1.72^{-1}$ (*3.18*) |
| Cohort 1969–76 | $1.88^{-1}$ (*3.77*) | 18.21 (*9.12*) | $9.69^{-1}$ (*7.28*) | $1.16^{-1}$ (*0.53*) |
| Education: low (below *Abitur*) | 1.00 | 1.00 | 1.00 | 1.00 |
| Education: high | 1.64 (*5.13*) | $1.50^{-1}$ (*2.13*) | $2.47^{-1}$ (*4.65*) | $1.58^{-1}$ (*3.93*) |
| Union: not member | 1.00 | 1.00 | 1.00 | 1.00 |
| Union: member | $3.74^{-1}$ (*15.92*) | $3.30^{-1}$ (*5.93*) | 1.13 (*0.64*) | $1.34^{-1}$ (*1.93*) |
| Class: working class | 1.00 | 1.00 | 1.00 | 1.00 |
| Service class: experts | 1.81 (*6.34*) | $1.78^{-1}$ (*2.76*) | $3.28^{-1}$ (*5.65*) | $1.78^{-1}$ (*4.11*) |
| Service class: social services | 1.34 (*3.24*) | $2.98^{-1}$ (*5.26*) | $4.00^{-1}$ (*6.77*) | $1.54^{-1}$ (*3.03*) |
| Service class: administration | 2.57 (*12.76*) | $1.01^{-1}$ (*0.05*) | $2.59^{-1}$ (*4.72*) | $1.28^{-1}$ (*2.09*) |
| Routine nonmanuals | 1.66 (*7.15*) | $1.49^{-1}$ (*2.03*) | $2.48^{-1}$ (*4.60*) | $1.25^{-1}$ (*1.81*) |
| Petty bourgeoisie | 3.89 (*15.17*) | $1.05^{-1}$ (*0.23*) | $4.09^{-1}$ (*6.40*) | $1.15^{-1}$ (*1.08*) |
| Foremen and technicians | 1.33 (*4.03*) | 1.08 (*0.59*) | $1.24^{-1}$ (*1.69*) | 1.00 (*0.00*) |
| Interactions with cohort | | | | |
| Co 1939–76 higher education | $1.95^{-1}$ (*5.85*) | $1.48^{-1}$ (*1.94*) | 1.32 (*1.35*) | $1.14^{-1}$ (*0.92*) |
| Co 1939–76 union member | 1.51 (*3.66*) | 1.61 (*2.11*) | 1.07 (*0.30*) | 1.14 (*0.69*) |
| Co 1939–76 working class | 1.05 (*3.46*) | $1.08^{-1}$ (*2.36*) | $1.14^{-1}$ (*3.79*) | $1.02^{-1}$ (*0.98*) |
| Constant | $2.38^{-1}$ | 9.87 | 23.57 | 3.54 |

*Note*: Z values in parentheses.

according to model 4.3.[8] The effects are expressed as multipliers of the odds ratio of choosing the first rather than the second alternative in the party contrast to which the column refers. The exponent '–1' indicates that the preference for the first party alternative is negatively affected by a given factor. Or, alternatively, it indicates that the preference for the

[8] The dependent variable in this model includes two additional categories not reported in the table: one for vote for other parties (mainly the small number of votes for one of the parties of the extreme right), and one for the larger number of respondents who refused to indicate their preferred party or who said they would not vote.

second party alternative is enhanced. Commenting on the results, I first focus on the variables whose effects have been found to be stable across surveys and cohorts. These are gender, employment status, and religion. They affect voting preferences in the same way in all ten surveys from 1976 to 1994 and for all age groups and cohorts interviewed in these surveys.

Table 6.4 shows that there is a clear gender difference in voting preferences. Controlling for all other factors, men prefer the CDU to all other parties more often than women. But there is no difference between men and women concerning the choice between the SPD and the Greens. The CDU is also the party preferred by those who are employed. All others—students, the unemployed, pensioners, and others not employed—tend to prefer the SPD or the Greens to the CDU. The unemployed, moreover, prefer the Greens to the SPD. The CDU is strongly preferred by those affiliated to one of the Christian churches, in particular the Catholic Church. Voters who regularly attend religious services have a closer affinity to the CDU than those who do not.

Having controlled for these various factors and in particular for the strong religious cleavage in party preferences in Germany, we can now turn to the class cleavage, which is the main focus of this chapter. As I have elaborated above, my interest goes beyond the traditional question of whether the historical split in party preferences between voters from the working classes and others, particularly from the petty bourgeoisie, has changed. Two further crucial questions relate to the political orientation of the service class and to the question of a potential class basis for the new Green Party. The model test has indicated changes for education, union membership, and social class across cohorts. Therefore we must be clear that the main effects of these variables relate to estimates obtained for the cohorts of voters used as a reference category in defining the interaction terms. These cohorts are voters born before the Second World War. The interaction terms then indicate how the voters in the postwar cohorts differ from those of the pre-war cohorts. The main results are as follows.

- For the cohort main effects, which indicate the general voting preferences of birth cohorts independent of other characteristics of these cohorts, we find an almost linear and quite strong trend for most of the contrasts. The younger the cohort, the more its members turn away from the CDU to the SPD or to the FDP; but they turn away even more strongly from both traditional major parties to the Greens. However, among those born after 1968 the trend away from the CDU (not from the SPD) seems to have stopped. (We have to be careful not to over-interpret the latter finding: the number of cases from the youngest birth cohorts is rather small in our data, and more than half of these respondents were interviewed at age 20 or younger. Their political orientation may not be very stable.)

- Among voters born before the Second World War, higher education is linked with a preference for either the FDP or the Greens over the CDU or the SPD. The least preferred party among the highly educated, however, is clearly the SPD, since the highly educated choose the CDU rather than the SPD. In the postwar cohorts, the highly educated make a clear move towards the left. The CDU is now the most disliked party. The preference for the Greens is intensified and—compared to the pre-war cohorts—there is a clear move away from the CDU to the SPD.
- Union members in the pre-war cohorts are the most distant from the CDU. They strongly prefer the SPD and (to only a slightly lesser extent) the Greens to the CDU. Controlling for the fact that the FDP receives a much smaller proportion of votes overall, union members also prefer the FDP to the CDU. However, among the union members in postwar cohorts, the distance from the CDU has shrunk somewhat.
- In interpreting the findings for social class, we should note that the estimates indicate the differences of a given class from the (skilled and unskilled) working class, which is defined as the reference point. From the CDU/SPD contrast we see that—compared to the skilled and unskilled working class—members of all other classes are less likely to vote for the SPD and more likely to vote for the CDU. The petty bourgeoisie is well known as the traditional ally of the CDU. However, there is also considerable variation among the nonmanual wage earners in their proximity to one of the traditional class parties. The administrative service class is much closer to the party preferences of the petty bourgeoisie. All others, particularly the social service segment of the service class, are clearly closer to the preferences of the working class.
- Compared to the working class, members of the various nonmanual classes are not only more likely to vote for the CDU rather than the SPD, they are also more likely than the working class to vote for either of the two smaller parties standing somewhat outside the classical class cleavage. In all contrasts in which the Greens or the FDP are involved, the coefficients for the nonmanual classes point to either the Greens or the FDP.
- We also find marked differences between the three segments of the service class regarding choices between one of the two major parties and one of the smaller parties. The administrative service class shows the closest proximity to the CDU and the widest distance from the Greens. The opposite is true for the social service segment of the service class. The experts are somewhere in between.
- Class effects change slightly from prewar to postwar cohorts. For the classical class cleavage, the parameter estimate for the interaction of

cohort and working class is positive. This means that the difference between workers and non-workers in voting preferences for the CDU has declined in the postwar cohort.[9] The difference between workers and non-workers in preference for the Greens also appears to have declined in the postwar cohort.

Summarizing the findings of Table 6.4, it is important to point out that education, union membership, and social class affect voting preferences in different ways. Their effects also vary in different ways from the older to the younger cohort. In the older cohort higher education means distance from the working-class party and affiliation with any of the other parties. In the younger cohort, the highly educated have changed sides on the classical class cleavage. They now affiliate rather with the working-class party and have a strong preference for the Greens. Union membership, in contrast, implies a strong alliance with the SPD against the CDU in the older cohort, an alliance that is weaker in the younger cohort. The effects of class position *per se* on party preference vary in relation to the varying nature of the class positions.

In Table 6.4, change in class voting across cohorts is represented by a simple split between working class and all other classes and a simple prewar/postwar cohort distinction. From models 4.1 and 4.2 in Table 6.3 we know that more differentiated class and cohort distinctions also produce significant improvement in fit over the baseline model of no change in class voting, particularly for the CDU/SPD contrast. As the estimates of these models reveal systematic patterns in the changing relationship between the class structure and the party system which are not revealed by the more parsimonious model 4.3, in the following Figures 6.1–6.3 I show how, according to model 4.1, the effects of cohort, education, union membership, and social class change across cohorts. I do not show the estimates for any other variables in model 4.1 because they are basically the same as in model 4.3. (This is also true for all other models I discuss in the remainder of the chapter.)

[9] Note that the interaction variable cohort 1939–76* working class has been constructed in such a way that respondents who were born after 1938 and have a working-class job are coded as 1 while non-working class respondents born before 1938 are coded 0. In all contrasts the estimates for this dummy variable have the same signs as the main effects for the various nonmanual classes. One could interpret this result as implying that—compared to their older workmates—workers in the younger cohort changed their party preferences in the direction of the nonmanual classes. However, if we had specified an interaction between membership in a *nonmanual* class and in cohort 1939–76, we would have obtained the same estimates for the dummy variable, but with an opposite sign. Such a result would then suggest that the nonmanual classes have moved somewhat in the direction of the working classes. From the data we cannot know who has moved—we only know that the difference between the working classes and the non-manual classes is smaller in the younger cohort.

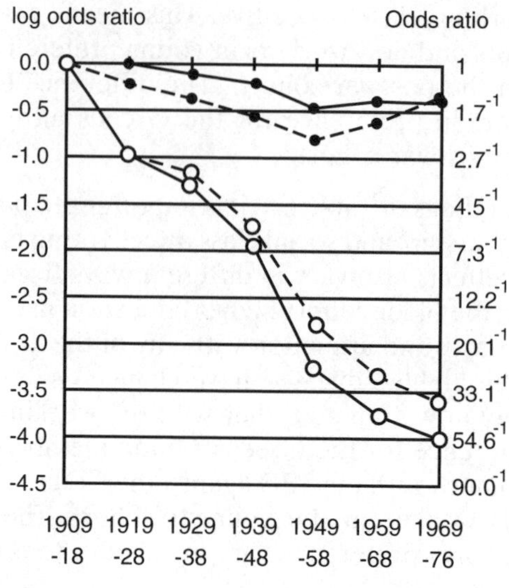


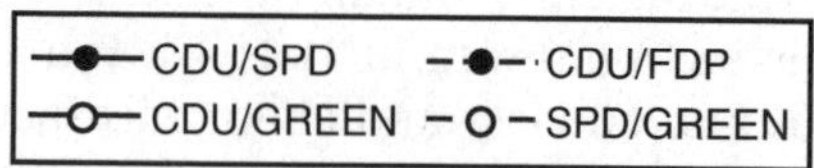


FIG. 6.1. Cohort effects on voting preferences between various party contrasts

Figure 6.1 shows the main effects of cohort for the various party contrasts. As already seen in Table 6.3 the main result is the postwar cohorts' turning away from *both* major parties and moving to the Greens. The cohort shifts from the CDU to the SPD are much weaker.

Figure 6.2 shows how the proximity of highly educated voters to the CDU and the proximity of union members to the SPD gradually disappears or declines from the older to the younger cohorts. In other words, the particular closeness of the older cohorts' *Bildungsbürgertum* to the CDU steadily declines and disappears in the postwar cohorts. The strength of affiliation of union members with the SPD also declines (again the result for the youngest cohort has to be treated with caution: numbers are very small and the duration of union membership is extremely short).

Figure 6.3 plots the changing class effects for the CDU/SPD contrast. The zero line in this figure represents the odds of CDU versus SPD voting preferences observed for the working class in the successive cohorts.

The most general finding is that, from the oldest to the youngest cohort, the distance between the voting preferences of the other classes and those

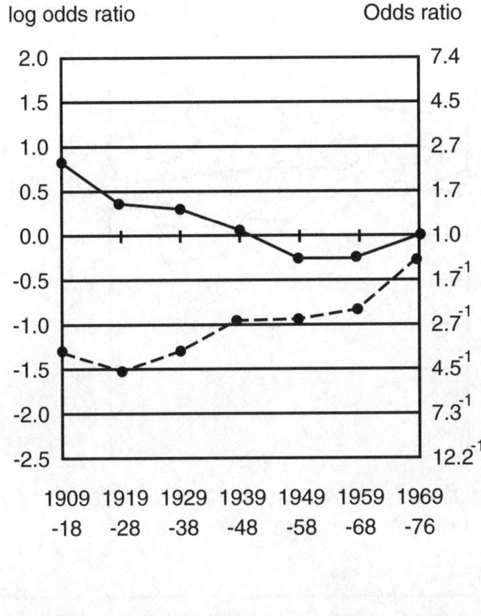


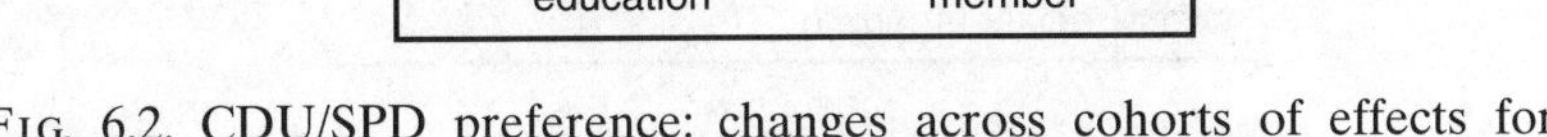


Fig. 6.2. CDU/SPD preference: changes across cohorts of effects for higher education and union membership

of the working class generally declines.[10] This observation is in accordance with the previous findings. Taken alone it does not help us yet to decide whether the non-working classes have moved closer to the SPD or whether the distance of workers to the CDU has declined from cohort to cohort. In both cases, we would find a convergence of the various class lines towards the zero line for the working class (the reference category). However, a closer examination shows that the extent of the convergence clearly varies among classes. For the petty bourgeoisie and the administrative service class, the *rapprochement* with the working class is relatively small. It is much larger for the other classes, in particular for the expert and the social service segments of the service class. In the post-Second World War cohorts, the social service segment is even more on the side of the SPD than the traditional allies of this party. If it was primarily the working class that had changed its party orientation, we should have found

[10] The figure does not show the estimates for the experts and social services in the youngest cohort because they are based on very small numbers.

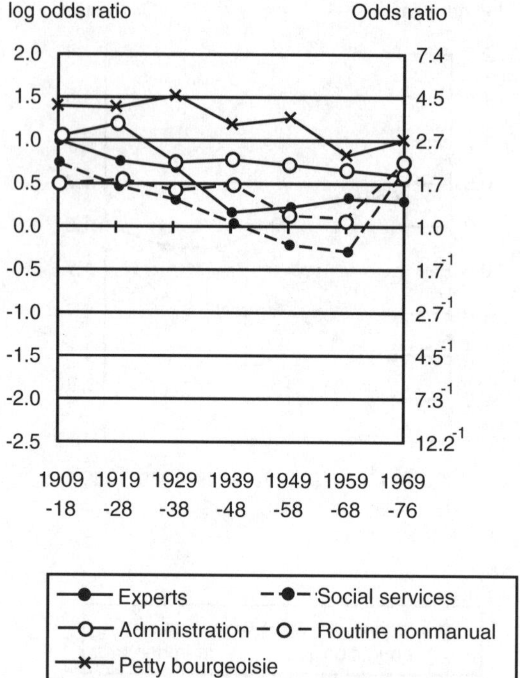


FIG. 6.3. Changes across cohorts of class effects on CDU versus SPD preference; classes contrasted to working class

a pattern of parallel convergence. This is clearly not the case. The picture is dominated by an increasingly divergent pattern of voting preferences among the non-working classes. In the succession of cohorts, the differences in party preferences, particularly among the three segments of the service class, become much larger. The declining gap between the manual workers and the nonmanual classes thus appears to be a consequence of a move by particular nonmanual classes towards the SPD rather than a result of an embourgeoisement of workers' party orientations (see also Klingemann 1984; Pappi 1986).

It is also interesting to note the variation in the time at which the trend curve turns into a more or less horizontal line for each of the classes. For the administrative service class, this happens in the 1929–38 cohort; for the experts, in the 1939–48 cohort; and for the social services, the decline continues up to the 1959–68 cohort. It is thus somewhat misleading to aggregate the cohorts across the same dividing line for all classes. Aggregating those born before the Second World War on the one hand, and those born in 1939 or later on the other, seems to be the least distorting option. For

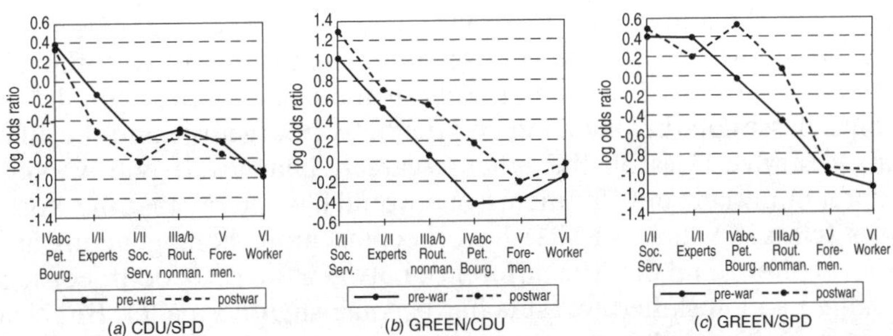


FIG. 6.4. Class effects on voting preferences for pre-war and postwar cohorts; classes contrasted to administrative service class

those born before 1939, the voting preferences of the nonmanual wage-earning classes are relatively similar and clearly more pro-CDU than the voting preferences of the working class. Among those born later, voting preferences among the service classes vary much more. The administrative service class keeps its alliance with the CDU while all others are much closer to the SPD.

Figure 6.4 shows selected results from model 4.2, in which cohorts have indeed been aggregated along this dividing line. However, attention is now directed to the diverging voting pattern among the segments of the service class. The zero line now stands for the administrative service class. The entries for the other classes show how they differ from the administrative service class in their party orientation and how they differ from one another. In each of the party contrasts shown in Figure 6.4(*a*)–(*c*), voters born before the Second World War (solid lines) are distinguished from those born later (broken lines). A first glance at these figures reveals that the social classes differ in their choice between the Greens and one of the major parties (Fig. 6.4(*b*) and (*c*)) at least as much as in their choice between the CDU and SPD (Fig. 6.4(*a*)). Secondly, in all contrasts the class-specific pattern of preferences is in general relatively similar for the pre-war and the postwar cohorts. For the following discussion of the results it is important to note that, in order to facilitate the interpretation of the findings, the succession of classes on the horizontal axes varies in Figure 6.4(*a*)–(*c*).

For the CDU/SPD choice (Fig. 6.4(*a*)), we again find considerable differences among the various segments of the service class. In the pre-war cohorts, the experts are still rather close to the administrative service class (which is defined as the reference category; the value of the effect for this class is thus by definition zero). In the postwar cohorts, they become more similar to voters holding social service jobs, and together with them they move towards the workers' party. Particularly in the younger cohorts, members of the administrative service class are now clearly closer to the voting preferences of the petty bourgeoisie than to those of any other class. The voting pattern of the antagonists of the classical class conflict—the working classes on the one hand and the petty bourgeoisie and the administrative service class on the other—scarcely changes. If one wanted to interpret minuscule developments, one would have to say that the working classes (classes V and VI/VII) have become more homogeneous in the younger cohorts and that the difference between the petty bourgeoisie and the skilled and unskilled workers has become slightly smaller. But clearly the most significant change between the pre-war and postwar cohorts concerning the classical class cleavage must be seen in the two large and identifiable segments of the service class—the experts and the social service professionals—narrowing the gap with the working class.

If we now move to the 'new politics' and contrast preferences for the CDU with those for the Greens in Figure 6.4(*b*), we find, among the pre-war cohorts, the largest gaps between the social services and the experts on the one hand and the other classes on the other. Here the workers and the petty bourgeoisie are on common ground: both dislike the Greens and prefer the CDU. The administrative service class and the routine non-manuals are relatively closer to the working class than to the experts and social services in their dislike of Green politics, while the experts and social services are the Greens' most decided supporters among the pre-war cohorts. For the postwar cohorts, we know from the cohort main effects that there is a general trend away from the major parties towards the Greens, but for all the classes explicitly shown in Figure 4*b* this trend is in fact stronger than for the reference class, the administrative service class. This move is particularly strong for the petty bourgeoisie and the routine nonmanual class.

If the choice is between the Greens and the SPD (Fig. 6.4(*c*)), once again the social services and the experts are the classes most in favour of the Greens, while members of the working class are their extreme opponents. Only in the older cohorts does the working class have some allies among the routine nonmanual class, while in this contrast the petty bourgeoisie and the administrative service class are to be found on the side of the Greens rather than among the supporters of the SPD. From the pre-war to the postwar cohorts we find again a class-specific *rapprochement* towards the Greens. As in the Green/CDU contrast, the largest moves towards the Greens are made by the petty bourgeoisie and the routine nonmanual class. There is scarcely any change for any of the segments of the service class or the working classes.

The findings presented so far would thus suggest the following conclusions. Concerning the traditional class cleavage, not much has changed except for the fact that the expert and social service segments of the service class have clearly approached the party of the workers among voters born and raised after the Second World War. The 'new politics' appears to have clear class dimensions as well. The social services and expert segments of the service class appear to constitute a class core of Green voting even in the pre-war cohorts. The success of Green recruiting among the other classes varies depending on the extent to which these classes have traditionally been allied with a specific party.

The working class, traditionally linked strongly with the SPD, clearly remains the most reliable supporter of this party if the choice is between the SPD and the Greens. The workers' opposition to the Greens becomes even clearer from the contrast between the CDU and the Greens. Of these two, workers prefer to affiliate with the petty bourgeoisie—their antagonist in the traditional class cleavage—and to vote for the CDU rather than join the Green segments of the service class. The reverse is true for the petty bourgeoisie. Choosing between the CDU and the Greens, this class gives the strongest support of all classes to the CDU, at least in the pre-war cohorts. But in choosing between the SPD and the Greens, the petty bourgeoisie affiliates with the core groups of Green voters rather than with its antagonist in the traditional class cleavage. The distance of the petty bourgeoisie from the Greens declines among the postwar-born cohorts. The management and administrative segment of the service class has voting preferences most like those of the petty bourgeoisie. However, it stands somewhat further away from the CDU than the petty bourgeoisie and does not follow the latter's move towards the Greens. The routine non-manual class is relatively close to the SPD in all contrasts among the pre-war cohorts, but—like the petty bourgeoisie—voters from this class among the postwar cohorts turn more towards the Greens than do voters from other classes.

## *Is Green Voting Class-Based or Value-Driven?*

The emergence and stabilization of the Green Party in Germany is most often explained in terms of new politics and the rise of postmaterialist values which are supposed to have replaced traditional class politics and materialist values. I have questioned this interpretation and underlined the class basis of Green voting. A number of central elements of the political ideology of the Green Party closely correspond to the claims for autonomy and the anti-bureaucratic orientations of the voters in expert and social service positions of the service class. In this sense, their preference for the Greens can be interpreted as interest-based in ways similar to the political affiliations of the working class or the petty bourgeoisie. The fact that the management and administrative segment of the service class shows similar preferences to the petty bourgeoisie supports this interpretation. The three segments of the service class primarily differ in their participation in bureaucratic power, and their different party orientations reflect this fact.

As discussed above, one crucial objection to such an interpretation is occupational self-selection. Having a job in one of the three segments of the service class may be a matter of self-selection of persons differing a priori in personal characteristics, and it might be these characteristics that explain both their choice of a specific domain of work within the service class and their Green preferences. For all the variables that we have controlled in the previous analyses, such a self-selection or spurious effect interpretation can be ruled out. The measured class effects and their changes across cohorts are net of the effects of all variables controlled in the model. This is particularly pertinent for higher education, which points to a pattern of Green voting even in pre-war cohorts and does so even more in postwar cohorts. But—as always—there might be other factors producing self-selection. As the 'new politics' are repeatedly related to the growth of postmaterialist value orientations, this should be a prime candidate to demolish the findings. To the extent that the inclination towards postmaterialist values *in toto* affects people in a given cohort, this development is caught by the cohort main effects of our models. But still the objection is that 'Postmaterialism is not a *product* of the "new class" but, rather, *shapes* the career choices of "young professionals", civil servants, managers and politicians' (Inglehart 1990: 67; emphasis added). 'Postmaterialist orientations are antecedent to, not consequent upon, occupation' (Scarbrough 1995: 149). If this is the crucial mechanism which explains Green Party preferences, then class differences should disappear when we control for postmaterialist value preferences. However, to the extent that class differences remain after such controls, the value interpretation remains deficient.

Figure 6.5(*a*)–(*c*) shows the results of this crucial test. For this figure I have replicated exactly the same analyses as for Figure 6.4(*a*)–(*c*), except for the addition of Inglehart's four-item postmaterialism index to the predictor variables in the multinomial party-choice model 4.2 of Table 6.3. Figure 6.5(*a*)–(*c*) now contains, for both the pre-war and postwar cohorts, two party preference lines: those with black symbols are identical to the lines in Figure 6.4(*a*)–(*c*) and correspond to the analyses without controlling for postmaterialism. As before, solid lines refer to pre-war cohorts, broken lines to postwar cohorts. The lines scarcely differ from each other. In all the contrasts, postmaterialist value orientations at best explain a very tiny fraction of the various classes' party preferences. The most systematic difference between the two analyses can be seen in the contrasts of both the SPD and the CDU with the Greens. If we control for postmaterialism, the voters with social service jobs appear to be slightly

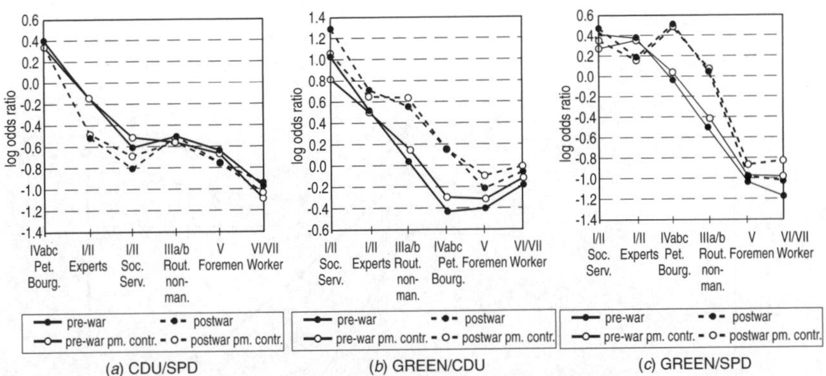


FIG. 6.5. Class effects on voting preferences for pre-war and postwar cohorts with and without control of postmaterialism

less pro-Green once their strong postmaterialist value orientations are taken into account. The contrary is true for workers: when their low levels of postmaterialism are taken into account, their voting pattern becomes slightly less anti-Green.

In Figure 6.6 we see how controlling for postmaterialism affects the cohort main effects for the various party contrasts. They are clearly more strongly affected than were the class effects in Figure 6.5(*a*)–(*c*). The larger the cohort effects are before controlling for postmaterialism, the more they decline when controlling for it.

The growing diffusion of postmaterialist value orientations among the younger cohorts thus explains part of the increased preference for the Greens among the younger cohorts and also part of their increased preference for the SPD over the CDU. This finding also indicates that the Inglehart index is indeed able to capture the effect of value change on party preferences. If class effects do not change when we control for postmaterialism, this cannot be completely due to the inability of the measures used to capture value change—even though better measurement instruments might be more efficient at capturing such changes.

The crucial result for the specific problem raised in this paper, however, is the one found in Figure 6.5(*a*)–(*c*). Postmaterialist value orientations do not explain the class bases of voting preferences, not even those for the Greens. There may be other sources of occupational self-selection. But at least I have ruled out the possibility that one of the prime predictors in the value-driven explanation of the Green vote also drives the process through which a class-based voting pattern in the different segments of the service class comes into being.

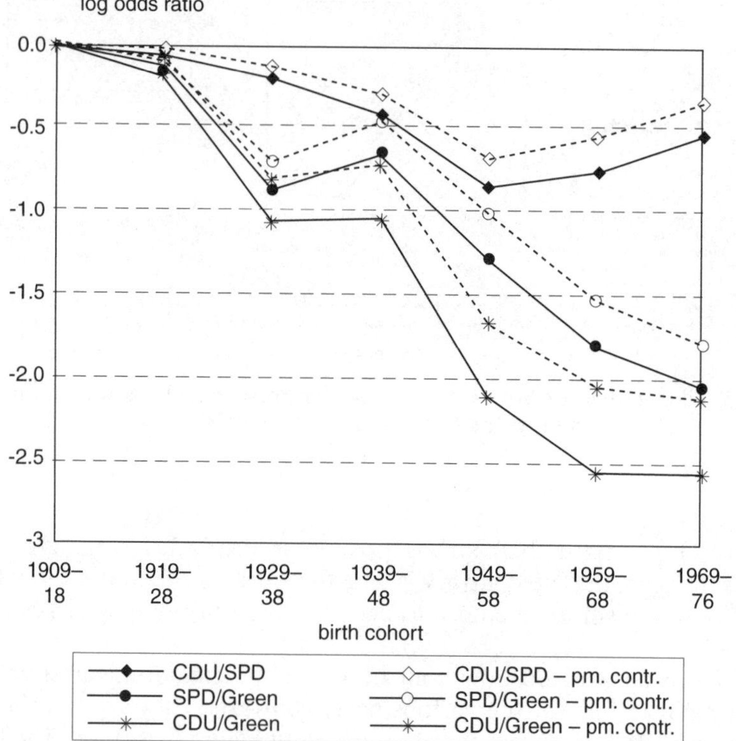


FIG. 6.6. Vote intention by cohort with and without controlling for value orientation

## SUMMARY AND CONCLUSIONS

The most relevant findings of this chapter are the following.

- Once other factors are controlled for, gender, employment status, and affiliation to the Christian churches appear to be long-term constants in their effects on party preferences of the West German electorate.
- Across the board, cohorts differ very strongly in their party preferences. In particular, the postwar cohorts are less likely to support the CDU and the SPD and more likely to support the Greens. The losses among the postwar cohorts are particularly high for the CDU because these cohorts are also more likely to prefer the SPD and the FDP to the CDU.
- Highly educated voters have changed their position with regard to the classical class parties. Among the pre-war cohorts, the *Bildungsbürgertum* has a clear anti-socialist orientation. It stands on the side of the

CDU, the FDP, and the Greens rather than the SPD. Among the postwar cohorts, the highly educated have moved to the left and have become even more Green.

- The three segments of the service class clearly differ from one another in party preferences. Managers and administrators share the party orientations of the petty bourgeoisie quite closely. The experts and, in particular, the professionals and semi-professionals in the social and cultural services strongly differ from them. This is true with respect to their position towards the parties of the classical class cleavage, and even more so with respect to preferences for the Greens. The social and cultural service professionals represent a kind of class core of Green voting.
- Among the antagonists of the classical class cleavage—the working class and the petty bourgeoisie—there is most likely some *rapprochement* from the pre-war to the postwar cohorts, but the changes in *direct* class effects are rather small. The more important change is that the strong affiliation of union members with the SPD declines in the postwar cohorts. This decline, however, is far from dramatic.
- From the pre-war to the postwar cohorts, the contours of the classical class cleavage—the alliances of the petty bourgeoisie, the administrators, and managers with the CDU and of the working class with the SPD—remain rather stable. But the experts and the social services move closer to the working-class party.
- We also find the alliances with or against the Greens to be relatively stable. The professionals and the semi-professionals stay with the Greens. The workers are most clearly against them. In the competition between the Greens and the CDU, the managers and administrators remained most loyal to the CDU; the experts and social service professionals moved away from the CDU to even closer proximity with the Greens. The petty bourgeoisie and the routine nonmanual class made the largest move towards the Greens.
- The growth of postmaterialist value orientations among the more recent cohorts explains some, but only a minor part, of the cohort shifts in party preferences; it explains practically nothing of the location of the various classes in the party space and of their moves within it.

What then are the more general conclusions we can draw from these results? For West Germany, claims of a markedly reduced relevance of class position for party choice would appear to be rather misplaced. The only change that could be interpreted as dealignment with respect to the classical class cleavage is the reduced impact of union membership on the choice between the SPD and the CDU, encountered among postwar cohorts. Even this change, however, cannot unmistakably be interpreted as dealignment. Postwar cohorts include respondents interviewed at rather young ages.[11] Their average duration of union membership is therefore much shorter than membership among pre-war cohorts. The smaller impact on party choice among postwar cohorts could therefore result from a shorter period of union membership rather than a general decline in the significance of membership. The connections between union membership and vote for the working-class party among the pre-war cohorts might also be particularly strong because of the common experience of persecution during the Nazi years. Given that we cannot decide between these explanations on the basis of the data presented here, an interpretation strictly in terms of dealignment seems premature.

Instead, the data argue for a quite astonishing constancy in the differences in party orientation among the antagonists of the classical class cleavage. We further find various groups of the so-called new middle classes located in a clearly identifiable and theoretically plausible position between the CDU and SPD. The fractions distinguished among the new middle classes also have clearly distinct positions with respect to the 'new politics', consistent with interests linked to their position in the class structure.

The changes observed in the association between class position and party preferences are quite consistent with the simple model of interests I have proposed. The differences we observe between the pre-war and the postwar cohorts can mostly be accounted for with a few changing elements on the supply side: the changes in the programmatic orientation of the SPD and the emergence of the Green Party. There is little need to revise the simplifying assumption of no demand-side change, except perhaps for two points. One concerns the declining role found for union membership in the classical cleavage. However, as argued before, it is not clear how to interpret this finding, and union membership relates to the mediating institutions between class and party rather than to the class conditions themselves. The second finding, not expected from the simple model, relates to the declining distance of the petty bourgeoisie from the Greens, a finding which must be clarified through further research.[12]

[11] Given the design of the study, the oldest ten-year group of the postwar cohorts (1939–48) was 28–37 years old in the first survey (1976). This cohort reached age 46 to 55 in the last survey (1994). The 1949–58 cohort is surveyed from age 18–27 to age 36–45; the next cohort is aged 18–35, and the youngest 18–25.

[12] The finding could be the result of a changing composition of this class: with the sectoral transformation, the proportion of self-employed workers in social service occupations might have increased. Even if self-employed, they are partly dependent on public finances and the welfare-state bureaucracies. This and other similarities with social service occupations might bring this group to party preferences similar to those of the professionals in the service class.

The elaboration of the Erikson–Goldthorpe schema proposed here and the findings obtained also suggest a reformulation of the assumptions of the so-called 'new politics' approach. Usually the 'new politics' are seen as a development that more or less replaces the class cleavage. New issues (postmaterialism, the environment, women's rights, and so on) and new political actors (new forms of political participation, new social movements, new parties) are seen as having replaced or at least weakened the old class-based political struggles (Hildebrandt and Dalton 1977; Dalton 1996; Poguntke 1989). I do not contest that new issues and new actors have emerged. But they have not seriously weakened the old tensions of the old cleavage, and more importantly, the 'new politics' appear to have a clear class basis, at least in Germany. Neither the old nor the new class cleavages appear to be seriously affected by value orientations, at least not those which can be captured by Inglehart's scale. Instead, we find a core class of Green voters. Interestingly enough, the class most opposed to the Greens is one of the key players in the old cleavage: the working class. The 'new politics' cleavage is thus at least partly one between old and new classes.

Another interesting observation is how the antagonists of the old cleavage form alliances when it comes to choices involving the 'new politics'. The workers are on the side of the petty bourgeoisie if the choice is between the Greens and the CDU. The petty bourgeoisie is on the side of the core classes of Green voters if the choice is between the Greens and the SPD. One explanation for this lack of reciprocity may be found in the internal heterogeneity of both the working class and the petty bourgeoisie. The petty bourgeoisie, particularly among younger cohorts, probably includes quite a number of self-employed workers in the semi-professions, who should align rather close to the social service segment of the service class. At the same time, social mobility studies have shown that quite a substantial proportion of working-class members grew up in peasant families, which could explain their conservative inclinations.

If the findings thus suggest a revision of some common assumptions of the 'new politics' discussion, they also question the assumption of the generally conservative political orientation of the service class, at least in the German context. First, they cast doubt on the assumption that the service class at large has a *homogeneous* political orientation. The orientations of its different segments clearly differ. Those in management and administration indeed have conservative preferences, but the experts and in particular those employed in the social and cultural services associate with either the left or the Green camp, at least when it comes to preferences among the parties of the contemporary German party system. Goldthorpe defends his expectation of a basically conservative political orientation of the service class by pointing to its privileged position, which its members should want to defend. The defence of interest is a plausible argument. But the question is, which interests precisely they would attempt to defend and whether this varies for the different segments of the service class: autonomy (at work) and limitation of apparatuses of control in society; the enhanced delivery of social and cultural services; investments in education through which they have themselves gained their privileged position and through which they may aspire to secure a similar position for their children? Some of these claims would appear very compatible with left and Green positions, and some are rather more 'conservative'. It is evident that we need more research on precisely how members of the different segments of the service class see their interests and how they are linked to the policies of the various parties; in particular, we need further investigation into potential differences between the new and old classes' reasons for preferring the SPD.

Moreover, I have only studied the class bases of party preferences. The 'new politics', however, have also been associated with new forms of political participation. There is not much research in Germany on how the latter are related to the various service class segments I have distinguished here. But it would not be surprising to find a class-based selectivity in social movement participation and in the practice of unconventional forms of political action similar to those, for instance, in The Netherlands (Kriesi 1989, De Graaf and Steijn 1997).

A further limitation of the present study is obviously the fact that the survey data used here only cover a relatively short and recent period in postwar German history. A decline in class voting may have occurred prior to the period examined in this study. As discussed above, there are studies covering a longer period of observation time and showing such a decline.[13] None of these studies, however, used a similarly refined class conception, studied the party choices in a similarly refined way, or controlled other factors affecting party choice in similar detail. Given the major social structural transformation that has occurred in postwar Germany, there are many factors that could have caused an apparent decline in relatively 'crude' measures of class voting. Moreover, if there were a long-term decline in class voting, why should it level off in 1976? At the very least, it would appear that the 'old' class cleavage has been complemented by a new class-linked cleavage structure precisely in the realm of 'new politics'.

[13] See the debate between Schnell and Kohler (1995, 1997), Müller (1997), and Jagodzinski and Quandt (1997). It should be noted that by controlling for cohort membership, the current analysis includes a time dimension stretching back to the interwar years. As cohort membership has a strong impact on party preference, in particular with respect to the so-called new politics, long-term declines in the class cleavages of party preferences should be captured by class effects varying with cohorts. However, it is largely the cohort main effects and not the cohort–class interaction effects that vary, and when the latter do so they mainly point into the direction of larger rather than smaller differences between fractions of the service class.

# 7

# Changes in Class Voting in Norway, 1957–1989

KRISTEN RINGDAL AND KJELL HINES

## INTRODUCTION

The literature on the social basis of voting behaviour, and on class voting in particular, is divided in terms of empirical findings. On the one hand, a series of analyses seem to show that structural cleavages in general have become less important for voting behaviour in the Western democracies (see Franklin *et al.* 1992), or more particularly, that class voting is declining (see Clark *et al.* 1993), while on the other, there are studies challenging this conclusion (see Hout *et al.* 1995). This chapter contributes to this debate by examining claims about the decline in class voting in Norway presented by Nieuwbeerta and De Graaf in this volume and the conclusions of previous studies of the social basis of voting in Norway which have adopted more traditional approaches to assessing levels of class voting (Valen 1981: ch. 7; Valen and Aardal 1983: ch. 3; Valen 1992; Listhaug 1993, 1989: ch. 3).

These studies all conclude that class has become less significant for voting behaviour, although it is still of some importance. However, they have analysed only the Socialist versus non-Socialist vote, often employing only a two-class (manual–nonmanual) measure of class position. In this chapter we examine class position and voting preferences in greater detail than has previously been the case. The main research question to be pursued is the following: do patterns of relative class voting in Norway change over time? If so, is the pattern of change best described as trend-

Earlier versions of this chapter were presented at the conference on The End of Class Politics, Centre for European Studies, Nuffield College Oxford, 13–14 February 1995 and at the Social Science History Association annual meeting, Chicago, 16–19 November 1995. The data used in this study come from the Norwegian Election Studies, 1957–89, provided by the Norwegian Social Science Data Service (NSD). Stein Rokkan (1957), Henry Valen (1965, 1977, 1981, 1985, 1989), Willy Martinussen (1969), Ragnar Waldahl (1973), and Bernt Aardal (1985, 1989) were responsible for planning the surveys. The fieldwork was carried out by the Norwegian Gallup Institute (1957–73), and by Statistics Norway (1977–89). None of the above is responsible for the analyses in this chapter or for our conclusions.

less fluctuation, or are there any systematic trends towards dealignment or realignment?

In this introduction we first briefly review relevant previous research. We then describe our own improvements on these approaches. As a key feature of our approach is the use of a more differentiated measure of voting than earlier studies, we then present a summary of relevant aspects of the Norwegian party system.

### *Previous Studies*

In his chapter on Norway in Franklin *et al.* (1992), Henry Valen examined the relationship between social structure and voting behaviour and included in his models a manual–nonmanual measure of class position and a left versus non-left measure of vote. His main conclusion was that the Norwegian data 'confirm the cross-national trend towards a declining relationship between left voting and social structure. . . . The analysis suggests that the decline of the left vote is largely due to structural changes' (Valen 1992: 326). He further concludes that the post-1945 birth cohorts differed substantially from earlier cohorts in their voting patterns. Although Valen found no support for the idea that a new cleavage based upon private versus public employment emerged during this period, he argued that the heated debate about Norway's entry into the EEC in 1970–2 was particularly disruptive of traditional party loyalties and the linkage between voting and structural characteristics.

Listhaug (1993, 1989) expanded on this approach by presenting trends for four indexes of class voting, again based upon a dichotomous vote, but using a four-class model. One of these indexes is equivalent to the Alford index, while the remaining three derive from comparisons of the level of Socialist voting among the 'old' and 'new' middle classes and farmers, with the Socialist vote among workers.[1] All of these indexes show a decline in class voting. The most stable pattern of class differences is between the old middle class and the working class. This measure is constant or weakly increasing until the 1980s. Listhaug interpreted differences between these measures as indicating that class differences between the old middle class and the farmers on the one hand, and the working class, on the other hand, are larger than between the new middle class and the workers. He also performed logistic regression analyses separately for the 1957 to 1985 election studies employing a dichotomous vote as the dependent variable and

[1] The 'old middle class' consists of self-employed, business owners, and members of the free professions. The 'new middle class' consists of salaried employees, clerical workers, and civil servants.

with class represented by the manual–nonmanual divide as one of the regressors. On this basis he concluded that the effect of class has weakened over time and that 'The long term factor which accounts for the decline in class voting is primarily the deterioration of socialist support in the working class', while the new middle class shows a constant socialist support throughout the period (1989: 43). He further argued that the growth of the size of the new middle class has contributed considerably to the decline in class voting as measured by the Alford index.

Thus both of the main studies of class voting in Norway indicate a trend towards dealignment, both in terms of absolute and relative class voting. They are limited in focus, however, in that they study dealignment using a dichotomous measure of vote and in some cases a similarly restricted measure of class position. Here, as earlier analyses have indicated that the level of aggregation of the party variable influences the results obtained, we use four party groups to represent the Norwegian multi-party system.[2] We also use a pooled dataset of all election surveys from 1957–89 which allows us to estimate trend parameters, whereas previous studies have analysed each election survey separately. As with many of the other chapters in this volume, we measure class position using a version of the seven-class schema devised by Erikson and Goldthorpe (1992*a*), which provides a more detailed evaluation of class effects.

The measure of class voting adopted is the total class-by-vote-by-election association. This definition corresponds to the idea of *total* class voting as defined in Hout *et al.* (1995 and Chapter 4 in this volume) and which is distinguished from *traditional* class voting, which refers to the tendency of the working class to vote for parties on the left and for the nonmanual classes to vote for parties on the right. (Although, unlike Hout *et al.*, our analysis does not include nonvoters.) To analyse the relationship between class and vote we employ a multinominal logit model, which allows the use of both discrete and continuous control variables. In our earlier analysis we have studied the class-by-vote association in isolation without controls for other variables.

[2] In an initial analysis of patterns of class voting in Norway (Ringdal and Hines 1995), we distinguished between three party groups (Socialist, Centre, and Conservative) and seven social classes. A topological model with eight different class-voting parameters was used to picture trends in class voting. Although the trends did not conform to a common pattern, two central parameters, the tendency of the working class to vote for socialist parties, and the tendency for the upper service class to vote for conservative parties, showed a steady decline over the period, as did a parameter indicating the aversion of unskilled workers to voting for Conservative parties. On the other hand, the tendency for farmers to support the Centre parties seemed to strengthen over time.

### *The Background to the Party System and the Construction of the Party Choice Variable*

The party system that existed from the 1920s to the 1960s can be described as a five-party system typical of the Nordic countries, consisting of the Conservatives, Liberals, Social Democrats, Agrarians, and the Communists. The history of the Norwegian multi-party system is illustrated in Figure 7.1. All recent party splits are represented in the figure, whereas two early defections from the Liberal Party are omitted. The Conservatives (*Høyre*) and the Liberals (*Venstre*) were both founded in 1884. The dominant party since the Second World War, the Labour Party (*Arbeiderpartiet*), was founded in 1887, but was not represented in the Storting until 1903. The Agrarian Party (*Bondepartiet*), later the Centre Party (*Senterpartiet*), was founded in 1920. The Labour Party joined the Comintern in 1919—the only party among the Nordic social democratic parties to do so—but left in 1923, and those members who wanted to remain formed the Norwegian Communist Party (*Norges Kommunistiske Parti*). A minor deviation from the five-party model is the Christian People's Party (*Kristelig Folkeparti*) founded in 1933 by a group of religious fundamentalists who broke with the Liberal Party.

The next party formation did not occur until 1961. Part of the Labour Party's left wing was excluded from the party and decided to form the Socialist People's Party (*Sosialistisk Folkeparti*). The reason for this split was the controversy within the Labour Party following from Norway's entry into NATO in 1949. A left wing also emerged within the Socialist People's Party when the party's youth organization adopted a doctrinarian Maoist position. This faction left the party at the party congress in 1969

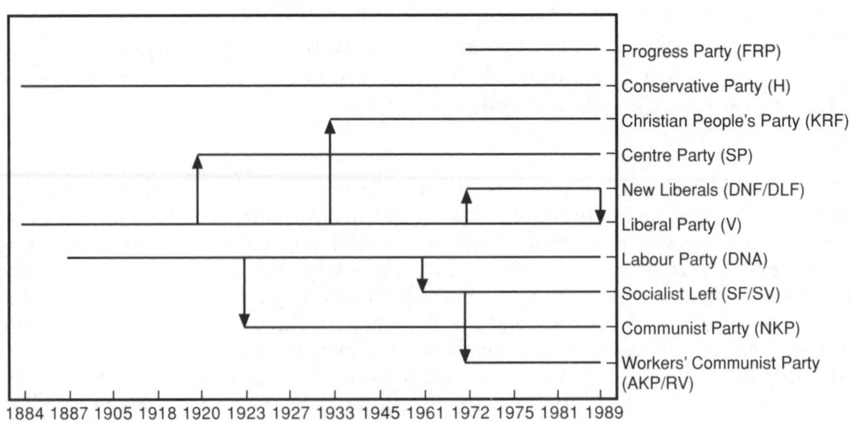


FIG. 7.1. The Norwegian multi-party system

to form the Workers' Communist Party (AKP) in 1972. Their electoral support has, however, remained marginal.

A further fragmentation of the party system followed the EEC referendum in 1972. Those who favoured EEC membership in the Liberal Party left and formed the New People's Party, later renamed the Liberal People's Party (DLF). The parties were reunited again before the general election in 1989. The Liberal Party has, however, had considerable problems with regaining their former electoral support. The groups on the left of the Labour Party were also affected by the EEC issue. Partly encouraged by the success in the referendum, the Socialist People's Party, the Communist Party, and former members of the Labour Party who were opposed to EEC membership formed a new party, the Socialist Left Party, in 1975. However, the Communists were not willing to dissolve their own party, and therefore left the unification process. In 1973, a new party to the right of the Conservative Party was also founded. It was named after its founder, Anders Lange, and later renamed the Progress Party (*Fremskrittspartiet*).

The pattern of voting displayed in each election survey since 1957 is shown in Table 7.1.[3] It can be seen that a long period of stable Labour government ended in 1965 with the victory of the coalition of non-socialist parties. The Labour Party also lost its campaign for EEC membership in the referendum in 1972. The result was a heavy loss of votes in the 1973 general election, mainly to the Socialist Left Party. From the mid-1970s, the Conservatives managed to attract working-class voters, as well as breaking some regional barriers to their support. The result was a gradual erosion of the left as well as the centre. The Progress Party ran a successful campaign at the local and regional elections in 1987, and gained voters particularly from the Conservatives. The success of the Progress Party lasted through the general election in 1989. The Socialist Left Party was also successful with the election campaign in 1989, and strengthened its position, particularly among public sector employees.

Given the evident complexity of developments in Norwegian politics over the years, it is inevitable that some simplification is required. A common depiction of the Norwegian party system is as three blocs of parties. The Labour Party and the Conservatives form the main competing parties, while the Liberal Party, the Centre Party, and the Christians form the political centre—although these three parties have participated in governing coalitions with the Conservatives since the middle of the 1960s. However, using three party groups blurs interesting differences between the Socialist Left and the Labour Party. The former has had a different recruitment profile from the Labour Party, attracting voters from

[3] The party choice variable controls for actual turnout for all elections except for that in 1957.

TABLE 7.1. *The marginal distributions of respondents' vote (%), the Norwegian Election Studies, 1957–1989 (N = 13,816)*

| Party | 1957 | 1965 | 1969 | 1973 | 1977 | 1981 | 1985 | 1989 |
|---|---|---|---|---|---|---|---|---|
| Communist | 1.0 | 0.6 | 0.6 | 0.7 | 0.5 | 0.8 | 0.5 | 0.0 |
| Socialist Left | 0.0 | 4.0 | 2.6 | 8.2 | 3.9 | 3.9 | 4.9 | 10.2 |
| Labour | 45.2 | 38.7 | 42.4 | 33.6 | 37.3 | 31.7 | 32.3 | 28.1 |
| Liberals | 7.5 | 9.2 | 8.0 | 6.0 | 4.2 | 4.3 | 3.5 | 3.6 |
| Christians | 8.0 | 5.0 | 6.8 | 11.3 | 9.8 | 7.3 | 8.3 | 7.4 |
| Centre Party | 7.6 | 10.8 | 11.8 | 13.6 | 7.9 | 6.0 | 5.9 | 5.1 |
| Conservatives | 12.8 | 15.7 | 14.5 | 12.1 | 19.8 | 26.6 | 25.7 | 18.4 |
| Progressives | 0.0 | 0.0 | 0.0 | 2.6 | 1.0 | 3.7 | 3.0 | 9.4 |
| Other parties | 0.0 | 0.0 | 0.0 | 0.0 | 0.3 | 0.3 | 0.3 | 1.6 |
| Did not vote | 7.3 | 9.9 | 8.0 | 10.0 | 13.1 | 12.7 | 12.0 | 10.9 |
| No answer | 10.6 | 6.1 | 5.1 | 2.0 | 2.3 | 2.8 | 3.6 | 5.4 |
| Total | 100.0 | 100.0 | 99.8 | 100.1 | 100.1 | 100.1 | 100.0 | 100.1 |
| N | 1,544 | 1,751 | 1,595 | 1,225 | 1,730 | 1,596 | 2,180 | 2,195 |
| Four party groups | | | | | | | | |
| Socialist Left | 1.3 | 5.5 | 3.6 | 10.0 | 5.2 | 5.6 | 6.4 | 12.4 |
| Labour | 55.0 | 46.1 | 48.9 | 38.2 | 44.2 | 37.6 | 38.4 | 34.2 |
| Centre | 28.2 | 29.7 | 30.8 | 35.1 | 25.9 | 20.8 | 21.0 | 19.5 |
| Conservative | 15.5 | 18.7 | 16.8 | 16.7 | 24.7 | 36.0 | 34.2 | 33.9 |
| Total | 100.0 | 100.0 | 100.1 | 100.0 | 100.0 | 100.0 | 100.0 | 100.0 |
| N | 1,268 | 1,470 | 1,385 | 1,077 | 1,459 | 1,345 | 1,833 | 1,801 |

*Notes*: Parties: Communist: NPK and AKP; Socialist Left: SF, SV, Sosialistisk valgforbund; Labour: DNA; Liberals: V, DLF, DNF; Centre Party: SP, Bondepartiet; Conservatives: H; Progressives: Fremskrittspartiet, Anders Langes parti; Did not vote: controlled against public register except for the 1957 election. Missing values in 1957 due to sample attrition in the post-election interview are estimated by pre-election indication of vote.

The four party groups: Socialist Left: NPK, AKP, SF, SV, Sosialistisk valgforbund; Labour: DNA; Centre: V, DLF, DNF, SP, KrF; Conservative: H, Fremskrittspartiet, Anders Langes parti.

the intellectuals as well as from the working class. We therefore incorporate this distinction into our coding of voting preferences. We thus have the following party groups: Socialist Left, Labour, Centre, and Conservative. Respondents who did not vote or did not answer the question on party choice are excluded from the analysis.

## DATA AND METHODS

### *Data: The Norwegian Election Studies*

The data used in this analysis are taken from the Norwegian Election Studies covering the Storting (parliamentary) elections.[4] All surveys were

[4] The 1977–89 Norwegian Election Studies are documented in Kiberg and Strømsnes (1992). The 1957 survey is documented in Leipart and Sande (1981).

designed to provide representative samples of the population of Norwegian voters. However, some of them form part of panels which results in smaller or larger overlap across the samples. Thus in the 1965–1969–1973 panel there is substantial overlap between the 1965 and the 1969 surveys, and the 1969 and 1973 surveys overlap completely. There are also panel designs involved in the 1981 to 1989 surveys, although the overlap is smaller.

### *The Measurement of Social Class*

The point of departure for this analysis, as with most other chapters in this volume, is Erikson and Goldthorpe's (1992*a*) widely used class schema. Because of the far from ideal occupational classification used in the Norwegian election studies, the resulting classes are not precisely comparable to Erikson–Goldthorpe classes. This is clearly problematic for cross-national comparisons such as that presented in Chapter 2, but less so for the analysis of trends within Norway where the main point is to obtain comparability across surveys conducted at different points in time. Thus, although more detailed occupational information is available in the 1981–93 surveys, we gave priority to covering a long time period equivalently by using only the occupational information common to all surveys from 1957 to 1989.

Occupational information in the surveys was obtained by showing respondents a card with a list of occupational positions from which they could choose the one which most closely approximated their own, or they could specify 'other'. 'Others' are coded as missing in the datafiles. In 1977, a 14-category card of occupational positions was used, and in 1981, 1985 and 1989, a 10-category card was used. In 1957, occupations were classified into 13 categories, and in 1965, into 55 categories and no cards were shown. Even within the 1965–69–73 panel there are variations in detail. All studies, however, take the 1957 codes as a point of departure. The 55 categories used in 1965, for example, constitute a more detailed version of the scheme developed for the 1957 survey. A satisfactory level of comparability can therefore be obtained by recoding the classifications in the different years to a relatively small set of class categories. The task of creating Erikson–Goldthorpe classes is also facilitated by the availability of information on self-employment (with and without employees) and location in a system of industrial classification in all surveys.

These procedures result in the following class categories: the upper service class (I), consisting of higher-grade professionals, administrators, and officials; the lower service class (II), consisting of lower-grade professionals and administrators; routine nonmanual workers (III); the petty bourgeoisie (IVab); farmers (IVc); skilled manual workers (V–VI); and unskilled manual workers (VIIab).[5] Class position was assigned to each respondent on the basis of his or her currrent occupation. If the respondent was not working at the time of the interview, class is based on his or her former occupation. If this is not available, the respondent is assigned to the class of his or her spouse.

The marginal distributions of social class correspond to the sorts of patterns observed more generally in advanced industrial societies. The upper service class (I) is small at the start of the period (3.5 per cent), but grows to more than 15 per cent by 1977. The lower service class (II) increases from 10 per cent in 1957 to around 15 per cent in the 1980s. Routine non-manual workers increase from 10 per cent in the early 1960s to about 18 per cent in the 1980s. In contrast, the petty bourgeoisie declined from around 9 per cent in 1957 to a low of 4 per cent in the early 1980s. The farmers show the most marked decline, from 17.5 per cent in 1957 to 6.7 per cent in 1989. The percentage of skilled manual workers (V–VI) is rather stable at around 22–24 per cent from the late 1960s onwards. The proportion of unskilled workers fell from about 35 per cent in 1957 to 17–19 per cent in the 1980s.

### *Analysis: The Multinominal Logit Model of Class Voting*

Voting is modelled by means of the multinominal logit model (Maddala 1983: 2.10). Instead of estimating the model simultaneously, we decomposed the model into three separate logistic regressions, corresponding to specified contrasts between the four main party groups.[6] For each dependent variable we estimated fourteen models, a set of seven models without control variables to obtain the gross effects of class and another set controlling for other socio-demographic covariates to obtain the net effects of class. The seven models are:[7]

[5] The manner in which occupations in the primary sector were recorded also creates some problems of comparability. In the 1981–9 studies, the ten categories used to record the respondents' occupational positions do not give information on self-employment in the primary sector separately. Only 'owners of own firms including farming' are singled out and recorded. Self-employed farmers could only be located indirectly by combining the information on occupational position with the information on sector of employment. In this way, self-employed fishermen were also identified and added to class IVc. The remaining people in the 'fishing, hunting' employment sector were added to the 'workers' category.

[6] We also estimated the identical model for the three-way (vote, class, survey) table by means of the Genlog routine in SPSS. The results were very similar to the ones reported in Table 7.3 except for the analysis of the preference of the Socialist Left to the Conservatives, where the extreme negative coefficients for some interaction terms for 1957 became less extreme. Genlog does not, however, handle situations with several additional control variables.

[7] This modelling approach relies heavily upon Hout *et al.* (1995). See their study for complete equations for all models.

1. the null model with only the intercept (gross effects), and intercept and control variables (net effects);
2. the simple trend model with the main effect of year;
3. the model of constant class voting (CCV) which includes the main effect of both year and class;
4. the uniform class differences model, which adds a class-by-year interaction to the CCV model;
5. the linear trend model, which allows the parameters for each class to vary linearly with time measured in four-year periods, starting from 1957;
6. the quadratic trend model, which adds a quadratic term to the linear trend model;
7. the saturated interaction model, which includes the full three-way class-by-vote-by-year interaction.

As the last model produces a large number of estimated parameters, we make use of the kappa index developed by Hout *et al.* (1995) to describe total class voting (see Chapter 4 in this volume). The total kappa is calculated for each year to yield an overall measure of class voting for our preferred models. In addition, separate or partisan kappas are estimated for each of the three distinct class–vote outcomes.

## RESULTS

We start by giving an overview of absolute and relative class voting as they appear in two-by-two class-by-party tables for Norway, 1957–89. We then present a set of logistic regression models to estimate the 'gross' effect of class, that is, without controlling for other variables. Lastly, we introduce controls for sex, age, cohort, education, and region.

### *Trends in Class Voting in Two-by-Two Class-by-Party Analyses*

In Chapter 2, the Scandinavian countries were found to score highest on indexes of class voting. Over time, however, the differences between the Scandinavian countries and other nations were found to have diminished. The results of our initial analysis are similar to those presented by Neuwbeerta and De Graaf (Chapter 2). This can be seen in Figure 7.2, which displays the Alford index and the log odds ratio over the nine surveys. The weakening of absolute class voting may be illustrated by the percentage of the working class (nonmanual) voting for left parties. This figure declined from 78 per cent in 1957 to 57 per cent in 1989. The Alford index starts similarly high at 43 in 1957 and declines monotonously, with one exception, to a low of 15 in 1989. The slope for the log odds ratio is

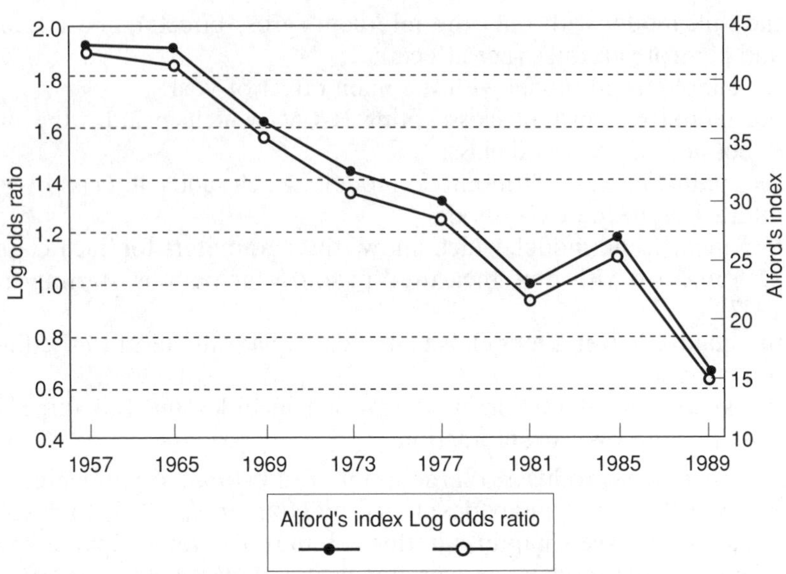


FIG. 7.2. Measures of class voting in two-by-two class–party tables

almost identical to the one for Alford's index. The log odds ratio starts at 1.9 in 1957 and shows a decline over the period. Thus in 1957, the odds of a manual voter voting Socialist was almost seven times higher than for nonmanual voters. By 1989 the same coefficient was only about twice as large. The generally smooth trend in the decline in class voting is somewhat broken, however, by the 1985 figures, which show a temporary resurgence of class voting.[8]

## *Multinomial Models of Class Voting*

The dependent variable in the multinomial model consists of the four voting categories—Socialist Left, Labour, Centre, and Conservative. These are represented by three separate logistic regressions. The dependent variable in the first logistic regression is the log of the probability of voting for

[8] Those who have read our earlier paper on class voting (Ringdal and Hines 1995) may have noticed a couple of differences between seemingly identical presentations of the Alford index and the log odds ratios. In the 1995 paper, the class-voting indices fall more steeply from 1957 to 1965 and they do not show the increase from 1981 to 1985 as seen in Figure 7.2. This discrepancy results from differences in the filtering of cases. Here we have used information on the current and earlier occupations of the respondent and the occupation of the spouse to allocate class positions, whereas in the 1995 paper we only included respondents with a registered occupation at the time of the interview.

the Socialists versus the Conservatives.[9] The second dependent variable is the log of the probability of voting Labour rather than Conservative, and the third dependent variable is the choice between the Centre parties and the Conservatives.

The two main independent variables, class and year of survey, are categorical. Class is decomposed into six dummy variables with class VII, unskilled workers, as the reference category. Year of survey is decomposed into eight dummies with the last one, 1989, as the reference category. The unconstrained interaction between these two categorical covariates is represented by forty-two dummy variables. The primary objective of this paper is to examine changes in these parameters over the time period. This involves testing for significant interaction terms. To avoid capitalizing on type I error, pooled tests for each set of dummies based on the Wald statistic have been performed.

Two sets of seven models were estimated, without control variables to obtain gross effects of class, and with controls to obtain net effects of class. The control variables represent the main socio-demographic factors found to contribute to differences in Norwegian voting behaviour. Region represents the territorial cleavage between the social and political centre located in the east (Østlandet) and the remaining regions, as well as the socio-cultural cleavage between the south/west on the one hand, and east and Trøndelag/North on the other hand. In this three-category representation of the main Norwegian regions, Trøndelag/North is used as the reference category. In addition, level of general education with four categories, high (*gymnas*) being the reference category; female, age and age squared, and birth cohorts, with cohort number three, 1945 onwards as the reference category, complete the list of control variables. The covariates are described in Table 7.2.

Fit statistics for the models of gross effects of class are presented in Table 7.3 and the net effects are presented in Table 7.4. The null model in Table 7.3 contains only the intercept, whereas the null model in Table 7.4 also includes the control variables. In the models with simple trends, only the year of survey is added as a categorical covariate. In both tables, the results for model 2 show that the constant class voting model picks up the bulk of the explained variation in the –2LL statistic. Nevertheless, the linear trend model represents a significant improvement in fit. Moreover, the probability value of the Wald statistic for the pooled class-by-survey interaction is very low, indicating that the class effects change over time. The next model, which adds a parameter for quadratic trend, does only marginally better than the linear trend model. Best of all, in terms of the –2LL statistic, is the unconstrained interaction model, but the linear trend model

[9] The equation for the first model is: $\log [P_1/(P_1 + P_4)] = \alpha + \Sigma\beta_j x$, where *xj* are of covariates, and *bj* logistic regression coefficients.

TABLE 7.2. *Description of the variables in the logit analysis*

| Name | Description | Type | Min. | Max. | Reference category |
|---|---|---|---|---|---|
| Vote4p | Vote, controlled for turnout | Cat. | 1 | 4 | 4 = Cons. |
| Class | EG class schema, 7 classes | Cat. | 1 | 7 | 1 = I |
| Survey | Year of survey | Cat. | 1 | 8 | 1 = 1957 |
| Year | Election periods of 4 years | Cont. | 1 | 8 | |
| Year2 | Year squared | Cont. | 1 | 64 | |
| Region | Main regions of Norway | Cat. | 1 | 3 | 3 = Trøndelag/North |
| Education | Level of general education | Cat. | 1 | 4 | 4 = high |
| Female | | Cat. | 0 | 1 | 1 = female |
| Age | Age in years | Cont. | 18 | 99 | — |
| Age2/100 | Age squared | Cont. | 3.2 | 98.0 | — |
| Cohort | Birth cohorts | Cat. | 1 | 3 | 3 = 1945– |

*Notes*: Vote4p: Socialist Left, Labour, Centre, Conservative; Class: II, II, III, IVab, IVc, V/VI, VII; Survey: 1957, 1965, 1969, 1973, 1977, 1981, 1985, 1989; Region: East, South/West, Trøndelag/North; Education: level 1 (elementary) . . . level 4 (gymnas). Cat.: categorical. Cont.: continuous.

TABLE 7.3. *Goodness of fit statistics for class-voting models, gross effects*

| | Soc. | | Party Labout/Cons. | | Contrasts Centre/Cons. | |
|---|---|---|---|---|---|---|
| | –2LL | df | –2LL | df | –2LL | df |
| [0] Null model | 3,372 | 3,400 | 9,754 | 7,407 | 7,607 | 5,486 |
| [1] Simple trend (year effects only) | 3,244 | 3,393 | 9,416 | 7,400 | 7,242 | 5,479 |
| [2] Constant class voting(CCV) | 3,019 | 3,387 | 8,185 | 7,394 | 6,792 | 5,473 |
| [3] Uniform class differences | 2,966 | 3,380 | 8,092 | 7,387 | 6,735 | 5,466 |
| [4] Linear trend in class effects | 2,933 | 3,381 | 8,083 | 7,388 | 6,717 | 5,467 |
| [5] Quadratic trend in class effects | 2,923 | 3,375 | 8,072 | 7,382 | 6,708 | 5,461 |
| [6] Unconstrained class by year interaction | 2,885 | 3,345 | 8,006 | 7,352 | 6,677 | 5,431 |
| Differences | | | | | | |
| [0]–[1] Year effect | 128 | 7 | 338 | 7 | 365 | 7 |
| [1]–[2] Class: main effect | 225 | 6 | 1231 | 6 | 450 | 6 |
| [2]–[3] Class: uniform differences | 53 | 7 | 93 | 7 | 57 | 7 |
| [2]–[4] Class: linear trend | 86 | 6 | 102 | 6 | 75 | 6 |
| [4]–[5] Class: quadratic trend | 96 | 12 | 113 | 12 | 84 | 12 |
| [2]–[6] Class: saturated interaction | 134 | 42 | 179 | 42 | 115 | 42 |
| [3]–[6] Class: non-uniform differences | 81 | 35 | 86 | 35 | 58 | 35 |
| [4]–[6] Class: non-linear interaction | 48 | 36 | 77 | 36 | 40 | 36 |
| Decomposition of saturated class by year interaction (per cent) | | | | | | |
| Linear trends | 64 | 14 | 57 | 14 | 65 | 14 |
| Addition for quadratic trend | 7 | 14 | 6 | 14 | 8 | 14 |
| Other non-linear | 28 | 71 | 37 | 71 | 27 | 71 |
| Sum | 100 | 100 | 100 | 100 | 100 | 100 |

TABLE 7.4. *Goodness of fit statistics for class-voting models, net effects*

| | Soc. | | Party Labour/Cons. | | Contrasts Centre/Cons. | |
|---|---|---|---|---|---|---|
| | –2LL | df | –2LL | df | –2LL | df |
| [0] Null model | 3,136 | 3,355 | 8,044 | 7,366 | 6,709 | 5,421 |
| [1] Simple trend (year effects only) | 3,001 | 3,348 | 8,000 | 7,359 | 6,575 | 5,414 |
| [2] Constant class voting (CCV) | 2,849 | 3,342 | 7,401 | 7,353 | 6,322 | 5,408 |
| [3] Uniform class differences | 2,812 | 3,335 | 7,351 | 7,346 | 6,291 | 5,401 |
| [4] Linear trend in class effects | 2,788 | 3,336 | 7,351 | 7,347 | 6,283 | 5,402 |
| [5] Quadratic trend in class effects | 2,777 | 3,330 | 7,343 | 7,341 | 6,278 | 5,396 |
| [6] Unconstrained class by year interaction | 2,738 | 3,300 | 7,273 | 7,311 | 6,252 | 5,366 |
| Differences | | | | | | |
| [0]–[1] Year effect | 135 | 7 | 44 | 7 | 135 | 7 |
| [1]–[2] Class: main effect | 152 | 6 | 599 | 6 | 252 | 6 |
| [2]–[3] Class: uniform differences | 38 | 7 | 51 | 7 | 31 | 7 |
| [2]–[4] Class: linear trend | 62 | 6 | 50 | 6 | 39 | 6 |
| [4]–[5] Class: quadratic trend | 73 | 12 | 58 | 12 | 44 | 12 |
| [2]–[6] Class: saturated interaction | 111 | 42 | 128 | 42 | 70 | 42 |
| [3]–[6] Class: non-uniform differences | 73 | 35 | 78 | 35 | 39 | 35 |
| [4]–[6] Class: non-linear interaction | 49 | 36 | 78 | 36 | 31 | 36 |
| Decomposition of saturated class by year interaction (per cent) | | | | | | |
| Linear trends | 56 | 14 | 39 | 14 | 56 | 14 |
| Addition for quadratic trend | 10 | 14 | 6 | 14 | 7 | 14 |
| Other non-linear | 35 | 71 | 55 | 71 | 37 | 71 |
| Sum | 100 | 100 | 100 | 100 | 100 | 100 |

*Note*: Covariates used to estimate net effects are: region, educational level, female, age, age squared, cohort (see Table 7.2 for further documentation of variables). The null model is the model with only the additional covariates.

seems to be an acceptable parsimonious alternative. The penultimate column in Table 7.3 shows that the linear trends pick up around two-thirds of the variation in the –2LL explained by the unconstrained interaction model. For the models with net effects of class in Table 7.4, the linear trend model picks up between 39 and 56 per cent of the variation explained by the interaction model. On the basis of this, we choose the linear trend model and the unconstrained interaction model for interpretation. As gross and net effects of class are rather similar, we will only present detailed results for the latter. In general, the gross effects are somewhat larger than the net effects, but the pattern of changes are very similar.

The next problem is how to sum up the multitude of coefficients, especially from the unconstrained interaction model. We will follow Hout *et al.* (1995) by applying their kappa statistics as a measure of class voting.[10]

[10] We note, however, that the kappa index does have some weaknesses. It is not a standardized measure, and it depends upon the choice of reference category for class.

Also, we plot the predicted logits (log odds ratios) from the unconstrained interaction model, as well as the significant linear trends.

In Figure 7.3, the total and the three partisan kappas are presented for the unconstrained interaction model with net effects of class. The total kappa shows considerable variation around a downward trend. From its peak value in 1957, it declines strongly until 1965, before weakly rising again, then dropping to its lowest value in the 1981 election. In 1985 it rises again to experience another drop in 1989. The variation in the total kappa is, however, mainly driven by the large variation in the partisan kappa for the choice between the Socialist Left and the Conservatives. The class effects for this regression were very large in 1957. However, the reason for this and the dramatic drop in the 1965 election is that, by then, the Socialist Left category contains voters of that party plus those voting for the Communist Party, whereas in 1957 the category consisted solely of the Communist voters, as the Socialist People's Party, the forerunner of the Socialist Left, was not formed until 1961. Very few nonmanual workers voted for the Communists in 1957, but for many of them, the Socialist Left was quite an acceptable choice in 1965, differing from the Labour Party mainly in terms of foreign policy.

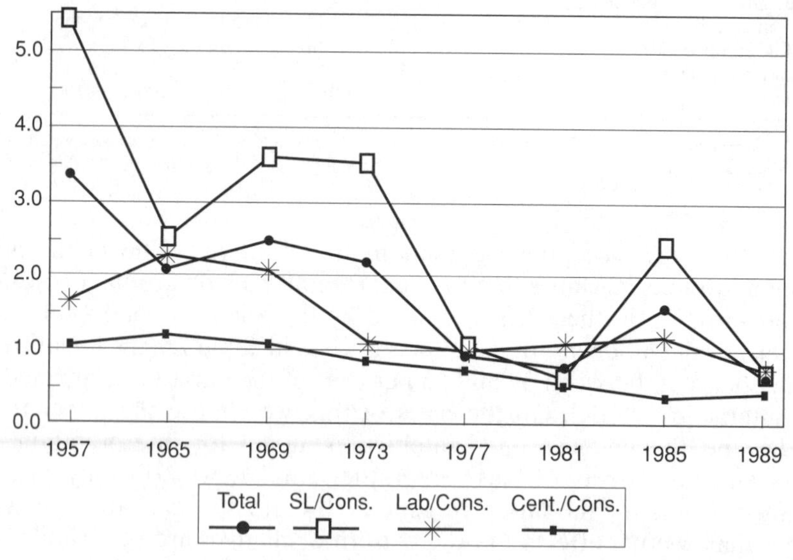


FIG. 7.3. The total and partisan kappas for the unconstrained interaction model, net effects of class

This means assessments of changes in patterns of class voting will be influenced by the choice of reference category. Moreover, as used here, kappa averages all class differences and therefore fails to highlight the theoretically most interesting ones.

The curve of the partisan kappas for the choice between the Labour Party and the Conservatives is our main indicator of change in traditional class voting. This curve is smoother and shows far less variation than that for the total kappa. The main impression is of a weak downward trend. Put another way, the kappa index is rather constant from 1957 to 1969, then it drops to a new stable level until a further drop in 1989. The kappa for the choice between the Centre parties and the Conservatives shows a slow, close-to-linear decline for the whole period. This coincides with the gradual acceptance of the Conservatives in the former strongholds of the Centre parties in the rural areas, especially in the south and west.

Figure 7.4 displays the predicted logits of preferring the Socialist Left to the Conservatives. These confirm the picture obtained with the kappas. The logits, especially for the service class, start very low in 1957, when the Socialist Left consisted of the Communists. The peak for all classes in their preference for the Socialist Left was in the 1973 election following the heated struggle over the issue of Norway joining the EEC the preceding year. As an aftermath of this struggle, a substantial part of the left wing of Labour Party joined forces with the Socialist Left. In the early 1980s, the political climate changed and the Conservatives gained support relative to the Socialists. The difference between class I and II on the one hand and class V/VI and VII on the other hand, clearly seems to diminish over the period, but this is less pronounced if we disregard the particularly high

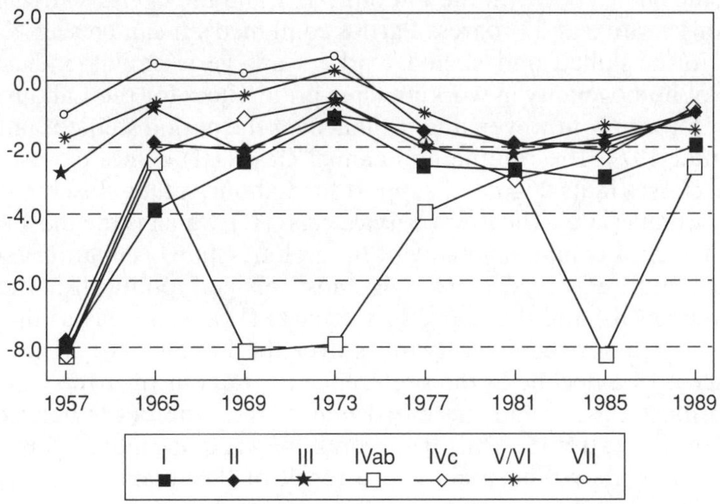


FIG. 7.4. The predicted logit of preferring Socialist Left to Conservative by class, net estimates

*Note*: Controls: sex, age, cohort, and region.

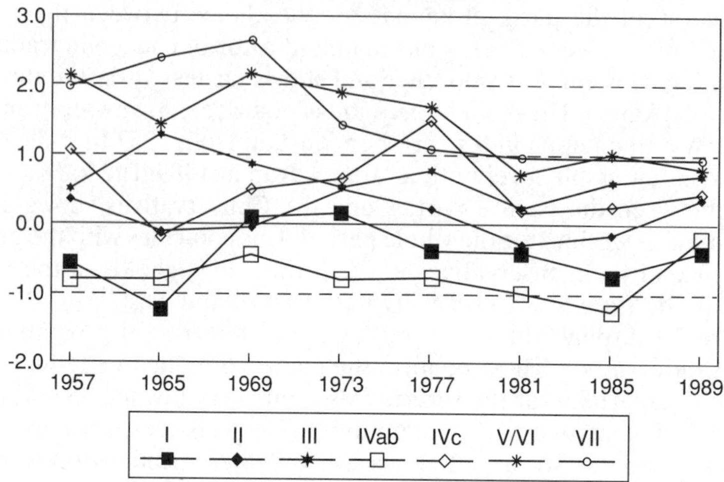


FIG. 7.5. The predicted logit of preferring Labour to Conservative by class, net estimates

*Note*: Controls: sex age, cohort, and region.

1957 figure. The self-employed vary considerable in their predicted support for the Socialist Left, probably because of small cell sizes.

Figure 7.5 contains the case closest to the concept of traditional class voting, the choice between the Labour Party and the Conservative parties (the Conservative and Progress Parties combined). It can be seen that the curves for unskilled and skilled workers are very similar, indicating a degree of homogeneity in working-class preferences for the Labour Party. This preference is, however, diminishing over the period studied, and especially after 1977. The routine nonmanual class (III) comes closest to the manual classes in its degree of support for Labour, rather closely followed by the farmers (IVc). The lower service class (II), which is the most rapidly expanding class containing many of the welfare-state occupations, such as teachers and registered nurses, is most divided politically. The self-employed (IVab) and the upper service class (I) are the classes that most consistently prefer the Conservatives over the Labour Party. The overall tendency is of a decline in the preference for Labour over the Conservatives in most classes, and the narrowing of the differences between the classes on the extremes. Thus the overall message of Figure 7.5 is that of a decline in class voting, mainly as a result of the weakening of Labour support in the working-class. The preference for the Conservatives in their core classes is, however, rather stable over the period.

Figure 7.6 presents the analysis contrasting the Centre parties (Centre Party, Liberals, Christian People's Party) with the Conservatives. The pref-

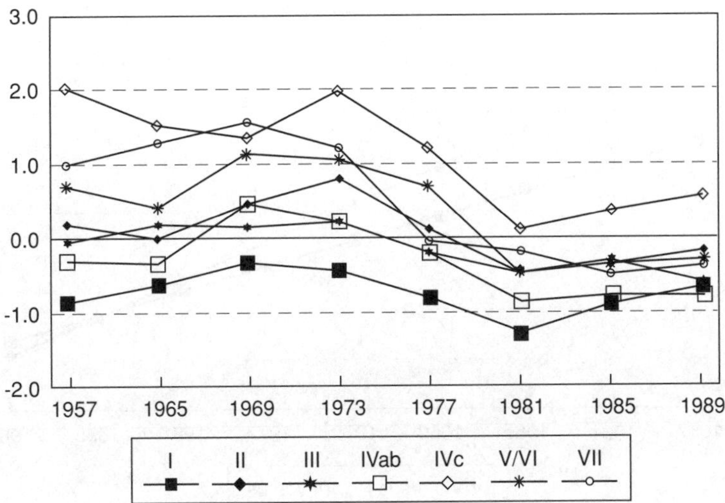


FIG. 7.6. The predicted logit of preferring Centre to Conservative by class, net estimates

*Note*: Controls: sex, age, cohort, and region.

erence for the Centre is strongest among farmers, but it declines between 1973 and 1981, while remaining rather stable or weakly increasing in the 1980s. In the bottom half of the figure are the curves for their opposites, the upper service class (I) and the self-employed (IVab), who are rather stable in their preference for the Conservatives. However, the figure reveals rather dramatic changes in the working-class. After 1973, working-class voters became gradually less inclined to prefer the Centre parties to the Conservatives. Before the 1977 election, the working class clearly favoured the Centre parties, whereas in the later period the Conservatives gained the upper hand. This reflects the Conservatives' ability to break down regional barriers and gain support outside the major towns. The difference between the extreme classes, the farmers (IVc) and the upper service class (I), also diminished over the period.

Finally we look at the results for the net effects of class in the linear trend model. Although the linear trends add significantly to the explained variation of the constant class voting model, many individual trend coefficients fail to reach significance at the 0.05 level. Those that are significant are presented in Figures 7.7–7.9. Since the upper service class provides an extreme position across all comparisons, it was chosen as the reference category. In other words, each curve represents the trend in the contrast between a given class and class I.

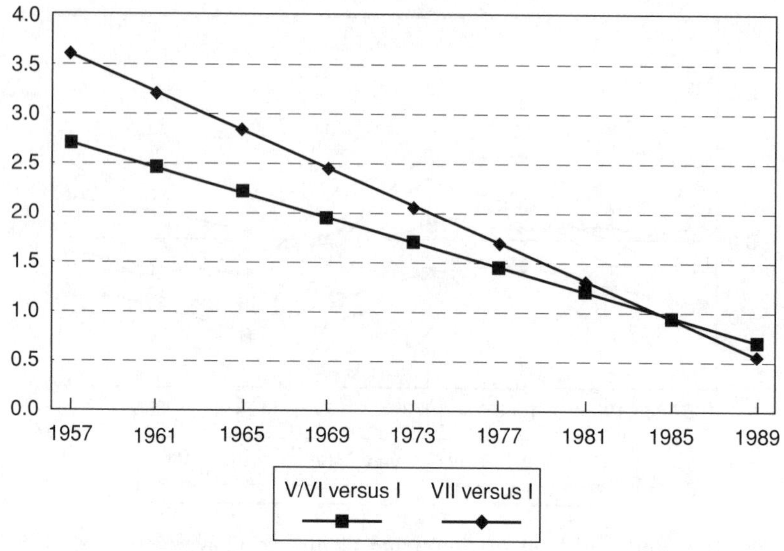


FIG. 7.7. Significant linear trends in preferring Socialist Left to Conservative, logit coefficients, net estimates

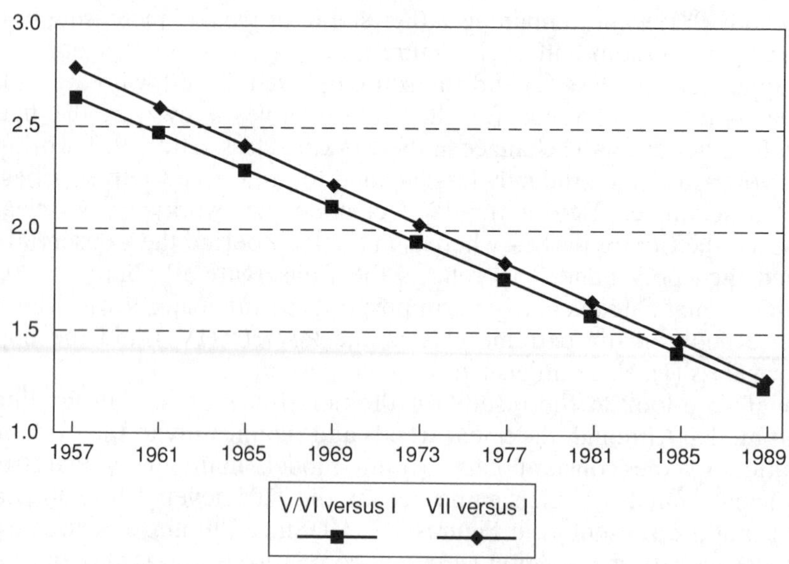


FIG. 7.8. Significant linear trends in preferring Labour to Conservative, logit coefficients, net estimates

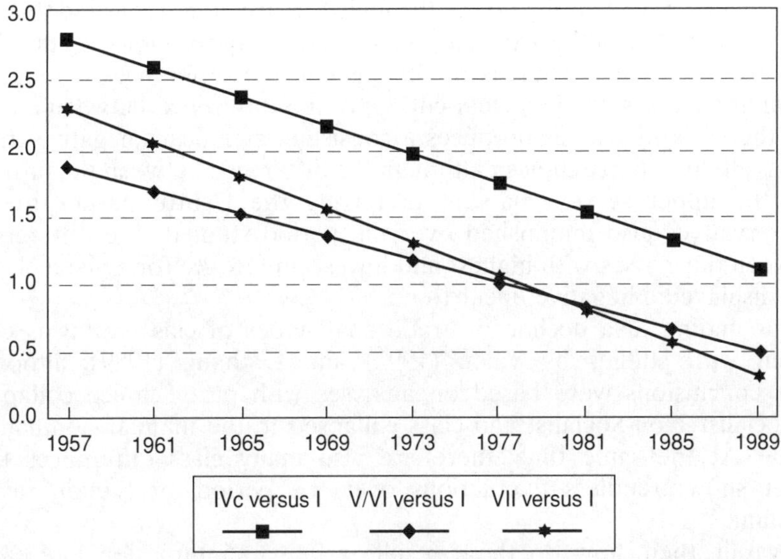


FIG. 7.9. Significant linear trends in preferring Centre to Conservative, logit coefficients, net estimates

The results in Figures 7.7 and 7.8 are very similar. The differences between the working class and the upper service class in preferring either the Socialist Left or the Labour Party to the Conservatives are more than halved over the period from 1957 to 1989. Figure 7.9 shows that the working class and the upper service class have also become more similar over time in choosing between the Centre parties and the Conservatives. The largest disparity in the figure, between the upper service class (I) and the farmers (IVc), also diminishes over time.

## DISCUSSION

The evidence presented here clearly indicates that the class–vote relationship in Norway changed between 1957 and 1989. We have seen the more or less uniform weakening of some parameters and the less patterned fluctuations in others. The total kappa, as well as each of the three partisan kappas, declined over the period studied, although the decline was not monotonic. However, the decline in the kappa that best represents traditional class voting was rather small, and the decline in class differences in preferences for the Centre versus the Conservatives, even smaller. Our examination of the logistic regressions indicated that the differences between the 'extreme' classes on each party choice seem to get narrower over time, whereas the changes in the differences among the remaining classes are less clear-cut. Only the difference between class I and the working classes produces a consistent significant negative trend across all three party choices, although the difference between the farmers and the upper service class in preferring the Centre parties to the Conservatives also diminished over the period studied. The differences between the classes with highest and lowest preference for a given choice also displayed a negative linear trend.

Our finding of a decline in 'traditional' types of class voting is consistent with studies by Valen (1992) and Listhaug (1989), although their conclusions were based on analyses with party choice collapsed to Socialist–Non-Socialist and class collapsed to the manual–nonmanual divide. At the same time, there are also many class differences that either show trendless fluctuations over the period, or remain rather constant.

Overall, then, how do these results relate to international research on class voting? Studies of relative class voting, such as Heath, Jowell, and Curtice (1985), Hout *et al.* (1995), Evans, Heath, and Payne (1996a) and Goldthorpe (Chapter 3 in this volume) have either demonstrated stability in relative class-voting, or demonstrated changes in class-voting parameters that may best be described as trendless fluctuations, or even realignment. Thus, on important points, our findings differ from these studies. They are, however, consistent with Nieuwbeerta and De Graaf's analysis of class voting in Norway (Chapter 2).

This does not, of course, indicate that class differences in voting behaviour in Norway have disappeared altogether, rather they appear to have come down to a more 'normal' European level. This means that the distinctiveness of the Scandinavian countries in terms of levels of class voting is waning. This change is probably a result of two different processes, taking place in two different periods of time. The first has been an easing of class conflict, while the second process has been a change in the character of class politics.

First, the high level of class voting in Norway in the 1950s can be understood by the role played by the strong and radical trade unions with close links to the Labour Party which made for highly ideologically loaded political debate. This was fuelled by the recent history of bitter labour conflicts in the 1920s and the 1930s. The Labour party came to power in 1936, after a compromise with the Agrarian party. They remained in power until 1965, an almost unbroken period with only a short interlude of bourgeois coalition government in 1963 (Rokkan 1966: 70–3). Support for the Labour Party remained at a level of about 45 per cent throughout the period from 1945 to 1969, and peaked at 48 per cent in the 1957 election.[11]

The years from 1952 to 1977 have in contrast been characterized as the era of the social democratic order (Furre 1991). The state assumed a high degree of responsibility for public welfare, including equalization of incomes. This was fuelled by stable economic growth. The policy regime included economic planning as well as a mixture of private and state ownership of industry. The corporate mode of decision-making (Rokkan 1966) also contributed to the mixing of private with public interests. There is no doubt that this form of social democracy eased class conflict. A political consensus over the welfare state also emerged. Thus, the bourgeois coalition government that came to power in 1965 was able to implement the extensive social security reform that had previously been planned by the Labour government. It is around this time that the strength of the left–right class cleavage declined.

Secondly, by the mid-1970s problems in the international economy had put the social democratic order under threat. Thus the fiscal policy of full employment was given up in 1977. To a certain extent, the electoral changes that have taken place from the mid-1970s onwards can be explained by a new type of conflict over the welfare state. The tax–welfare backlash seems to have struck most heavily among younger male workers (see the curve for classes V/VI and VII in Figure 7.5). On the other hand, growth in welfare occupations has supplied work opportunities for women, mainly in the postwar generations (Esping-Andersen 1990: 221–9). The result has been a new gender gap in the labour market as well as in voting behaviour, with women supporting the parties of the left and males the parties of the right (see the curves for classes I and II in Figure 7.4, and Listhaug *et al.* 1985).

Moreover, the decline in the size of the working class has itself presented a strategic challenge for the socialist and social democratic parties (Przeworski and Sprague 1986; Kitschelt 1994). Thus according to Kitschelt (1994: 290), the Norwegian Labour Party has opted for the 'pivoting' strategy, that is, placing itself in the political centre and thereby attracting the maximum number of votes. However, this strategy also leaves the bulk of the 'symbolic and client processing' occupations (included in, but not entirely corresponding to classes I and II in the Erikson–Goldthorpe schema) open to the Socialist Left Party. The composition of the electorate

[11] This dominance was helped by the presence of a weak and divided right (Castles 1978). In Norway, the parties of the centre have represented the interests of the periphery, that is, agriculture and the popular movements of teetotalism, religion, and the New-Norwegian language, while the Conservatives were based in the urban bourgeoisie. This split among the bourgeois parties eased the road to power for the social democrats.

of the Socialist Left Party has undergone the most dramatic change of all (Valen *et al.* 1990: 98–109). The party started out with an electorate quite similar to the electorate of the Labour Party. The proportion of manual workers was 65 per cent in 1965, which had dropped to 29 per cent in 1989. On the other hand, the proportion of public sector employees rose from 9 per cent to 35 per cent. This change in electoral composition is also reflected in the party's programme. Ecology played a major part in the successful election campaign in 1989, while Marxist ideology was played down. Another challenge has come from right-wing authoritarian politics, represented by the Progress Party, which seems to appeal mostly to manual and routine nonmanual occupations. Despite these changes, however, it would be premature to conclude that class-based politics is going to disappear completely: although, overall levels of class voting have declined. Norway may simply be approaching an equilibrium level of class voting similar to that in many other West European nations.

# 8

# The Class Politics of Swedish Welfare Policies

STEFAN SVALLFORS

## INTRODUCTION

One of the most important arenas for contemporary class politics is the welfare state. Those who are less endowed with various resources connected with class positions, and more exposed to the risks connected with labour market dependency, may be expected to turn to the state in order to safeguard their interests. In the same vein, we would expect groups with larger market resources to be more likely to oppose redistribution.

While these facts may be agreed upon by people of different theoretical persuasions, there is considerably less agreement on whether this particular conflict pattern has been, and will be, stable over time. As we shall see, arguments have been put forward implying that the class politics of welfare policies is changing. It has been argued, from a variety of different quarters, that we are witnessing either the dissolution of class conflicts, or their replacement by other forms of social conflict. If there is some semblance of truth in such claims, effects should be clear for views about the welfare state among ordinary citizens. We would expect the link between class positions and attitudes towards welfare policies to become weaker, and/or to be replaced by stronger links between other structural positions than class and people's attitudes.

In this chapter, we analyse how attitudes to the welfare state have changed since the early 1980s in a particularly interesting case, Sweden. Sweden has long occupied a privileged position as the archetypal welfare state within discourse and research on social policies. In terms of budget outlays, social rights, taxation levels, social expenditure, income equalization, or almost any other measure used to distinguish a highly developed welfare state, Sweden invariably comes out as one of the highest ranking nations (Esping-Andersen 1990; Kangas 1991; Schmidt 1989;

This chapter is an extensively revised version of 'The End of Class Politics? Structural Cleavages and Attitudes to Swedish Welfare Policies', *Acta Sociologica*, 38 (1995): 53–74, by permission of Scandinavian University Press, Oslo, Norway. This research has been supported by the Swedish Council for Social Research.

Saunders 1994). Influential interpretations have explained these characteristics in terms of the strong position of the Swedish labour movement, which has been strong enough to wrest substantial concessions from more privileged groups in society (Stephens 1979; Esping-Andersen and Korpi 1984; Esping-Andersen 1985).

Recent developments in Sweden indicate that this model welfare state has come under increasing strain and may actually be crumbling. The sharp rise in unemployment during the 1990s means that full employment, once the cornerstone of the Swedish welfare model, is no longer there. The rise in unemployment also creates severe financial problems for welfare policies, as, at the same time, it undermines the tax base and creates pressure on outlays for unemployment benefits and labour market policies. Far-ranging proposals for restructuring and cutting back universal welfare policies have also been proposed or even implemented.

The recent problems of the Swedish welfare state have also, in some quarters, been taken as indications of increasing problems of legitimacy for welfare policies. More specifically, it has been argued that the former class basis of the Swedish model is eroding, and leaving place for a much more multifaceted and fragmented conflict of interests which is undermining the basic characteristics of 'the Swedish model' (SOU 1990: 44: ch. 11).

The aim of this chapter is to test if the alleged dissolving of class conflict actually has any empirical backing. The data come from surveys on attitudes to welfare policies that have been conducted in Sweden over the last decade. In the next section, recent debates on class politics in relation to attitudes are reviewed in order to distil the main arguments. The following sections contain the empirical analysis, first through a summary of changes in gross percentages and construction of attitudinal indices, and then through an assessment of how the links between various structural cleavages and attitudes have changed over the period. In the concluding section the main results are summarized and their wider implications discussed.

## STRUCTURAL DETERMINANTS AND ATTITUDINAL CLEAVAGES: RECENT INTERPRETATIONS

Theses on the demise of class conflict may be grouped into two main variants (Evans 1993*a*). According to the first, the decline in class politics is but one instance of a general loosening of the grip of structural conditions on values, commitments, and attitudes, sometimes captured in terms such as 'postmodernity' or 'postmaterialism'. According to the second, the structural bases of politics persist, but the former privileged role of class has been overtaken by other social cleavages. Let us discuss each in turn.[1]

According to Offe (1987) there has been a steady erosion of the social and normative underpinnings of the welfare state. Offe argues that the welfare state cannot, in the long run, rely on pure self-interest in the population to back an extensive and redistributive welfare state. Instead explanations of welfare-state stability should be sought at a normative level, where limited self-interest can be transformed into normative commitments of a collective and egalitarian kind. Following fast urbanization and increased social mobility, environments that would induce such orientations have been destroyed and are unlikely to develop again. The ensuing 'destructuration of collectivities' encompass a 'process of fragmentation, pluralization, and ultimately individualization of socio-economic conditions and interest dispositions' (Offe 1987: 527).

Beck (1992) puts forward a very similar argument in his analysis of the emerging 'risk society'. He states that our present condition entails an individualized inequality: processes of inequality are still present, but the mechanisms linking this inequality to collective mobilization and identity formation have been undermined. The combined effects of greater physical and social mobility and individualizing tendencies within the labour market and the social insurance system are likely to create a society where class loses its impact as a base for identities and interests .

From a quite different theoretical framework, Inglehart (1990) reaches virtually the same conclusions regarding the waning importance of class. He links this to the broader syndrome of 'postmaterialism', a development in which traditional motivations of material and social security lose their power as driving forces behind human actions and aspirations. The postmaterialist value syndrome crosscuts materialist concerns and blurs class distinctions, as groups with higher socio-economic positions tend to embrace postmaterialism to a larger extent than the working class. Clark and Lipset (1991; Clark *et al.* 1993) and Pakulski (1993) advance similar arguments. They see traditional hierarchies declining, both at work and in the wider community. Combined with larger social mobility and rising affluence, this gives rise to a 'fragmentation of stratification', a conclusion strikingly similar to Offe's.

In the Swedish context, the official commission for the study of power endorses similar notions about the waning of hierarchical divisions in Swedish society (Petersson 1989; SOU 1990: 44). The election surveys also supply a never-ending stream of empirical analyses of what they see as the

[1] Sometimes, both arguments are advanced by the same author, as where a displacement of class by other cleavages is supposed to take place within a framework of a general decline of the structural roots of politics.

change from class voting to issue voting (Holmberg 1981, 1984; Holmberg and Gilljam 1987; Gilljam and Holmberg 1990, 1993).

A quite different strand in the recent critique of class analysis can be found among those who have argued that other structural divisions are superseding the role formerly occupied by class. These authors maintain that social and structural conditions will still have an important impact on how people come to define themselves and think about politics. But divisions other than class have, due to social and political developments, come to the fore. As will be shown, many of these developments are directly linked to the institutionalization of welfare policies.

The candidates for new privileged divisions have been many. In feminist discourse, it is implicitly or explicitly argued that gender will or has already become an important social division crosscutting class demarcations. In relation to the welfare state, there are principally two ways in which gender could be decisive in structuring identities and interests (Hoel and Knutsen 1989). The first links the issues to the self-interest among women. As employees of the welfare state, as welfare clients, or as family members relieved of heavy and unrewarded care work, women are often more dependent on the welfare state than men are (Hernes 1987*a*, 1987*b*; Borchorst and Siim 1987). The other starts from the socialization experiences of women compared to men, which allegedly make them more inclined to embrace a 'rationality of caring' involving concern, consideration, and devotion to others (Prokop 1976; Waerness 1987). The institutionalization of welfare policies brings into the public domain what were previously private matters of care for and obligation to others, transforming a 'moral economy of domesticity' into support for state welfare (Piven 1985).

In relation to Sweden, Esping-Andersen has explicitly stated what often remains implicit within feminist discourse by arguing that class conflicts over welfare policies are increasingly diluted by an emerging gender conflict. The heavy concentration of women within the welfare-state sector creates severe strains between a welfare state mainly populated by women and a private sector dominated by men. According to Esping-Andersen, the outcome of this conflict may prove destructive for the underpinnings of the welfare state: 'Swedish social democracy can only hope that the bonds of marriage are strong enough to weather the storm of economic warfare' (Esping-Andersen 1990: 227).

In this respect, issues of gender are tightly wedded to the question of private and public sector location. The divisions between public and private employees, just like the gender division, can be divided, on the one hand, into arguments that emphasize self-interest among those employed by the public sector in guarding their employment, wages, and working conditions (Dunleavy 1980; Zetterberg 1985), and, on the other hand, into those pointing to a special kind of socialization experience within the public sector, which creates bonds of sympathy and solidarity between public sector employees and their clients, patients, and other 'welfare dependants' (Lafferty 1988). According to some authors, this suggests possibilities for alliances between welfare clients and state bureaucrats (Kolberg and Pettersen 1981; Zetterberg 1985; Dunleavy 1986; Piven and Cloward 1986; Joppke 1987). The coincidence of interests between non-manual groups within the public sector and people dependent on state support for their survival transforms the former class-based conflict. Private sector workers are increasingly likely to side with their private sector colleagues against public sector employees and those supported by the welfare state (Dunleavy 1986: 142).

Some writers have pointed to Sweden as a nation where conflicts of interests between private and public sector should be especially acute, taking into account the heavy tax pressure and the large group of those supported by the welfare state (Zetterberg 1985; Taylor-Gooby 1991). What, from the perspective of those employed by or dependent on the welfare state may look as necessary functions, could from the perspective of the privately employed simply appear as a cumbersome tax burden.

The last new cleavage to be discussed here is the one emanating from different positions in the consumption sector. In particular, the question of housing markets and their impact on wealth distribution and, possibly, interests and identities has been highlighted (Kemeny 1981; Saunders 1986, 1990). Saunders (1986: 323) is explicit in his emphasis on housing being 'the most basic element in the analysis of consumption relations', and in his insistence that those relying on a 'privatized mode of consumption' are in a fundamentally different social situation from the minority 'cast adrift on the water-logged raft of what remains of the welfare state' (Saunders 1986: 318).

In his 1986 textbook, Saunders is convinced that these facts will translate into ideological and political divisions blurring and superseding class distinctions (Saunders 1986: 312–19). Four years later, however, Saunders is much less convinced that consumption cleavages will overtake the role of class in structuring identities and attitudes. His own empirical analysis seems clearly to 'confirm previous studies that the electoral significance of housing tenure is secondary to that of class' (Saunders 1990: 234). Furthermore, there are no signs of home ownership implying a more conservative ideological outlook. Specifically, there is nothing to support the claim that home owners are less supportive of the welfare state (Saunders 1990: 248–54). In the light of Saunders's previous claims, it is worth quoting his own summary of the empirical results: 'Home owners do not vote distinctively, nor do they subscribe to a specific set of anti-collectivist political values' (Saunders 1990: 255).

The volte-face performed by Saunders is indicative of the problems many of the anti-class theorists seem to have in substantiating their claims empirically. Dunleavy, for example, concludes that 'the evidential basis for a sectoral interpretation must remain tentative in character', as his grandly designed theory of production sector cleavages fails in the end to receive any empirical support (Dunleavy 1980: 549).

As the chapters in this volume demonstrate, claims of a radical decline in the class basis of voting are clearly exaggerated. Other research, from Britain, Scandinavia, and Australia, suggests also that class is still by far the most important cleavage in structuring attitudes to welfare and inequality (Marshall *et al.* 1988; Heath *et al.* 1991; Svallfors 1991; 1993*a*; 1993*b*; 1993*c*; Evans 1993*b*; Matheson 1993; Glans 1993). Findings such as these have led authors not convinced by the decline-of-class thesis to launch a spirited counterattack. Thus Goldthorpe and Marshall review a wide range of empirical studies and conclude that there is no evidence that 'classes in Britain—the working class included—have shown any weakening in either their social cohesion or their ideological distinctiveness' (Goldthorpe and Marshall 1992: 392).

Attitudes to the welfare state should in more than one respect constitute an ideal test case for adjudicating between the various claims that have been offered by class theorists and their opponents. As Matheson points out, contemporary class conflicts are most often pursued on the terrain of the welfare state, involving 'attitudes and behaviours towards state intervention in economic and social life with the effect of overriding the distribution of resources via market mechanisms, especially the labour market' (Matheson 1993: 57). So class theorists should have few objections to the use of attitudes to the welfare state in assessing the continuing relevance of class analysis.

Neither should the proponents of various forms of the decline-of-class thesis. In fact, the reason for factors such as gender, sector, or housing being potentially important cleavages is that they have been institutionalized as social cleavages in and through the welfare state. Specific traits of female care responsibilities and the gendered labour market segmentation, the self-interest or special socialization among public sector employees, the system of subsidies and transfers prevailing within housing markets, are all linked to welfare policies in various ways. So if the new social cleavages are having an impact on the way in which people view and assess their world, this should be clearly visible in welfare-state attitudes.

Even those who want to argue that we find a general decline in structural determination of values and attitudes should find attitudes to the welfare state a suitable field for empirically testing their claims. As was pointed out earlier, theorists such as Offe (1987) explicitly argue that the decline in class structuration of values and commitments leads to severe problems of legitimacy for welfare policies. Once the formerly homogeneous and solidaristic classes have been broken down to a set of individualized and self-interested actors, the normative underpinnings of the welfare state cannot be sustained. So any tendency towards fragmentation of interests should have a substantial impact on attitudes to welfare policies.

Attitudes to the welfare state also have some advantages as indicators of ideological conflict compared to voting. As argued by Evans, 'it is not justifiable to infer changes in the ideological differences between classes from voting patterns: the class-vote link is not only a product of the ideological distinctiveness of classes, but also of the distinctiveness of parties. If parties fail to present manifestos which appeal to the interests of different classes, then there is no reason for there to be a strong class-vote link' (Evans 1993*b*: 451–2).

While there have been some attempts to analyse the development of ideological cleavages over time, such as Evans (1993*b*), most analyses have used one-point cross-sectional data. Specifically, there has been no attempt to study changes in the structural determination of welfare-state attitudes in Sweden. The conclusion by Svallfors (1991) that class and 'class-related' factors such as education and income are still most important in structuring attitudes to the welfare state relies on a single snapshot of attitudes from the mid-1980s. This, it could be argued, is biasing the analysis against the proponents of the decline-of-class thesis. Even if class is still the most important factor in structuring attitudes, it may be possible to detect tendencies towards fragmentation and new cleavages. In this chapter, by using data covering more than a decade, it may be possible to examine competing claims more thoroughly.

## THE CONTEXT: TRENDS AND PATTERNS IN ATTITUDES TOWARDS WELFARE, 1981–1992

The data on which the analysis builds come from three national surveys conducted in Sweden in 1981, 1986, and 1992.[2] The analysis concentrates on the last two surveys, since they both contain a very broad spectrum of welfare-state attitudes. Some of these items were picked from the 1981 survey, which makes it possible to make comparisons on some issues over the whole eleven-year period. The purpose of the two later surveys was to

[2] The response rate was 76.6%, 66.3%, and 76.0%, respectively (details of sampling and non-responses are found in Hadenius 1986: appendix 1; Svallfors 1989: appendix A; Svallfors 1992: 5, appendix). The lower response rate for 1986 is potentially a source of concern. It turns out, however, that the structure of non-responses in 1986 is similar to that in 1992, with a slight under-representation of high-income earners and a slight over-representation of people living in Stockholm. The biases therefore seem to be rather constant over the period, with a probable weak 'right-wing' bias in the sample owing to the higher response rate among high-income earners.

pose questions dealing with a broad range of welfare-policy issues, instead of following the standard practice of using just a few single indicators of attitude to the welfare state. In this way, the intention was to bring out the complexity and possible ambivalence and contradictions in attitudes instead of relying on a simplified notion of 'for or against the welfare state' (Svallfors 1989). The present analysis rests on a subset of all these questions, a number of rather specific questions dealing with the level of public expenditure on various welfare policies, the service-delivery aspects of welfare policies, the preferred way of financing various welfare services, and issues of suspected abuse of welfare benefits and services.

Table 8.1 shows attitudes to public spending on various welfare policies over the period from 1981. The table gives the proportion of the public that supports increased expenditure on various programmes and the percentage balance of support, that is, the proportion that supports an increase in expenditure minus the proportion that wishes to reduce it.

The main impression from the table is stability. The same programmes tend to appear towards the bottom or the top end of the list in all three surveys, and percentage changes are mostly very small. Two exceptions to this are views on spending for support for the elderly and for lower-level schooling. In both cases there are clear indications of an increasing willingness to increase expenditure over the time period. There are no clear signs of any diminishing willingness to have high welfare expenditures,

TABLE 8.1. *Attitudes to public expenditure*

| Percentage wishing to increase expenditure services and balance* | 1981 | 1986 | 1992 |
|---|---|---|---|
| Medical and health care | 44.6 (+42) | 47.3 (+44) | 52.7 (+48) |
| Support for elderly (pensions, care for the elderly) | 30.2 (+29) | 37.0 (+34) | 60.3 (+58) |
| Support for families with children (child allowances, child-care) | 31.3 (+19) | 42.6 (+34) | 31.8 (+17) |
| Housing allowances | 12.6 (−23) | 13.0 (−23) | 13.1 (−25) |
| Social assistance | 16.2 (−5) | 16.7 (−5) | 13.2 (−13) |
| Research and higher education | 39.4 (+33) | 45.4 (+40) | 37.6 (+30) |
| Comprehensive and secondary schooling | 26.2 (+20) | 32.2 (+31) | 50.1 (+49) |
| Employment policies | 69.3 (+63) | 56.0 (+46) | 61.7 (+55) |
| State and local government administration | 2.4 (−54) | 1.9 (−53) | 2.5 (−68) |
| Housing costs deductions | — | — | 13.1 (−17) |
| N | *c*960 | *c*980 | *c*1,500 |

*Note*: Replies to the question 'Taxes are used for different purposes. Do you think that the amount of tax money used for the following purposes should increase, remain the same, or decrease'?, 1981–1992.

* Difference between those wishing to increase and those wishing to decrease expenditure in parentheses.

even if public support for families with children shows a U-turn, ending in 1992 at the same level as it started in 1981.

An indication of the ambivalence towards the welfare state is found in the extremely low support for spending on government administration. Many Swedes want higher social spending, but few seem prepared to pay for the administration of this spending. This ambivalence is also shown in the much lower support for programmes targeted at low-income or poor people, such as housing allowances and social assistance. This is not necessarily proof of lack of compassion for those with low incomes, but more likely an expression of suspicion that the recipients are not genuinely deserving, a theme which will appear again shortly.

In Table 8.2, attitudes to the question of service delivery are displayed. There is a clear trend towards increasing support for private enterprises as best suited to handle welfare policies. This trend is clearest in child-care and care for the elderly, where the percentage thinking that private enterprises are better has doubled, from 10.0 per cent and 5.2 per cent, respectively, in 1986. This has, however, not been reflected in a comparable decline in support for 'state and local authorities'. Instead the most clear-cut finding on this issue is the decline in support for the family as best suited to handle child-care and care for the elderly. Support for the family is down from 29.4 per cent to 11.2 per cent when it comes to child-care and from 10.6 per cent to 4.6 per cent when it comes to care for the elderly. In light of recent ideological and practical developments in the Swedish welfare state, where more emphasis is put on family and community care (Johansson 1994), these findings are rather surprising.

On the question of how to finance welfare policies, we find even greater stability. As shown in Table 8.3, changes from 1986 to 1992 are very small.

TABLE 8.2. *Attitudes to service delivery*

| Service | State or local authorities | | Private enterprises | | Family and relatives | | Other[a] | |
|---|---|---|---|---|---|---|---|---|
| | 1986 | 1992 | 1986 | 1992 | 1986 | 1992 | 1986 | 1992 |
| Education | 84.8 | 81.5 | 7.6 | 11.2 | 0.0 | 0.0 | 6.6 | 6.3 |
| Health services | 83.3 | 77.5 | 8.8 | 14.2 | 0.0 | 0.0 | 2.5 | 2.5 |
| Child-care | 48.6 | 48.4 | 10.0 | 20.4 | 29.4 | 11.2 | 12.0 | 20.0 |
| Care for elderly | 75.5 | 75.9 | 5.2 | 9.9 | 10.6 | 4.6 | 8.7 | 9.6 |
| Social work | 87.8 | 85.5 | 2.0 | 4.4 | 1.8 | 2.1 | 8.4 | 8.0 |

(n = 1986 ca 960, 1992 ca 1410)

*Notes*: [a] Cooperatives, Trade unions, charity organizations, Various combinations of answers.

Replies to the question 'Who in general do you consider best suited to deliver the following services'. 1986 and 1992.

Sample size of *c*960 in 1986; *c*1,410 in 1992.

In 1992 as in 1986 it is only regarding child-care that we find any substantial support for increased user fees in financing. The new area in the 1992 survey, care for the elderly, shows the highest support for continuing collective financing.

As is shown in Table 8.4, however, while attitudes to welfare spending, state services, and collective financing on the whole show a strong support for welfare policies, there is widespread suspicion of fraud or laziness among those receiving welfare benefits and services. The reduced level of suspicion in 1992 regarding abuse of unemployment benefits can almost certainly be explained by the higher unemployment figures in that year. It should be borne in mind, though, that only the last question—on falsely reporting illness—really suggests outright fraud. The other questions probably rather tap into a belief that there is overspending on the undeserving.

How, then, do all these various attitudes go together? Are they all part of the same pattern, so that people who want higher spending in one area

TABLE 8.3. *Attitudes to financing welfare policies, 1986 and 1992*

| Service | 1986 | 1992 |
|---|---|---|
| Education | 79.0 | 74.6 |
| Health services | 89.9 | 90.3 |
| Child-care | 63.3 | 63.4 |
| Care for the elderly | — | 91.9 |
| N | *c*970 | *c*1,490 |

*Notes*: Replies to the question 'How do you think the following services should be financed?' *Percentage answering 'Primarily through taxes and employer contributions'*.

TABLE 8.4. *Attitudes to abuse of welfare policies, 1986 and 1992*

| Proposition | 1986 | 1992 |
|---|---|---|
| Many of those using health services are not all that ill. | 54.9 | 59.5 |
| Many of those receiving unemployment benefits could get a job if they only wanted to. | 81.8 | 70.2 |
| Many of those receiving social assistance are not really poor. | 72.4 | 70.1 |
| Many of those receiving housing allowances should move to smaller and cheaper dwellings. | 58.5 | 64.6 |
| Many of those who report themselves ill are not really ill. | 68.3 | 70.5 |
| N | *c*980 | *c*1,500 |

*Notes*: Replies to the question 'How usual do you think it is that social benefits and services are used by people who don't really need them?' *Percentage agreeing with certain propositions.*

also want it in another; and are those who are more in favour of the state handling services also more in favour of collective financing and less suspicious of abuse?

One way to describe the relations between the various items is through principal-components analysis, where the covariation among observed variables is reduced to a smaller set of underlying dimensions. Tables 8.5 and 8.6 present the results of principal-components analyses for the years 1986 and 1992.[3]

Great stability is found in the attitudinal patterns. The same items tend to correlate with the same factors in 1986 as in 1992, which indicates that the attitudinal patterns are not just meaningless flux. The first factor in both 1986 and 1992 is easy to interpret as a 'suspicion factor'. All the items on abuse of welfare policies load on this factor. Factor 3 in 1986 and factor 2 in 1992 are clearly capturing the service-delivery aspects of welfare-state attitudes. Factor 4 in 1986 and factor 5 in 1992 refer to issues concerning the financing of welfare policies, albeit in a somewhat less clear-cut way in 1992.

The expenditure items separate into three factors. The last factor in both 1986 and 1992 correlates with the two questions on education. It is easy to see why they should form a factor of their own since education serves a qualifying and credentialist function rather than the compensatory function of other welfare policies. The remaining spending issues separate into two factors (no. 2 1986/no. 3 1992 and no. 5 1986/no. 4 1992). The first of these could be interpreted as a 'support factor', where support for specific groups such as families with children, persons of low income, or the unemployed are in question. These issues also correlate strongly with support for spending on administration. The other deals with spending on 'semi-public goods' such as care for the elderly and health care. The questions on primary schooling and employment policies also load fairly high on this factor, especially in 1992. The difference between these two factors is that the first deals with some specific groups, the 'risk' of being a member of which varies considerably between various sectors of the population. The second deals with groups, such as the old and the sick, of which we are all future potential members.

There are some correlations in the analysis that deviate from the interpretation just presented. All issues dealing with child-care, for example, tend to correlate on the same factor (no. 2 in 1986 and no. 5 1992) in a way that cuts across the interpretation just given. We also find that in 1992, the issue of financing health care correlates more clearly with the issue of spending on health care than with the other two finance questions.

[3] The service-delivery questions (state and local government versus all other) and the financing questions are dichotomized. The expenditure issues are trichotomized (increase, remain the same, decrease). The abuse issues have four categories, from strongly agree to strongly disagree.

TABLE 8.5. *Dimensional analysis of attitudes to welfare policies, 1986 (Factor loadings x 100)*

| Factor | I | II | III | IV | V | VI |
|---|---|---|---|---|---|---|
| Expenditure | | | | | | |
| 1. Medical and health care | –06 | 09 | 20 | 16 | **74** | 01 |
| 2. Support for the elderly | –01 | 22 | 09 | –05 | **73** | 10 |
| 3. Support for families with children | –09 | 38 | –13 | 39 | 22 | 13 |
| 4. Housing allowances | –21 | **71** | 00 | 04 | 12 | –02 |
| 5. Social assistance | –21 | **61** | 04 | 12 | 24 | –05 |
| 6. Research and higher education | –05 | –04 | 00 | –01 | 00 | **79** |
| 7. Comprehensive and secondary schooling | –11 | 09 | –04 | 09 | 10 | **73** |
| 8. Employment policies | 01 | **46** | 25 | 14 | 29 | 02 |
| 9. State and local government administration | –02 | **66** | 19 | 00 | 02 | 05 |
| Service delivery | | | | | | |
| 1. Education | –10 | –18 | **56** | 28 | 13 | 05 |
| 2. Health care | –03 | 16 | **59** | 21 | 18 | –16 |
| 3. Child-care | –05 | **46** | **55** | 12 | –23 | 03 |
| 4. Care for elderly | –01 | 18 | **80** | –04 | 01 | 06 |
| 5. Social work | –08 | 08 | **69** | –04 | 01 | 02 |
| Financing | | | | | | |
| 1. Education | –22 | –09 | 16 | **74** | –04 | 18 |
| 2. Health services | –06 | 22 | 14 | **61** | 28 | –22 |
| 3. Child-care | –10 | **47** | 10 | **60** | –08 | 07 |
| Abuse | | | | | | |
| 1. Health services | **74** | –01 | 03 | –11 | 00 | –09 |
| 2. Unemployment benefits | **79** | –07 | –14 | –07 | –02 | –05 |
| 3. Social assistance | **80** | –11 | –06 | –03 | –03 | –05 |
| 4. Housing allowances | **67** | –27 | 02 | –06 | –04 | –06 |
| 5. Sickness benefits | **77** | –04 | –07 | –12 | –03 | –02 |
| Eigenvalue | 4.74 | 2.46 | 1.59 | 1.26 | 1.17 | 1.14 |
| $R^2$ | 21.5 | 11.2 | 7.2 | 5.7 | 5.3 | 5.2 |

*Notes*: *Principal components analysis with varimax rotation; factor loadings > 40 in bold.*

This is brought out even more clearly when using a second method to discern attitudinal patterns: the cluster analysis displayed in Figures 8.1 and 8.2. These contain dendrograms, which are a way of graphically displaying which variables correlate strongly and which do not.[4]

[4] The names and numbers of the variables are the same as in Tables 8.5 and 8.6, which means that, for example, 'Finance 2' at the bottom of Figure 8.1 refers to the question on how to finance health services. Variables that are clustered far to the left

TABLE 8.6. *Dimensional analysis of attitudes to welfare policies, 1992 (Factor loadings x 100)*

| Factor | I | II | III | IV | V | VI |
|---|---|---|---|---|---|---|
| Expenditure | | | | | | |
| 1. Medical and health care | –04 | 12 | 09 | **76** | 11 | 00 |
| 2. Support for the elderly | 00 | 03 | 18 | **77** | –07 | 07 |
| 3. Support for families with children | –07 | –04 | **57** | 20 | **44** | –02 |
| 4. Housing allowances | –16 | 11 | **76** | 08 | 15 | –06 |
| 5. Social assistance | –25 | 13 | **67** | 12 | –02 | 02 |
| 6. Research and higher education | –08 | 00 | 04 | –09 | –07 | **80** |
| 7. Comprehensive and secondary schooling | –09 | –11 | –02 | 38 | 31 | **60** |
| 8. Employment policies | –02 | 33 | 38 | 34 | –14 | –05 |
| 9. State and local government administration | 00 | 09 | **62** | –00 | 02 | 08 |
| Service delivery | | | | | | |
| 1. Education | –05 | **62** | –12 | –03 | 25 | 14 |
| 2. Health care | –10 | **74** | 13 | 10 | 07 | –15 |
| 3. Child-care | –05 | **57** | 30 | 08 | 26 | 21 |
| 4. Care for elderly | –02 | **76** | 07 | 10 | 02 | –06 |
| 5. Social work | –10 | **70** | 18 | 07 | –10 | 09 |
| Financing | | | | | | |
| 1. Education | –22 | 13 | 01 | –06 | **72** | 30 |
| 2. Health services | –12 | 29 | –05 | **46** | 33 | –30 |
| 3. Child-care | –15 | 17 | 33 | 14 | **64** | –18 |
| Abuse | | | | | | |
| 1. Health services | **77** | –05 | 06 | –06 | –13 | –02 |
| 2. Unemployment benefits | **80** | –12 | –04 | –01 | –07 | –11 |
| 3. Social assistance | **81** | –12 | –04 | –01 | –07 | –11 |
| 4. Housing allowances | **64** | 00 | –33 | –03 | –21 | 04 |
| 5. Sickness benefits | **82** | –10 | –13 | –08 | –01 | 00 |
| Eigenvalue | 4.94 | 2.54 | 1.74 | 1.37 | 1.17 | 1.14 |
| $R^2$ | 22.4 | 11.5 | 7.9 | 6.2 | 5.3 | 5.2 |

*Notes*: *Principal components analysis with varimax rotation; factor loadings > 40 in bold.*

What can be deduced from the two dendrograms? The first thing to underline is that just as in the principal-components analysis, there is considerable stability in the attitudinal patterns. The same variables tend to cluster in almost the same way in 1992 as in 1986. There are some exceptions to this which will be discussed.

in the dendrogram, as for example 'Abuse 2' and 'Abuse 3', have very high correlations, while variables that are clustered far to the right in the dendrogram have very low correlations. The analysis used the average linkage method for estimating clusters.

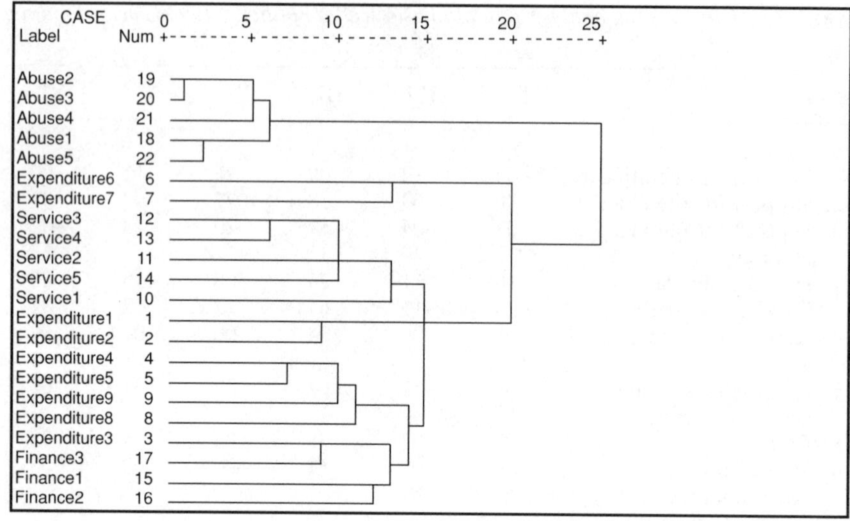


FIG. 8.1. Dendrogram using average linkage (Between Groups), 1986

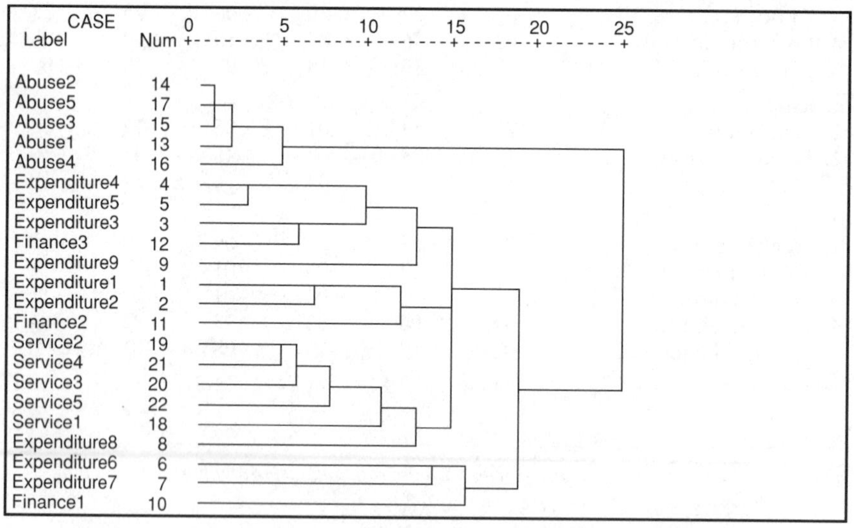


FIG. 8.2. Dendrogram using average linkage (Between Groups), 1992

A second implication is that while the items on welfare abuse are very highly correlated among themselves, they have very low correlations with all the other welfare-state attitudes. Not until the very largest clustering distance do the abuse items cluster with any of the other variables. The attitudes on abuse of welfare policies are to some extent insulated from broader patterns of attitudes to welfare policies. A person who thinks that welfare is widely abused can still have almost any attitude on any other welfare policy issue.

One change that can be detected from 1986 to 1992 is that in 1992 the finance items no longer form a cluster. Instead they tend to follow the area to which they relate, so that financing of child-care (Finance 3) goes with spending on child-care (Expenditure 3); financing of health care (Finance 2) with spending on health care (Expenditure 1); and financing of education (Finance 1) with the expenditure on education items (Expenditure 6 and 7). So what is apparent from the cluster analysis is that there are two principal ways in which these variables are linked. One is through the *aspect* of welfare policy they capture: service delivery, spending, financing, or abuse. The other is through the *recipient group* they target: parents, the infirm or elderly, students, for example.

That abuse questions tend to have high correlations, or that service-delivery questions do, is of course not very surprising or interesting in itself. The interesting finding is rather that so many aspects of attitudes to welfare policies do not correlate very strongly. It is not the case that people are generally for or against the welfare state; their attitudes vary across different attitudinal dimensions in a way that creates a very mixed pattern, but not necessarily one that is incoherent or incomprehensible.

In order to compare attitudes in various groups, a number of additive indices were constructed with support from the dimensional analyses. Three indices, measuring, respectively, suspicions of welfare abuse, attitudes towards service delivery, and attitudes towards the financing of welfare policies were created. The 'Suspicion index' contains all the abuse items, recoded into 0 (agree) and 1 (disagree) and summed. The 'Service index' contains all the service delivery questions, recoded into 1 ('State and local authority') and 0 (all others) and summed. The 'Finance index' contains the three questions on how to pay for services, recoded into 0 (Increasing user fees) and 1 (Taxes and employer contributions) and summed. Measures of reliability (Cronbach's alpha), as displayed in the Appendix (Table 8.A1), indicate that there are some problems with the 'Finance index' in 1992, as we might expect from the dimensional analysis. For purposes of comparability, it nevertheless seems reasonable to retain the index, while bearing in mind the problems of reliability when interpreting the results.

All of the spending issues, except the two on education, were collapsed into one 'Spending index'. All items were recoded into 2 ('increase'), 1 ('remain the same' and 'don't know'), and 0 ('decrease') and then summed. The two questions on education do not correlate strongly at all with the other issues; they result in lower measures of reliability when brought into the index. Neither are they able to form an index of their own: attempts result in unacceptably low reliability (alpha = 0.34 in 1992).[5] It would be possible, if one were to follow the results from the factor analysis slavishly, to keep the two items on health and care for the elderly separate from the others summarized in the spending index (cf. Svallfors 1991). This results, however, in rather low levels of reliability (alpha = 0.51 in 1986), and adds little of substance to the interpretation which follows.

The way the indices are created, higher index values always mean more attitudinal support for welfare policies. A person with the highest possible values on all indices wishes to increase spending on all listed areas, would like the state and local authorities to handle all listed services, wants to keep financing mainly through taxes and employer contributions, and does not suspect that any of the listed welfare polices is subject to abuse. Index distributions are displayed in the Appendix (Table 8.A1).

## STRUCTURAL DIVISIONS AND ATTITUDES TO WELFARE POLICIES

From the previous discussion, a few general hypotheses may be derived concerning the link between various structural divisions and attitudes to welfare policies. The first derives from suggestions of increasing fragmentation of interests and identities and simply states that the link between class and attitudes will become weaker over time.

H1: Over the time period studied, there will be a decline in association between class and attitudes, expressed as smaller regression coefficients for the class dummies and lower levels of explained variance.

The second hypothesis comes from the discussion about non-class cleavages and states that over time we will find a stronger link between various non-class cleavages and attitudes to welfare policies. This suggestion may be stated in a strong form, implying that other social cleavages will supersede the class–attitudes link, or in a weaker form, which only assumes that we will find a tendency towards stronger links between non-class cleavages and attitudes.

H2*a*: Over the time period studied, the link between class and attitudes will be superseded by the link between new cleavages and attitudes, expressed as a substantial, and increasing, reduction in class regression coefficients once other cleavages are brought into the equation.

[5] An interesting finding from separate analyses of these two items is that class patterns are 'reversed' compared to what we find on the other spending items. Higher non-manuals wish to spend more on education than manual workers, which is especially clear in the case of research and higher education. This is hardly surprising given the class distribution profile of higher education, but it illustrates the importance of keeping education separate from other spending items.

H2*b*: Over the time period studied, the link between new cleavages and attitudes will become stronger. This will be expressed through larger regression coefficients and higher levels of explained variance.

The alternative assumption, or null hypothesis, is that over the time period studied we will find practically no change in the relation between class and attitudes, and that in 1992, just as in 1981 and 1986, class will have a stronger impact on welfare attitudes than will non-class variables.

The indicator of class position used is the Swedish socio-economic classification (SEI). This classification separates occupations along several dimensions: employers from self-employed and employed, farmers from other self-employed, groups of employers according to firm size, manual workers from nonmanual occupations, and occupations with different education or skill requirements (SCB 1982). The classification is very similar to the class schema developed by Goldthorpe and his collaborators (Goldthorpe 1980, 1987; Erikson and Goldthorpe 1992*a*). The eighteen categories distinguished in the SEI are here collapsed into six categories: unskilled workers, skilled workers, lower nonmanual workers, intermediate nonmanual workers, higher nonmanual workers, and the self-employed. The data for 1986 do not allow separation of employers from the self-employed, while farmers are such a small group that they are included with the other self-employed, with whom they share many attitudes. Since no data on spouse's class were collected in the 1986 survey, class coding is based on respondent's own occupation. Pensioners, the unemployed, and respondents not in the labour force are classified according to their last occupation.

In addition to class, the analyses compare men with women, public sector employees with those working in the private sector and home-owners with those who rent—all divisions which have been proposed by advocates of the rise of non-class cleavages. Three categories of dependants on the welfare state are also discerned: the unemployed, the retired, and all others. The retired and the unemployed seem to be the main distinct categories of people that are more or less completely dependent on public benefits. Other categories of people not currently in the labour market, such as home-makers and students, are not as dependent on cash benefits from the state and are thus allocated to the same category as those currently in the labour market.[6]

The only attitudinal index where it is possible to conduct any multivariate analysis on the 1981 data is the 'Spending index'. This means that

[6] There are, of course, other variables that would be relevant if the primary purpose of this analysis was simply to explain variation in attitudes to welfare policies. Factors such as income and education, which are related to but not reducible to class, or position in the life-cycle as indicated by age, are clearly relevant in structuring attitudes to welfare policies (Svallfors 1989, 1991). Their status in relation to the theoretical debates pursued here, however, is not clear-cut.

the time-span for most indicators is shorter than is ideal for tracing the development of cleavage structures over time. The limited time-span is to some extent compensated by the fact that we have data covering a broad range of welfare issues. The present analysis should at least be indicative of whether we find a general tendency towards the dissolution of class differences across a range of issues.

The class, gender, sector, housing, and dependent-on-public-support variables were transformed into a set of dummy variables and used in regression models with the four attitude indices that were created in the previous section. Tables 8.7 to 8.9 display the results of these regressions. Table 8.7 includes only the class dummy variables for all indices and years; Table 8.8 includes only non-class variables; Table 8.9 includes both class and non-class variables. Group means are presented in the Appendix (Table 8.A2).

There are several dimensions along which we can compare the results in the tables: across variables, indices, or years. On the spending index, we find that class differences are as we would expect them to be, with workers being most supportive of welfare spending and higher nonmanuals and the self-employed least supportive. A comparison of Tables 8.7 and 8.8 also indicates that class has a somewhat stronger association with the index than the non-class variables. However, the association between class and attitudes becomes somewhat weaker between 1981 and 1992, whereas the private–public sector cleavage, from being completely negligible in 1981, becomes somewhat more important over time. The impact of gender and housing on attitudes declines somewhat, but gender differences are still significant in 1992, even after controlling for class and public sector employment.

While class differences have declined on the spending index, they have grown on the service index. Workers are just as supportive of state handling of services in 1992 as they were in 1986, while all other groups except the higher nonmanuals became less supportive of the state-handling services. We also find, in both 1986 and 1992, that public sector employees and the retired are significantly more supportive of the state than people working in the private sector and those not retired. While the differences between private and public sector employees have become smaller over the six-year period, contrasts between the retired and the rest have become clearer. The most striking finding, however, is the extremely small differences between men and women. Arguments within feminist theory would certainly have suggested otherwise. Another remarkable finding is that in 1992, home-owners are significantly *less* 'privatized' than those who rent, contrary to what would be expected from the debate on consumption groupings. In general, class and non-class variables have effects that are of about the same magnitude and largely independent of each other—as

TABLE 8.7. *Class determinants and attitudinal indexes*

| | Welfare Attitudes | | | | | | | | |
|---|---|---|---|---|---|---|---|---|---|
| | Spending index | | | Service index | | Finance index | | Suspicion index | |
| | 1981 | 1986 | 1992 | 1986 | 1992 | 1986 | 1992 | 1986 | 1992 |
| Skilled workers | –0.65[b] | –0.28 | –0.29 | 0.15 | –0.02 | –0.14 | 0.00 | –0.05 | –0.10 |
| Lower nonmanuals | –1.10[a] | –0.60[c] | –0.73[a] | 0.06 | –0.49[a] | –0.12 | –0.08 | –0.15 | 0.07 |
| Middle nonmanuals | –1.67[a] | –1.24[a] | –1.47[a] | –0.18 | –0.43[a] | –0.20[c] | –0.18[b] | 0.12 | 0.04 |
| Higher nonmanuals | –2.39[a] | –2.42[a] | –1.89[a] | –0.57[a] | –0.60[a] | –0.42[a] | –0.11 | 0.24 | 0.48[a] |
| Self-employed | –1.63[a] | –1.54[a] | –1.42[a] | –0.39[b] | –0.75[a] | –0.46[a] | –0.28[a] | –0.60[a] | –0.58[c] |
| (Reference category is unskilled worker) | | | | | | | | | |
| Constant | 8.57[a] | 8.43[a] | 8.48[a] | 3.92[a] | 3.99[a] | 2.45[b] | 2.37[a] | 1.71[a] | 1.66[a] |
| $R^2$ (%) | 11.4 | 9.3 | 7.9 | 2.6 | 3.6 | 3.1 | 1.2 | 1.9 | 2.2 |

*Notes*: Multiple regression (ordinary least squares); unstandardized regression coefficients.
Levels of significance: [a] = *t*-value significant at 0.001 level; [b] *t*-value significant at 0.01 level; [c] *t*-value significant at 0.05 level.

TABLE 8.8. *Non-class determinants and attitudinal indexes*

| | Welfare Attitudes | | | | | | | | |
|---|---|---|---|---|---|---|---|---|---|
| | Spending index | | | Service index | | Finance index | | Suspicion index | |
| | 1981 | 1986 | 1992 | 1986 | 1992 | 1986 | 1992 | 1986 | 1992 |
| Gender (men = 0) | 0.72[a] | 0.69[a] | 0.53[a] | 0.08 | 0.03 | 0.11 | 0.03 | 0.08 | 0.32[a] |
| Sector (private = 0) | –0.05 | 0.28 | 0.62[a] | 0.38[a] | 0.30[a] | 0.16[c] | 0.15[b] | 0.32[b] | 0.14 |
| Housing (owner = 0) | 0.42[b] | 0.68[a] | 0.34[b] | 0.02 | –0.18[c] | –0.02 | 0.05 | 0.36[b] | 0.02 |
| Unemployed | — | 1.18[b] | 1.23[a] | 0.32 | 0.12 | 0.44[b] | 0.22[c] | 0.06 | 0.55[b] |
| Retired | 0.72[a] | 0.94[a] | 0.73[a] | 0.30[b] | 0.66[a] | 0.03 | –0.02 | –0.18 | –0.26[c] |
| (Reference category for unemployed and retired is 'others') | | | | | | | | | |
| Constant | 7.14[a] | 6.86[a] | 6.87[a] | 3.59[a] | 3.49[a] | 2.17[a] | 2.17[a] | 1.39[a] | 1.44[a] |
| $R^2$ (%) | 4.8 | 6.8 | 5.5 | 2.8 | 4.0 | 1.9 | 1.2 | 2.4 | 2.1 |

*Notes*: Multiple regression (ordinary least squares); unstandardized regression coefficients.

Levels of significance: [a] = *t*-value significant at 0.001 level; [b] *t*-value significant at 0.01 level; [c] *t*-value significant at 0.05 level.

TABLE 8.9. *Structural determinants and attitudinal indexes*

| | Welfare Attitudes | | | | | | | | |
|---|---|---|---|---|---|---|---|---|---|
| | Spending index | | | Service index | | Finance index | | Suspicion index | |
| | 1981 | 1986 | 1992 | 1986 | 1992 | 1986 | 1992 | 1986 | 1992 |
| Skilled workers | –0.47[c] | –0.05 | –0.16 | 0.18 | 0.02 | –0.12 | 0.01 | 0.00 | –0.06 |
| Lower nonmanuals | –1.03[a] | –0.63[b] | –0.61[b] | 0.02 | –0.47[a] | –0.13 | –0.06 | –0.16 | 0.05 |
| Middle nonmanuals | –1.52[a] | –1.07[a] | –1.33[a] | –0.24 | –0.43[a] | –0.22[c] | –0.17[c] | 0.11 | 0.11 |
| Higher nonmanuals | –2.06[a] | –2.07[a] | –1.71[a] | –0.59[a] | –0.60[a] | –0.42[a] | –0.10 | 0.29 | 0.56[a] |
| Self-employed | –1.48[a] | –1.29[a] | –0.98[a] | –0.31[c] | –0.73[a] | –0.40[a] | –0.21[c] | –0.44[c] | –0.42[b] |
| (Reference category is unskilled worker) | | | | | | | | | |
| Gender (men = 0) | 0.41[b] | 0.48[b] | 0.36[b] | 0.03 | –0.02 | 0.03 | 0.01 | 0.09 | 0.32[a] |
| Sector (private = 0) | 0.05 | 0.37[c] | 0.63[a] | 0.41[a] | 0.23[b] | 0.17[c] | 0.14[b] | 0.24[c] | 0.05 |
| Housing (owner = 0) | 0.24 | 0.51[b] | 0.19 | –0.03 | –0.26[b] | –0.06 | 0.03 | 0.36[b] | 0.02 |
| Unemployed | — | 0.82[c] | 0.86[b] | 0.21 | –0.06 | 0.37[c] | 0.18 | 0.07 | 0.58[b] |
| Retired | 0.60[b] | 0.88[a] | 0.59[a] | 0.29[c] | 0.62[a] | 0.04 | –0.02 | –0.12 | –0.21 |
| (Others left out) | | | | | | | | | |
| Constant | 8.07[a] | 7.58[a] | 7.68[a] | 3.71[a] | 3.88[a] | 2.37[a] | 2.27[a] | 1.44[a] | 1.44[a] |
| $R^2$ (%) | 13.4 | 13.7 | 11.3 | 5.2 | 7.4 | 4.4 | 2.0 | 3.7 | 3.8 |

*Notes*: Multiple regression (ordinary least squares); unstandardized regression coefficients.

Levels of significance: [a] = *t*-value significant at 0.001 level; [b] *t*-value significant at 0.01 level; [c] *t*-value significant at 0.05 level.

shown by the very small changes in coefficients from Table 8.7 to Table 8.9, or from Table 8.8 to Table 8.9.

On the finance index, we find that group differences are very small (in 1992, the F-values of the models barely reach statistical significance). The only striking finding is perhaps that higher nonmanuals in 1992 are almost as supportive of collective financing as workers are. Six years before they resembled the self-employed in being less supportive of collective financing.

Finally, the suspicion index displays a class pattern that is to some extent 'reversed' compared to the other indices. The higher nonmanuals are the least suspicious group, something which is clearer in 1992 than it was six years earlier. Among the non-class variables, gender and unemployment have grown in importance, while the impact from housing and sector on attitudes has declined.

If we compare the indices, we find that attitude differences are clearest for the spending index, less so for the service index, and the finance and suspicion indices display very modest group differences. This could be interpreted as indicating a fairly strong consensus on the importance of keeping collective financing and on the perceived abuse of welfare policies, but with more marked attitudinal conflict about how much to devote to various welfare policies and some conflict also on the question about who is best suited to handle services.

Comparisons across the 1981–92 period reveal a general picture of stability in group differences. No general tendencies towards decreasing class differences can be detected, even if results on the spending index might indicate a slight shift from class towards sectorally based conflicts. Since these changes are rather small, it would seem unwise to draw any firm conclusions. Other differences across both variables and indices are remarkably stable.

Nor is there any general trend for any of the non-class cleavages to be gaining in importance. The findings point in different directions on different indices. With respect to housing, the trend is actually the reverse of that predicted by proponents of consumption group theory. Private versus public sector differences display an unclear pattern of growth in some areas and decline in others. The gender cleavage is of fairly modest importance in 1992 as in 1986. The unemployed, as a group the most supportive of welfare policies on six indices out of nine (as shown in Appendix, Table 8.A2), do not in general become more distinct from other groups over time. The modest impact of retirement on attitudes is also rather similar over time.

It seems, then, as if none of the three hypotheses formulated in the beginning of the section receives any clear support. Stability, rather than dramatic or unequivocal change, characterizes cleavages over Swedish welfare policies, at least in the relatively short time-span we have been able to analyse.

## CONCLUSIONS

This has been, above all, a tale of stability. Gross percentage distributions, patterns between different variables, attitude differences between various groups: they all show a large measure of stability. These are findings that contradict much of the debate on recent changes in cleavage structures. Neither those who are convinced that political differences between men and women will come to the fore in times of welfare crisis, nor those who believe that new consumption groups will replace class as the most important social cleavage, receive much support from this analysis. Regarding gender cleavages, it should be noted that women (as men) constitute a very heterogeneous group. To say the very least, owing to the very different class positions among women, it is unlikely that all of them will perceive their interests as necessarily being best defended by a universal and costly welfare state. Regarding housing, even Saunders, who in 1986 believed it to be 'the most basic element in the analysis of consumption relations' (Saunders 1986: 323) was forced by the weight of his own evidence to admit its minor importance (Saunders 1990). Contrary to what Saunders seems to believe, however, it would appear that findings such as his own, or those presented in this article, cast serious doubts on the viability of the whole consumption group framework.

Being employed by the public sector, retired, or unemployed, and thus in various ways directly dependent on the welfare state for economic sustenance clearly has some implications for attitudes to the welfare state, as shown above. However, there are no unequivocal signs that divisions between private and the public sector employees are widening, and the unemployed do not seem to be more marginalized in their attitudes during the early 1990s than they were in the mid-1980s.

Why, then, do all the brave predictions about the decline of class politics fail to receive any strong empirical support? On the one hand, it should be noted that much of the recent theorizing has been based on a less than solid empirical foundation. Some of the authors simply ignore the data, and rely on suggestive theorizing, some of which seems to endorse a fairly idealized picture of the homogeneous and solidaristic classes that could be found in the heyday of welfare policy reform (a typical example is Offe 1987 referred to above). As pointed out by Marshall *et al.* (1988: 202–6), findings such as these receive no support from historical research, which instead emphasizes that internal heterogeneity and divisions built on sectional self-interest have always been endemic within the working class, something which has still not precluded solidaristic forms of collective action. Both the purely solidaristic worker of yesterday and the asocial individual maximizer of today seem to be products of a 'dualistic historical thinking' by certain social theorists rather than referring to any social reality (Marshall *et al.* 1988: 206).

As we have seen elsewhere in this volume, even some of the research which does take empirical work into account relies on faulty analysis. By using flawed indicators such as the Alford index, or by relying on inadequate class indicators and categorizations, a veritable mass of research artefacts has been produced under the banner of the decline-of-class thesis (i.e. by Inglehart 1990 and by Clark and Lipset 1991).

Another unfortunate tendency among those critical of class analysis is to extrapolate from specific national experiences, seemingly unaware of the limits of how far such experiences can support general arguments. What has been brought out with increasing clarity in comparative social research is the considerable influence of national institutions on processes of class formation and emergence or dilution of new conflict lines, but so far, this has had a limited impact on theory. In this respect, it is hard to avoid the impression of a certain German bias in the arguments about the dissolution of the structural bases of politics, as well as a certain British bias in the argument about new structural conflicts coming to the fore.

In the German case, institutionalist arguments would suggest that (West) Germany is indeed quite different from other West European nations in the extent to which class conflicts have been contained in an extensive web of institutions geared towards social harmony (Crouch 1980; Hancock 1989; Stjernø 1995). Results from empirical work on attitudes also indicate that this has led to less ideological conflict between various groups than is found elsewhere (Coughlin 1980: 157; Svallfors 1993*a*; Matheson 1993: ch. 7; Hayes 1995). Any arguments about an increasing fragmentation of interests that rely mainly (or only) on the German case should therefore be regarded with some suspicion until trends can be shown to extend beyond the German borders.

The British case is almost the opposite of the German in the extent to which conflicts between private and sector employees, between home owners and those who rent, or between welfare dependants and taxpayers, have added to rather than diluted existing class conflicts. The structure of the British welfare state, with its strong emphasis on providing specific consumption subsidies and universal services rather than generalized income transfers, and a strong duality between state benefits at a sustenance level and private/occupational insurances of an income-replacement kind, would seem particularly likely to create precisely such a multifaceted conflict over the welfare state (Dunleavy 1986, 1989; Papadakis and Taylor-Gooby 1987).

The charge of parochialism could, of course, be brought against the present analysis as well, preoccupied as it is with Swedish data. Perhaps Sweden is unusual in still being dominated by class cleavages? Swedish history certainly points to some distinctive traits, such as the absence of religious, ethnic, or regional cleavages which led to the party system being set up on a pure class basis to a far greater extent than in continental Europe. This class-based party system, in combination with strong and centralized trade unions, may have prevented new structural cleavages coming to the fore, or slowed the process of fragmentation of interests and identities. Present-day comparative studies also indicate that, contrary to assumptions about Swedish classlessness or consensus, Sweden displays clearer class divisions in attitudes to inequality and redistribution than nations such as Britain, (West) Germany, and Australia (Svallfors 1993*a*, 1993*b*, 1993*c*).

Those not persuaded by the arguments in this chapter could also point to the short time-span in the analysis, which means that a slow and gradual decline in class differences may be hard to detect. As pointed out, it would have been preferable to cover a longer time period, but this was unfortunately impossible due to lack of data. However, as can be seen from the other chapters in this volume, as well as in previously published research referred to earlier, accumulated findings from other countries—often using much longer time series—are not consistent with claims about any *generalized* decline in class voting or class-based ideologies. The proponents of the variants of the decline-of-class thesis have produced surprisingly little substantive empirical evidence to support their case. The burden of proof must by now surely lie with those who believe that class conflicts are progressively diluted.

In the meantime, social research would perhaps be better served by putting more effort into explaining the 'remarkable persistence of class-linked inequalities and of class-differentiated patterns of social action, even within periods of rapid change at the level of economic structure, social institutions, and political conjunctures' (Goldthorpe and Marshall 1992: 393), than by searching for new structural cleavages or envisaging the end of class politics.[7] No matter how unfashionable it would appear in some quarters, what we need to explain is inertia, not fluidity; stability, not change.

[7] A fruitful starting-point for such explanations concerning attitudes to welfare policies could be found in recent theorizing about risk, risk categories, and risk coalitions, especially in the influential historical analysis by Baldwin (1990: introduction; see also Svallfors 1996: ch. 2). A second, but related, starting-point would be the version of rational action theory recently proposed by Goldthorpe (1996*b*, 1998).

# APPENDIX

TABLE 8.A1. *Index distributions 1981, 1986, and 1992 (per cent)*

| Index value | Spending index 1981 | 1986 | 1992 | Service index 1986 | 1992 | Finance index 1986 | 1992 | Suspicion index 1986 | 1992 |
|---|---|---|---|---|---|---|---|---|---|
| 0 | 0.1 | 0.3 | 0.1 | 3.9 | 5.0 | 6.8 | 4.4 | 31.6 | 37.0 |
| 1 | 0.0 | 0.7 | 0.7 | 3.5 | 6.2 | 11.9 | 15.7 | 25.5 | 20.0 |
| 2 | 0.7 | 0.7 | 1.1 | 8.5 | 10.0 | 26.8 | 26.8 | 16.2 | 14.0 |
| 3 | 2.6 | 2.2 | 2.9 | 16.2 | 15.1 | 54.4 | 53.1 | 9.2 | 10.2 |
| 4 | 4.6 | 6.1 | 4.9 | 25.3 | 20.6 | | | 8.5 | 7.7 |
| 5 | 10.1 | 6.6 | 9.1 | 42.7 | 43.1 | | | 8.9 | 10.1 |
| 6 | 13.5 | 13.3 | 11.9 | | | | | | |
| 7 | 16.1 | 15.2 | 14.7 | | | | | | |
| 8 | 14.8 | 17.3 | 15.4 | | | | | | |
| 9 | 12.5 | 14.7 | 14.9 | | | | | | |
| 10 | 12.5 | 9.6 | 11.8 | | | | | | |
| 11 | 6.6 | 6.2 | 6.1 | | | | | | |
| 12 | 4.3 | 4.3 | 4.1 | | | | | | |
| 13 | 1.6 | 2.3 | 1.9 | | | | | | |
| 14 | 0.0 | 0.4 | 0.3 | | | | | | |
| Mean | 7.74 | 7.75 | 7.72 | 3.84 | 3.69 | 2.29 | 2.28 | 1.64 | 1.65 |
| Standard deviation | 2.36 | 2.47 | 2.47 | 1.36 | 1.50 | 0.92 | 0.89 | 1.62 | 1.72 |
| Cronbach's Alpha | 0.66 | 0.68 | 0.68 | 0.71 | 0.76 | 0.61 | 0.53 | 0.75 | 0.79 |

TABLE 8.A2. *Index values in various subgroups*

| | Welfare Attitudes | | | | | | | | |
|---|---|---|---|---|---|---|---|---|---|
| | Spending index | | | Service index | | Finance index | | Abuse index | |
| | 1981 | 1986 | 1992 | 1986 | 1992 | 1986 | 1992 | 1986 | 1992 |
| Men | 7.37 | 7.41 | 7.42 | 3.76 | 3.65 | 2.22 | 2.26 | 1.61 | 1.49 |
| Women | 8.15 | 8.15 | 8.05 | 3.93 | 3.74 | 2.36 | 2.32 | 1.64 | 1.82 |
| Unskilled worker | 8.72 | 8.48 | 8.54 | 4.01 | 4.04 | 2.48 | 2.40 | 1.71 | 1.63 |
| Skilled worker | 7.92 | 8.15 | 8.19 | 4.07 | 3.95 | 2.31 | 2.38 | 1.66 | 1.55 |
| Lower nonmanual | 7.47 | 7.83 | 7.74 | 3.99 | 3.49 | 2.32 | 2.29 | 1.56 | 1.73 |
| Middle nonmanual | 6.90 | 7.19 | 7.00 | 3.74 | 3.56 | 2.25 | 2.18 | 1.82 | 1.70 |
| Higher nonmanual | 6.18 | 6.01 | 6.59 | 3.35 | 3.39 | 2.02 | 2.28 | 1.95 | 2.16 |
| Self-employed | 6.92 | 6.89 | 7.06 | 3.53 | 3.29 | 1.98 | 2.06 | 1.10 | 1.05 |
| Private sector | 7.69 | 7.54 | 7.33 | 3.69 | 3.54 | 2.21 | 2.21 | 1.53 | 1.54 |
| Public sector | 7.78 | 7.97 | 8.10 | 4.07 | 3.84 | 2.40 | 2.37 | 1.86 | 1.77 |
| Owner | 7.55 | 7.50 | 7.57 | 3.87 | 3.76 | 2.31 | 2.26 | 1.54 | 1.64 |
| Renter | 8.02 | 8.15 | 7.96 | 3.83 | 3.57 | 2.28 | 2.32 | 1.86 | 1.68 |
| Employed | — | 7.53 | 7.54 | 3.77 | 3.57 | 2.27 | 2.28 | 1.68 | 1.68 |
| Unemployed | 8.44 | 8.77 | 8.67 | 4.07 | 3.61 | 2.69 | 2.49 | 1.78 | 2.17 |
| Retired | 7.58 | 8.45 | 8.19 | 4.03 | 4.23 | 2.29 | 2.25 | 1.45 | 1.39 |

# PART III

## The New Class Politics of Post-communism

# 9

# The Politics of Interests and Class Realignment in the Czech Republic, 1992–1996

PETR MATEJU, BLANKA REHAKOVA, AND GEOFFREY EVANS

## INTRODUCTION: THE CHANGING CHARACTER OF CZECH ELECTORAL POLITICS

The electoral success of the Social Democrats in the 1996 Czech parliamentary elections surprised both politicians and political scientists. The Czech Social Democratic Party (CSSD) received 26 per cent of votes, which was exactly four times more than in the 1992 elections. The Civic Democratic Party (ODS), a liberal conservative party, the designer of Czech economic reform and the Social Democrats' main competitor, received slightly below 30 per cent of votes in both 1992 and 1996. Although it remained the strongest party on the Czech political stage, the electoral success of Social Democrats made its position far weaker than after the 1992 elections.

The period between 1992 and 1996 also saw the emergence of two processes relevant to voting behaviour: (1) the crystallization of the content of left–right political orientations, and (2) a general shift in perceptions of the relationship between the market and the state. Voters on the left have thus become more egalitarian in their views of distributive justice while those on the right of the political spectrum display more anti-egalitarian attitudes (Mateju and Vlachova 1997). Figure 9.1 provides a simple illustration of this crystallization process.[1] There is also

This research received support from the Grant Agency of the Czech Republic (grants 403/96/K120 and 403/96/0386). The authors wish to thank Czech Television and SC&C for permission to use data from the exit polls of 1992 and 1996, Klara Vlachova and Jindrich Krejci for their help in the preparation of the datasets for analyses and for their valuable comments on the first draft of the paper.

[1] The index of 'egalitarian inclinations' was constructed from answers to two five-point items: 'The fairest way of distributing wealth and income would be to give everyone equal shares', and 'The most important thing is that people get what they need, even if this means allocating money from those who earned more than they need'.

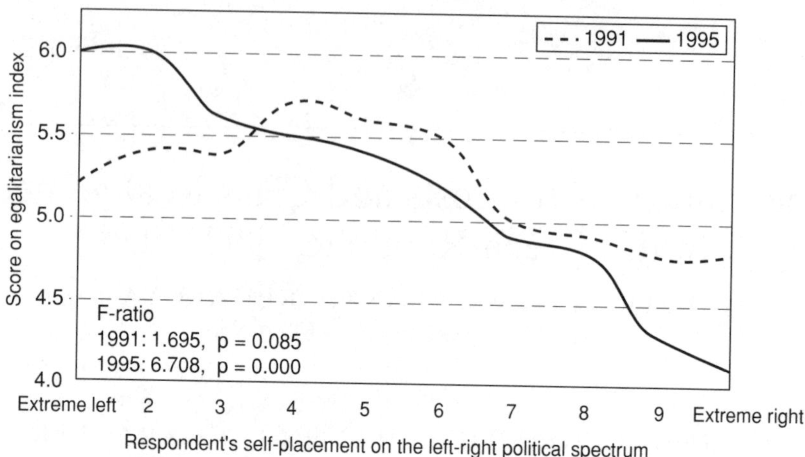


FIG 9.1. Attitudes towards egalitarian norms of distribution along the left–right political spectrum in the Czech Republic, 1991 and 1995

*Note*: Average values of the index of egalitarianism.
*Source*: Social Justice Survey 1991, 1995.

evidence that the Czech population has generally become far more 'paternalist', endorsing stronger state intervention in the economy (Vecernik 1996).[2]

It would appear then that the Czech public is developing an understanding of Czech politics as a left–right division defined by the sorts of conflicts—between interventionist and free market strategies, between redistributive and *laissez-faire* policies—which underlie such divisions in the West. What is unclear, however, is whether these developments in attitudes towards the market and inequality in response to the difficulties incurred during marketization—and which are clearly class-related in their consequences (see Evans 1997, Mateju 1996*a* Rehakova and Vlachova 1995)—have contributed to a growth in the association between social class and voting behaviour. So although the general pattern of change in voting behaviour over this period can certainly be attributed in large part to a *general shift* among the electorate towards political parties that emphasized state intervention and welfare, the increase of votes for the

Responses were coded so that scores on the index ranged from 2 (anti-egalitarian) to 10 (egalitarian).

[2] The International Social Justice Project surveys carried out in 1991 and 1995 showed, for example, that the proportion of individuals strongly endorsing market mechanisms as a driving force for the economy dropped from 60 to 34%.

left might also reflect the crystallization of an association between social class and political partisanship as a result of the post-communist transformation. Our aim in this chapter is to examine this thesis.

## PERSPECTIVES ON VOTING IN POST-COMMUNIST COUNTRIES

Explanations of the relationship between social position and voting behaviour in post-communist countries can be grouped into two distinct types. One identifies the groups of 'winners' and 'losers' that differ substantially in their support for pro-reform parties on the basis of *subjective* factors such as the expression of relative deprivation. The core argument of this position is that the winner–loser split defined by subjective appraisals of changing life-chances does not correspond very closely with objective class boundaries (Wnuk-Lipinski 1993, Kis 1994, Mateju 1996*b*). Recent analyses (Rehakova and Vlachova 1995, Mateju 1996*a*) of responses to transition in Central European societies have indicated that many people experienced a significant change in their positions in social hierarchies and, in particular, in their life-chances, without displaying evidence of objective class mobility or objective change in their status. Since political behaviour is affected at least as strongly by what is perceived as by what actually exists, this suggests that *perceptions* of social position and mobility, which are at most weakly related to objective positions, contribute significantly to the formation of groups of 'winners' and 'losers' in the market transition currently under way in Eastern Europe. Consistent with this idea, in 1993 in four Central European countries (the Czech Republic, Hungary, Poland, and Slovakia) *subjective* socio-economic mobility was found to be the strongest predictor of voting, while the effect of objective class position was markedly smaller than is typically the case in Western democracies (Mateju 1996*b*).

A second approach to the explanation of voting behaviour in post-communist countries emphasizes the increasing significance of *objective* class-based inequalities as a basis of economic interests (Evans and Whitefield 1993; Evans 1997). According to this perspective, in market societies left-wing political parties can expect to obtain their support differentially from social classes whose members experience economic insecurity and, consequently, are strongly affected by the presence or absence of left-wing redistributive policies resulting in a more egalitarian distribution of income and wealth. As the working class in post-communist societies lose out in the market-place, they can be expected to connect their experiences to their policy preferences and hence to express increasingly a relative preference for parties that present interventionist and redistributive policy programmes. Thus post-communist countries experiencing the early stage of capitalism are likely to be characterized by class *polarization* between disadvantaged classes—the working class and peasants—and those who benefit more obviously and immediately from marketization—the professional and entrepreneurial classes.

Several theories support this view of changes in post-communist politics. For example, the principal argument of the *Theory of the Two Axes* (i.e. Szelenyi, *et al.* 1996, 1997) is that there have been two types of cleavages in the political field of post-communist societies: the *liberal–conservative* cleavage, opening up ground for political struggles over value orientations, moral and cultural norms, and so on and the *left–right* cleavage, supplying the arguments for political struggles over economic interests (see also Evans and Whitefield 1993; Kitschelt 1992). According to Szelenyi and his collaborators, politics in post-communist countries is currently experiencing a shift from the prevalence of the liberal–conservative axis (politics of symbols) to the rule of the left-right axis (politics of interests):

> The first epoch after the fall of communism is dominated by concerns with liberty, identity and community; thus it is divided along the Liberal/Conservative axis and not shaped significantly by class. Economic interests and class cleavages do exist in the background, and as civil liberties are guaranteed economic conflicts move to the fore. As a result, politics moves from a politics of symbols to a politics of interest, the Left/Right divide in politics and the class determination of political attitudes gain in importance. In other words, the closer the former state socialist countries move to the model of democratic market societies, the more meaningful the notion of Left and Right becomes and the greater role economic interests and class cleavages play in electoral politics. (Szelenyi *et al.* 1997: 212)

As already emphasized, there is no reason to regard these two theoretical perspectives—subjective and objective—as mutually exclusive. In our view, both perspectives provide a relevant theoretical framework for the analysis of voting behaviour. A distinction should be made, however, regarding the *relative* explanatory power of each of these perspectives in *different stages* of the post-communist transformation. In the early periods of the transformation, the role of subjective factors (subjective mobility, relative deprivation, perception of change in life-chances, and so on) in the determination of voting behaviour is likely to be stronger than the role of objective class. As the new post-socialist class structure emerges and the politics of symbols is transformed into the politics of interests, however, objective class is becoming a more and more important factor in voting behaviour. And, as we have already seen in the introduction, not only has the left–right axis survived, but between 1992–6 it crystallized, and in the process gained a traditional left-right character. Individuals identifying themselves with the left developed a more consistent egalitarian distributive ideology and became more suspicious of the liberal and conservative view of the role of the market, while adherents of the right have taken a step further in building a more consistent meritocratic ideology of distributive justice. In other words, the almost universal 'pro-market euphoria' of the early stage of the transformation has faded and different social groups and classes have begun to develop their own views of the ideal socio-economic order. Thus it is likely that the re-emergence of the traditional content of the left–right political spectrum has gone hand in hand with the crystallization of traditional class interests.

There are at least four processes which imply that these class interests have been growing rather than declining during the post-communist transformation.

1. Restitution and privatization have led to the emergence of a class of proprietors and entrepreneurs. The growth of this new class contributes to the formation rather than the decline of traditional class cleavages and interests.
2. The working class has lost its ideologically based 'leading role' in society and has become the group most vulnerable to economic turbulence (the decline of traditionally 'preferred' industries, unemployment, inflation, and so on). This development necessarily causes a crystallization rather than an erosion of traditional working-class consciousness. Moreover, owing to delayed modernization of industrial structures in post-communist countries, the size of the working class has not been declining, which means that it still represents quite a significant social force in post-communist politics.
3. The transition to the market has brought an increase in wage, income, and wealth inequality. This increase in social and economic inequality is reinforcing rather than hindering the crystallization of class-based interests.
4. The market transition is bringing about a transfromation from a socialist economy of scarcity to a capitalist economy of abundance, which means, among other things, that after more than forty years supply is becoming higher than demand—not to mention the dramatic changes in the variety of the commodities and services on offer. Such a development supports the growth of materialist rather than postmaterialist values.

Taken together, these general processes create conditions for the strengthening of class-based voting behaviour and for the crystallization of a 'traditional' left–right political spectrum. Hence, we may expect a polarization over time in the effect of class position on electoral behaviour. However, there are also specific features of Czech experience which may have been important in shaping these processes: first, because the Communist regime in the Czech Republic collapsed without its previous economic or political erosion, both political and economic reform have been more profound and more consistent than elsewhere in Eastern Europe. So although the social policy of the right-wing Czech government has been deliberately more of a modern-liberal than conservative type, maintaining the lowest poverty rate in Eastern Europe,[3] and Czech economic policy has successfully controlled both inflation and unemployment,[4] there has been an increase in economic inequality and a corresponding increase in the popular desire for stronger welfare and social policy programmes. Secondly, the Czech Republic was also among the most egalitarian of the communist countries.[5] The consequences of the market-transition in terms of the increase in wage, income, and wealth inequality have therefore been felt particularly strongly (see e.g. Rehakova 1997). Consequently, increasing social and economic inequality has reinforced egalitarian beliefs, particularly among those who feel they have lost out in the new system.

The analysis that follows focuses on two questions: first, we ask whether class position had an increasing effect on electoral behaviour between 1992–6, such that the working class became relatively more left-wing in its party preferences and the middle classes became relatively more right-wing. In other words, we ask whether there was evidence of a traditional form of class–party polarization. Secondly, we consider to what extent any change in the association between class and party can be explained by the political struggle between the ODS and Social Democrats, the two major rivals on the Czech political stage.

## DATA, VARIABLES, AND METHODS OF ANALYSIS

The surveys used in this analysis are two exit polls carried out during the 1992 and 1996 Czech elections.[6] These polls were designed to provide esti-

[3] See Vecernik (1996) for a comparison of different indicators of poverty among post-communist countries.

[4] According to the Institute for Comparative Economic Studies in Vienna (WIIW), the Czech Republic faced inflation of about 8.5% in 1996 (which is the lowest inflation rate after Slovakia, which had 7% predicted inflation in 1996), with by far the lowest unemployment rate (3% compared to 11% in Hungary, 13% in Slovakia, 14% in Poland and Slovenia).

[5] The pro-egalitarian inclinations of the Czech population also have historical roots stretching further back than just to the Communist era and its ideology: Mateju and Vlachova (Mateju 1993, Mateju and Vlachova 1995) emphasize the egalitarian interpretation of reform advocated by the early Protestant movement in Bohemia, while Havelka (1995) points to the 'social incompleteness' of the Czech social structure due to the loss of its national gentry in the late fifteenth and early sixteenth century, when the Hapsburgs won the battle for the Czech crown.

[6] The 1992 exit poll was carried out by INFAS, IVVM, and Factum for Czechoslovak Television. The 1996 exit poll was conducted by IFES and SC&C for Czech television.

mates of the election results to be presented and discussed on Czechoslovak (1992)/Czech (1996) television before the official results were released. Both surveys were based on a representative sample of electoral districts and contained information on respondents' voting behaviour, occupation, age, sex, and religion. The 1992 poll contains 11,058 unweighted cases from the Czech part of the former Czechoslovakia, the 1996 survey contains 13,792 cases.

For the analysis, both data files were merged and weighted to the actual election results. To achieve comparability of results between the two years, two decisions had to be taken. First, the results of 1992 elections to the Czech National Council (CNR) were used instead of the results of elections to the Federal Assembly (FS).[7] Secondly, the number of parties was reduced to manageable and comparable levels (from twenty-one in 1992 and sixteen in 1996). The key for the inclusion of a party in the analysis was that it received enough votes to meet the required threshold to enter the parliament in 1996.[8] In 1992 all left-wing parties except the Social Democrats created a coalition 'Left Bloc' (The Communist Party of Bohemia and Moravia (KSCM) and the Party of the Democratic Left (SDL) ) while in 1996 they contested the elections separately. Both the Left Bloc (LB) and the Party of the Democratic Left (SDL) were defeated in 1996 (with 1.4 per cent and 0.13 per cent respectively) while Communists entered parliament with 10.3 per cent of valid votes. For the sake of comparability between 1992 and 1996, we created a 'Left Bloc' category for both years. For 1992 this represents the 'Left Bloc' coalition (KSCM, LB, and SDL) while in 1996 it brings together the votes for the LB, SDL, and KSCM. (See Appendix, Table 9.A1 for the explanation of acronyms for names of political parties.) Voting preference was then defined in two different ways:

- 1 = Left (CSSD, KSCM, LB, SDL) = 1, non-Left (all other parties on the list) = 2;
- Social Democrats = 1, *ODS* = 2; other parties excluded.

[7] In 1992 two ballots were carried out in each part of the former Czechoslovakia: the ballot for elections to the Czechoslovak Federal Assembly and the ballot for elections to the Czech National Council (in the Czech Republic) and to the Slovak National Council (in Slovakia).

[8] Two more parties reached the threshold in 1992 than in 1996: a Moravian nationalist party (HSD–SMS with 5.8% of the vote in 1992), and the Liberal and Social Union (LSU—with 6.5%), a party without a clear political programme. HSD–SMS split after the 1992 elections and its successors (MNS–HSS and MSMS–MNS) together received less than 1% of the vote in 1996. The LSU was transformed into the LSNS (Liberal Social and National Party) and integrated with the Free Democrats (SD) before the elections in 1996. The new party (SD–LSNS) received only 2% of the vote.

Four independent variables were employed in the analysis: class, sex, age cohort, and region. Class was defined in such a way as to distinguish between the four main social classes of the economically active population (professional, routine nonmanual, self-employed, and workers).[9] In order to keep a large category of retired persons in the analysis, we added the category 'retired'; other economically non-active persons (mostly students and housewives) were excluded. To control for the effects of demographic factors, two dichotomous variables were used in the models: Sex (1 = male, 2 = female) and Age (1 = 18 to 44, 2 = 45 and above).[10] Since the Prague region differs markedly in voting behaviour from other regions, we controlled for the centre–periphery effect by including the dichotomous variable Region (1 = Prague region; 2 = other regions). The distributions of dependent and independent variables are displayed in the Appendix, Table 9.A2.

Three analytic strategies were adopted. We started with simple two-way classifications for each year showing the distributions of votes for the main political parties across social classes. Loglinear models were then used to assess the change in the effect of class on voting preferences. Finally, logit models were estimated to assess the effect of class on selected electoral choices when controlling for effects of age, sex, and region. For these analyses, four class contrasts were specified: (1) professional versus routine nonmanual, (2) the self-employed versus employed (i.e. professional, routine nonmanual, and workers), (3) workers versus all other economically active respondents, and (4) the retired versus the economically active.

## RESULTS

Tables 9.1 and 9.2 show the percentage of votes cast for political parties by class position in 1992 and 1996. Two types of change can be seen over this period: (1) the concentration of votes on a smaller number of political parties, and (2) changes in the association between a respondent's class and political party he or she voted for.

First, in 1992 eight parties met the required threshold (5 per cent of valid votes), while no less than 21 per cent of voters failed to obtain direct representation in parliament. In 1996, the number of parties that obtained the required number of votes dropped to six, and the number of votes that did

[9] This variable was created from the 'Social class' item in which respondents were asked to say which class they belonged to by choosing one of a series of class categories. This method of eliciting class positions prevented any closer approximation of the Erikson–Goldthorpe class schema.

[10] Only two age cohorts were defined in order to reduce the number of cells in the multiway arrays analysed by the logit models.

TABLE 9.1. *Voting in the Czech elections by social class, 1992 (percentages)*

| Party | Social class | | | | | | |
|---|---|---|---|---|---|---|---|
| | Professional | Routine-nonmanual | Self-employed | Worker | Retired | Other inactive | Total |
| ODS | 31.7 | 33.7 | 42.7 | 22.8 | 27.1 | 29.5 | 29.0 |
| ODA | 12.9 | 7.9 | 7.0 | 3.4 | 4.1 | 4.9 | 5.8 |
| KDU–CSL | 6.4 | 5.1 | 1.7 | 6.1 | 9.3 | 5.4 | 6.1 |
| CSSD | 7.2 | 7.3 | 2.4 | 7.1 | 6.2 | 4.9 | 6.3 |
| Left Bloc[a] | 13.8 | 14.2 | 5.4 | 13.3 | 18.5 | 11.5 | 13.8 |
| SPR–RSC | 1.8 | 5.2 | 6.2 | 9.5 | 1.7 | 6.9 | 5.8 |
| LSU | 7.2 | 6.1 | 2.5 | 8.6 | 3.8 | 6.7 | 6.3 |
| HSD–SMS | 4.0 | 4.7 | 4.6 | 7.9 | 3.7 | 6.7 | 5.7 |
| Other parties | 15.0 | 16.3 | 27.4 | 21.3 | 25.6 | 23.6 | 21.3 |
| Total | 8.2 | 22.2 | 6.7 | 29.4 | 19.7 | 13.9 | (N = 11, 292) |

*Notes*: Parties below the line break did not gain representation in the Czech National Council.

[a] The coalition 'Left bloc' (KSCM, LB, and SDL).

TABLE 9.2. *Voting in the Czech elections by social class, 1996*

| Party | Social class | | | | | | |
|---|---|---|---|---|---|---|---|
| | Professional | Routine-nonmanual | Self-employed | Worker | Retired | Other inactive | Total |
| ODS | 36.2 | 29.8 | 44.8 | 18.9 | 27.5 | 32.7 | 29.5 |
| ODA | 11.8 | 7.1 | 8.7 | 3.9 | 3.2 | 9.1 | 6.3 |
| KDU–CSL | 9.8 | 6.2 | 4.7 | 8.2 | 10.5 | 9.1 | 8.1 |
| CSSD | 22.3 | 29.9 | 17.7 | 35.0 | 21.4 | 24.0 | 26.3 |
| Left Bloc[a] | 9.4 | 10.2 | 5.5 | 11.7 | 19.5 | 8.2 | 11.7 |
| SPR–RSC | 2.0 | 8.2 | 9.7 | 12.7 | 3.9 | 8.3 | 8.0 |
| SD–LSNS[b] | 3.3 | 1.8 | 2.0 | 1.9 | 1.9 | 1.9 | 2.0 |
| Moravian parties[c] | 0.7 | 0.7 | 0.5 | 1.1 | 0.3 | 0.8 | 0.7 |
| Other parties | 4.3 | 6.1 | 6.4 | 6.6 | 11.8 | 5.8 | 7.4 |
| Total | 6.9 | 23.6 | 11.6 | 21.2 | 22.4 | 14.3 | (N = 13, 930) |

*Notes*: Parties below the line break did not gain representation in the parliament of the Czech Republic.

[a] The sum of votes for the KSCM, LB, and SDL, the parties that were in the coalition in 1992.

[b] Free Democrats, Liberal, National, and Social Party the successor to the LSU.

[c] HSMS–MNS and MNS–HSS, the successors to the HSD–SMS.

not convert into seats in the parliament dropped to 10 per cent. The Social Democratic Party which profited most from the concentration of votes, gained 20 per cent more votes in 1996 than in 1992, while the right-wing coalition (ODS, ODA, KDU–CSL) gained only 3 per cent.

Secondly, the distribution of the vote by classes suggests that voters' behaviour was more class-structured in 1996 than in 1992. For example, it can be seen that support for the Social Democrats was at a similar level among both professionals and workers in 1992, but was 13 per cent higher among the latter in 1996. Conversely, support for the ODS among professionals was only 9 per cent higher than the workers in 1992 but this too had jumped to 17 per cent in 1996. We do not need to rely on such impressionistic evidence, however, as the loglinear models presented in Table 9.3 indicate more precisely that these two main political rivals, the ODS and the Social Democrats, were indeed the parties that contributed most to the crystallization of class voting between 1992 and 1996.

Table 9.3 shows how the change in the fit of the independence model between 1992 and 1996 depends on the type of contrast used to distinguish between blocks of political parties. Most remarkable is the change in the fit that occurs when contrasting the ODS with the Social Democrats (ODS × CSSD × other, and ODS × CSSD). The change in the social profiles of these two major political rivals appears to be the major factor contributing to the growth of the class–party association in the Czech Republic between the two elections. It would appear that the political struggle between the ODS and the Social Democrats was at least in part—although not purely—a class-based political struggle. Table 9.3 also shows that the change in the $L^2(S)$ for the independence model based on the

TABLE 9.3. *Tests of the independence model between social class and political party for various classifications of political parties*

| Classification of political parties | df | $L^2(S)^a$ 1992 | 1996 | $\Delta L^2$ (%) |
|---|---|---|---|---|
| Full (see Tables 9.1 and 9.2) | 40 | 761.1 | 919.9 | 20.9 |
| Right coalition × CSSD × extreme × other | 15 | 254.9 | 457.1 | 79.3 |
| Right coalition × left × other | 10 | 329.6 | 386.0 | 17.1 |
| Right coalition × other | 5 | 182.6 | 338.3 | 85.1 |
| Left × other | 5 | 118.8 | 227.2 | 91.2 |
| ODS × CSSD × other | 10 | 167.3 | 372.2 | 222.2 |
| ODS × CSSD (other parties excluded) | 5 | 179.4 | 508.1 | 283.2 |

*Notes*: [a] $L^2$ for independence model standardized on N = 10,000.

Definition of blocks of parties: Right coalition: ODS, ODA, KDU–CSL; Extreme: Left Bloc and SPR–RSC in 1992; KSCM, LB, SDL, SPR–RSC in 1996; Left: CSSD and Left Bloc in 1992; CSSD, KSCM, SDL in 1996.

contrast between left-wing versus other parties, the most popular contrast used in comparative analyses of voting behaviour, is not smaller than the $L^2(S)$ from the models based on more detailed classifications, except those directly contrasting the CSSD and the ODS.

These results provide the answers to the question of whether the association between class and party was strengthened, weakened, or remained constant between the two elections. Also, however, we need to examine the pattern of change in party voting among members of particular social classes *relative* to the political affinities of other classes.

A simple way to assess this question empirically is to calculate and compare the odds for the most important electoral choices (e.g. the chance of voting for one of the left-wing parties rather than for any other party: the chance of voting for the CSSD rather than for the ODS, for instance) We may ask, for example, what were the probabilities of a vote for the Social Democrats rather than for the ODS in particular social classes in 1992, and how did the probabilities of this particular electoral choice differ between classes? Repeating the same analysis for the year 1996, we can evaluate the extent of change in the class basis of electoral choices between elections, as well as the intensity of change in any particular electoral choice for each class.

Table 9.4 provides such an analysis for three distinct classifications of political parties. The odds of voting for some of the left-wing parties rather than for any other party (panel A) make it possible to identify two patterns that describe changes in voting behaviour between the two elections: a strong *overall* shift towards left-wing political parties (the odds for the population increased from 0.25 to 0.61), and a *class-based* change in this particular electoral choice. As we have already seen, in both years the self-employed were least likely to vote for the left (the odds of voting left rather than non-left for this class were 0.09 in 1992 and 0.30 in 1996).[11] In 1992, however, there were no statistically significant differences in left versus non-left voting between professionals (0.26), routine nonmanual workers (0.27), and manual workers (0.25). Yet by 1996 all three classes differed significantly in their affinity to left-wing parties (0.46, 0.67, 0.88). Also interesting is the finding that while in 1992 the most 'leftist' were the retired (0.33), in 1996 they were displaced by the working class (0.88 for workers, 0.70 for the retired).

This picture becomes even sharper when we look at the odds of voting for the Social Democrats rather than for some of the right-wing coalition

[11] The numbers in parentheses are odds for left versus non-left voting for individual classes without controlling for sex, age, and region. Thus, for example, the value 0.5 means that the members of a particular class are 0.5 less likely to vote for the left than for the non-left, while the value 1.5 would mean that they are 1.5 more likely to vote for the left than for non-left political party.

TABLE 9.4. *The odds of various types of left versus non-left electoral choices by social class, 1992 and 1996*

*A. Odds: Left/other*

| Social class | 1992 | 1996 | 1996/1992 |
|---|---|---|---|
| Professionals | 0.264 | 0.464 | 1.76 |
| Routine nonmanuals | 0.273 | 0.669 | 2.45 |
| Self-employed | 0.085 | 0.302 | 3.55 |
| Workers | 0.254 | 0.876 | 3.45 |
| Retired | 0.328 | 0.692 | 2.54 |
| Other | 0.196 | 0.477 | 2.43 |
| Total | 0.252 | 0.612 | 2.43 |

*Note*: Calculated from the classification 'Left-wing parties—all other parties'.

*B. Odds: CSSD/Right coalition*

| Social class | 1992 | 1996 | 1996/1992 |
|---|---|---|---|
| Professionals | 0.141 | 0.386 | 2.74 |
| Routine nonmanuals | 0.158 | 0.694 | 4.39 |
| Self-employed | 0.047 | 0.304 | 6.47 |
| Workers | 0.220 | 1.132 | 5.14 |
| Retired | 0.153 | 0.519 | 3.39 |
| Other | 0.123 | 0.470 | 3.82 |
| Total | 0.154 | 0.597 | 3.88 |

*Note*: Calculated from the classification 'Right-wing coalition—CSSD—extreme parties—all other parties'.

*C. Odds: CSSD/ODS*

| Social class | 1992 | 1996 | 1996/1992 |
|---|---|---|---|
| Professionals | 0.227 | 0.619 | 2.73 |
| Routine nonmanuals | 0.219 | 1.003 | 4.58 |
| Self-employed | 0.056 | 0.395 | 7.05 |
| Workers | 0.311 | 1.852 | 5.96 |
| Retired | 0.229 | 0.778 | 3.40 |
| Other | 0.167 | 0.733 | 4.39 |
| Total | 0.217 | 0.889 | 4.10 |

*Note*: Calculated from the full classification used in Table 9.1 and Table 9.2.

parties (panel B) or for the ODS alone (panel C). It is particularly important to notice here that the two social classes that have made the strongest move in their electoral choice towards the CSSD were the workers and the self-employed. While the change in the electoral choice of the former confirms expectations based on the polarization hypothesis, the *relative* shift of the self-employed towards the left-wing CSSD contradicts it.

We now use logit models to examine these changes in the voting behaviour of social classes while controlling for the effects of other potentially important variables (age, sex, and region). Table 9.5 presents the results of models contrasting voting left versus non-left and the Social Democrats versus the Civic Democratic Party.

### *Left Versus Non-left*

Model 1 examines left versus non-left electoral choice and fits extremely well ($L^2 = 63.4$ with 64 degrees of freedom; $p = 0.497$), though it is very far from a saturated model. Only two classes show distinct gender differences: workers compared to other economically active persons and the retired relative to the economically active. As far as the change between 1992 and 1996 (the term Choice by Year) is concerned, the model suggests a difference between classes (the term Choice by Year by Class improves the model fit significantly) as well as between men and women (represented by the term Choice by Year by Sex).

If we look at the odds presented in Table 9.4 we can see that while in 1992 there was virtually no difference between professionals and routine nonmanual workers (0.98 lower odds for the former than the latter which is not significant), in 1996 the two classes show significantly distinct propensities for left voting (0.78 lower for professionals than for routine non-manual workers). The difference between the self-employed, the class with the weakest affinity for the left-wing parties in 1992, and employees diminished in 1996, because—as is shown below—the self-employed moved towards the left more than other classes. At the same time, however, the difference between workers and other economically active respondents increased. These are presented in Figure 9.2, which also shows that the difference in the affinity for left-wing parties between workers and other economically active persons is more pronounced among women than among men.

The most important development between 1992 and 1996 was that all classes moved markedly towards the left. Model 1 in Table 9.5 shows, however, that this shift was not independent of class and gender—see Figure 9.3. This figure shows relative odds for selected class differences. If the value of the relative odds is one or close to one, there is no difference between the two groups being compared, if it is significantly lower or higher than one, there is a significant difference between them.

First, women moved towards the left more than men, regardless of their class. Secondly, surprisingly, the class that made the strongest move to the

TABLE 9.5. *Estimated odds from models 1 and 2*

| Class | Age | Sex | Region | Left vs. non-left | | | Social Democrats vs. ODS | | |
|---|---|---|---|---|---|---|---|---|---|
| | | | | 1992 | 1996 | 96/92[a] | 1992 | 1996 | 96/92[a] |
| | 18–44 | M | Prague | 0.198 | 0.307 | 1.56 | 0.125 | 0.318 | 2.54 |
| | | M | Other | 0.327 | 0.508 | 1.56 | 0.250 | 0.634 | 2.54 |
| | | F | Prague | 0.155 | 0.283 | 1.83 | 0.125 | 0.318 | 2.54 |
| | | F | Other | 0.256 | 0.467 | 1.83 | 0.249 | 0.632 | 2.54 |
| Professional | 45+ | M | Prague | 0.258 | 0.401 | 1.56 | 0.205 | 0.521 | 2.54 |
| | | M | Other | 0.426 | 0.663 | 1.56 | 0.408 | 1.036 | 2.54 |
| | | F | Prague | 0.202 | 0.369 | 1.83 | 0.204 | 0.519 | 2.54 |
| | | F | Other | 0.334 | 0.610 | 1.83 | 0.407 | 1.034 | 2.54 |
| | 18–44 | M | Prague | 0.202 | 0.428 | 2.11 | 0.129 | 0.565 | 4.35 |
| | | M | Other | 0.335 | 0.707 | 2.11 | 0.258 | 1.123 | 4.35 |
| | | F | Prague | 0.159 | 0.393 | 2.48 | 0.129 | 0.565 | 4.35 |
| Routine | | F | Other | 0.262 | 0.651 | 2.48 | 0.257 | 1.122 | 4.35 |
| Nonmanual | 45+ | M | Prague | 0.264 | 0.558 | 2.11 | 0.145 | 0.632 | 4.35 |
| | | M | Other | 0.437 | 0.923 | 2.11 | 0.289 | 1.258 | 4.35 |
| | | F | Prague | 0.207 | 0.513 | 2.48 | 0.145 | 0.631 | 4.35 |
| | | F | Other | 0.342 | 0.849 | 2.48 | 0.288 | 1.254 | 4.35 |
| | 18–44 | M | Prague | 0.057 | 0.187 | 3.28 | 0.037 | 0.258 | 7.02 |
| | | M | Other | 0.094 | 0.310 | 3.28 | 0.073 | 0.513 | 7.02 |
| | | F | Prague | 0.050 | 0.191 | 3.85 | 0.037 | 0.258 | 7.02 |
| | | F | Other | 0.082 | 0.316 | 3.85 | 0.073 | 0.513 | 7.02 |
| Self-Employed | 45+ | M | Prague | 0.074 | 0.244 | 3.28 | 0.028 | 0.194 | 7.02 |
| | | M | Other | 0.123 | 0.404 | 3.28 | 0.055 | 0.386 | 7.02 |
| | | F | Prague | 0.065 | 0.250 | 3.85 | 0.028 | 0.194 | 7.02 |
| | | F | Other | 0.107 | 0.412 | 3.85 | 0.055 | 0.386 | 7.02 |
| | 18–44 | M | Prague | 0.152 | 0.467 | 3.06 | 0.164 | 1.943 | 5.76 |
| | | M | Other | 0.252 | 0.772 | 3.06 | 0.326 | 1.876 | 5.76 |
| | | F | Prague | 0.162 | 0.584 | 3.60 | 0.163 | 0.939 | 5.76 |
| | | F | Other | 0.269 | 0.966 | 3.60 | 0.325 | 1.871 | 5.76 |
| Worker | 45+ | M | Prague | 0.199 | 0.608 | 3.06 | 0.182 | 1.049 | 5.76 |
| | | M | Other | 0.329 | 1.007 | 3.06 | 0.362 | 2.086 | 5.76 |
| | | F | Prague | 0.212 | 0.762 | 3.60 | 0.181 | 1.046 | 5.76 |
| | | F | Other | 0.350 | 1.260 | 3.60 | 0.361 | 2.081 | 5.76 |
| | 18–44 | M | Prague | 0.238 | 0.440 | 1.85 | 0.156 | 0.536 | 3.46 |
| | | M | Other | 0.343 | 0.727 | 1.85 | 0.309 | 1.068 | 3.46 |
| | | F | Prague | 0.139 | 0.303 | 2.17 | 0.099 | 0.343 | 3.46 |
| Retired | | F | Other | 0.230 | 0.500 | 2.17 | 0.198 | 0.683 | 3.46 |
| | 45+ | M | Prague | 0.310 | 0.573 | 1.85 | 0.172 | 0.598 | 3.46 |
| | | M | Other | 0.513 | 0.948 | 1.85 | 0.344 | 1.188 | 3.46 |
| | | F | Prague | 0.181 | 0.394 | 2.17 | 0.110 | 0.382 | 3.46 |
| | | F | Other | 0.300 | 0.652 | 2.17 | 0.219 | 0.760 | 3.46 |

*Note*: [a] 96/92: the odds in 1996 divided by the odds in 1992.

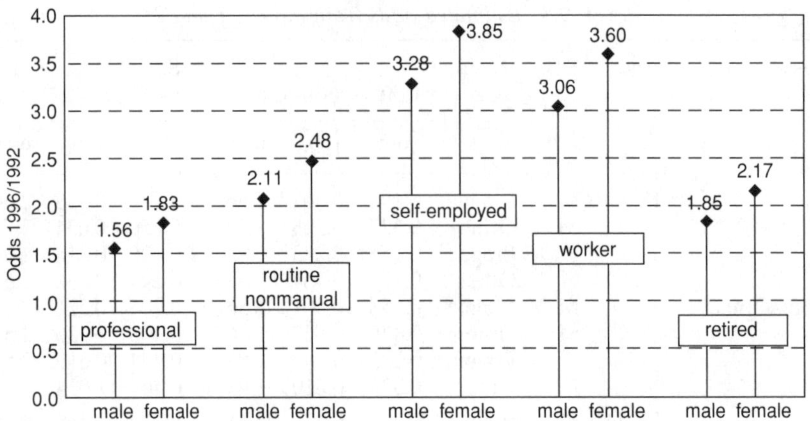


FIG 9.2. The change in left versus non-left votes between 1992 and 1996

FIG 9.3. Selected class differences for the left versus non-left votes

left was the self-employed (the ratio between the two odds is 3.28 for self-employed men and 3.85 for self-employed women). The working class also moved towards the left-wing parties more than other economically active groups. Thus, the multivarate analysis of left versus non-left electoral decisions confirms that the changes in the voting behaviour of professionals and workers correspond to the class and party polarization hypothesis, whereas the move towards the left among the self-employed does not.

Unsurprisingly, other variables also had effects on vote: women moved towards the left-wing parties more than men, regardless of social class, age, and region; in both years, older generations were more left-wing than younger people (the odds over 1:30) regardless of social class, sex, and region; and in both years, voters in Prague were consistently less likely to vote for the left than people in other regions (the odds are 0.60).

### *The Social Democrats versus the Civic Democratic Party*

As shown in the bivariate distributions, the change in the association between class and party was primarily due to the crystallization of class profiles of the two major competitors' electorates: the Civic Democratic Party (ODS), the strongest party on the right side of the political spectrum, and the Social Democrats (CSSD), the party that succeeded in building a strong left-wing opposition between the two elections. Model 2 examines this electoral choice and again shows an acceptable fit ($L^2 = 74.6$ with 64 degrees of freedom; $p = 0.172$). As with Model 1, all independent variables proved to be significant factors determining the time-invariant component of the effect of class on the odds of voting for the CSSD rather than for the ODS. However, the *change* in the odds between 1992 and 1996 turns out to vary significantly only between social classes (the term Choice by Year by Class).

The estimated odds from Model 2 (see Table 9.5) show regularities similar to those of Model 1 for the left versus non-left choice, but with divisions between classes that are far bigger than for the left versus non-left comparison. In 1992 the self-employed were the class with the strongest propensity to prefer the ODS over the CSSD: in this class for every 100 votes cast for the CSSD as many as 1,750 ballots were cast for the ODS. In other classes this ratio was much smaller: about 100:445 among professionals, routine nonmanuals, and the retired, and about 100:323 among workers. Although the ODS remained the most typical electoral choice among the self-employed, the propensity of its members to vote for the Social Democrats rather than for the ODS increased in 1996: by then, for every 100 votes among the self-employed cast for the CSSD only 252 were cast for the ODS. Professionals, on the contrary, were the class showing the most stable affinity for the ODS (the odds CSSD:ODS were 100:438 in 1992, and 100:162 in 1996), followed by the retired (100:435 in 1992, 100:128 in 1996) and routine nonmanual workers (100:454 in 1992, 100:100 in 1996). For workers, however, the ratio flipped from a strong preference for the ODS over the CSSD in 1992 to a preference for the CSSD over the ODS in 1996 (100:323 in 1992, 100:54 in 1996).

The results displayed in Figure 9.4 provide a simple picture of the most important changes in class-based differences in voting preferences for the

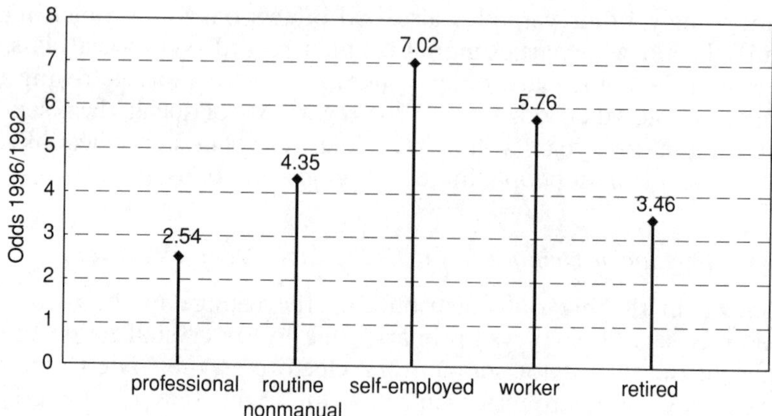


FIG 9.4. The change in CSSD versus ODS votes between 1992 and 1996

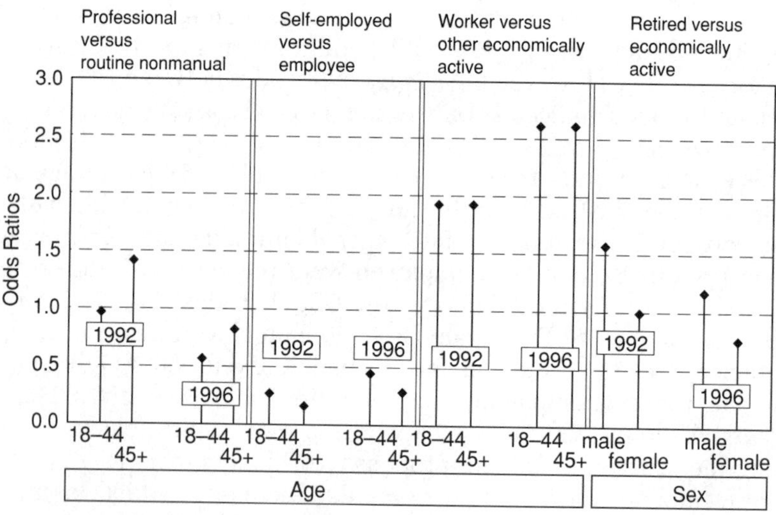


FIG 9.5. Selected class differences for CSSD versus ODS votes

Social Democrats over the ODS. The most striking thing here is the strength of the relative shift of the self-employed from the ODS towards the CSSD. Also rather surprising is the finding that pensioners turned to the Social Democrats to a lesser degree than did other social groups.

Finally, age and sex show an interesting pattern of interaction with class position (see Fig. 9.5). In 1992 younger generations of professionals and routine nonmanuals did not differ significantly in the degree of their affinity for the Social Democrats (in fact, both groups showed a strong affinity for the ODS). In 1996, however, younger members of these two classes did differ significantly. The electoral choice of the younger generation of routine nonmanual workers was closer to the CSSD than was that of younger professionals. The story is different among the older generation. In 1992, the older generation of professionals showed a stronger affinity for the Social Democrats than did older routine nonmanual workers, while in 1996 the older generations of these classes no longer differed in their electoral choice between the two biggest political rivals. What we are witnessing here would appear to be the tendency of the younger generation of professionals and routine nonmanual workers to express their class-based partisanship more strongly than is the case among the older generation.

## CONCLUSIONS

The central question addressed in this paper was whether the remarkable increase in the number of votes for the Social Democrats in the Czech Republic between the 1992 and 1996 election years was accompanied by a process of class–party realignment caused by the crystallization of political interests and attitudes in the electorate. We have seen that behind the apparent stability in the general pattern of self-placement on the left–right political axis, there was a significant change in the content of left–right political orientations: those expressing an affinity for the left became more egalitarian in their views of economic and social inequality, while those on the right of the political spectrum developed more anti-egalitarian attitudes. Consistent with this, we inferred that any changes in voting behaviour between the two elections were likely to have been caused by, among other things, the increasing role of class interests in the formation of voting preferences.

The empirical analysis of change in the pattern of the relative affinities of social classes for political parties indicated that the massive shift towards the left was both universal and class specific. It was universal because electoral choices changed in the same direction in all social classes. It was class specific at the same time because social classes differed in the intensity of the change in their voting preferences. While in 1992 the differences between the propensity of professionals, routine nonmanuals, and workers to vote for the left rather than for any other party were not statistically significant, in 1996 all of these classes differed significantly in their affinities for the left-wing parties. Over time, routine nonmanual workers moved left more than professionals, workers more than other economically active persons, those still in the labour force more than the retired, and—surprisingly—the self-employed more than employees. We also found that the shift to the left was gender specific: women moved to the left more than men, regardless of social class, age, and region. The change in the propensity to vote for the Social Democrats rather than for the Civic Democratic Party showed a similar pattern, although this was specifically only class-based. The probability of voting for the Social Democrats rather than for the Civic Democratic Party (ODS) increased more among routine nonmanual workers than among professionals, more among the working class than others, more among the self-employed than employees, and more among those in the labour-force than the retired.

The analysis further indicated that the two main political rivals, the ODS and the Social Democrats, were the parties that contributed most to the crystallization of class voting between 1992 and 1996.[12] This suggests that the political struggle between the ODS and the Social Democrats was not simply a political battle fuelled by the personally tempered combat of the two party leaders (Vaclav Klaus and Milos Zeman), as political commentators have tended to assume, but was also, if not primarily, a truly class-based political struggle. The findings clearly show that the change in social profiles of the constituencies of these two major political rivals on the Czech political stage contributed most to the growth of the class–party association in the Czech Republic between the two elections.

On the whole, then, the class-based nature of the shift to the left is consistent with the idea that a 'traditional', left–right class-based polarization has taken place in the Czech Republic. The only group that changed its electoral choices in a direction that contradicts this hypothesis were self-employed voters. This class provided the strongest shift towards the Social Democrats, though it still remains the class with the strongest affinity for the liberal-conservative ODS. The reasons for the relative leftward shift by the self-employed have yet to be clarified, but these quite probably reflect the changing composition of the self-employed between 1992 and 1996. This class was the only one which varied as a proportion of the electorate to any degree over the period, almost doubling in size from 7.8 per cent to 13.5 per cent. It may well have changed its class character also.

Thus although our evidence indicates that there was not a universal pattern of 'traditional' class-party polarization over the four years between

[12] Some additional analyses suggest also that the tendency to stick with the right was more class-based than the move to the left. This may reflect the fact that the Social Democrats gained a significant number of votes not only from the right-wing parties, but also from the small parties that disappeared from the political scene after the 1992 elections. Many of the votes obtained from these sources might have been an expression of discontent with some specific aspects of the coalition parties' politics and with the image of their leaders.

1992 and 1996, it points clearly to a polarization between the major social classes—between the working class and the professional and managerial class—with a substantial block of routine nonmanual positions falling between these two opposing groups. Importantly, these patterns of change are also most pronounced among younger voters. These findings would appear to be consistent with the idea that class interests are playing an increasingly important role in political choices during the process of marketization. Rather than the class–party dealignment supposedly characteristic of advanced industrial societies, our interpretation points towards the idea that over time voting behaviour in post-communist countries becomes more interest than symbol driven, leading to an increasing alignment in class-voting. This point has even more significance when we take into account the fact that the Czech economic system has considerably more positive prospects than is the case in most other post-communist societies—which might therefore display, if anything, greater degrees of class polarization. And given the uncertainties apparent in the post-communist economic situation, even in the Czech case this polarization is unlikely to be reduced in the near future.

# APPENDIX

TABLE 9.A1. *Acronyms for Political Parties*

| Acronym | Name of the party | Note |
|---|---|---|
| ODS | Civic Democratic Party | Right, liberal-conservative |
| ODA | Civic Democratic Alliance | Right, liberal-conservative |
| KDU–CSL | Christian Democratic Union–Czech People's Party | Right, Christian-democratic |
| CSSD | Czechoslovak (Czech) Social Democratic Party | Left, social democratic |
| LB | Left Bloc | Coalition of extreme-left parties in 1992; extreme-left party in 1996 |
| KSCM | Communist Party of Bohemia ad Moravia | Extreme left |
| SDL | Party of the Democratic Left | Extreme left |
| SPR–RSC | The Union for Republic–Czechoslovak Party of Republicans | Extreme right, populist |
| LSU | Liberal Social Union | Centre, liberal-socialist |
| HSD–SMS | The Movement for Self-Governing Democracy–Association for Moravia and Silesia | Centre, nationalist |
| SD–LSNS | Free Democrats–Liberal, National, and Social Party | Centre, liberal (German type) |
| HSMS–MNS | The Movement for Self-Governing Moravia and Silesia–Moravian National Union | Centre, nationalist |
| MNS–HSS | Moravian National Party–The Movement for Silesian and Moravian Unity | |

TABLE 9.A2. *Distribution of Variables used in the analysis (percentages)*

| Variable | 1992 | 1996 | Variable | 1992 | 1996 |
|---|---|---|---|---|---|
| Left vs. non-left vote | | | Sex | | |
| Left | 20.6 | 38.2 | Male | 52.3 | 52.0 |
| Non-left | 79.4 | 61.8 | Female | 47.7 | 48.0 |
| N | 10,990 | 14,071 | N | 11,051 | 13,793 |
| Social Democrat vs. ODS vote | | | Age | | |
| ODS | 82.0 | 52.9 | 18–44 | 63.6 | 51.6 |
| Social Democrats | 18.0 | 47.1 | 45 and above | 34.4 | 48.4 |
| N | 3,985 | 7,888 | N | 11,002 | 13,960 |
| Class | | | Region | | |
| Professional | 9.5 | 8.1 | Prague | 22.5 | 19.7 |
| Routine-nonmanual | 25.8 | 27.5 | Other | 77.5 | 80.3 |
| Self-employed | 7.8 | 13.5 | N | 11,292 | 13,960 |
| Worker | 34.1 | 24.8 | | | |
| Retired | 22.8 | 26.1 | | | |
| N | 9,728 | 11,939 | | | |

# 10

# The Emergence of Class Politics and Class Voting in Post-communist Russia

GEOFFREY EVANS AND STEPHEN WHITEFIELD

## INTRODUCTION

Unlike many chapters in this book which concern established Western democracies, the question for Russia is not whether the relationship between class and partisanship is declining but whether it is increasing. There are important differences in the context of Russian politics that explain why this question should be the starting-point of investigation. First, democracy in Russia is new and support for parties and political candidates for office, as well as the parties and candidates themselves, is in its infancy. The sorts of links, therefore, between voters and politicians that are often assumed to be essential to the emergence of class bases to partisanship should have been weak in origin but likely to grow over time. Secondly, the Russian economy has only in the last six years made significant strides towards the creation of the sort of economy which will approximate to the market conditions in which Western class divisions are politically salient. For each of these reasons, as democracy and the market develop, we may expect class bases to partisanship to be increasing in Russia and in this chapter we consider whether this expectation is empirically justified.

There is a further reason, however, why the relationship between class and vote in Russia should be of interest and this relates to the character of explanations of the emergence and transformation of class political alignments. If class is an important factor in vote, why is this so? If it changes in importance, what accounts for the change? Answers to these questions in the Western literature have tended to fall into one of two camps: those that privilege sociological factors and those that emphasize

The research presented in this chapter was commissioned as part of the Economic and Social Research Council's East–West Programme, Phase 2: Grant no. Y 309 25 3025, 'Emerging Forms of Political Representation and Participation in Eastern Europe' and by the INTAS Project, 'Ethnicity, Nationality and Citizenship in the Former Soviet Union'.

the political. The former highlights the primacy of changes in the class system itself: it can be considered a 'bottom-up' approach to the structuring of political divisions. The latter, by contrast, argues that class partisanship derives from the strategies of parties themselves, or from the changing character of political institutions: it can be characterized as 'top-down' in nature.

The bottom-up sociological approach to explaining political change can take several forms, including reference to changing characteristics and composition of class positions, or the growth of alternative social bases of interests that cross-cut class position, or the changing social psychology of the voter as a result of the growth of mass higher education or affluence. All of these approaches, however, share the assumption that changes in social structure, or in the economic experiences of classes, are the source of changes in the relationship between party and class.

The top-down political explanation for the strength of class voting has also been put by a number of scholars. Sartori (1969), pointing to the fact that the multiple possible forms of social experience and identity make sociological explanation underdetermined, argues that the salience of any one factor, including class, is therefore an effect of the willingness of organizations such as parties to politicize it. As he puts it: 'Class conditions are only a facilitating condition. To put it bluntly, it is not the "objective" class (class conditions) that creates the party, but the party that creates the "subjective" class (class consciousness)' (Sartori 1969: 84). In a similar vein, Przeworski has claimed that 'individual voting behaviour is an effect of the activities of political parties. More precisely, the relative salience of class as a determinant of voting behaviour is a cumulative consequence of strategies pursued by political parties of the left' (Przeworski 1985: 100–1). Without this party decision, class is much less strongly associated with vote.

In addition to analysing the extent of class voting in Russia and how it may have changed over time, therefore, this chapter also considers the relative merits of these bottom-up and top-down accounts of class partisanship. The two explanations present stark alternatives. On the one hand, the sociological account would hold that any growth in class voting would need to be explained by reference to some changing characteristics of class or class experience. On the other hand, the political account would appeal to the strategies of parties or elites, independently of changing class experience. Each of these perspectives, however, might be considered insufficient in the circumstances of post-communist Russia in which, as we argued in the opening paragraph, there is simultaneous marketization which is clearly beneficial for members of some classes and costly for others (see also Evans 1997), the emergence of democratic competition for votes, and the initial and developing experience of voters with both. These conditions suggest a process in which Russians are likely to be learning a great deal about where they stand: by relating their market experience to their views about the desirability of marketization in Russia; and, in turn, relating these to their partisanship. As distinct from either of the views above, and following on from previous research (Whitefield and Evans 1994*a*), we would point to the possibility that the growth in class voting over time in Russia is a consequence of political learning among Russians involving a dual process of, on the one hand, recognition of divergent experiences of the costs and benefits of marketization by people in different social classes, and a growing capacity over time and electoral iterations to orient these on parties and candidates, on the other.

This political-learning approach does not rely on the importance of party behaviour and strategy in defining the structure of voters' choices. Rather, it argues that parties and presidential contenders do not decide the initial conditions for voters' choice of parties; indeed, they have every incentive to seek to orient themselves on the sorts of experiences that voters themselves find most salient and central to their lives, such as the economy in most states, or ethnic or religious divisions in states where these are of great historic and social significance. Parties which signal a stance on such questions are more likely to be rewarded. While this may change over time, in the short period since the start of post-communist party systems the primacy of social experience is likely to be maintained, and if social differences intensify, so parties or candidates should differentiate themselves further on the relevant issue to maintain their profile. Voters, on this account, do not need parties to instruct them in what is relevant, though parties may—and must if they wish to win support—contribute to the learning process by making clear where they stand. In the Russian case, this explanation would point to the growth over time of the class bases of partisanship in response to three factors: growing experience of class difference; growing understanding of the relationship between class experience and the view of the market itself; and growing recognition of the stances taken by parties. The political learning account does not, therefore, give causal precedence to party strategies when accounting for growth in class partisanship, but does not exclude them from contributing to that growth.

The rest of the chapter proceeds along these lines to analyse the extent of class voting in Russia and how it may have changed over the years 1993–6. It also considers how any such changes may be explained by reference to the sociological, political, and learning accounts just outlined. The analysis points to the importance of a number of factors, including differential class–market experience, in producing a growing increase in class partisanship, and thus provides some support to the sociological explanation. However, this account can only explain a part of the change and the rest appears to be the result of a greater capacity among voters to link their economic experience with their economic norms and to link these in turn with their class position and with a corresponding party or political candidate. The sources of such learning may be multifarious, from parties to the media, to more informal group, family or individual experience. The analysis does indicate, however, that the increase is not simply the effect of shifts in candidate strategy or institutional design, and in this sense, a political learning account is supported over the purely top-down explanation.

## CLASS AND POLITICS: THE RUSSIAN CASE

The issues involved when accounting for class voting are essentially the same in Russia as in the broader context just outlined. Is class significantly related to partisanship and is its significance changing? If so, is this for bottom-up 'sociological', or top-down 'political' reasons—or, as we shall ultimately argue, because of learning among Russians about both politics and markets? Certainly, in the Russian case, each kind of explanation has a degree of initial plausibility.

It should be noted that a number of commentators have, by reference to both political and sociological peculiarities of Russia, denied *any* importance of class to partisanship. From the political perspective, Russian politics has, until 1996, been locked in the politics of 'revolutionary transformation' while '[c]onventional cleavages, which demarcate the contours of stable party systems, emerge only after consolidation of the new economic and political system' (McFaul 1997: 3). For McFaul, this is particularly true of the presidential competition that forms the focus of our analysis. Class, in other words, cannot become a source of differentiation among voters until politicians shift their campaigns from the issue of the break from communism to those of the differentiated market. As McFaul puts it, this 'crystallized divide has impeded interest-based party development . . . When politics are polarized, all ideological divisions, class divisions, and/or ethnic identities are subsumed by two broad categories: reform or anti-reform, status quo or status quo ante' (McFaul 1996: 322). It is worth noting that McFaul does not provide any analysis of mass electoral behaviour that might substantiate such a claim; nor would our own analysis of party campaign strategy (Whitefield and Evans 1998) accord with McFaul's claim that it lacked any basis in social interests.

From a sociological perspective, other commentators have pointed to the continuing weakness of Russian civil society and the absence of any societal basis as yet for the mobilization of class differences (Sakwa 1996).

Until this occurs, class-based partisanship and clear links of parties to social groups are expected to be weak. As Rose, Tikhomirov, and Mishler conclude: 'If 70 years of communist rule did little else, it made traditional social structural cleavages of limited significance in post-communist Russia' (Rose *et al.* 1997: 807). The Communists in particular, they argued, were not a class party (ibid. 1997: 817).

We consider whether this claim that class is of no importance to partisanship—whether for bottom-up sociological or top-down political reasons—in the analysis below. It is worth pointing out that some scholars have already come to different conclusions and have shown that class does have an impact on vote (Wyman *et al.* 1995; White *et al.* 1997*b*). Of equal importance, however, is the question of whether class differences may have grown over time—and why—and here no detailed analysis has yet been undertaken. However, the arguments outlined above have clear implications for prognoses about changes in the effects of class on partisanship.

First, Russia has undergone a major economic transformation from plan to market, starting during the Gorbachev period but intensifying dramatically after 1991. Though it is ongoing, much of this transition was concentrated in the period covered by this study, between 1993 and 1996, when the effects of price liberalization, privatization, and both massive inflation and subsequent (temporary) price stabilization were experienced. During this time, Russian citizens were confronted for the first time in many generations with cut-backs in social services and state provision and the real possibility of unemployment along with widespread non-payment of wages and benefits. The social conditions, in other words, for market-based occupational class differentiation were clearly in place along with the possibility that the impact of markets might lead to increasing polarization of economic experience between classes over the three years. If class is a factor in vote, therefore, and if it is of growing importance to voting over time, one plausible sociological explanation is that this results from different—and polarizing—class experiences of marketization.

Secondly, Russians have experienced a major political transformation, and much of this has also been concentrated in the three-year period of this study. Three elections have taken place: the Duma elections of 1993 and 1995, and the presidential elections of 1996. It can be argued that the central issues in these elections have shifted from a simple pro-change versus revanchist division in the first, where class divisions may be less likely to be important, to much more variegated factors in subsequent years, where parties are more likely to compete by emphasizing social differences. There is evidence of elite polarization over this period in which parties have sought to present more distinctive positions to the electorate

(Breslauer 1993; Brown 1993; Vite 1994; Sakwa 1996). With each election, there has been a very significant growth in the degree to which Russians have developed partisan attachments, at least when conceived as preferences for parties rather than party memberships or strong party support. Moreover, parties have increasingly differentiated themselves on issues related to the economy over time (Petrenko *et al.* 1995). One party in particular has experienced a particular revival in its electoral fortunes: the Communist Party moved from illegality between 1991 and 1993 to winning the largest share of the vote in the Duma elections of 1995 and contending strongly for the presidency in 1996, and has done so by, in part, emphasizing its stance as a spokesman for the economic losers in the transition (Sakwa 1996; Timoshenko 1995). However, it is not only the left that has chosen to take a class perspective on politics in this period; such appeals can also be found among pro-market parties and politicians anxious to mobilize entrepreneurs and others held to be benefiting from the transition (Sakwa 1996; Timoshenko 1995; White *et al.* 1997*a*: 232–3). It is equally plausible, therefore, to argue that the salience of class—and any putative growth in this over time—is the result of a growing capacity of political elites and parties to transmit effective interest-based appeals to voters and, in particular, of the growing strength of the Communists as a party which mobilizes voters on class grounds.

Between these wholly sociological and political explanations, as we have already pointed out, lies another which emphasizes the element of political learning among Russian classes. On this view, class experience or party strategy alone would not be sufficient to account for the growth of class voting. Rather, classes would need to interpret their market experience in terms of their class position and translate such experience into a political stance towards the market *per se* which they saw reflected in the posture adopted by political parties or presidential candidates. Such a view would also have an expectation of growing class bases to partisanship but would explain it not by reference just to political strategies of elites or the effects of the economy but as an interaction between the two which leads to voters gaining more experience and understanding of the new Russian market democracy.

The rest of the paper investigates the relationship between class, markets, and partisanship in Russia over these years and seeks to cast light on the relative merits of these competing explanations of changes. The data is drawn from three national random samples of the population of Russia undertaken in 1993, 1995, and 1996, commissioned by the authors. (Further details of sampling and fieldwork can be found in the Appendix.) We first examine the relationship between class and partisanship, and show the changing strength of association between them over time. Next we examine the extent of variation in class experience of marketization over time, and consider whether such class differences in experience can account for observed changes in the class–vote relationship. Having concluded that they do not fully account for such changes, we examine whether changes in the class–vote relationship can be accounted for by reference to an increasing connection made by our Russian respondents between their market experience and their support for markets and their voting preferences. The evidence indicates that the relationship between class position, partisanship, and support for marketization polarizes over time. This is taken to suggest that the growing level of class alignment in Russian politics results from a process of learning by Russian voters, in which they increasingly link their experiences with an understanding of markets and of the stances of politicians towards it. The evidence, therefore, is compatible with the political-learning model we have outlined and cannot be explained simply as an effect of either sociological factors or political strategies alone.

## MEASURING CLASS AND PARTISANSHIP IN THE RUSSIAN CONTEXT

In our view, class is best understood as a related set of occupational characteristics, uniting workers in different sectors of the economy, especially those of employed versus self-employed, salaried versus waged, supervisory versus supervised, with benefits or without, which give rise to differentiated economic strategies and life-chances (see, for example, Evans 1992, 1996, 1997). These characteristics in turn are contingently related to others such as social status or income, but are not defined by them (see Evans 1998). As with most other chapters in this book, therefore, class refers to a combination of distinctions in employment status (that is, between employers, self-employed, employees) and also within the broad category of employees. Class position is measured using the algorithm developed by Goldthorpe and Heath (1992), with British OPCS (Office of Population, Censuses, and Surveys) occupational unit groups augmented by use of ISCO (International Standard Classification of Occupation) codes, and by local information so as to take into account both the range of agricultural occupations in the region and modifications suggested by the remaining intricacies of the former communist occupational structure. From the resulting schema are derived the standard eleven categories. As with other chapters of this book, these classes are in turn aggregated to form a more parsimonious representation of the key aspects of the class structure; in the analysis reported below we use five categories: the service class (class I); lower service and routine nonmanual workers (classes II and

III);[1] petty bourgeoisie (class IVa and IVb); working class (classes V, VI, and VIIa); and, following conventional terminology in Eastern Europe, peasants (classes IVc and VIIb). To allow for the possibility that the complexities of the Erikson–Goldthorpe schema are unnecessary to describe the class–vote relationship in Russia, we also examine the effect on partisanship of a simplified dichotomous measure of class, where these categories are formed by combining workers and peasants from the five-class schema to form the 'working class', and the rest to form the 'middle class'.

Allocation to class position is derived from respondents' own occupation and employment statuses, as recent research suggests that in Eastern Europe allocation on an individual basis is likely to be the most effective strategy (see Marshall *et al.* 1995). Individuals who are at present not working are allocated a class position on the basis of their most recent job. The distributions of class positions show considerable stability over time and bear comparison with other countries discussed in this book. Fluctuations in size remain small and are most troublesome only when considering the small category—the petty bourgeoisie—where small numbers make reliable estimates difficult to obtain.

Inevitably, the application of a class schema developed in the West to a situation in which the characteristics of occupations are likely to reflect, among other things, both former communist reward principles and embryonic capitalist development is fraught with difficulty (although for encouraging signs with regard to the operationalization of the class schema in Eastern Europe, see Erikson and Goldthorpe 1992*a*; Evans 1997; Evans and Mills 1999). It is likely therefore that the concept of class is going to be less effectively operationalized in Eastern European countries than it is in Britain. None the less, at this stage in our understanding of class relations in post-communist societies, the insights to be gained from even imperfect measures are likely to make their use worthwhile. After all, the main consequence of any weaknesses in the present system of measurement is that divisions between classes are likely to be underestimated, compared with those which would be obtained with improved indicators of class position. Thus refinements in the ways that class is operationalized in Eastern Europe are unlikely to undermine arguments concerning the non-significance of class in the region; rather they should serve to enhance the importance attributed to class position as a basis of interests.[2]

[1] The aggregation of classes II and III reflects the difficulty of confidently classifying respondents into one or other of these classes. The choice of different aggregation procedures has no effect on the substantive interpretation of the findings.

[2] Further analyses of class structure in Russia in which class positions are allocated using self-identified class positions that to some degree proxy those in the Goldthorpe schema—manual workers, manager, entrepreneur, intelligentsia, peasant—do not appear to produce substantively different results from those reported here (see

Partisanship is measured using responses to questions on intended vote in 1993 and 1995, and to actual vote in 1996, when the survey took place just after the presidential elections. The dependent variable in the analysis is support for presidential candidates rather than parties, because the proportion of respondents able to express a party preference in 1993 was too small to allow meaningful analysis (and is generally somewhat smaller than the proportion who have a presidential preference), and because examining support for parties would exclude Yeltsin supporters, as he does not have his own party.

For the analysis, blocs were created comprising Yeltsin/Gaidar/ Yavlinsky and Yeltsin/Yavlinksy (1995 and 1996, respectively) and Zhirinovsky/Lebed. Combining the supporters of these candidates does not imply that there are no differences between their constituent components on social grounds, only that these differences are not class related—analyses reported elsewhere indicate that they were sufficiently similar in their ideological appeal to justify their combination (Whitefield and Evans 1998).

The use of measures of presidential rather than party preference might be expected to affect the findings in two ways: first, by increasing the effects of personalized attachments; and, secondly, by including in the 1996 analysis politically less committed respondents who expressed a preference because the presidential election had just occurred, but who in previous years might not have done so. The effects of these possible biases might be expected to diminish the extent of the class–vote relationship, so that any increase in its salience over time is likely, if anything, to be greater than we find.

## EXAMINING THE RELATIONSHIP BETWEEN CLASS AND VOTING PREFERENCE

An initial estimate of the relationship between class and vote and how it may have changed over the three years in which the survey was carried out is given in Table 10.1, which shows a comparison of the aggregated versions of the working and middle classes for the three presidential candidates/blocs. These data show some important shifts in the relative alignments of the two classes with particular candidates. For example, there is a big increase in the differences in working-class and middle-class votes going to Yeltsin on the one hand—from a ratio of 0.89 of working class to

Whitefield and Evans 1999). In Eastern Europe more generally, it would appear, these rather different ways of operationalizing class position are closely associated empirically (Evans 1997).

middle class in 1993, to 0.85 in 1995, and to 0.71 in 1996. By contrast, the relative share of these votes going to the anti-reform candidates, Rutskoi and Zyuganov, shows precisely the opposite direction with a ratio of middle-class to working-class votes of 0.93 in 1993, 0.86 in 1995, and 0.68 in 1996. Class differences are also evident in the composition of the Zhirinovsky and Zhirinovsky/Lebed bloc, but in this case the tendency appears to be towards diminishing rather than growing class differences in support. The evidence from Table 10.1 overall, however, is that—at least for the comparison between Rutskoi/Zyuganov and Yeltsin—there appears to be an increasing class basis to partisan alignment in Russian politics during the period we are investigating.

This is consistent with the findings of a series of logistic regressions shown in Table 10.2. These models compare two pairs of presidential candidates/blocs by two classes over time. In the contrast between Yeltsin versus Zhirinovsky and Zhirinovsky/Lebed, class differences are significant for 1993 and 1996, but not for 1995, with the working class less likely to support Yeltsin in these years. There is, in other words, no evidence of a trend in the strength of this association.

The direction of the effect is the same for the comparison of Yeltsin with Rutskoi or Zyuganov. However, in this case the tendency is for the strength of association of class with partisan choice between these candidates to grow considerably over time. Indeed, taking these candidate comparisons on the simple two-class model currently under discussion, there is clear evidence of a considerable degree of class polarization in this parameter over the three years of our studies.

However, the deficiencies of a two-class model compared with the more differentiated Erikson–Goldthorpe schema have been discussed in a number of earlier chapters and it is worth investigating whether the pattern of class polarization can be identified more precisely when the two broad categories have been disaggregated into classes defined in terms of more specific distinctions in employment relations. The use of a more detailed class schema may refine our understanding of which classes may be particularly responsible for the increasing class basis of the vote. So, for example, rather than all manual workers, whether the industrial working class or the agricultural sector, or the several middle classes as a whole, moving towards Zyuganov or Yeltsin, particular sub-classes may be responsible for the changes observed. The apparent similarities in the working-class basis of the Zhirinovsky/Lebed and the Zyuganov votes may also conceal important distinctions in sub-class composition. To investigate these issues, Table 10.3 presents another set of logistic regressions of the same partisan contrasts onto the five-class schema. The results do suggest some informative modifications to the simple two-class picture presented above, although the petty bourgeoisie, in

TABLE 10.1. *Intended (or reported) votes for presidential candidates by class by year (per cent)*

| Class | 1993 | | | 1995 | | | 1996 | | |
|---|---|---|---|---|---|---|---|---|---|
| | Yeltsin | Zhirinovsky | Rutskoi | Yeltsin | Zhirinovsky | Zyuganov | Yeltsin | Zhirinovsky | Zyuganov |
| I Service class | 66.7 | 5.2 | 28.1 | 70.4 | 11.2 | 18.3 | 55.5 | 21.7 | 22.8 |
| II Lower service/ routine nonmanual | 58.0 | 6.8 | 35.2 | 74.1 | 12.7 | 13.2 | 51.4 | 18.6 | 30.0 |
| III Petty bourgeoisie | 66.7 | 9.1 | 24.2 | 54.8 | 38.7 | 6.5 | 50.0 | 28.6 | 21.4 |
| IV Peasants | 36.8 | 15.8 | 47.4 | 75.0 | 10.0 | 15.0 | 32.7 | 15.8 | 51.5 |
| V Working class | 59.2 | 10.5 | 30.3 | 59.8 | 18.9 | 21.3 | 39.4 | 26.9 | 33.7 |
| Combined classes: | | | | | | | | | |
| I, II, III | 61.3 | 6.5 | 32.2 | 71.0 | 14.1 | 14.9 | 52.9 | 20.1 | 27.0 |
| IV, V | 56.8 | 11.1 | 32.1 | 60.9 | 18.2 | 20.8 | 38.4 | 25.3 | 36.3 |
| N | 465 | 67 | 252 | 443 | 105 | 115 | 642 | 318 | 443 |

TABLE 10.2. *Logistic regressions of vote onto two-class schema for selected partisan comparisons by year*

| Class | 1993 Yeltsin (1) vs. Zhirinov. (0) β (s.e.) | 1995 Yeltsin (1) vs. Zhir./Leb. (0) β (s.e.) | 1996 Yeltsin (1) vs. Zhir./Leb. (0) β (s.e.) | 1993 Yeltsin (1) vs. Rutskoi (0) β (s.e.) | 1995 Yeltsin (1) vs. Zyuganov (0) β (s.e.) | 1996 Yeltsin (1) vs. Zyuganov (0) β (s.e.) |
|---|---|---|---|---|---|---|
| Middle class | 0.61 (0.26)[b] | 0.41 (0.22) | 0.55 (0.14)[a] | 0.07 (0.16) | 0.48 (0.21)[b] | 0.62 (0.13)[a] |
| Working class | — | — | — | — | — | — |
| Model chi-square (4 df) | 5.44[b] | 3.45 | 15.83[a] | 0.22 | 5.28[b] | 24.71[a] |

*Notes*: [a] = significant at $p < 0.01$; [b] = significant at $p < 0.05$.
Middle-class effects are relative to the working-class reference category.

TABLE 10.3. *Logistic regressions of vote onto five-class schema by year*

| Class | 1993 Yeltsin (1) vs. Zhirinov. (0) β (s.e.) | 1995 Yeltsin (1) vs. Zhir./Leb. (0) β (s.e.) | 1996 Yeltsin (1) vs. Zhir./Leb. (0) β (s.e.) | 1993 Yeltsin (1) vs. Rutskoi (0) β (s.e.) | 1995 Yeltsin (1) vs. Zyuganov (0) β (s.e.) | 1996 Yeltsin (1) vs. Zyuganov (0) β (s.e.) |
|---|---|---|---|---|---|---|
| Service class | 0.82 (0.44) | 0.68 (0.30)[b] | 0.56 (0.19)[a] | 0.19 (0.23) | 0.31 (0.26) | 0.74 (0.18)[a] |
| Lower service/ routine nonmanual | 0.41 (0.31) | 0.61 (0.28)[b] | 0.64 (0.17)[a] | –0.17 (0.18) | 0.69 (0.27)[b] | 0.39 (0.15)[a] |
| Petty bourgeoisie | 0.26 (0.64) | –0.80 (0.41)[b] | 0.18 (0.46) | 0.34 (0.43) | 1.10 (0.76) | 0.69 (0.50) |
| Peasants | –0.88 (0.52) | 0.86 (0.77) | 0.34 (0.32) | –0.92 (0.38)[b] | 0.57 (0.65) | –0.61 (0.24)[b] |
| Working class | — | — | — | — | — | — |
| Model chi -square (4 df) | 9.01 | 16.20[a] | 17.98[a] | 9.59[b] | 8.52 | 34.72[a] |

*Notes*: [a] = significant at $p < 0.01$; [b] = significant at $p < 0.05$.
Class effects are relative to the working class reference category.

particular, is so small a category that its effects cannot confidently be interpreted.

Taking the Yeltsin versus Zhirinovsky and Zhirinovsky/Lebed comparisons first, there are no significant effects for the five-class schema as a whole in 1993. Significant differences are found in 1995 and 1996, in which both the service class and routine nonmanual workers are significantly more likely than the working-class reference group to be Yeltsin supporters. Peasants do not differ from workers in their partisan orientation with regard to these competitors. This picture is confirmed for 1996. There is no evidence, however, of an *increasing* class–vote polarization when looking at the beta coefficients for the social classes in each year. These tend to move up or down in no particular pattern and are not significantly different across the three years. The service and routine nonmanual classes are distinctive in their support for Yeltsin over Zhirinovsky/Lebed, but this does not appear to be increasing over time.

The situation with respect to the Yeltsin versus Rutskoi/Zyuganov comparison is different in a number of respects. In 1993, the model as a whole does (just) achieve statistical significance and within this there is a pronounced effect for peasants who, by comparison with all other social classes at this time, are more likely to support Rutskoi. This distinctiveness of the peasantry from the others disappears in 1995 when the model as a whole is not significant (there were, however, only twenty peasants with presidential preferences in this year). By 1996, however, differences become very clear-cut, with peasants again much more likely to support Zyuganov than the working class, whereas the service and routine nonmanual classes are much more likely to support Yeltsin. This picture of growing class differences for these comparisons across the spectrum is further supported when looking at the coefficients for the distinctive groups which increase considerably over time, especially for the service and routine nonmanual categories. The former in particular show a pattern of increasing polarization from the voting preferences of manual workers over the period studied.

The use of the Erikson–Goldthorpe schema, therefore, tends to confirm the growing class polarization in support for Yeltsin versus Rutskoi/Zyuganov observed using a two-class schema, but indicates more precisely where it is targeted and points to important differences in the class character of support for Zhirinovsky/Lebed versus Rutskoi/Zyuganov. We can conclude that class differences are of importance and increasingly so for some partisan divisions in Russia—those divisions which arguably reflect the traditional distinction between left and right on economic policy preferences. The next step is to explain why these changes in the class basis of Yeltsin versus Rutskoi/Zyuganov voting preferences have been occurring.

## CLASSES AND MARKET EXPERIENCE IN RUSSIA, 1993–1996

The bottom-up sociological argument outlined in the introduction affords one plausible means of explaining the growing importance of class to vote over time and the changes in the class composition of partisan differences. Simply put, class is more important and some classes are more closely linked with particular candidates because of the differential effects of market experience on classes over the three years. In terms of their market experience, classes are becoming more polarized and this translates into polarization in their voting preferences. To explain this changing relationship, therefore, we need to show that classes have become increasingly differentiated in market-related experiences.

To test this proposition, we use comparable measures of market experience obtained in each survey. These measures index respondents' estimation of the shifts in their household's standard of living over the previous five years and expectations of its living standards over the coming five years. A further question asks respondents to evaluate the workings of the market economy in Russia 'so far'. All responses are given on five-point scales (coded one through five); a high score indicates a positive response. If the sociological account is correct, we should expect to find not only clear class differences on these measures, but differences growing among classes proportionate to the changes that we have already noted in the class–vote relationship.

Table 10.4 shows predictable differences between classes on each of the measures of market experience and these differences seem in the main to be growing over time. Thus class perceptions of their families' living standards over the previous five years do not differ much in 1993, though the petty bourgeoisie are clearly more positive than the working class (a gap of 0.58). By 1996, however, divisions had widened considerably, with the petty bourgeoisie now far higher in their appraisal (0.99) than the working class—as are the service class (up from 0.16 in 1993 to 0.58). Such differences are similar to those found when respondents were asked to assess their households' prospects with respect to living standards over the next five years; again, entrepreneurs and to a lesser degree those in the service class were more likely to look favourably on their future than peasants by 1996. These class distinctions are less clearly drawn, not surprisingly, when respondents were asked about the performance of the market in their country more generally.

Table 10.5 summarizes these changes using ordinary least squares (OLS) models in which economic experience is regressed onto class position in each year. There is clear evidence of polarization in class experiences of the costs and benefits of marketization—all of the most relevant differences—that is, between the working class/peasants and service/routine nonmanual and petty bourgeoisie—accentuate significantly between 1993 and 1996. For example, class differences on the market evaluation question move from non-significance in 1993, to petty bourgeois distinctiveness in 1995, to clear differences between the service class and petty bourgeoisie and workers in one direction, and workers and peasants in the other in 1996. Again, a similar picture holds for the future assessments of living standards. The most pronounced rises, however, are for class appraisals of recent changes in living standards, where differences are not only already significant in 1993 but increase considerably over time. These effects are clearly stronger than those for the less immediately personal and salient

TABLE 10.4. *Market experience by class by year*

| Class | Mean Scores of Social Groups | | | | | | | | |
|---|---|---|---|---|---|---|---|---|---|
| | Past five years[a] | | | Next five years[b] | | | Current evaluation[c] | | |
| | 1993 | 1995 | 1996 | 1993 | 1995 | 1996 | 1993 | 1995 | 1996 |
| Service class | 2.21 (1.19) | 2.21 (1.28) | 2.46 (1.28) | 2.80 (1.03) | 2.95 (0.94) | 3.08 (0.94) | 2.21 (0.89) | 2.30 (0.99) | 2.72 (1.03) |
| Lower service/routine nonmanual | 2.18 (1.20) | 1.98 (1.16) | 2.07 (1.17) | 2.83 (1.03) | 2.81 (0.98) | 2.88 (0.89) | 2.22 (0.95) | 2.27 (0.97) | 2.58 (0.98) |
| Petty bourgeoisie | 2.63 (1.36) | 2.73 (1.28) | 2.87 (1.36) | 2.82 (1.13) | 3.27 (0.92) | 3.35 (1.05) | 2.50 (0.90) | 2.68 (1.04) | 3.10 (0.98) |
| Working class | 2.05 (1.05) | 1.77 (1.04) | 1.88 (1.07) | 2.72 (1.03) | 2.70 (0.94) | 2.83 (0.91) | 2.29 (1.02) | 2.15 (0.87) | 2.64 (1.00) |
| Peasants | 1.91 (1.00) | 1.67 (1.00) | 1.63 (0.88) | 2.78 (1.11) | 2.43 (0.94) | 2.67 (0.87) | 2.32 (1.04) | 2.34 (1.04) | 2.40 (0.90) |

*Notes*: [a] Respondents were asked 'Compared with five years ago, has your household's standard of living fallen a great deal, fallen a little, stayed about the same, risen a little, or has it risen a lot?'

[b] Respondents were asked 'And looking ahead over the next five years, do you think that your household's standard of living will fall a great deal from its current level, fall a little, stay about the same as it is now, rise a little, or rise a lot from its current level?'

[c] Respondents were asked 'And how would you evaluate the actual experience of the market economy so far?'

A high score indicates a higher standard of living (on a scale from 1 to 5). Standard errors are in parentheses.

TABLE 10.5. *Regressions of market experience onto class by year*

| Class | Past five years | | | Next five years | | | Current evaluation | | |
|---|---|---|---|---|---|---|---|---|---|
| | 1993 β (s.e.) | 1995 β (s.e.) | 1996 β (s.e.) | 1993 β (s.e.) | 1995 β (s.e.) | 1996 β (s.e.) | 1993 β (s.e.) | 1995 β (s.e.) | 1996 β (s.e.) |
| Service class | 0.16 (0.08)[b] | 0.45 (0.07)[a] | 0.59 (0.07)[a] | 0.08 (0.07) | 0.24 (0.06)[a] | 0.25 (0.06)[a] | –0.09 (0.07) | 0.15 (0.06)[b] | 0.09 (0.07) |
| Lower service/ routine nonmanual | 0.13 (0.06)[b] | 0.21 (0.07)[a] | 0.19 (0.06)[a] | 0.11 (0.06) | 0.11 (0.06)[b] | 0.05 (0.05) | –0.07 (0.05) | 0.12 (0.05)[b] | –0.06 (0.06) |
| Petty bourgeoisie | 0.56 (0.14)[a] | 0.99 (0.14)[a] | 0.99 (0.21)[a] | 0.09 (0.13) | 0.54 (0.12)[a] | 0.52 (0.17)[a] | 0.21 (0.12) | 0.53 (0.12)[a] | 0.46 (0.18)[b] |
| Peasants | –0.14 (0.11) | –0.09 (0.13) | –0.24 (0.11)[b] | 0.05 (0.10) | –0.27 (0.11)[b] | –0.15 (0.09) | 0.03 (0.10) | 0.19 (0.11) | –0.24 (0.10)[b] |
| Working class | — | — | — | — | — | — | — | — | — |
| $R^2$ | 0.01[a] | 0.04[a] | 0.05[a] | 0.00 | 0.02[a] | 0.02[a] | 0.00 | 0.01[a] | 0.01[a] |

*Notes*: Class effects are relative to the working-class reference category. A high score indicates more positive experiences. Coefficients are unstandardized betas.

[a] = significant at $p < 0.01$; [b] = significant at $p < 0.05$.

TABLE 10.6. *Logistic regressions of vote onto class and economic experiences by year*

| Class and economic experience | 1993 Yeltsin (1) vs. Rutskoi (0) β (s.e.) | 1995 Yeltsin (1) vs. Zyuganov (0) β (s.e.) | 1996 Yeltsin (1) vs. Zyuganov (0) β (s.e.) |
|---|---|---|---|
| Service class | 0.09 (0.25) | 0.10 (0.28) | 0.59 (0.21)[a] |
| Lower service/routine nonmanual | –0.21 (0.20) | 0.49 (0.29) | 0.42 (0.17)[b] |
| Petty bourgeoisie | 0.07 (0.47) | 0.13 (0.84) | 0.01 (0.59) |
| Peasants | –1.13 (0.43)[a] | 0.44 (0.71) | –0.45 (0.27) |
| Working class | — | — | — |
| Market Experience | | | |
| Current evaluation | 0.67 (0.11)[a] | 0.85 (0.15)[a] | 0.80 (0.08)[a] |
| Past five years | 0.38 (0.09)[a] | 0.30 (0.12)[b] | 0.26 (0.07)[a] |
| Next five years | 0.19 (0.09)[b] | 0.32 (0.12)[a] | 0.54 (0.09)[a] |
| Model chi-square (7 df) | 123.09[a] | 80.59[a] | 300.79[a] |

*Notes*: [a] = significant at $p < 0.01$; [b] = significant at $p < 0.05$.

economic experiences captured in the other two measures of economic experience.

We can conclude, therefore, that the effects of the market are different for different classes and that these effects have been accentuated over time.[3] This suggests that changes in the class–vote relationship might well be accounted for by reference to such polarizing class differences in economic experience. To answer this question more convincingly, however, requires an analysis of the ability of economic experience and expectations to account for the growing class basis to partisanship. This can be evaluated by including these variables in an expanded version of the logistic regressions shown in Table 10.3. If the sociological account is valid, then we would expect growing differences between classes in voting preferences to be accounted for (that is, reduced to statistical non-significance) by growing class divisions in economic experiences and expectations. So, for example, if the polarization in partisanship between the service class and the working class results from differential experience of the economic costs and benefits incurred through marketization, then controlling for these costs and benefits should remove the class coefficient. Table 10.6 presents models of class voting for Yeltsin versus Rutskoi/Zyuganov which control for economic experience.

The results of the analyses shown in Table 10.6 do not fully support the

[3] Elsewhere we have also shown that Russians on the whole perceive economic inequality between classes to be both large and growing over this period (Whitefield and Evans 1999).

bottom-up argument. Economic experiences are significantly related to vote in each year, as one might expect, and the coefficients for class differences from the working-class reference category are reduced to some degree. However, there remain significant and substantively interesting class differences in 1996 that were not there in 1993. In particular, the service class and routine nonmanual workers move away from the working class in voting intentions between 1993 and 1996 even when economic experiences are controlled for. These experiences cannot therefore explain this aspect of class-based political polarization. In other words, though a part of the explanation of partisanship, differential economic experience is not in itself an adequate explanation for the fact that class became an increasing source of partisanship between 1993 and 1996.

## CLASS PARTISANSHIP AND SOCIAL LEARNING IN RUSSIA, 1993–1996

The alternative to the sociological account was outlined in the introduction. This emphasized the importance of political factors in explaining the changing importance of class to partisanship and some of these were regarded as equally plausible initial contenders for accounting for the changing class–vote relationship; in 1993 Russians had limited experience of democracy and its parties, one of which, the Communist Party, was actually banned for the period before the surveys took place. So, with several electoral iterations, Russians may have learned by dint of their own experience or from the improved availability and sophistication of party appeals, more about the class position of the competing candidates and about the relationship between politics and markets.

Indeed, it is important also to point out that Russians were inexperienced not only about democracy in 1993, but about markets as well. While they may have been differentiated by their economic experience and expectations, as the last section has shown, given the newness of the market, it may have taken time for Russians to relate their experience to a set of broader economic orientations or norms; in other words, to decide how to relate their economic experience to support for the market *per se*. And, furthermore, time may have been needed to relate such orientations, in turn, to their support for presidential candidates. While not providing an explanation here of the sources of such learning, it is worth considering whether Russians have managed over time to relate their economic experiences more closely to their orientations and political preferences.

If this were the case, rather than economic experiences themselves being the cause of increased class voting, this would be the effect of increasing

TABLE 10.7. *Regression of market support onto market experience by year*

| Economic experience | 1993 | | 1995 | | 1996 | |
|---|---|---|---|---|---|---|
| | r | β (s.e.) | r | β (s.e.) | r | β (s.e.) |
| Current evaluation | 0.35 | 0.32 (0.02) | 0.40 | 0.41 (0.03) | 0.49 | 0.43 (0.02) |
| Past five years | 0.26 | 0.14 (0.02) | 0.24 | 0.10 (0.02) | 0.34 | 0.14 (0.02) |
| Next five years | 0.22 | 0.11 (0.02) | 0.26 | 0.21 (0.03) | 0.31 | 0.15 (0.03) |
| $R^2$ | | 0.16 | | 0.20 | | 0.27 |

*Notes*: All coefficients are significant at $p < 0.01$.

r: Pearson r.

political and economic understanding brought about by sources such as parties, candidates, and the media, as well as by more grassroots learning and reorientation by the individuals and households who make up social classes. In a similar vein, we have already demonstrated the effects of learning with respect to both markets and political choices on the outcome of the 1993 Russian election (Whitefield and Evans 1994*a*) and our analysis here is consistent with that view.

To test this explanation, we first consider the relationship between market experience (as measured by the responses to the three questions in Table 10.4) and market support, where respondents are asked to say whether they support the aim of building a market economy in Russia. The strength of the relationship for the sample as a whole is shown in the models presented in Table 10.7. The $R^2$s in this table indicate quite clearly that the association between market experience and market support has grown considerably over time. The betas increase less noticeably only because of the increasing strength of the relationship between different aspects of market experience over time, which tends to reduce the net effect of any given coefficient (as can be seen from Table 10.7, zero-order correlations with market support increase to a greater degree over the three surveys). This suggests to us that Russians are learning—whether as a result of their own reflection or from the educational activities of politicians or both—to link their policy preferences more closely to their economic experiences.

The next step is to see whether this increasing association between economic experience and norms is associated with growing class differentiation with respect to norms. Table 10.8 shows that this is the case. Class differences exist in 1993, with the service class being the most supportive of the market, followed by the routine nonmanual, petty bourgeoisie, and working classes, and with peasants the least supportive. More importantly, from the size of the beta coefficients we can see that, again, these differ-

TABLE 10.8. *Means and regressions for market support by class by year*

| Class | 1993 | | 1995 | | 1996 | |
|---|---|---|---|---|---|---|
| | Mean | β (s.e.) | Mean | β (s.e.) | Mean | β (s.e.) |
| Service class | 3.71 | 0.30 (0.08)[a] | 3.51 | 0.46 (0.07)[a] | 3.67 | 0.45 (0.07)[a] |
| Lower service/ routine nonmanual | 3.55 | 0.14 (0.06)[b] | 3.35 | 0.29 (0.07)[a] | 3.44 | 0.21 (0.06)[a] |
| Petty bourgeoisie | 3.65 | 0.24 (0.13) | 3.69 | 0.66 (0.15)[a] | 4.10 | 0.87 (0.20)[a] |
| Peasants | 3.15 | −0.19 (0.11)[b] | 2.88 | −0.17 (0.13) | 2.80 | −0.42 (0.10)[a] |
| Working class | 3.41 | — | 2.95 | — | 3.23 | — |
| $R^2$ | 0.016[a] | | 0.035[a] | | 0.048[a] | |

*Notes*: [a] = significant at $p < 0.01$; [b] = significant at $p < 0.05$.
A high score indicates a more positive attitude towards the market (on a scale from 1 to 5).

ences are clearly growing over time. By 1996 they are similar in magnitude to the relation between class position and far more nuanced (and hence more discriminating) measures of left–right economic preferences observed in the West (Evans *et al.* 1996; Heath, Evans, and Martin 1994).

The penultimate stage in the argument is to show that such distinctions in norms are also increasingly found with respect to partisanship. Table 10.9 gives the mean scores on market support by vote or intended vote. Again, differences are both evident and increasing. Yeltsin (or Yeltsin bloc) supporters are most strongly pro-market and Rutskoi or Zyuganov supporters least so. Interestingly, Zhirinovsky (or Zhirinovsky/Lebed) supporters tend to move away from Rutskoi and Zyuganov over time and stand between them and Yeltsin. The difference between Yeltsin and Rutskoi in 1993 is 0.81; by 1995 this has grown to 1.32, and this order of difference remains in 1996.

Voters seem to be increasingly able—again, either because of their own capacity to learn over several iterations or because of the activity of candidates themselves—to relate their normative perspectives to their electoral choices. It is plausible, therefore, that growing differences in partisanship between classes over time could be accounted for by differences in their normative support for the market.

This proposition is tested by again regressing candidate preferences onto class position, but this time adding market support to the effects of class position. If the learning hypothesis is correct, then we would expect growing class-voting differences to be accounted for by the increasing capacity of voters to relate their experience to their norms and their norms

TABLE 10.9. *Support for the market by political preferences by year (means)*

| Political preferences | Mean score on support for market | | |
|---|---|---|---|
| | 1993 | 1995 | 1996 |
| Yeltsin (93)<br>Yelt./Yav./Gaid. (95)<br>Yeltsin/Yav. (96) | 4.00 | 3.65 | 3.81 |
| Zhirinovsky (93)<br>Zhirinov./Leb. (95)<br>Zhirinov./Leb. (96) | 3.19 | 3.19 | 3.48 |
| Rutskoi (93)<br>Zyuganov (95)<br>Zyuganov (96) | 3.19 | 2.33 | 2.69 |
| Yeltsin (1) vs.<br>Rutskoi–Zyuganov (0) regressed onto support for market (log odds ratios and chi-square) | 0.74<br>100.8 (1 df)[a] | 0.90<br>112.3 (1 df)[a] | 1.05<br>311.5 (1 df)[a] |

[a] = significant at $p < 0.01$.

to their presidential preferences. The analyses presented in Table 10.10 are consistent with this argument.

First, note that the effect of market support is highly significant for each of the years and is of growing magnitude. Secondly, and more importantly, it has the effect of removing the significant effects of class on vote. Once market support is controlled for, class differences largely disappear. Most significantly, this holds true for the differences between the working class and peasants on the one hand and the service class on the other in 1996, which, as shown above, were significantly different even after class differences in market experience were taken into account. Increasing class alignment can thus be understood as a consequence of class polarization in experiences, in the increasing links between those experiences and attitudes towards the market, and of increasing links between those attitudes and presidential support.

## CONCLUSIONS

This chapter paper has focused on characterizing the extent and development of class bases to partisanship in Russia, and with explaining how and why this should be growing. We have argued that the growing importance of class in Russia is not simply the result of individuals' class-based

TABLE 10.10. *Logistic regressions of vote onto class and market support by year*

| Class and market experience | Yeltsin (1) vs. Rutskoi (0) | Yeltsin (1) vs. Zyuganov (0) | Yeltsin (1) vs. Zyuganov (0) |
|---|---|---|---|
| | 1993 | 1995 | 1996 |
| | β (s.e.) | β (s.e.) | β (s.e.) |
| Service class | 0.04 (0.26) | 0.01 (0.30) | 0.34 (0.22) |
| Lower service/routine nonmanual | –0.24 (0.20) | 0.36 (0.31) | 0.24 (0.18) |
| Petty bourgeoisie | 0.02 (0.49) | –0.02 (0.86) | –0.40 (0.59) |
| Peasants | –0.97 (0.44)[b] | 1.10 (0.74) | –0.27 (0.28) |
| Working class | — | — | — |
| Market Experience | | | |
| Current evaluation | 0.51 (0.11)[a] | 0.45 (0.16)[a] | 0.53 (0.08)[a] |
| Past five years | 0.34 (0.09)[a] | 0.22 (0.13) | 0.18 (0.08)[b] |
| Next five years | 0.14 (0.09) | 0.24 (0.13) | 0.49 (0.09)[a] |
| Market support | 0.50 (0.09)[a] | 0.74 (0.11)[a] | 0.73 (0.08)[a] |
| Model chi-square (8 df) | 156.71[a] | 132.49[a] | 385.44[a] |

*Notes*: [a] = significant at $p < 0.01$; [b] = significant at $p < 0.05$.

A high score indicates more positive experiences and a more positive attitude towards the market.

differences in economic experiences, but also of an increasing tendency to relate these experiences to broader ideological perspectives and, in turn, to presidential preferences. Class differences in partisanship in Russia are mediated via class differences in support for the market and the increasing association of policy-related preferences with market experience as a result, we propose, of social and political learning. The Russian electorate has become more 'politically sophisticated' over time as well as more economically differentiated and it is this conjunction of influences that accounts for the increasing strength and pattern of the class–vote relationship.

The factors that account for this increased sophistication could include a wide range of influences—either individual reflection or partisan education in turbulent economic and political times or both—and their elucidation must await further research. On the basis of this evidence, however, we can say that, as distinct from some commentators on post-communist Russian politics, we do find social divisions based on class emerging in Russia. These cannot be accounted for by the existence of a developed civil society; nor are they likely to be the effect of partisan activity alone, given the weak level of development of parties and the incentives to parties or presidents to converge on what is of greatest concern to voters rather than to pursue their own agendas. Rather, in a highly uncertain economic and political environment, parties, presidential contenders, and voters have moved towards increasingly clear stances on the issue of the economy and the market and have at the same time evolved more effective strategies of signalling and recognition. Russian electoral politics has become more structured over time as a result of the growing capacity of voters to relate their economic experience to their class position and to find political contenders that reflect their policy-related preferences.

# APPENDIX
## The Surveys

TABLE 10.A1. *The surveys*

| Date | Sampling frame | Sample design and procedure | Response rates | |
|---|---|---|---|---|
| Summer 1993 | Adult population (18+): lists of 'privatization vouchers' | 1. 10 regions<br>2. 56 settlements<br>3. Individuals sampled from list of vouchers | Names issued<br>Non-contact<br>Refused<br>Achieved<br>Response rate | 2,420<br>264<br>126<br>2,030<br>0.84 |
| Summer 1995 | Adult population (18+): 1989 census of households (stages 1, 2); electoral register (stage 3); list of households (stage 4) | 1. 4 economic-geographical zones; 15 clusters;<br>2. 49 raions + 2 (Moscow and St Petersburg) sampling points;<br>3. 51 communities;<br>4. Multistage probability sampling and random route with Kish Grid selection | Names issued<br>Non-contact<br>Refused<br>Achieved<br>Response rate | 2,600<br>397<br>200<br>2,003<br>0.77 |
| Summer 1996 | Adult population (18+): the electoral lists | 1. 4 economic-geographical zones; 15 clusters;<br>2. 49 raions + 2 (Moscow and St Petersburg) sampling points;<br>3. 51 communities;<br>4. Multistage probability sampling and random route with Kish Grid selection | Names issued<br>Non-contact<br>Refused<br>Achieved<br>Response rate | 2,658<br>389<br>249<br>2,020<br>0.76 |

# PART IV

## Reappraisal, Commentary, and Conclusions

# 11

# Resolving Disputes About Class Voting in Britain and the United States: Definitions, Models, and Data

DAVID L. WEAKLIEM AND ANTHONY F. HEATH

## INTRODUCTION

Measuring the influence of social class on voting might seem to be a relatively straightforward enterprise by the standards of social scientific research. There is abundant data and little doubt about how the dependent variable should be measured. While the measurement of social class is more complex, the performance of different definitions of class can be evaluated empirically, and once one is chosen, the measurement of trends in class voting should not, it seems, be difficult.

As readers of this volume know, this is not the case. There has been a great deal of controversy about trends in class voting, especially in Britain and the United States. Some of the disagreement can be traced to differences in methods. We will not review these issues here, except to say that we accept the arguments for the use of loglinear and related models to measure class voting. Yet even among researchers who use these techniques, conclusions differ. Weakliem (1995*a*), using data from the British Election Survey (BES), finds a small but statistically significant downward trend in class voting since 1964, along with a good deal of short-term fluctuation. Goldthorpe (Chapter 3), also using BES data, holds that there is no trend and little fluctuation. Weakliem and Heath (Chapter 5), using Gallup data covering 1935–92, find a definite decline in class voting since the 1950s, preceded by a substantial increase between 1935 and 1951. Turning to the United States, Hout, Manza, and Brooks (Chapter 4; see also Hout *et al.* 1995), using the American National Election Studies

The data were obtained from the ESRC data archive (Essex), the Roper Center for Public Opinion Research (Storrs, Connecticut), and the Inter-University Consortium for Political and Social Research (Ann Arbor, Michigan). We thank Jane Roberts and Fern Bennett for help in obtaining the data, and Tracy Schauer for research assistance. We also thank Nuffield College for financial support.

(ANES), find no general decline in class voting since 1948, but do find a realignment of classes. Weakliem and Heath, on the other hand, using Gallup polls and the General Social Survey (GSS), find a substantial and relatively steady decline from the 1930s to the 1980s.

These differences raise the disturbing possibility that results of statistical analyses are strongly affected by small changes in methods, definitions of class, or characteristics of the sample. It is possible, however, that the differences in results based on different samples are small enough to be explained by sampling error, and that some differences in conclusions are matters of emphasis rather than real disagreement. It is therefore important to explain the differences and see if the various results can be reconciled, and this is the object of the present chapter. We begin by comparing our results from the analysis of Gallup/GSS data for the United States with those of Hout, Manza, and Brooks. We then provide parallel analyses of Gallup and BES data for Britain. Finally, we use a detailed occupational breakdown of the BES data to explore the consequences of using different class schemas. In doing so we attempt to resolve some of the differences in interpretation between Goldthorpe, Hout, Manza, and Brooks, and Weakliem and Heath, which appear in Chapters 3–5.

## DATA

The BES and ANES data have been used extensively in voting research. In his chapter, Goldthorpe analyses tables of class by vote in British general elections from 1964 to 1992. He distinguishes seven classes according to the principles discussed in his earlier work (Goldthorpe 1987: 40–3): high-level managers and professionals ('service class'), lower-level managers and professionals, routine nonmanual, small proprietors, foremen and technicians, skilled workers, and semi- and unskilled workers. Respondents are classified by the 'head of household's' occupation. Hout, Manza, and Brooks analyse the relationship between class and vote in American Presidential elections from 1948 to 1992 using a similar definition of class. They distinguish six classes: professional, managers and administrators, routine white collar, proprietors, foremen and craft workers, and semi- and unskilled workers. They classify respondents by their own occupations, and exclude housewives, students, and retired people.

Weakliem and Heath analyse tables of class by vote for British general elections from 1935 to 1992, with the exception of 1950, and American presidential elections from 1936 to 1992. They also include a British survey of voting intentions in 1943 in order to shed some light on class polarization during the gap between the elections of 1935 and 1945. The Gallup surveys contain less detail on respondents' occupations than do the BES and ANES surveys, but it was possible to distinguish four classes in the British data: proprietors and executives, professionals, white collar, and manual, and six in the American: farmers and farm labourers, professionals, managers and proprietors, white collar, skilled manual, and semi- and unskilled manual.[1] The Gallup surveys obtained information on respondent's occupation until 1952 in the United States and 1970 in Britain, and then switched to 'head of household's' occupation, but this change had no discernible effect on estimates of class voting.

In the United States, the classification of parties is straightforward. Important third-party candidates ran in 1948, 1968, 1980, and 1992, but none of the parties contested more than one election, so they cannot be systematically analysed. In Britain, Social Democrats are included with the Liberals in 1983 and 1987, producing a three-party classification into Conservatives, Labour, and Liberals.[2] Hout, Manza, and Brooks, and Weakliem and Heath also consider nonvoters, but they are omitted here in order to simplify the discussion.

## ANALYSIS

### *United States*

#### *General Indexes of Class Voting*

The most familiar measure of class voting is the Alford index (Alford 1963), defined as the percentage of manual workers supporting the left minus the percentage of nonmanual workers supporting the left. However, while the simplicity of the Alford index makes it useful for descriptive purposes, its reliance on dichotomies of class and party makes it unsuitable for more rigorous analysis (Korpi 1972). One of the advantages of loglinear and related models is that they can be applied to tables of any dimension and consequently eliminate the need to dichotomize classes and parties.[3]

A useful model for the comparison of tables has been suggested by Erikson and Goldthorpe (1992*a*: 91–2) and Xie (1992) and applied to class

[1] In Britain, farm owners are counted as proprietors and farm labourers as manual workers.

[2] Northern Ireland, which has a distinct party system, was not included in the original surveys. Voters for the Plaid Cymru and Scottish Nationalist Party were not numerous enough to be included in the analysis.

[3] Clark *et al.* (1993: 308) assert that these techniques rely on 'dichotomising variables rather than using all available continuous data'. This statement presumably refers to the treatment of control variables such as education, which are treated as categorical (although not necessarily dichotomous). Loglinear and association models do not, however, treat the core variables of class and party as dichotomous.

voting by Goldthorpe in his chapter. The 'uniform difference' model, as Erikson and Goldthorpe call it, assumes that changes in class voting take the form of uniform convergence or divergence of all classes and parties. For example, suppose that the Labour vote among manual workers is twice as large as would be expected if class and vote were independent and the Conservative vote among managers is three times as large as expected. In a later election, suppose that the ratio of actual to expected Labour vote among manual workers falls to 1.5, or three-quarters as large as before. If the uniform difference model holds, the ratio of actual to expected Conservative votes among managers will also decline to three-quarters of its previous value, or 2.25. The strength of association between class and party in an election is summarized by a single parameter, β. Unlike the Alford index, β cannot be compared between nations, but only among elections in a given nation.

The estimated values of β for the United States based on the Gallup/GSS, ANES for all voters, and ANES excluding blacks are shown in Figure 11.1. Using the Gallup/GSS data, there is a fairly steady decline in class voting. With the ANES data for all voters, there seems to be some downward trend but it is considerably weaker. Weakliem and Heath, however, noting that class voting has traditionally been very weak among

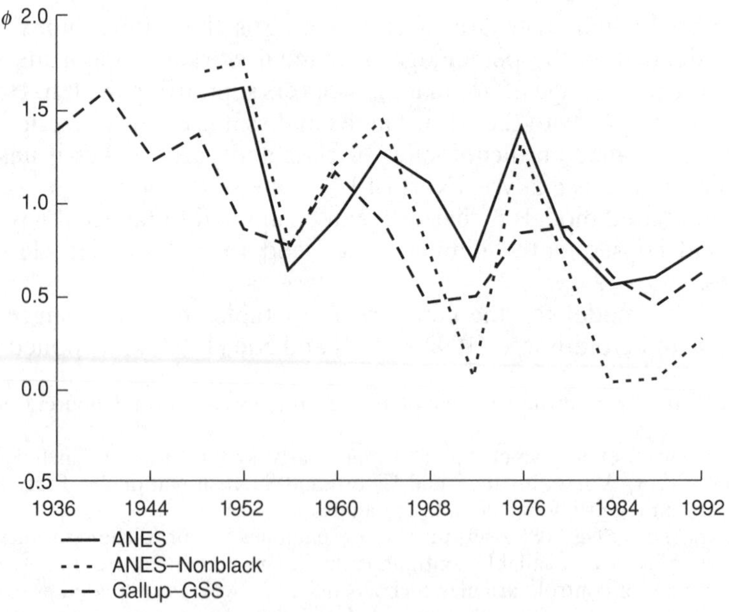


FIG. 11.1. Uniform difference estimates of class voting, United States

blacks, excluded them from their analysis. If blacks are omitted from the ANES sample, the downward trend in class voting becomes more pronounced. That is, strong and increasing support for the Democratic Party among blacks, who are concentrated in manual and lower white-collar occupations, partly offsets the decline in class voting among whites.

Hout, Manza, and Brooks base much of their analysis of class voting on another measure, kappa (κ). Suppose that $n_{ij}$ is the number of voters from class *i* who support party *j*. If one takes any combination of two classes and two parties, the odds ratio $n_{11}n_{22}/n_{12}n_{21}$ represents the difference between those two classes in support for those parties. Kappa is the standard deviation of the logarithms of the odds ratios from all possible pairs of classes and parties. If class has no effect on vote, the logarithms of all odds ratios will be zero, so the standard deviation will be zero as well. Kappa has no upper bound, since the odds ratio will approach infinity as the numbers in the denominator approach zero.

Kappa is intended to measure the change in the effects of class on voting without making any assumption about the specific nature of the change. In this sense, it is similar to the $R^2$ in a regression equation. The uniform difference model, on the other hand, assumes a specific type of change, since the estimates of β reflect only those changes that amount to simple increases or decreases in class polarization, not those that involve changes in the relative positions of classes or parties. If the uniform difference model is accurate, trends in β and κ should be similar, but κ will be affected to a greater extent by sampling error because it includes more parameters to be estimated. If the uniform difference model is not valid, however, the two measures can diverge substantially. The conceptual differences between the measures will be discussed at more length below, but it is instructive to simply compare estimates of β and κ. Table 11.1 shows the correlations among estimates of β and κ derived from the ANES and Gallup/GSS data.

These results confirm that the exclusion of blacks makes a substantial difference; for both β and κ, the correlations with the Gallup/GSS estimates and with time are stronger when blacks are excluded. It is more difficult to say whether there are systematic differences between κ and β. If they measured different things, one would expect high correlations among measures of the same type. This does not seem to be the case: in fact, the κ estimated from the ANES data (nonblacks) is more highly correlated with β than the κ estimated from the Gallup/GSS data. These results suggest that both indexes are measuring the same thing, but that β is better in the sense of having less random error. However, the residual $L^2$ from the uniform difference model is statistically significant (110.5 with 45 degrees of freedom), meaning that some changes in class voting are

TABLE 11.1. *Correlations among indexes of class voting and time, United States*

| Index of class voting | Index of class voting | | | | | | |
|---|---|---|---|---|---|---|---|
| | 1 | 2 | 3 | 4 | 5 | 6 | 7 |
| 1 ANES (UNIDIFF) | 1.000 | 0.909 | 0.766 | 0.712 | 0.574 | 0.589 | –0.623 |
| 2 ANES-Nonblack (UNIDIFF) | 0.909 | 1.000 | 0.580 | 0.707 | 0.772 | 0.658 | –0.777 |
| 3 ANES (κ) | 0.766 | 0.580 | 1.000 | 0.868 | 0.386 | 0.476 | –0.460 |
| 4 ANES–nonblack (κ) | 0.712 | 0.707 | 0.868 | 1.000 | 0.638 | 0.494 | –0.509 |
| 5 Gallup/GSS–nonblack (UNIDIFF) | 0.574 | 0.772 | 0.386 | 0.638 | 1.000 | 0.898 | –0.810 |
| 6 Gallup/GSS–Nonblack (κ) | 0.589 | 0.658 | 0.476 | 0.494 | 0.770 | 1.000 | –0.789 |
| 7 Year | –0.623 | –0.777 | –0.460 | –0.509 | –0.646 | –0.650 | 1.00 |

*Note*: Figures above the diagonal are based on listwise deletion of missing cases (i.e. 1948–88 elections); those below on pairwise deletion.

not captured by the uniform difference model. Hence, it is necessary to consider more flexible models of change in class voting.

### *Multidimensional Models of Change*

As mentioned above, although β and κ sometimes yield similar results, there are important conceptual differences between them. Kappa is intended to indicate the extent to which class affects vote, without specifying anything about the relations between particular classes and parties. It does not, however, detect all changes in class voting. If class-voting alignments exactly reversed themselves, with the most radical class becoming the most conservative and vice versa, κ would remain unchanged. The ability to distinguish the 'direction' of class voting is an important advantage of the uniform difference model. Consequently, it would be useful to have models that keep this property but are less restrictive than the uniform difference model. One possibility is based on the 'association model', which is a modified loglinear model based on the assumption that class and party categories can be placed on a numerical scale.[4]

For example, one might expect that the political preferences of routine nonmanual workers would be somewhere in between those of professionals and managers and the manual working class, and that the class

[4] Technically, association models are logmultiplicative rather than loglinear models. For the sake of simplicity, we will not make this terminological distinction.

composition of Liberal voters would be somewhere in between that of Labour and Conservative voters. One approach to analysis would be to convert the categorical variables into continuous variables by giving scores to the classes and parties and using these in standard regression or correlation methods. Association models do something similar, but rather than using pre-defined scores, they obtain the estimates of the 'positions' that best explain the association between variables.[5] Formally, if classes are indexed by $i$, parties by $j$, and elections by $k$, the association model can be written:

$$\log(n_{ijk}) = \log(N_k) + C_{ik} + P_{jk} + \Sigma\phi_{mk}\gamma_{mi}\tau_{mj}. \qquad (11.1)$$

Because there is no natural scale for the row and column scores, they must be standardized in some way, conventionally by giving them mean zero and variance one. Given the row and column scores, $\phi$ can be understood as a measure of the strength of association between the variables. The simplest and most commonly used version of the association model contains only one dimension. The one-dimensional association model is similar to the uniform difference model in that it produces a single index of class voting. An association model with more than one dimension, however, allows change to occur along different class–party alignments. For example, there might be two distinct sets of class scores, one opposing manual workers to nonmanual workers with farmers falling in the middle, and the second opposing both manual and nonmanual workers to farmers. It is possible that class voting could increase along one dimension while decreasing along the other. For example, the urban–rural alignment might yield to the manual–nonmanual alignment. In this case, both $\kappa$ and the uniform difference model might show little change, as the two movements would partly counteract each other. A two-dimensional association model, however, could show both types of changes at once.

The class and party scores may be estimated to produce the best fit, or they may be assigned in advance to focus on a contrast of particular interest. In the United States, since there are only two parties, the party scores amount to a simple contrast between Democrats and Republicans. Note that it is possible to have several distinct sets of class scores associated with a single set of party scores. In Britain, with three parties, it is possible to estimate party scores along two distinct dimensions. In order to simplify interpretation of the results, however, we define two sets of scores in advance: Labour versus all others and Liberal versus all others. Class scores on the first dimension can be understood as a class's propensity to support Labour rather than the Conservatives, and scores

[5] Goodman (1987, 1991) provides more detailed discussion of association models and comparisons to related techniques such as correspondence analysis.

on the second dimension as its propensity to support the Liberals over the Conservatives.

The Alford index and other measures based on a single contrast can be understood as special cases of the association model. In effect, these measures look at the strength of association along a dimension defined as specific sets of row and column scores. For example, following Alford, one could give a score of –1 to all manual occupations and all left parties, and a score of +1 to all nonmanual occupations and all centre and right parties. Model (11.1) could then be estimated, and $\phi$ would be approximately proportional to the Alford index. The idea of using pre-defined scores with some clear theoretical interpretation is attractive, but it can produce misleading results unless other dimensions of theoretical or practical importance are included. Harrop and Miller (1987: 187) observe that 'Marx's apocalyptic vision of a simple political dichotomy between workers and capitalists would show up as a decline in class divisions on the standard Alford index calculated on . . . manual and non-manual employees'. In terms of association models, including just the manual/nonmanual contrast would not enable one to distinguish between a simple decline in class voting and a realignment along the lines of Marx's prediction. In this scenario, adding an additional dimension distinguishing workers and capitalists would eliminate the apparent changes involving the manual/nonmanual dimension.

*Results from Multidimensional Association Models*

In the ANES data, the $L^2$ statistic for the hypothesis of no association between class and party is 282.1 with 60 degrees of freedom. A loglinear model of constant class voting yields an $L^2$ of 142.8 with 55 degrees of freedom. The one-dimensional association model allowing changes in $\phi$, which with only two parties is equivalent to the uniform difference model, produces an $L^2$ of 110.5 with 45 degrees of freedom, and adding a second dimension reduces the $L^2$ to 25.0 with 30 degrees of freedom. In the Gallup data, the model of no association between class and party yields an $L^2$ of 1820.6 with 95 degrees of freedom. A model of constant class voting produces an $L^2$ of 365.8 with 90 degrees of freedom. Allowing change in $\phi$ reduces the $L^2$ to 219.0 with 76 degrees of freedom, and adding a second dimension with change in $\phi$ reduces it further, to 116.2 with 59 degrees of freedom. Including a third dimension produces a smaller but statistically significant improvement in fit, reducing the $L^2$ to 72.1. Since the estimates involving the third dimension proved difficult to interpret, we consider only the first two dimensions in subsequent discussion.[6] The fact that

[6] The Gallup/GSS contains more cases than the ANES dataset (about 70,000 as opposed to 20,000), making it more difficult to find a simple model that fits the data using standard significance tests.

TABLE 11.2. *Class scores from association model, United States*

| Class | Dimension 1 | | Dimension 2 | |
|---|---|---|---|---|
| | Gallup | ANES | Gallup | ANES |
| Professionals | –0.966 | –0.854 | 1.164 | 1.260 |
| Business | –1.145 | –0.978 | –0.062 | –0.860 |
| White collar | –0.069 | –0.164 | 0.039 | 0.582 |
| Farm/proprietors | –0.094 | –0.482 | –1.803 | –1.430 |
| Skilled manual | 0.879 | 1.231 | 0.53 | –0.073 |
| Semi/unskilled | 1.395 | 1.242 | 0.698 | 0.524 |

adding a second dimension produces a substantial improvement in both datasets is consistent with Hout, Manza, and Brooks's claim that there has been some realignment of classes rather than simple convergence or divergence.

The estimated class scores for the first two dimensions based on the two datasets are shown in Table 11.2. Although the ANES and Gallup occupational classifications are not identical, the scores on the first dimension are remarkably similar, with a correlation of 0.96. The correlation is quite high on the second dimension as well (0.89), although the differences involving the business and white-collar classes are large enough to be worthy of notice. At least in this case, estimates of class positions in the association model are not very sensitive to small differences in the definition of class. Substantively, the first dimension shows the familiar contrast between manual workers and managers and professionals. White-collar workers are roughly in the middle, as are farmers in the Gallup/GSS data. The classification used in the ANES data does not include a separate category for farmers, but combines farm owners with owners of other businesses. Small proprietors are somewhat closer to managers and professionals than to manual workers. Nevertheless, the estimated positions of the Gallup/GSS farmer and ANES small-proprietor classes are close enough for the two groups to be taken as rough equivalents. In both datasets, the second dimension is dominated by a contrast between professionals and farmers/proprietors. Moreover, both show that unskilled workers are somewhat closer to professionals on the second dimension. The major difference between the estimates on the second dimension is that managers are estimated to be closer to proprietors in the ANES data and roughly in the middle in the Gallup/GSS.

The preceding results can be understood in a purely descriptive sense as a summary of the relative political propensities of the different classes. The class scores, however, can also be interpreted in light of expectations about economic, cultural, and political differences among the classes. The class scores on the first dimension seem to correspond to differences in economic interest as conventionally understood. The scores on the second dimension might be taken as representing the cultural divisions discussed by authors such as Inglehart (1990). However, if cultural liberalism is a result of education and affluence, as Inglehart maintains, the position of unskilled manual workers is surprising. An alternative interpretation of the second dimension is that it reflects relations to the state (Dunleavy and Husbands 1985: 21–5). Unskilled workers are likely to benefit from state services such as income or medical assistance, while many professionals are either employed by the state or by organizations that receive large amounts of state funding such as universities or hospitals. Thus, both benefit from the expansion of government spending on social services, in contrast to the other classes. All accounts of 'new politics', however, agree in implying that the second dimension should have become stronger relative to the first in recent elections.

Figure 11.2 displays the estimated strength of association along the first dimension for the Gallup/GSS and ANES data. The patterns of change are quite similar. Both sets of estimates show a clear downward trend, and they generally agree on short-term changes as well: for example, both show low levels of class voting in 1968 and 1972, followed by an increase in 1976. There are, however, some larger differences between them, notably in 1952, when the Gallup series shows a sharp drop in class voting. In comparing the results from the two datasets, it is important to remember that

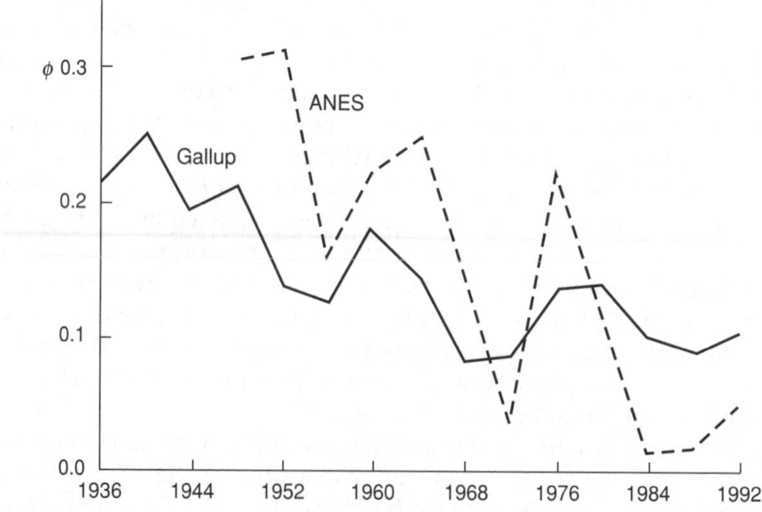


FIG. 11.2. Estimates of class voting along first dimension, United States

all estimates are subject to sampling error. That is, different samples drawn from exactly the same population could be expected to show somewhat different levels of class voting simply as a result of chance. Moreover, the range of normal sampling error is surprisingly large in samples of a few thousand. For example, although the ANES estimates show a large increase in class voting between 1956 and 1960, this difference is not statistically significant—that is, a difference of that size could occur by chance if the true level of class voting were the same in both elections. Thus, we could not expect perfect agreement between the ANES and Gallup estimates, but must ask if they are similar enough to be regarded as measurements of the same thing. To answer this question, we can estimate the following multivariate regression model:

$$\phi_d = \alpha_d + \beta\phi^* + \varepsilon_d, \qquad (11.2)$$

where the subscript $d$ indicates the dataset, $\phi_d$ is the observed value of class voting, $\phi^*$ is the unobserved true value of class voting, and $\varepsilon$ is a random error term. This model assumes that both estimates reflect the same underlying quantity. Differences in the average value of the estimates in the different data sets are represented by $\alpha$, and differences in the strength of the relationship to the unobserved variable are represented by $\beta$.[7] The residual variance from this regression will have a chi-square distribution, making it possible to say whether the fit of the model is adequate. If the fit is adequate, that means that the differences in estimates from the two datasets are small enough to be explained by ordinary sampling error; if it is not, there are some systematic differences between the two sets of estimates.

Fitting the model while forcing $\alpha$ and $\beta$ to be the same in both datasets produces a residual chi-square of 32.75 with 11 degrees of freedom. Allowing $\alpha$ to differ while forcing $\beta$ to remain the same reduces the residual chi-square to 12.6 with 10 degrees of freedom, which is an acceptable fit ($p = 0.247$). Allowing $\beta$ to differ as well improves the chi-square by only 0.2, far short of statistical significance. That is, the estimated value of $\phi$ is consistently larger in the Gallup data, but after allowing for sampling error, *changes* in $\phi$ are the same in both datasets. As a result, the two sets of estimates can be combined to obtain a more accurate picture of changes in class voting. The estimated values of $\phi^*$ from 1948 to 1988 are: 0.337, 0.221, 0.160, 0.276, 0.212, 0.080, 0.058, 0.199, 0.180, 0.048, and 0.032.[8]

[7] This parameter is not related to the $\beta$ parameter in the uniform difference model.

[8] These estimates use the ANES as a baseline. The value of $\alpha$, which represents the difference in the Gallup and ANES estimates, is 0.082. Because positive values of $\alpha$ are strongly implied by theory, we also considered the possibility that the relationship is multiplicative rather than additive, which would mean that negative values of $\alpha$ are impossible. The multiplicative model, however, did not fit quite as well as the additive model, and the results were otherwise very similar.

There is a clear trend in $\phi^*$, but the short-term fluctuation is also highly significant. In 1956, 1968, and 1972 class voting was significantly below the values predicted by a linear trend, and in 1976 and 1980 it was above the trend. Although most discussions of change in class voting have focused on trends, in quantitative terms, short-term fluctuation is equally important.

Estimates of $\phi$ for the second dimension from the ANES and GSS/Gallup data are shown in Figure 11.3. Again, the estimates are similar, with both showing a tendency to increase over time. Applying model (11.2) and allowing $\alpha$ to differ while forcing $\beta$ to remain the same yields a chi-square of 18.4 with 10 degrees of freedom, which is large enough to raise some doubts about the model ($p = 0.048$) Allowing $\beta$ to differ reduces the $L^2$ to only 18.2 with 9 degrees of freedom. Because of the size of the chi-square statistics, it is not clear whether the two sets of estimates can be regarded as identical, but they are certainly similar. In only one year, 1968, is the difference larger than could be expected to occur by chance. As with the first dimension, there is a significant trend, but also substantial short-term fluctuation. For example, the value of $\phi$ is large, indicating relatively strong support for the Democrats among professionals, in 1972, but then declines in 1976 and 1980 before recovering in the 1980s. The estimated values of $\phi^*$ from 1948 to 1988 are: –0.058, –0.059, –0.138, 0.012, 0.018, 0.073, 0.214, 0.086, 0.040, 0.098, and 0.184.

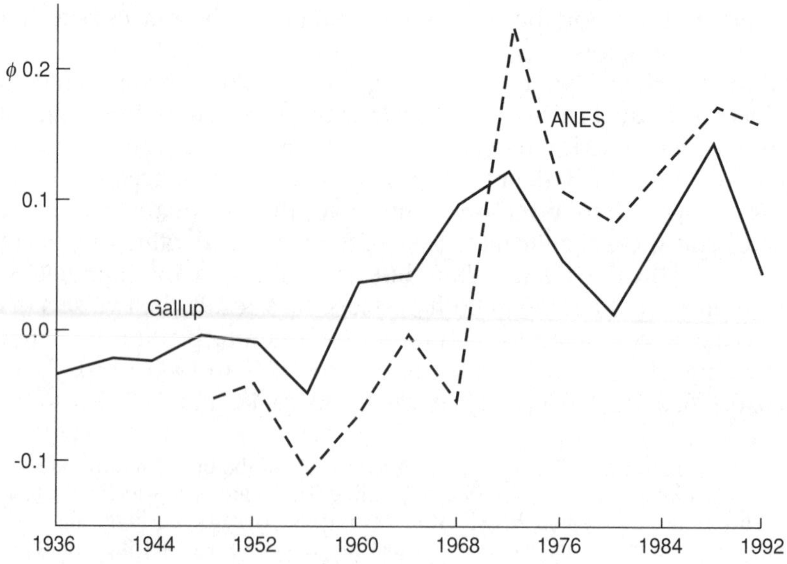


FIG. 11.3. Estimates of class voting along second dimension, United States

To summarize, both datasets tell the same, or very similar, stories about changes along two dimensions of the association model. Class polarization along the first dimension, which corresponds to the traditional division of middle class and working class, declined in the United States between 1948 and 1988. Both datasets also reveal a second dimension on which professionals are opposed to independent farmers or proprietors. Compared to other classes, professionals have tended to move towards the Democrats, while at the same time farmers or proprietors have tended to move towards the Republicans.

*Discussion*

Before turning to the British data, we will discuss the methodological and substantive conclusions that can be drawn from the preceding analysis. We found a decline in class polarization along the first dimension, along with two significant deviations from the general pattern: professionals, and to some extent white-collar workers, have moved towards the Democrats and farmers towards the Republicans. The fact that both can be modelled as changes along the second dimension means that the two movements have been simultaneous: in general, when professionals have shifted towards the Democrats, relative to other classes, farmers and proprietors have shifted away. Hout, Manza, and Brooks also found that professionals and white-collar workers had shifted towards the Democrats, although they express the change as the development of new Republican and Democratic 'coalitions'.

The main point of disagreement is that Hout, Manza, and Brooks argue that class voting has not really declined in the United States. Our calculations, reported in Table 11.1, show that this conclusion is too strong and that their preferred measure of total class voting, κ, has tended to decline over time. While some decline is visible with the ANES data, the evidence is much stronger when the Gallup data is included as well. Yet both the present analysis and Hout, Manza, and Brooks agree that there has been some realignment, or shifts in the relative position of classes. Hence, speaking of an increase or decrease in class voting is at best a simplification. What can clearly be said, however, is that the traditional alignment of working class versus middle class has become weaker in the United States.

These results are consistent with Lipset's (1981) and Inglehart's (1990) accounts of changes in the relations between class and political choice. These authors argue that the traditional alignment has become weaker, but a new alignment cutting across the manual/nonmanual division has become stronger. Thus, in Lipset's (1981: 510) term, there are 'two lefts', one drawn largely from the working class and the other from the middle class. While our results for the United States are compatible with such accounts, existing accounts are not specified clearly enough to permit conclusions about specific versions of the general perspective. Virtually all authors suggest that professionals are furthest to the left on the second dimension, but there is much less clarity and agreement about the positions of other classes. Some imply that the contrast is between professionals and *all* other classes, others that it is primarily between professionals and manual workers. Inglehart (1990: 162–76), however, finds that 'postmaterialist' attitudes, which he sees as the source of the new left, are quite widespread among younger managers in several nations.[9] In this case the second dimension should oppose both managers and professionals to manual workers and the traditional petty bourgeoisie. Our results are not entirely consistent with any of these views, since they show skilled manual workers as roughly in the middle, unskilled workers as slightly to the Democratic side, and proprietors or farmers on the Republican side of the second dimension. As discussed above, the results are also consistent with a quite different interpretation of the second dimension as involving economic relations to the state. Finally, it should be noted that one might interpret the second dimension as a statistical artefact. On this view, two classes, professionals and farmers/proprietors, have changed their political positions relative to the other classes. Although the shifts have occurred at about the same time, that does not prove that they are actually connected. Thus, the realignment might represent several class-specific factors, rather than a more general pattern of social change.

Turning to methodological issues, the major finding is that the ANES and Gallup/GSS results are consistent in the period when both are available. Hence, the Gallup estimates of class voting can be taken as reliable substitutes for the ANES estimates, making it possible to consider the 1936–44 elections. Since the ANES surveys currently include only twelve presidential elections, the opportunity to add three data points is a substantial advance. The comparability of estimates from different sources is an important finding, given the substantial sampling error in estimates of class voting from the ANES.[10]

## *Britain*

### *Results from Multidimensional Association Models*

Unlike the United States, Britain has three significant parties. As discussed above, we use two sets of party scores, which can be understood as Labour/Conservative and Liberal/Conservative contrasts. Using the

[9] This finding is to be expected if, as Inglehart (1990) believes, education and material security are the major sources of postmaterialism.

[10] We also find that the inclusion or exclusion of blacks makes a difference in estimates of class voting derived from cross-tabulations. It is probably less important when individual-level data are used along with a control for race, as in Hout *et al.*'s analyses.

TABLE 11.3. *Class scores from association model, Britain*

| Class | Labour/Conservative | Liberal/Conservative |
|---|---|---|
| A. Goldthorpe Classes (BES) | | |
| Upper service | –1.078 | –0.346 |
| Lower service | –0.517 | 0.219 |
| Nonmanual | –0.266 | –0.269 |
| Proprietors | –1.105 | –1.915 |
| Manual foremen | 0.507 | 0.326 |
| Skilled manual | 1.235 | 1.091 |
| Unskilled manual | 1.224 | 0.894 |
| B. Gallup Classes | | |
| Managers and proprietors | –0.898 | –1.365 |
| Professionals | –0.568 | 0.186 |
| Nonmanual | 0.108 | 0.148 |
| Manual | 1.358 | 1.031 |

BES data with the seven-class schema, a model of no association between class and party produces an $L^2$ of 2,484 with 108 degrees of freedom, while the model of constant class voting produces an $L^2$ of 270.4 with 96 degrees of freedom. A model allowing changes in association along both the Labour versus Conservative and Liberal versus Conservative dimensions improves the $L^2$ to 83.5 with 80 degrees of freedom, which is a satisfactory fit ($p = 0.375$). With the Gallup data, the model of no class voting gives an $L^2$ of 5,349 with 84 degrees of freedom, and a model of constant class voting gives an $L^2$ of 297.5 with 78 degrees of freedom. Allowing changes in the $\phi$ parameters improves it to 135.1 with 54 degrees of freedom. This model can still be rejected using standard significance tests, indicating the existence of some realignment that cannot be modelled by the Labour/Conservative and Liberal/Conservative dimensions. Most of this change appears to involve shifts in the relative position of managers and professionals which were completed before the BES series began in 1964. Even in the post-1964 period, however, the model does not fit the Gallup data as well as the BES.[11] Nevertheless, it accounts for most of the association between class and vote, so we will consider the parameter estimates from this model before moving on to more complicated ones.

The estimated class scores from each dataset are shown in Table 11.3, while estimates of the strength of association ($\phi$) along the Labour–Conservative dimension are shown in Figure 11.4.

[11] For 1964–87 period, the two-dimensional model applied to the Gallup data produces an $L^2$ of 61.3 with 32 degrees of freedom.

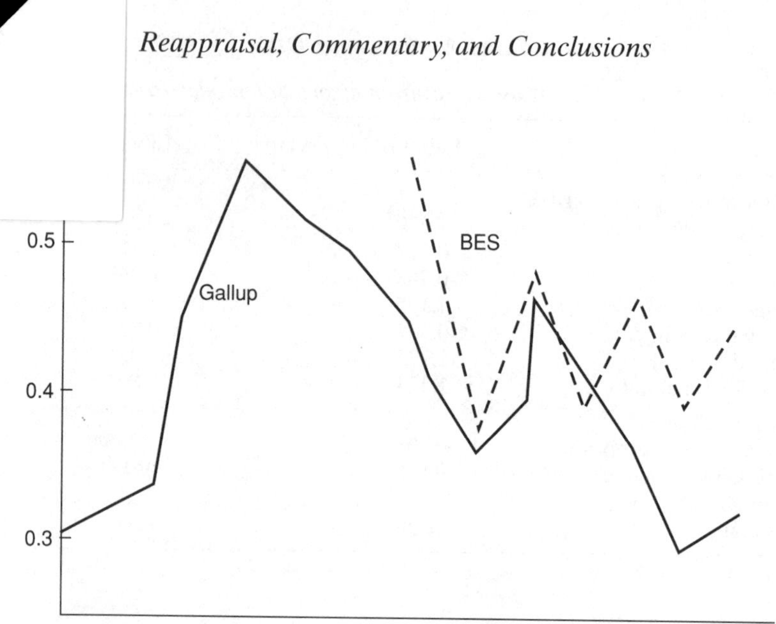


FIG. 11.4. Estimates of class voting along Labour/Conservative Dimension, Britain

As expected, in the BES data the upper service class and small proprietors are the most anti-Labour, and manual workers are the most pro-Labour. In the Gallup data, managers, directors, and proprietors are the most anti-Labour, followed closely by professionals, while manual workers are the most pro-Labour. There are only nine elections, 1964–92, for which we have data from both surveys. The Gallup figures give a stronger impression of a steady downward trend during this period; in the BES, class voting appears to fall between 1964 and 1970, and then to fluctuate without any trend. However, given the sampling error in the estimates and the fact that there are only nine elections, judging the similarity of the estimates by inspection is difficult. Fitting the multivariate regression model (11.2) above to scores on the first dimension produces a chi-square of 9.0 with 8 degrees of freedom when $\alpha$ is allowed to differ and $\beta$ is the same in both datasets.[12] That is, the Gallup and BES estimates of changes in Labour versus Conservative class voting are not significantly different in the 1964–92 period. If the BES and Gallup estimates are combined, which our results indicate they can be, there is clearly a downward trend in class voting over the period. It is, however, of only moderate size,

[12] The fact that the $\alpha$ parameter is significantly different from zero is of little interest because the class schemas are not the same.

as inspection of Figure 11.4 indicates. In our earlier work using the BES we rejected the claim of class dealignment (Heath *et al.* 1985; Weakliem 1989), but more recently we have concluded that a limited dealignment has occurred since the early 1960s (Heath *et al.* 1991: 77; Weakliem 1995*a*). These results reinforce our more recent conclusions.

The exact form of the downward trend is theoretically interesting, since some accounts of dealignment emphasize long-term developments, suggesting a linear trend, and others emphasize the impact of particular historical events, suggesting a discontinuous pattern. Distinguishing among the different possibilities is difficult, however, given the size of the errors in the estimates for individual years. Using only the BES data, a model with a contrast between the elections of the 1960s and all subsequent elections fits better than the linear trend model. On the other hand, using only the Gallup data, a model with a contrast between the elections pre- and post-1979 fits better than the linear trend model. When estimates from both samples are combined, the linear trend model fits better than either two-period model. Thus, the most reasonable summary is that the trend in class voting since 1964 has been approximately linear. There has, however, been a good deal of short-term fluctuation in class voting: estimates from both samples show a sharp drop in 1970 and a sharp increase in October 1974. The existence of these short-term changes means that one must be cautious in making claims about the precise nature of any trends.

On the Liberal/Conservative dimension, the class scores from both datasets show manual workers as the most pro-Liberal class. These results may seem surprising, since the Liberals receive a larger share of the vote of professionals and white-collar workers than of the working class. Relative to the Conservatives, however, the Liberals did best in the working class. For example, in the combined 1964–92 BES sample, the Liberals received only 14.6 per cent of the vote in the working class against 22.5 per cent in the higher service class, but the ratio of Liberal to Conservative votes was 1:2 among skilled manual workers and 1:2.8 in the higher service class. The difference in class schemas seems to be important here, since the Gallup estimates show a substantial difference between managers and proprietors and professionals, and the BES estimates show a large difference between the petty bourgeoisie and the service class. Since different segments of the middle class show very different tendencies to support the Liberals over the Conservatives, the exact way in which groups are combined might be expected to have a significant effect on estimates of class voting.

Estimates of class voting on the Liberal/Conservative dimension are displayed in Figure 11.5. The estimates from the Gallup and BES data are not particularly close, and in several cases are strikingly different. Applying the multivariate regression procedure and allowing $\alpha$ to differ while forcing $\beta$

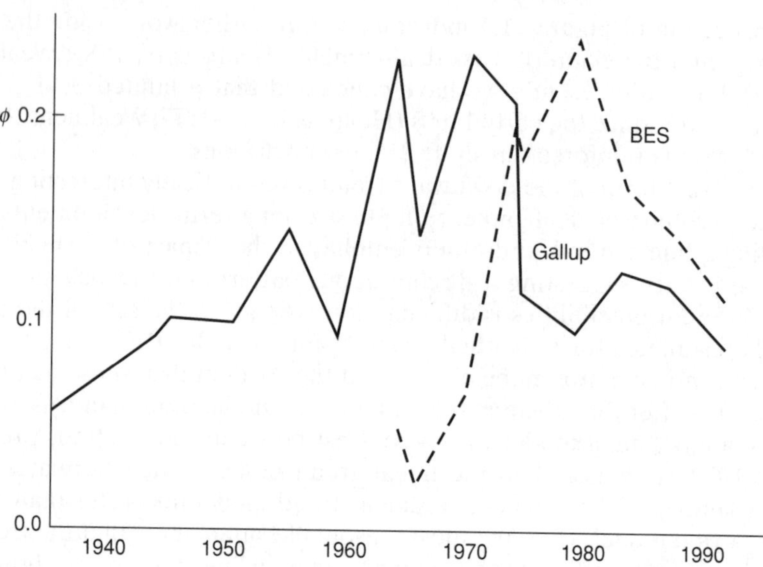


FIG. 11.5. Estimates of class voting along Liberal/Conservative dimension, Britai

to remain the same yields a chi-square of 24.4 with 8 degrees of freedom, while allowing β to differ reduces it to 22.4 with 7 degrees of freedom, still not an acceptable fit. That is, the patterns of change in class voting estimated from the two datasets are significantly different. Given these differences, little can be said about the pattern of change except that any trend is dominated by short-term fluctuation. It is also noteworthy that in both datasets, the values of ϕ for the Liberal/Conservative dimension are much smaller than those for the Labour/Conservative dimension, indicating that class is a less powerful predictor of the choice between Liberals and Conservatives. In other words, Liberal voters are not very different from Conservative voters in terms of class position, and the Liberals have not acquired a strongly distinctive class base of support, although in principle they would seem well placed to appeal to the middle-class leftism discussed by Lipset (1981) and Inglehart (1990).

The models considered until now have not allowed for the type of realignment found in the United States. To model such changes, it is necessary to estimate a second set of class scores for the Labour/non-Labour and Liberal/non-Liberal dimensions. This modification produces a statistically significant improvement in fit in the Gallup data, reducing the $L^2$ to 39.6 with 22 degrees of freedom.[13] The party scores on the Labour/

[13] The deviations from this model are still too large to be plausibly explained by sampling error ($p = 0.005$). It is possible that the model still fails to capture some of the changes in the association between class and party. Another possibility is that the quota

non-Labour dimension contrast managers to professionals, with white-collar and manual workers falling almost exactly in the middle. Controlling for the general changes in class voting, professionals have moved towards Labour since the 1930s, while managers and proprietors have moved away. This general pattern is similar to that found in the United States, and suggests an increasing political division within the middle class, but the size of the shift is much smaller. Moreover, there is a good deal of fluctuation in the strength of the dimension, and it is not clear that the trend has continued since the mid-1960s. On the Liberal/non-Liberal dimension, the changes are statistically significant, but even smaller, and there is no clear trend. Thus, there is no evidence of substantial long-term realignment involving the Liberals.

Applying similar models to the BES data produced a statistically significant improvement in fit on the Labour/non-Labour dimension, but not on the Liberal/non-Liberal. The estimated changes in Labour voting are difficult to interpret. The results suggest that the upper service class, foremen and technicians, and skilled workers moved towards Labour in 1979 and away from Labour in 1983–92 after allowing for changes in general class voting. This change probably represents idiosyncratic features of those particular elections rather than any general realignment. It should be noted that the contrasting trends for managers and professionals found in the Gallup data could not be expected to show up in the BES, since both groups are included in the service class. Consequently, a test of the 'two lefts' model of class voting in Britain requires a more detailed class schema, to which we now turn.

### *Alternative Definitions of Class*

The definition of class will clearly make a difference to estimates of the level of class voting. It is important to note, however, that estimates of change will not necessarily be affected. Suppose that we begin with a highly disaggregated set of groups which various class schemas aggregate in different ways. If the size of all groups remains the same and any change involves a general convergence or divergence of all groups, then estimated changes in class voting will remain the same regardless of how the groups are combined. If the relative size of the groups changes, estimates of different class schemas will be influenced by 'composition effects'. For example, if unskilled manual workers give more support to the left than do skilled manual workers and the number of unskilled manual workers declines while the number of skilled workers remains constant, then a class defined as all manual workers will appear to move to the right. All class

samples used in the Gallup surveys tend to produce more sampling variation than would be found using random samples. If this is the case, then a chi-square test would tend to reject even a true model. In either case, any remaining discrepancies are too small to be of much substantive importance.

schemas will probably be influenced by composition effects to some extent, since even very narrowly defined occupational groups sometimes have distinctive patterns of voting. The extent to which composition effects influence conclusions is an empirical matter.

If changes in class voting involve some type of realignment, the choice of class schema will be important even if there is no change in occupational distributions. For example, if managers and professionals move in opposite directions, that realignment simply cannot be detected using a class schema that combines managers and professionals into a single class. In other cases, realignment could appear as an increase or decrease in class voting. For example, a shift of routine white-collar workers to the left would produce an apparent decline in class voting when using a manual/nonmanual division. Changes due to composition effects are not necessarily spurious or trivial—if the classes with the most extreme voting patterns become smaller, then class divisions have in a sense become less important—but they need to be distinguished from changes in the effect of class locations on individual behaviour.

In order to assess the consequences of using different class schemas, we consider the detailed classification into socio-economic groups (SEGs) used in the BES data.[14] The SEGs can be combined to produce approximations of the Goldthorpe and Gallup class schemas used in the preceding analyses, as well as the manual/nonmanual distinction used in many voting studies. In this section, we will compare estimates of class voting using the full SEG system, the seven Goldthorpe classes, the four Gallup classes, and the manual/nonmanual contrast. Although the SEGs are recorded only in the BES, the results will give a sense of how much difference the definition of class makes to estimates of change in class voting.

Fitting a model of constant class voting to the SEG data yields an $L^2$ of 345.6 with 288 degrees of freedom. Fitting an association model allowing changes on the Labour/Conservative and Liberal/Conservative dimension produces a statistically significant improvement, to 304.4 with 272 degrees of freedom. The estimated changes in class voting are similar to those obtained with the seven-class schema used above, but the impression of a trend is weakened. The correlations of estimates of Labour/Conservative class voting from the BES using the SEGs and the seven-class, four-class, and two-class schemas are shown in Table 11.4.

Estimates using the three collapsed schemas are all very close, with cor-

[14] The eighteen SEG categories are: large employers, managers in large establishments, small employers, managers in small establishments, self-employed professionals, employee professionals, intermediate nonmanual occupations, nonmanual supervisors, clerical, personal service, manual foremen, skilled manual, semi-skilled manual, own-account manual, farmers and farm managers, own-account farmers, farm labourers, and the armed forces.

TABLE 11.4. *Correlations among strength of Labour/Conservative class voting estimated under different class schemas, 1964–1992*

| Class schema | Class schema | | | | |
|---|---|---|---|---|---|
| | 1 | 2 | 3 | 4 | 5 |
| 1 manual/nonmanual | 1.000 | | | | |
| 2 Four-class | 0.994 | 1.000 | | | |
| 3 Seven-class (Goldthorpe) | 0.965 | 0.977 | 1.000 | | |
| 4 SEG (eighteen categories) | 0.816 | 0.834 | 0.906 | 1.000 | |
| 5 Year | –0.633 | –0.635 | –0.573 | –0.226 | 1.000 |

relations of 0.95 or above. All have similar correlations with the SEG estimates, although the seven-class schema comes closest. The correlation with time, however, is considerably lower for the SEG categories than for any of the other class schemas. In other words, estimated declines in class voting since 1964 using the seven-class, four-class, or two-class schemas are partly spurious, presumably as the result of composition effects. The estimated trend in class voting based on the SEG categories is small and not statistically significant.

Examination of the marginal frequencies shows that all of the class schemas combine SEGs with diverse political dispositions. For example, self-employed manual workers are near the middle in political terms. Goldthorpe's schema includes them in the petty bourgeoisie, along with several much more conservative groups. The other schemas combine them with other manual workers, who are well to their left. Consequently, the rapid growth in the number of self-employed manual workers since 1964 has tended to pull Goldthorpe's 'petty bourgeoisie' to the left and Gallup's 'manual workers' to the right, in both cases causing an apparent decline in class voting. Other rapidly growing groups that influence the estimates in similar ways include managers in large establishments and intermediate nonmanual workers.

These results suggest that some of the estimated decline in class voting since the 1960s in Britain is spurious. It is unlikely, however, that all of the apparent decline is the result of composition effects. Even using the full SEG classification, the estimated trend in class voting is negative. The increase in Labour/Conservative class voting between 1935 and 1951 seen in the Gallup data is almost certainly not the result of composition effects. If there was any change in the occupational composition of Britain during those years, it was probably similar to that which has occurred since the 1960s—a decline in the number of self-employed professionals and employers and an increase in the number of employed nonmanual

TABLE 11.5. *Correlations among strength of Liberal/Conservative class voting estimated under different class schemas, 1964–1992*

| Class schema | Class schema | | | | |
|---|---|---|---|---|---|
| | 1 | 2 | 3 | 4 | 5 |
| 1 Manual/nonmanual | 1.000 | | | | |
| 2 Four-class | 0.927 | 1.000 | | | |
| 3 Seven-class (Goldthorpe) | 0.822 | 0.652 | 1.000 | | |
| 4 SEG (eighteen categories) | 0.927 | 0.874 | 0.922 | 1.000 | |
| 5 Year | 0.377 | 0.422 | 0.400 | 0.496 | 1.000 |

workers. These changes would tend to produce an apparent decline in class voting. Hence, the estimates in Figure 11.4 may even understate the increase in class voting during the 1950s.

The correlations of estimates of Liberal/Conservative class voting using different class schemas are displayed in Table 11.5. As in the case of Labour/Conservative class voting, the correlations are generally high. Given the large differences between the Gallup and BES estimates discussed above, the correlation between estimates based on the four-class and seven-class schemas is of particular interest. Although the correlation is positive and moderately large (0.65), it is considerably smaller than the correlation of either with the estimates based on the full SEG classification. This suggests that conclusions about changes in the class basis of the Liberal vote may be significantly influenced by the class schema used. In contrast, conclusions about the class composition of the Labour and Conservative electorates appear to be robust across various definitions of class.

The detail of the SEG categories is useful in testing hypotheses about realignment. Given theories of 'new politics' and the results for the United States, a realignment involving professionals versus the traditional middle class is of particular interest. Hence, we defined a new class dimension on which employed professionals scored 1, employers, farmers, and own-account workers scored –1, and all other SEG groups scored zero. By estimating the strength of this dimension by election, we can test the hypothesis that professionals shifted towards the left and employers to the right relative to other classes.

Including this additional dimension failed to improve the fit significantly (the change in $L^2$ is 17.6 with 16 degrees of freedom). There was marginally significant evidence of change on the Labour/Conservative dimension when 1964 and 1966 were contrasted to all later years. The estimates indicated that professionals moved towards Labour and employers moved away after 1966. On the Liberal/Conservative dimension, there was no evidence of systematic change. This finding, although negative, is important given the widespread impression that Liberals gained support among professionals after the Social Democratic break from Labour. The direction of the estimated changes on the Labour/Conservative dimension is consistent with 'new politics' accounts. Any such realignment, however, was quite limited and occurred before 1970. These conclusions are consistent with the findings based on the Gallup data discussed above. Experiments with other pre-defined dimensions also showed no evidence of substantial realignment. Thus, while the strength of class voting has varied since 1964, there has been little or no change in the basic pattern of association, in contrast to the United States.

*Discussion*

We found that the different datasets produced similar estimates of changes in class voting involving the Labour and Conservative Parties. This does not mean that the extra data is redundant, however. First, by combining the estimates from different datasets, we can reduce the error in the estimates of class voting. Secondly, if the Gallup estimates of class voting are accepted as good substitutes for estimates based on the BES, it becomes possible to consider a much longer period of time. These results are particularly impressive given the substantial differences between the definitions of class used in the two datasets. At the same time, the datasets yield substantially different conclusions about changes involving the Liberals. Our analysis of the BES data using detailed socio-economic groups suggests that this is at least partly a consequence of the different definitions of class. Consequently, any claims about changes in the class basis of the Liberal vote must be treated with great caution.

Considering Labour versus Conservative voting, we find a statistically significant decline in class differences since 1964, in contrast to Goldthorpe, who argues that there is no tendency towards dealignment. The difference in conclusions does not depend on the difference in models: the uniform difference estimates of class voting are very similar to the estimates of Labour/Conservative class voting in the association model. The main reason for the difference in conclusions is the additional evidence provided by the Gallup data. When using the BES with the seven-class schema, a small but statistically significant downward trend is found, but this is the result largely of the high level of class voting in 1964.[15] However, because the Gallup and BES estimates of class voting are not significantly different in 1964–92, it is reasonable to take both as equally accurate

[15] This result is based on the head of household classification used by Goldthorpe. However, when respondents are classified by their own occupation, the estimated decline is not significant.

estimates of the same underlying quantity. With more data the error in the estimates of class voting is reduced, making it easier to distinguish any trends that may exist. When the Gallup data are taken into account, the evidence for a decline in class voting becomes much stronger, especially since class voting in the 1950s is estimated to be even greater than in 1964. Nevertheless, the estimated decline in class voting since the 1950s is of modest size, and the results in the preceding section suggest that some of it reflects composition effects.

## CONCLUSIONS

Our purpose in this chapter was to explain the differences among the three studies of class voting in Britain and/or the United States that appear in this volume. We found that systematic differences in the data were not the major cause of differences in conclusions. On the contrary, estimates of class voting in the United States were very similar in the ANES and Gallup/GSS data, despite some differences in the definitions of class. In Britain, where the definitions of class differed substantially, estimates of class voting involving Labour were still not discernibly different, although estimates involving the Liberals were quite different. The differences between the conclusions of Hout, Manza, and Brooks, and Weakliem and Heath about the course of class voting in the United States are mainly owing to the conceptual difference between kappa and association models The traditional class alignment has become weaker, but another alignment has been growing stronger, so the total effect of class, as embodied in $\kappa$, does not show a strong trend. In Britain, either dataset by itself gives some evidence of dealignment in Labour voting and combining them gives stronger evidence. Whether the dealignment is 'large' or not is a matter for individual judgement, but it is clear that class still plays an important role in party choice. In fact, rather than converging on a common pattern of low class voting, Britain and the United States have become more different over the last sixty years. Because the class scores are standardized, the scale of $\phi$ is roughly equivalent in the United States and Britain. Comparison of Figures 11.2 and 11.4 indicates that in the 1930s and 1940s the traditional class alignment had about as much impact on Democratic versus Republican voting in the United States as on Labour versus Conservative voting in Britain. Since that time, however, its impact in the United States has declined considerably. In Britain, class voting increased until the early 1950s, and the decline since then merely restored it to the level of the 1930s.

We now turn from discussion of our specific findings to consider their more general implication for research and theory on class voting. As we observed at the start of Chapter 5, a great deal of theory about class voting has been based on a very limited selection of data, primarily the ANES, the BES, and the Eurobarometer surveys. Thus, although there is a large literature on the general decline of class, there is little evidence, and most of it is of recent vintage. Our main object in compiling the Gallup data series was to obtain estimates of class voting for times before the standard surveys were available. In addition, having an additional source for recent years makes it easier to distinguish among trend, real fluctuation in class voting, and sampling error. Although we were sceptical of arguments about the general decline of class, the additional data support the case that there has been some recent decline in the traditional class alignment in Britain and the United States. But before declaring that the conventional view is correct, one needs to consider trends over the entire period, including the years before the BES and ANES began. Over the whole period, patterns of change are not at all similar in the two nations. In the United States, there is a fairly steady decline in class voting along the working-class/middle-class dimension; in Britain, there is no linear trend, but an increase followed by a decline. The magnitudes of the decline in class voting since the 1950s are also quite different. Moreover, there has been substantial realignment in the United States, but much less in Britain.

The substantial differences between the United States and Britain count against accounts that relate change in class voting to social changes characteristic of all industrial societies, such as Inglehart (1990) or Clark and Lipset (1991). This is not to say that general social changes have no consistent effect on politics: Inglehart (1990) has presented strong evidence that changes in public opinion in many nations have something in common. The widespread appearance of movements related to the environment, gender equality, and the rights of ethnic minorities suggests that non-material issues of several kinds have generally become more important in recent years. Our disagreement concerns the connection of such concerns to class politics. The assumption in many discussions is that material and non-material concerns, or class and other identities, are inversely related: the more interested one is in non-material issues, the less interested in material ones. This, however, is merely an assumption, and the most serious empirical investigation, that of Marsh (1975), fails to support it. If people can care about both material and non-material issues, or identify with both class and other groups, the changes in public opinion discussed by Inglehart (1990) have no clear implications for class voting.

While our results count against the idea that changes in class voting in all industrial societies are dominated by a single trend, they also count against suggestions that changes in class voting reflect no more than the specific circumstances of individual elections. While there is a good deal of short-term fluctuation, there are also some general tendencies that endure over longer periods of time. Changes in class voting can be represented by increases or decreases along one or two dimensions. Shifts involving distinctive behaviour by a particular class are of relatively little importance, contrary to some rational-choice theories and many journalistic accounts of election results. Moreover, the changes in general class voting bear no obvious relationship to changes in party programmes or the ideology of party leaders (see Chapter 5 for more detailed analysis of this point).

The distinct patterns of class voting in the United States and Britain cannot be explained as a simple reflection of economic growth, the shift to a service economy, or other general social changes common to both countries. On the other hand, it seems that the changes are too regular to be explained exclusively by short-term political factors. Since none of the existing accounts seems adequate, we will sketch an alternative that holds out some promise of explaining our results. In most accounts, an appeal to working-class economic interests necessarily means a call for government intervention to redistribute income. It was not until the twentieth century, however, that this connection was generally accepted. A popular 'radical' position in the early nineteenth century was that working-class interests were best served by small government and low taxes. Andrew Jackson's Democrats and Gladstone's Liberals appear to have gained substantial working-class support with such appeals (Benson 1961; Biagini 1991). This position was based on the idea that government was generally corrupt and biased towards the rich, so that direct government action would deliver few benefits to ordinary people while undercutting working-class organization. In contemporary politics, this view has come to be associated with conservative parties. Hence, if this idea is widely accepted in the working class, class voting will be low. We suggest that the decline in class voting in the last few decades may reflect declining general confidence in government. To some extent, this change in attitudes may result from objective conditions, including the increasing cost of the welfare state and slower economic growth. However, while the objective conditions are similar in both nations, the decline in class voting is much more pronounced in the United States. The difference may reflect the fact that anti-government sentiments have traditionally been stronger in the United States, making it easier for them to re-emerge under similar conditions.

The differences in the American and British trends during the 1930s and 1940s, which are difficult to explain in conventional terms, are consistent with our analysis. In the United States, the New Deal seemed to show that effective government action to serve working-class interests was possible, while in Britain, the difficulties of the Labour government of 1929–31 seemed to show the opposite. It was the British experience in the Second World War, not the Depression, that made government intervention in the economy seem effective. Thus, it is reasonable to suppose that the idea of government as a fair and effective agent of redistribution was strongest during the New Deal in the United States, and during the postwar years in Britain.

In itself, the level of class voting has nothing to do with the overall support for the parties. Low levels of class voting mean simply that the left gains similar amounts of support in all classes, whether that support is high or low. However, it is usually assumed that high class voting is associated with greater overall support for the left. In the conventional account of class voting, the left has a natural advantage on economic issues because a majority of the population stands to gain from redistribution. Conservative parties can win only by diverting attention to non-economic issues. Our account also implies that class voting and overall support for the left will be correlated. Assuming that the left party stands for more government intervention, increasingly negative attitudes towards government will be associated with less support for the left in the working class.[16]

The conventional view of class voting suggests that the influence of class will generally decline, and that left parties will fare badly unless they shift their emphasis to non-economic issues, because traditional class interests are simply not very important to voters today. Our account, in contrast, implies that the influence of class on voting *could* increase again, and that this would probably be associated with gains for the left. For this to happen, however, confidence in the effectiveness of government action would have to increase. Our proposed explanation cannot be rigorously evaluated with the present data. It is clear, however, that there is much to be explained. Trends in class voting are more diverse over time and space than is generally recognized. Neither conventional 'sociological' accounts emphasizing uniform long-term trends, nor 'political' accounts emphasizing unpredictable short-term fluctuations, seem likely to be able to account for the changes we have found.

[16] Support could be expected to decline in the middle class as well, but less sharply. People who favour redistribution out of moral commitment are more likely to continue to support the left even if they think that government action is inefficient.

# 12

# Critical Commentary: Four Perspectives on The End of Class Politics?

PETER MAIR, SEYMOUR MARTIN LIPSET, MICHAEL HOUT, AND JOHN H. GOLDTHORPE

This chapter consists of commentaries on the general project addressed by the contributions to this book, in which Peter Mair, Seymour Martin Lipset, Michael Hout, and John Goldthorpe reflect on issues arising from the foregoing empirical chapters. All of these contributions were made in the form of oral presentations on the issues raised by the papers presented at the conference on 'The End of Class Politics?' at Nuffield College, with later modifications as more studies were added to the range of analyses presented there. Inevitably, therefore, despite a certain amount of editing, the style in this chapter is less formal than in the rest of the book. It is also intentionally *critical* in tone—the speakers were asked explicitly to consider the *limitations* of the work contained here rather than to be congratulatory in their appraisal. A risky strategy for an editor to take perhaps, but none the less—or perhaps because of this injunction—the issues considered by our assembled discussants expand upon those appearing in the empirically focused chapters in several ways and thus merit reproduction in their own right.

The first comment is from Peter Mair, who presents a perspective from political science rather than the sociological emphasis characteristic of most of the book's other contributors.

### Peter Mair

Let me say first that I have a strong interest in the analysis of class politics, but with two caveats. The first is that my interest is, obviously, from a political science rather than a sociological point of view. And the second is that my interest is as a comparativist, which means that I am concerned with differences in degrees of class politics, however measured, and more especially in explanations of such differences.

There are two sorts of comparison that are of interest here, two sorts of differences: the first is the obvious one of comparisons across countries, while the other is comparisons over time. In principle, both work on the same logic, and in principle we should be able to get insights into explanations, whether comparing over time or whether comparing across countries. And, in principle, both are susceptible to the same sorts of explanations, to the same sorts of analyses, to the same sorts of theories. What I have found in the work reported in this volume, is that while there has been an immense amount of attention to over-time comparison, there has been relatively little cross-country comparison. Thus the first problem of this work is that, with the exception of Paul Nieuwbeerta and Nan Dirk De Graaf's chapter, we are missing a lot of countries. The project is mainly concerned with the United States and with Protestant Europe. Catholic Europe or continental Europe does not get much of a look in, and that makes for a very narrow basis from which to generalize. For instance, we miss the whole world of religion in politics, we miss variations in party systems and of political systems, and in a politics which is influenced as much by religion as it is by class, perhaps even more so by religion than by class. So if you want to talk about or generalize about the end of class politics or the end of class voting, whatever it might be, generalizations which apply within Protestant Europe and the United States are very limited generalizations, and that is why my Dutch colleagues' paper is, in a sense, the most interesting one for me, because it does attempt to generalize.

The second problem I have, which may not really be a problem at all, is that there is little of politics as such. That is understandable; sociologists are promiscuous in different ways to political scientists. There is an element of politics, but the rest of it is sociology. And so while there is a great deal on class voting, there is far less on class politics. I suggest therefore that the contributors look at a chapter by Sartori in a book edited by Lipset thirty years ago, which is cited in only one of the empirical chapters. I think it is a very important essay. It is called 'From the sociology of politics to political sociology' (Sartori 1969). From Sartori's perspective, what we have here is the sociology of politics, it is not political sociology *per se.* So at most what we have is an analysis of the end of class voting, but we do not have anything about the end of class politics. Having said that, let us look first at class voting and what the idea of class voting implies, and perhaps more importantly, what the idea of class voting does not imply.

Let us begin with what class voting does imply, and I think Hout, Manza, and Brooks's chapter is very important here, because to my mind class voting implies that a class, however defined—manual, nonmanual, one of the seven Erikson–Goldthorpe classes—votes more or less as one, that is, that the class acts as a group—people in a class vote in the same way as other people in that class, more or less. The stronger the class, the more they act as one. In other words, knowing the class of person A, you can more or less predict how that person would have voted at time *t*: because you know how the class voted, you know how the individual within the class voted. Now once at that level—a very simple level of class voting—refinement of categories becomes very important, because then you can become more accurate.

So that is what class voting implies. What it does not imply, to my mind, is that there is any necessary consistency over time in partisan terms, and that is why Hout, Manza, and Brooks's point is particularly interesting. In other words, even if the object of class voting changes from one election to another, such that all managers vote for conservatives at time *t*, and for liberals at time $t + 1$, it is still class voting. They have shifted the object of their preferences, but they are still voting as a class. What this means is that the existence of class voting of itself does not imply that there is a consistent link between class and party, or between class and a bloc of parties, or between class and a type of party. Hence, as long as a class votes as one, there is class voting—regardless of whether the object changes over time or whether the object changes from one country to another, and whether we talk about the object as a bloc of parties or as a type of party or as an individual party. That is, to my mind, the minimum element of class voting.

But if we want to go beyond that and look not only at whether class voting exists, but also at consistency over time or across countries; if, in other words, we want to turn to the class–party link or to the class–bloc link, or to the class–type link, then we get into another set of questions—another arena—which moves beyond simple class voting. To hypothesize that a link exists between class and party, or to hypothesize that the link between class and party/bloc/type is important, is to begin to ask a very different question than that involved in the question of whether class voting as such exists. Once you begin to try to chart or explain variations in class and party or class and blocs of party, you get much closer to the question of class politics and you are moving away from simply analysing class voting.

If we hypothesize that certain classes will be more likely to vote for left-wing parties, while other classes will be more likely to vote for parties in the centre or right, then when we sit down to compare data across countries and time we obviously find a set of relationships that varies considerably. How do we account for this variation? Let us look again at the Nieuwbeerta and De Graaf chapter which hypothesizes two basic reasons why these relationships might vary from country to country or over time (and I think the comparison over time must be regarded as equivalent to the comparison between countries). The first of these is derived from social-structural differences, but, at least according to Nieuwbeerta and De

Graaf's evidence, this does not really pan out. In other words, and putting it very baldly, social-structural differences do not account for differences in class voting. From a political science point of view that is good to see, although in a sense we knew it already—at least theoretically. From a political science perspective, politics is clearly something much more than just a natural outgrowth of social structure. In effect, there is something else which lies in between social structure and politics, and Mike Hout's commentary has some nice lines on this in which he underlines the importance of also understanding the intermediary role of political parties. He also says that it is difficult to see realignment as the 'natural' outcome of social changes in all industrial societies, and elsewhere, in the Hout, Manza, and Brooks chapter, that trends in class voting do not directly reflect economic and social conditions but also depend on the nature of political discussions. In other words, there is no automatic connection between society and politics. This was Sartori's point thirty years ago, and it is still valid today. Indeed, it would be a very impoverished perspective if we were to view politics as simply a function of social structure. For example, we would find it difficult to explain why there is not then a strong socialist party in the United States, or in Ireland, given that there is such a party in Sweden or that there was—perhaps still is—such a party in Britain.

The second factor that Nieuwbeerta and De Graaf cite to account for cross-national variations in class voting is the difference in voting preferences. But this, in turn, begs the question of why there should be differences in voting preferences between classes, and that is where you come back to politics, since you simply cannot explain differences in voting preferences from a purely class point of view—or even from a purely social-structural point of view. On the contrary, you need to look at politics as such: you need to look at the cleavage structure and how that changes; you need to look at the parties themselves—or at blocs of parties—and how they interact, as organizations, policy makers, and campaigners; you need to look at what competitors do; and you need to look at the political and institutional context in which this competition takes place. All of these factors will help to explain why social structure translates into politics differently from one country to another. It is, in short, because the translation agency is so different, and this again is Sartori's point: translation is not just an automatic or a neutral process. And it is only by addressing questions like this that one can also address the question of whether there is a decline in class politics or an end to class politics. Without addressing questions like this, you can at most deal with questions about class voting. And if you are only interested in class voting, if that is the end-point, then I think that it is more important—following Hout, Manza, and Brooks—to know whether the class votes as one at time *t* than it is to know whether there is any consistency in the direction of class voting, whether across time or across space.

To conclude, the contributions to this book have provided a model discussion of class voting. But they have not been about class politics: that is another world. These authors may not want to enter that other world, but they should at least recognize that it exists.

## Seymour Martin Lipset

In my comments I would like to draw back from the expertly conducted and detailed empirical analysis we have seen in the rest of this book and consider *why* class voting is more important in certain countries than in others.

First, I think it makes sense to consider what we mean by class and class politics. One of the things we have not talked about here is 'what is class?'. The contributors to this volume have a clearly defined notion of objective class and of the indicators used to measure it. But I would say that the research reported here examines just one aspect of stratification. Stratification involves diverse rankings from high to low and what most of the chapters do is to treat one aspect of stratification, namely occupation, and classifications linked to occupation. But of course, stratification can occur in terms of power, in terms of income, in terms of education, and in terms of the status system or *Stand*. There is nothing wrong, obviously, with focusing on a particular aspect of stratification and politics, but I think one has to recognize that this is not necessarily what some theories of class and politics—such as those, for example, associated with Marx and Weber—mean when they talk of class politics. One might consider, in particular, the whole question of class consciousness and under what conditions class consciousness occurs. Discussing the rise and decline of class politics, involves dealing with the rise and decline of class consciousness.

Consider, for example, the *status structure*. Different countries have very different status structures, and from a comparative historical point of view, I would argue that status has been more important in determining the nature of the class–party link than occupation. Countries in which *Stände* have been more important are more likely to generate class consciousness. Thus there is an interesting phenomenon in Germany, and I suppose it is true in Sweden as well, of the *selbstständiger Arbeiter* or what we would call in English artisans, self-employed workers. In Germany, a shoemaker would never have worn a tie, whereas a grocer would, and this meant they were in different classes. The self-employed manual workers voted Social Democratic. The self-employed small business people voted for one of the bourgeois parties, even though in income terms they might be the same class, and in terms of their relationships to the means of production they were in the same class. But the social structure defined one as a worker and the other as middle class, and this in turn very much affected how they voted. People in Germany and Sweden are used to defining people occupationally—as *Herr Arbeiter*, or *Herr Professor*. The social structure defined class position fairly explicitly and this in turn produced links to class-based parties.

Another issue relates to Peter Mair's comments apropos of Catholic Europe. It surely is a truism that if you examine the cleavage structures of countries where there is only one basic cleavage, class, this is going to be by definition most important. Take a country like Sweden, in which class voting and class membership in unions is very important. Sweden has no Catholics—almost everyone in Sweden is a Swede and a Lutheran—and while there are other sub-variations (gender, education), the kind of issues which promote cleavage structures linked to social characteristics other than class do not exist. That is, Sweden has a relatively simple cleavage structure. Britain has a slightly more complex, but still relatively simple one. But Catholic Europe, Southern Europe, has a much more complicated structure, as have countries with ethnic minorities and/or regional or cultural variations. And in so far as these cleavages contribute to the structuring of politics, they necessarily reduce the impact of occupational class.

Germany is again an interesting case. The former West Germany had a large Catholic population, and the Catholic party, the Christian Democrats, were and are very strong in that region. The correlation between class and politics in West Germany was and remains low. The former East Germany—that is, mainly Prussia—is Protestant and, like Sweden, the correlation between class and politics has been high. This difference was not because these regions had different social class or occupational structures, but because of the presence of a varying cleavage in West Germany. Religion had been and remains a major source of cleavage in West Germany, but not in East Germany.

Or consider Canada. In Canada class has very little importance. If you examine national data on voting patterns for Canada, class almost disappears as a factor. One of the reasons for this is that Canada has a complex cleavage structure. Canada is a much more regionally differentiated society than the United States. *Within* provinces there are some reasonably strong correlations between class and vote. However, in the country as a whole there is little correlation. This is because provinces vary, much like different countries, with respect to the pattern of association between classes and parties. In addition, religion and ethnicity play major roles in Canadian politics, and these operate to reduce the class–vote correlation.

But among the factors impinging on class voting are not only those pertaining to the nature of class position, or the presence of other cleavages, there are also several other contextual factors relevant to the relationship of classes and parties. Consider the following class-related statistics about Britain. Between 1979 and 1989 there was an increase in the proportion of British people who were middle class in terms of the market research rankings—that is, those who fall in groups AB and $C_1$—from 33 per cent to 40 per cent. Owner-occupied housing increased from 52 per cent to 67 per cent. The proportion of the population who owned shares in companies went up from 6 per cent to 22 per cent. On the other hand, the proportion of the population belonging to trade unions fell from 30 per cent to only 17 per cent. More than a half of trade union membership in Britain is now middle class rather than working class. These are basic changes affecting what I would say are attributes of class structure, so that in Britain there has been an upgrading of the class structure and of the context in which politics takes place. And I think this changing context—the shape of the class structure—is important.

I would also say that the extent of *class organization* is a crucial factor. The most important form of class organization is of course the trade unions. And the proportion of the working class who belong to unions is a measure of class formation—all the voting studies show that people who belong to trade unions are more likely to vote with their class (i.e. left) than non-unionists. But of course, TU organizations are not the only ones that are relevant: professional organizations, business organizations, there are all types of interest groups. The degree of organization in a society will of course affect class.

Finally, though it has already been discussed in the larger context, there is the *political context* and what its effects might be. Certain parties appeal to voters in class terms, others do not, but whether they do or not affects the nature of the system. If parties become less class-orientated in their appeal, this will reduce the class–vote relation. I was struck some years ago when talking to the new president of Brazil, Fernando Enrique Cardoso (a first-rate sociologist) about my work trying to deal with the old issue of why there is no socialism in the United States; why it never had a significant socialist or labour party. I was outlining to Fernando Enrique theories about the reasons for this American exceptionalism. And he said that what I was saying does not only apply to the United States, it applies to the Americas, that is, Latin America. He said the Americas as a whole, not just the United States, are different from Europe. He then told me an interesting story. He and his friends, most of whom were Marxist and socialist, met when the military dictatorship was collapsing, to decide what they would do politically to form a new party. They consciously decided not to create a socialist party, even though they were all socialists. The reason they decided not to do so was because they were convinced that socialist parties do not work in the Americas, because there is not the kind of class structure needed for a socialist party to succeed. To succeed in Latin America, left parties have to be populist parties, like the Democratic Party. The model to follow is the North American rather than the European. So even though they wanted a party that would appeal to the lower classes and the less privileged, the way in which it presented itself had to be different from those adopted in Britain, Sweden, and other European societies. Now I am not convinced that this is right, but the fact that Cardoso believed that the populist strategy they adopted was the only viable strategy is *in itself* consequential for the relationship between classes and parties. Again, therefore, it points to the role of context in conditioning the relationships between class and politics. And hence if one is talking about holding constant factors which may affect this issue of whether occupational classes increase or decrease in their impact on politics, there is an almost infinite number of factors which come into the picture. All of these things affect class politics and need to be considered when interpreting the relationship between classes and parties.

## Michael Hout

I was struck at the meeting at Nuffield College, when someone asked Paul Nieuwbeerta: 'when will class voting disappear in Britain?' And he said: 'in 2020'. I was reminded of a passage in *Life on the Mississippi*, where Mark Twain reviews a study that had been done by the army corps of engineers on the Mississippi river in which someone had measured the silt level in the Mississippi in one period and five years later he had measured it again, and made the extrapolation that by the year 1974 the Mississippi river would be nothing but mud. At which point Mark Twain said: 'There is something fascinating about science. It yields such wholesale returns of speculation on such trivial investments of fact'. Much of this book is all fact and no speculation, and I want to redress that imbalance. But in the line of the leopard who cannot change his spots, my speculation is going to be guided by the UNIDIFF model, and particularly the sage comment of Robert Erikson at that same Nuffield meeting, who said: 'isn't the UNIDIFF model in any year just proportional to how much the parties differentiate themselves in the minds of the voters?'

Now Peter Mair might actually recognize what I am about to do as politics or he might not. But in the currency in which I trade, it is as political as I am likely to get. Let us start with the uniform model that David Weakliem and Anthony Heath use, transformed to logit form:

$$\ln(F_{ijt}/F_{ij't}) = P_{0jt} - P_{0j't} + F_{1t}K_{1i}(P_{1j} - P_{1j'}) + F_{2t}K_{2i}(P_{2j} - P_{2j'}) \qquad [1]$$

where $i$ indexes classes, $j$ indexes parties, and $t$ indexes years (see the Weakliem and Heath chapter for other definitions). Note that the association parameters—the $F_{1t}$ and $F_{2t}$ terms—are subscripted by time but that the party scores—$P_{1j}$, $P_{2j}$, $P_{1j'}$, and $P_{2j'}$—are not.

What I want to do now is to think about the possibility that Robert Erikson is right—that parties differentiate themselves on class in some elections but not others. Robert's conjecture implies that model [1] lets the wrong parameter vary with time. The $t$ subscript should be on the difference between parties—$P_{1j} - P_{1j'}$ and $P_{2j} - P_{2j'}$—not on the association parameters. And so we should rewrite the model this way:

$$\ln(F_{ijt}/F_{ij't}) = P_{0jt} - P_{0j't} + F_1K_{1i}(P_{1j} - P_{1j'})_t + F_2K_{2i}(P_{2j} - P_{2j'})_t \qquad [2]$$

It turns out that this model and model [1] imply the same expected log-odds, but they are substantively different models. We perhaps should be thinking of the results we have all reported in the papers collected here in the terms of model [2] instead of model [1]. More importantly, though, we should invest our effort in getting good observations on $(P_{1j} - P_{1j'})_t$ and $(P_{2j} - P_{2j'})_t$ instead of continuing to infer them from our models. With measures instead of parameters we can test ideas about how party appeals explain class voting. Instead of speculating on the existence of 'two lefts' or trying to read the tea-leaves of the association model's parameters, for example, we might go out and measure how parties make materialist, post-materialist, and immaterialist appeals to classes.

As an example of this approach, I have proposed a measure taken out of the British Election Surveys, from the appendix in Heath *et al.* (1991): 'Would you describe party j nowadays as good for one class or as good for all classes?' This item could serve as a party-specific measure of the class dimension and how differentiated the electorate perceives the parties to be on that dimension. We might also try and get multiple indicators of the key dimensions of parties' class appeals—again there are relevant and established scales available for this purpose in the British Election Study. And then, of course, we would have to come up with parallel measures for other dimensions and what they mean. This, I think, could be a fruitful way of proceeding if we want to explain rather than just summarize the relations between classes and parties.

However, it is important to realize also that in the real world of politics the parties tend to actually blend their appeals and bring out their messages in ways calculated to differentiate themselves from one another. For example, in the week prior to the 1992 election, George Bush was campaigning outside the factory gates of an autoplant near Detroit, and he made a statement which sunk him in a certain sense, because it made him seem a little crazy. But it did go to the issue of cross-class appeals in the blending of materialist and postmaterialist sorts of issues. Talking about Albert Gore, who had written a book about environmental policy, Bush said, 'Why do I call this guy a bozo? It is because if these bozos are elected we will be up to our necks in little owls and no one will have a job.' In pitting protection of endangered species like the spotted owl against jobs in the timber industry, Bush was trying to undercut the Democrats' appeal to factory workers. More skilfully done, campaign rhetoric might succeed in splitting the Democrats' blue-green coalition by convincing blue-collar workers that, if forced to choose, the Democrats would protect owls not jobs.

Another thing to consider while in this speculative vein is the question asked rhetorically by Terry Clarke and Marty Lipset some years ago: 'are classes dying?'. In one sense I think we have addressed that issue in this book in that we continue to be able to find strong evidence of classes in our data. Is *traditional* class voting declining? Yes. But I have four caveats on that: the first is that classes respond differently to the new politics. That leaves a class basis, albeit a realigned class basis, to the new politics, and this is not just a result of educational differences between classes. On this I think that Peter Mair's distinction, between class voting and class politics, is extremely useful, and goes to the point I was trying to make much better than I was able to articulate.

Another caveat is that the dramatic declines in Scandinavia have a regression to the mean quality rather than a dealignment quality, by which I mean that the dealignment that Kristen Ringdal and Kjell Hines find in Norway leaves it looking like Britain, not like Canada, and we have to keep that in mind, so that before we talk of dealignment in Norway we should recognize that it has come down to a sort of average level of class voting rather than a zero level of class voting. We should also, when discussing these questions, distinguish a dealignment from the right from a dealignment from the left. In the United States it is professionals and routine white-collar workers who move towards the Democrats, whereas in Norway it is the skilled workers who move towards the Conservatives. And I think that maybe directionality might teach us something if we attend to it.

Finally, how are we going to go about this? I would like to emphasize a line from *Political Man*, where Marty Lipset (1981: 230) says: 'Even though many parties renounce the principle of class conflict or loyalty, any analysis of their appeals and their support suggests that they do represent the interests of different classes'. Our work in this volume is all about support and has tended to ignore appeals. The little conjecture I have presented with respect to the association model is one way, within our paradigm, of dealing with the issue of appeals, but I think if we keep in mind the general point of the two-sidedness of the class-voting, or class-politics, association, we will make further progress more effectively.

**John Goldthorpe**

One thing at all events has been made clear by this book, and that is that the debate on class and party support in modern democracies is a very complex one. As we have seen, empirical, technical, and theoretical issues are heavily interwoven. What one might also add is that, as this controversy has been fought out, social-scientific arguments have often been conducted in a more or less explicit political context. Not much has been said about this here, but I think one should mention it if only, as it were, to clear it out of the way. Many of those who have claimed a weakening in the class–vote link have seen themselves as engaging in a latter-day version of the debate with Marx or even, in some cases, in a kind of triumphalist celebration of the demise of socialism in the West. And again there are others, themselves one-time Marxists, who have seen their vision of the future fade, and then, in making their adieus to the working class have, in their despair, rejected any other conception of class-based politics than the Marxist one. In my view, such entirely politically motivated arguments are of little value or interest. One can cut through them very simply by saying that it is entirely possible to question the thesis of the decline of class politics without ever having been a Marxist; and that it is possible, also, to assert this thesis without ever having been an academic cold warrior, or without now being an ex-Marxist postmodernist. I think that both of the propositions I have just made are demonstrated in the contributions presented.

So let me then go on to the empirical and technical issues that have arisen. Clearly, the central empirical question with which we have been preoccupied is simply that of whether the class–party link has or has not been weakening over time in Western democracies—where, I should add, class is defined in relation, in some way or other, to the positions that individuals hold in labour markets and production units. In various studies published in the 1960s and 1970s—what Nieuwbeerta and De Graaf have called the first- and second-generation studies—it was usually contended, whether on the basis of national or cross-national research, that the class–party link was in decline, that a process of class dealignment in electoral politics was in trend. And I have to say to Peter Mair that this claim was made most often and most prominently by political scientists and not by sociologists; the sociologists did the political scientists the courtesy of taking their argument seriously, and of subjecting it to critical scrutiny.

What has then been subsequently shown, in the third-generation studies, is, first, that this earlier work was seriously limited in that analysts were able to consider only two types of party (usually left and non-left) and only two classes (usually, manual and nonmanual); and, secondly, that they confounded the net, or intrinsic, class–vote association (and changes therein) with the effects of the distribution of the electorate over classes and over parties (and changes therein). Further, from the 1980s onwards, one could say that the application of more sophisticated statistical techniques, chiefly various forms of loglinear modelling, overcame both of these problems that had vitiated the earlier work; and that at the same time the amount of data available, in the form of class-by-vote tables, extending over lengthy periods, greatly improved. The consequence of this was, then, that the empirical picture changed quite significantly. It is now, I would argue, no longer at all certain that throughout the Western world a general, secular decline in the association between class and party support can be observed. There are some—and I am certainly among them—who would be far more impressed by the evidence of cross-national variation in this respect. In some nations, at least over certain periods, class dealignment is indeed apparent. But in other nations this is not so. In these other cases it is sometimes a 'trendless fluctuation' in the class–vote association that would seem to be the best description of what has been happening; or, perhaps, the interesting finding is of a one-off shift in the level of class voting; or yet again what stands out may be a process of class *re*alignment rather than dealignment—although in this latter respect I would be very sceptical indeed of any discussion of the decline in 'traditional' class voting as opposed to some other kind. I suspect that the use of this word is subject to the same difficulty as it often is in discussing English society: what is described as traditional turns out, on examination, to be something that was invented at the end of the last century.

All this seems to me to provide a very good example of just how better analytical techniques and better quality data can very substantially improve the quality of our empirical findings, and in ways that obviously have relevance for major sociological questions which we wish to address. Indeed, I think that the work contained in this collection is an example that could—and, I hope, will—figure in methods textbooks, in order to show that using the right techniques with good data can have a very important pay-off. But, having said that, I have also to say that, especially in the light of the contributions to this volume, I do now feel that we may be reaching the stage where the Mertonian process of 'displacement of goals' is setting in. We are now in some danger of becoming so involved in the fascinating practice of modelling class-by-vote tables that we are losing sight of what it is exactly that we want to do this for. So the question that

I want to pose is whether, or how far, the technical refinements into which we are now entering are really all that relevant to the arguments that are at the heart of the debate on class and electoral politics.

To take this question further, we need to remind ourselves of the theoretical issues that are involved here. We should recognize that those who have advanced the thesis of the decline of class politics have not regarded this as just a matter of brute empirical fact. Rather, and very properly, they have treated this thesis as being a derivation from more ambitious and wider-ranging theoretical arguments. I think that at least four such arguments can be identified. First, class voting declines because, as industrial societies develop, new structural cleavages supersede cleavages of class—such as, for example, sectoral cleavages, setting those who work or who, in crucial respects, consume within the public sector against those who do not. Then secondly, class voting declines because, with increasing material welfare, the economic issues chiefly associated with class become of reduced political salience, and party support becomes more closely linked with differing value commitments—for example, those expressed in the so-called 'new agendas' of environmentalism, feminism, and so on. Thirdly, class voting declines because, with greater mobility, social and geographical, the primordial affiliations of family, local community, and workplace are all weakened, and voters are thus allowed to choose their party in a more individualistic and more rational way than before: as political consumers, they buy parties according to what their particular policies or programmes have to offer at particular times and, like consumers, they may, therefore, be fickle. Fourthly, class voting declines because in advanced industrial or 'postindustrial' societies class becomes, in general, a waning force in shaping social identities and social actions, in particular as class inequalities of condition and opportunity progressively diminish.

These different theoretical arguments underlying the thesis of the decline of class politics are not entirely consistent one with another. Nevertheless, whether you take them together or severally, what they clearly imply is that in Western democracies the class–vote association should be in quite generalized, quite continuous, and even, one might argue, accelerating decline. In other words, if these commendably strong arguments are indeed correct, then I wonder whether the kinds of recherché debates that we have been having on empirical matters should be necessary or even possible. In other words, the trends in the class–vote association that are implied by these arguments are not of a kind that will only be visible if one starts the analysis in the 1930s. They are not of a kind that will be visible only if, after complex treatment of the data from many nations and many time points, one closes one eye and squints with the other. The trends that are implied here should not be ones that, if they are apparent in some nations, do not then seem to show up in others. And they should not be ones that, if they exist at all, are almost invariably overlaid with short-term fluctuations in the level of class voting of a clearly stronger kind. So I do wonder if the very fact that we have had to engage in these very elaborate discussions about what the empirical evidence shows is not in itself evidence that strong arguments simply do not hold. It seems to me that even on the most favourable interpretation that can be given to the findings presented in this volume, these arguments find very little support; or that, at the very best, if there is anything in them, the effects that they claim must be seen as being powerfully offset by other factors of which they do not take any serious account.

What I would argue, then, is that those who still want to maintain the idea that there is some pervasive underlying tendency for the class–vote link to weaken have to take up the task of explaining just what these offsetting, countervailing factors are, such that this tendency is not at all easy to perceive. For my own part, though, I would see very little reason to retain any of the theoretical arguments I have outlined. What they seek to explain may well not exist in the first place; and, furthermore, the processes they invoke to explain it are often themselves of a highly questionable character. For example, I find it strange that decreasing class inequalities of condition or opportunity should be invoked in this respect or, again, the growing electoral impact of new agendas. One could, to put it very harshly, claim that one has here the invocation of non-facts to explain non-facts. I would, of course, recognize that there are some rather general features of change in modern societies that do have a similarly generalized influence on electoral politics. For example, one could cite here the decline in the size of industrial working classes and the growth of the service class, or salariat, of professional, administrative, and managerial employees. This does seem to be something that is happening across Western societies. Or again, one might cite the increasing 'globalization' of the economy, which creates severe problems for any parties favouring other than free-market economic policies. Both these tendencies can go some way to explaining the general decline in the fortunes of labour and social-democratic parties across the Western world. But of course, these are features which, so to speak, bear on the *margins* of the class-by-vote table rather than on the interactions; and so far as the latter are concerned, I have to say that I remain a strong supporter of the null hypothesis: nothing very much is happening. Or, in other words, I find it difficult to believe that there are any processes generic to industrial or postindustrial societies that are at work reducing the net association between class and party support or indeed affecting it systematically in any other way.

Looking to the future, so far at least as comparative work is concerned, I believe that this has to be conducted with a greater degree of attention than hitherto for national specificities. And so, again contrary to Peter

Mair, I think that Nieuwbeerta and De Graaf's chapter indicates that the Dutch approach has reached its limits. We should indeed seek to apply and test similar hypotheses from nation to nation, using similar modelling techniques, and also to use similar class categories—of, I would hope, a relatively refined kind. But at the same time we should aim to do full justice to the very wide differences that exist in national party structures, rather than operating simply with left–right dichotomies. In this way, we can then hope to trace out the detail of the pattern of class–party affinities and aversions and of changes therein. What I would guess we will typically find (and some of the chapters, especially on the Scandinavian countries, already suggest this) is that where changes in class voting do occur, these are not, for the most part, of a highly generalized kind—that is, ones that apply across the entire electorate—but rather they are changes that refer to the members of particular classes showing a greater or a lesser propensity to support a particular party. And further, when we come to try to explain these changes, I would guess that what we will find is that nationally specific factors loom very large in our explanations, and especially factors that relate less to social-structural changes, whether of class, status, or whatever, than to political changes or at all events to changes or differences in the way in which political parties have responded to social-structural shifts. And so to this extent, I would agree with Peter Mair that, as it were, politics will come back into its own. But again I have to wave the sociological flag and to say that some of the worst examples of 'sociologism' were indeed displayed by the political scientists who first advocated the decline of the class politics thesis. So, ironically, it is the sociologists who, by effectively undermining this thesis empirically, have in fact played the leading role in reasserting the primacy or, at all events, the autonomy of the political.

# 13

# Class and Vote: Disrupting the Orthodoxy

GEOFFREY EVANS

## INTRODUCTION

This book has concerned itself with debunking the over-generalized theories and untested assumptions that have had an unjustifiable prominence in academic and journalistic discussions of the social bases of politics. As part of this aim, the studies presented here have revealed many important differences cross-nationally in the changing nature of the class basis of voting. The explanation of these variations is the focus of much of the interpretative analysis contained within the book, as are their implications for strategies of party competition. None the less, the emphasis in most of the preceding chapters has been on the careful *description* of patterns of voting behaviour over time. The reason for this is simple: it is necessary to know what it is we are trying to explain before we try to explain it.[1] Much of this book has been devoted to doing just that rather than assuming, as have so many commentators, that the empirical phenomena to be explained are generic to advanced industrial societies. Moreover, and importantly, observation of cross-national variation in the pattern of and trends in levels of class voting rules out, in and of itself, many popular interpretations of developments in class politics: description is itself a test of theory.

Many theories have been put forward to account for class dealignment, but it is those that invoke sociological explanations that we have been in the best position to evaluate. Examples of such tests can be seen in Nieuwbeerta and De Graaf's analysis of the variations in the composition of the

[1] We might also take this refinement of what sort of changes there are to be explained even further: a recent paper by Weakliem and Heath (1995) on class voting in different regions of Britain found that over time Wales and Scotland had some class dealignment whereas in the south of England levels of alignment had been virtually constant. Thus the explanandum in Britain might be better characterized as why class voting has declined in Scotland and Wales but not elsewhere. The complexities introduced into characterizations of national trends by regional variation are also well demonstrated by the quite different structure of party competition and its social bases in Northern Ireland (see Evans and Duffy 1997).

class structure and its relationship to changing patterns of class vote, Hout, Manza, and Brooks's examination of the impact of trade union membership, and Müller's analysis of trade union membership, postmaterialism, and 'new politics', as well as in the various other chapters that control for non-class characteristics in their analyses. Most of these sociological explanations point towards relatively gradual change in the social bases of politics over time. This contrasts with the sort of change we might predict on the basis of political explanations of levels of class voting. The effects of political actors—that is, parties—are more likely to be short term, and exhibit discontinuity as incumbents change office. It is difficult to test such accounts given the present state of knowledge in this area and the character of the available survey evidence. Peter Mair is right to argue that at some point politics has to brought into the picture, but the survey-based modelling of the impact of parties on voting behaviour requires particularly careful specification and interpretation if it is to be convincing.[2]

Even the analysis of sociological explanations is not a straightforward task. In this volume we have used two rather different strategies. One is the systematic comparative modelling presented in Chapter 2. The other is the intensive national case studies that make up most of the rest of the book.[3] One of the aims of this project has been to juxtapose these two approaches and assess their effectiveness in answering questions about over-time change in class voting.

## HAS THERE BEEN A GENERALIZED DECLINE IN CLASS VOTING IN ADVANCED INDUSTRIAL SOCIETIES?

Nieuwbeerta and De Graaf's ambitious comparative chapter has deservedly been the subject of commentary in Chapter 12 and, implicitly, the target of the more narrowly focused analyses reported elsewhere in the book. Certainly, their collection of twenty countries over forty-five years is a remarkable dataset. Nevertheless, if we look a little more closely at the number of years and surveys actually included for most countries in the data we see that in only ten cases is there information covering ten or more years; in only five cases do we have information over twenty or more

[2] Evans *et al.* (1991, 1999) provide examples of a single-country, over-time analysis bearing on this issue.

[3] Strictly speaking, this is not quite accurate as Weakliem and Heath's chapters examine up to three countries. Nevertheless, their approach analyses these countries in great detail as separate cases and makes no attempt to impose the same party structure cross-nationally.

years. Many countries have one survey (France, Belgium), or perhaps two (Ireland, Finland). Given these limitations, what can the analysis tell us? For Nieuwbeerta and De Graaf (Chapter 2) it tells us that:

> our analysis showed unequivocally that in countries where class voting was rather strong after the Second World War, there were substantial declines in levels of class voting. In most of these countries, the fluctuations in class voting can in our view be regarded as part of an overall declining trend, and not as trendless fluctuations.

But is this actually the case? Among the five countries with data from a reasonably extensive time-span, we find three where a linear trend is significant: Britain, Norway, and Germany. Of these, it has been shown on several occasions that in Britain there was a one-off drop in class voting between 1966–70 and no clear-cut evidence of systematic change since that time (see Evans *et al.* 1991, 1996; Heath *et al.* 1995, and Chapter 3 in this volume). While in his exceptionally careful and detailed analysis of West Germany over more or less the same period as Nieuwbeerta and De Graaf (1976–94 and 1969–90, respectively) Walter Müller shows that class dealignment—as opposed to realignment—did not occur: 'we do not find any evidence of a trend or of any other significant variation in the pattern of class voting in the series of our ten surveys taken between 1976 and 1994. . . . What we find, then, is a remarkable stability in the main effects of most variables throughout the almost twenty years surveyed here' (Chapter 6).

Only in Norway do the results of the relevant case study fit the Nieuwbeerta and De Graaf picture. Other evidence presented by Robert Erikson at the Nuffield Conference is also consistent with a similar decline in Sweden.[4] As Michael Hout has commented, the Scandinavian cases do seem to have 'regressed to the mean'. But that is the only context in which dealignment has occurred, and from an exceptional level in the first place. Compare this to Dalton's (1996: 186) reference to the declining class basis of politics as the 'new "conventional wisdom"' of comparative electoral research. Clearly, while it may have become a convention, it is perhaps not one to which the epithet 'wisdom' can plausibly be attached.

Of course, Nieuwbeerta and De Graaf might argue that many of their coefficients are 'in the right direction' even if not significant by conventional criteria. But on inspection this only worsens the case for a generalized decline in class politics. The fact that the really big changes are found in Finland (from 1972–5) and Ireland (1989–90) suggests two things: (1) massive error and unreliability/instability in the data and estimates; or (2) dramatic changes in the class–vote relationship over a remarkably short

[4] Robert Erikson's unpublished analysis presented at the conference at Nuffield College indicates that in Sweden there was a significant decline in the UNIDIFF parameter in the 1960s.

period. If we take these findings seriously as indicative of long-term trends, we would infer, as Paul Nieuwbeerta implied at the Nuffield meeting (see Michael Hout's comment), that class voting should have long-since disappeared in Finland and Ireland. But we know from other sources that, at least in Ireland (Evans and Sinnott 1999), this is simply not the case. It would appear that, at most, the short-term effects shown in these analyses reflect a discontinuous and reversible feature of party politics and the choices offered to voters; more likely, they reflect characteristics of the surveys themselves. Thus they suggest either a far more voluntaristic model of voting, perhaps reflecting rather specific political events, than Nieuwbeerta and De Graaf appear to endorse; or that inferring trends from one- or three-year time-spans is more than a little unwise.

We must therefore conclude that, heroic though it is, Nieuwbeerta and De Graaf's application of a programme of standardized comparative modelling fails to provide firm evidence of any general decline in class voting. The door is still open, of course, for further research of this type using more datasets to give better estimates of changes across more countries. But even this would have to surmount a further serious limitation—one that has been exposed repeatedly in the case studies presented above which have represented the spectrum of political choices somewhat more accurately by allowing party systems to amount to more than left versus non-left, or any other dichotomy. This is that the structure of the party system is likely to be crucial to the way in which parties orientate their appeal: is the left party competing with another left party, or is it competing with a centre party? Does one party monopolize the left vote, or is it divided? In other words, what is the 'opportunity structure' in which parties compete? Cross-national variations in these opportunity structures are likely to affect appeals and social bases in more nuanced ways than are afforded by the left versus non-left approach to class voting—a point made clear in Herbert Kitschelt's two recent major works on the ways in which party strategy reflects the opportunity structures provided by the main dimensions of competition and the institutional context in West European party systems (Kitschelt 1994, 1995).[5]

In other words, comparative research is fundamental to explanation, but if in engaging in such research we distort part of what makes the comparison worthwhile—that is, the differences in party systems between countries—then we have rather defeated the object. A focus only on 'traditional' class voting and on a rather rigid specification of what counts as left and right can be misleading if claims for its general relevance are

[5] On this point, I find Peter Mair's sympathetic response to Nieuwbeerta and De Graaf's approach surprising. As a political scientist he might have been expected to protest at the minimal representation of political choice in Nieuwbeerta and De Graaf's analysis.

overstated. This is not, of course, to say that we cannot compare over-time changes across countries; rather it is to argue that important differences between countries need not be sacrificed to do so. A trend is a trend whether it is based on the choice between ten parties or two.[6] Obviously, with more parties, there is more scope for realignment and the complexities of interpretation that might ensue, but the reality is that party systems are simply somewhat more complex than Nieuwbeerta and De Graaf's specification allows. Perhaps if instead of comparing the effects of using more or less complex measures of social class they examined the impact of using more or less complex measures of party systems, they would be able to provide rather more convincing evidence that they have not undermined the validity of their analysis by oversimplifying their dependent variable. For now, however, the only substantive inference we might want to draw concerning the decline of class voting is that Scandinavia has changed, and is now more like Britain.[7]

If the broad-ranging systematic comparative strategy does not withstand close scrutiny, an alternative is to draw together information from the detailed country studies. We have already seen examples of how their findings diverge from the thesis of a general decline in levels of class voting. What they also show, however, is that in some countries patterns of class voting have changed in more subtle ways. In some cases this has involved a realignment of class–party affiliations and in others movement both towards and away from convergence in the voting behaviour of classes. For example, despite using different datasets, both Chapters 4 and 5 show that in the United States there is a specific phenomenon—of class–party realignment—to be explained. Such realignment is not to be found in either of the equivalent analyses of British voting patterns; neither is the long-term trend in class differences in turnout and the inverse correlation with class voting. Even where we have not seen evidence of realignment, class voting has not remained constant: in Britain there is evidence of a curvilinear pattern of long-term over-time change, with an increase followed by a decrease. France presents a simpler picture: levels of class voting change less markedly over time and the only long-

[6] The important point here is that potentially relevant conditions vary much more when comparing nations than they do when looking at over-time change. Usually, for example, the electoral system does not change to any great degree in the latter. The complexities that arise when nations are compared are not in principle insurmountable, but there are clearly problems when a deficit of cases—a commonplace in the study of party systems—inhibits controlled comparisons.

[7] The reasons for this are in themselves a source of interest: does it reflect the success of the welfare state in these countries? Stefan Svallfors would not think so. His short-term but broad-ranging analysis of the social bases of welfare attitudes shows a complex picture that provides no clear support for a decline in class divisions over welfare itself.

term realignment is the rightward shift of farmers. Germany displays, according to Walter Müller, an 'astonishing' degree of temporal continuity in its class cleavages, but what can also be seen is that the 'new politics' parties, themselves have developed class bases—and, of course, the two post-communist societies examined here are different again (see below).

The secular model of change evidently does not account for these observed patterns. In other words, there are marked cross-national differences in what is to be explained in these countries which cannot be accounted for by theories that are general to advanced industrial societies and which discuss class voting only in terms of 'more' or 'less'.

What then does this tell us about other work in this area, of those numerous commentators in political science and sociology who have either asserted or 'discovered' that class is obsolete, or at least obsolescent, as an influence on the behaviour of voters and parties? There are the commentators who seem to have at best a limited grasp of the empirical issues. In this camp we can put authors such as Beck (1992); Pakulski and Waters (1996); Eder (1993); and Baumann (1982). To the limited degree that they connect their speculations about class to any testable proposition, they can be relatively easily dismissed. More significant are those commentators who have engaged more closely with evidence. Dalton's (1996: 191–2) conclusion that 'the sociological transformation of advanced industrial societies is weakening class alignments' summarizes the kernel of this approach. But of course, these processes—to the extent that they are occurring at all—imply a generalized and continuing secular trend. At the very least, the case studies in this book remove from contention as an explanation of changes in class voting the sociological thesis of declining class distinctiveness derived from processes of social change generic to advanced industrial societies: hence the title of this concluding chapter.

But what about *other* approaches to explanation, particularly those which refer to the impact of political actors? There are several influential scholars who have rejected the sociological, relatively deterministic account of the transition to postindustrial politics in favour of more voluntaristic models of socio-political relations. Kitschelt (1994, 1995) argues explicitly that the electoral fortunes of European social democratic parties are largely determined by their strategic appeals and choice of objectives in the arena of party competition, rather than by secular trends in the class structure and social system—a line of reasoning that echoes Przeworski's (1985: 100–101) emphasis on the importance of organization, and especially parties, in the creation of constituencies.[8] From this perspective there

[8] As Peter Mair has pointed out, this view of the relation between classes and parties was also expressed some time ago by Giovanni Sartori (1969).

is reason to believe that even in advanced industrial societies class voting might increase as well as decrease—a key difference from the sociological approaches considered above. More specifically, it implies that the adoption of class-relevant policy programmes should be associated with an increase in the class basis of partisanship.

The possibility that strategy can impact on class-voting patterns, particularly in the short term, is an explicit part of the message advanced by Goldthorpe in his chapter on Britain (Chapter 3) and the authors of the 1997 British Election Study (see Evans *et al.* 1999).[9] It is very different from the accounts of (probably terminal) decline in class voting rooted in gradual social change and is not constrained to be just downward in its impact. But this is not to say that sociological changes have no impact. Changes in the relative *sizes* of classes might well have implications for party strategy: particularly the declining size of the working class. It is clear, for example, that the British Labour Party has followed several West European left-wing parties down the road to centrist social democracy—a move consistent with Downs's (1957) model of competition for the median voter. As Labour moved to the centre it should have picked up support and squeezed the centre party, the Liberal Democrats. Far from being the representative of an interest group—the working class—Labour's transformation recasts it as a 'catch-all' party. The momentum for this shift comes from four consecutive election defeats but its deeper origins lie in the changing shape of the social structure which makes a parliamentary majority derived from working-class particularism far less likely than it would have been only twenty years previously.

What we might then expect to see is a decline in certain forms of class voting because of a change to a 'catch-all' strategy by parties on the left in response to the shrinking class basis of support for those parties. In some systems such moves leave open the space for left parties to attract support from marginalized working-class groups; in other, first-past-the-post systems, we might expect the start-up costs for electorally viable left parties to be too great. What happens then? In its most developed form, the United States, we have seen evidence of the growth of a new class–vote cleavage—between those who vote and those who do not—as a deficit of

[9] Goldthorpe also considers whether the swings in popularity which occurred in the 1997 General Election in Britain call into question the claims of analyses based on older data. The answer is probably not—at least with respect to the conclusions regarding sociological explanations of the changing magnitude of class voting: across-the-board changes, such as those that occurred in these two elections, are not the same as changes in the pattern of association between class and vote; and significant social change does not often occur over four- or five-year periods. So if any systematic change in the class–vote relation has occurred, it would most likely be attributable to the effects of party strategy. The same inference more than likely applies to the results of the recent presidential elections in France.

working-class interest representation leads to increased class differences in participation. This is not the same as the class voting of old, but it is a form of class voting.

A further complication arises when considering the relationship between actual and potential levels of class voting. The political choices offered to voters may shape the nature of class *voting*. But this does not mean that they shape the nature of class-based differences in *political interests*. Lack of representation can reduce class divisions in party support without affecting class divisions in political interests. Thus a fall in the class basis of partisanship should not be taken as evidence of declining differences between classes in political preferences—particularly when representativeness and political entrepreneurship are constrained by the electoral system. Stefan Svallfors's chapter examines such perceived class interests and shows constancy over time (Chapter 8); similar work elsewhere suggests a similar stable pattern (Evans 1993*a*), while others (Vanneman and Cannon 1987; see also Evans 1993*c*) add comparative support for the idea that class divisions in political orientations can be constant while their impact on partisanship can vary as a result of political rather than sociological factors. The potential for class politics thus remains even when parties fail to seize upon it.

Also, of course, the fact that the middle class has grown in size is not necessarily cause to forget class politics. Working-class politics is just one version of class politics. The strategic rationality of appealing to middle-class interests is simply a new twist on an old theme. The aim of political actors under these conditions is to steal middle-class votes while keeping working-class votes—the classic dilemma of the social democratic parties described by Przeworski and Sprague in *Paper Stones* (1986). But in the days of a larger working class, it was clearly more important for parties of the right to seize working-class votes while not losing the middle class—a strategy characterized by Disraeli's tribute to the 'angels in marble' who provided the British Conservative Party with their 'against-the-odds' electoral successes for many years—an epithet seized upon to good effect by McKenzie and Silver (1967) in their interpretation of the pattern of class–party competition in the age of large working classes (and which rather contradicts Przeworski's well-known assertion of the distinctive role of left parties in conditioning the incidence of class voting).

The notion that the changing shape of the class structure influences party strategy, which in turn eventually impacts upon the form of the class–vote relation, is an area ripe for a theoretically informed examination of the relationship between the decision to vote and the choices available to members of different classes. So far, though, the empirical basis for such an approach is not convincing. More theoretically orientated scholars, such as Przeworski and Kitschelt, have addressed these issues on the basis of somewhat scanty analyses of cross-national survey data on voting.[10] Where such evidence is reviewed, it does not provide support for the view that party strategy is consequential for the strength of the class–vote relation: thus according to Dalton, 'the revival of economic issues and the class-based appeals of parties in response to economic recession . . . has not significantly revived class voting in the 1980s and 1990s' (1996: 175–6). Similarly, in Chapter 5 of this volume Weakliem and Heath model the link between party polarization over class-related ideology and the extent of class voting by obtaining measures of party positions. However, they could find no evidence of a consistent association between the distance the parties were apart on a 'class dimension' of ideology and levels of class voting in either Britain or the United States. So although a pattern consistent with the accentuating effects of ideological polarization can be found in the United States in the 1930s, where there were high levels of party polarization and high levels of class voting, and in the 1950s, where party differentiation was low and class voting was also low, it does not hold up elsewhere. High levels of ideological polarization were also to be found in Britain in the 1930s—in 1935 Labour ran with its most left-wing programme ever—but class voting was low. Then in the 1950s when ideological differentiation fell, there were higher levels of class voting—Weakliem and Heath's Gallup poll data suggest this was the peak of class voting in Britain. More recently, in the 1980s the parties in both countries again polarized but class voting did not follow suit. So in three of the four instances where there were high levels of ideological differentiation between parties, we had low levels of class voting. Clearly, a straightforward political explanation in which voters respond to the gap between parties does not work. We need to specify under which conditions polarization between the parties leads to more pronounced class voting. In other words, what is it about the United States in the 1930s and 1950s that makes it conform to expectations, and what is it about the other cases that makes them fail to do so? Any explanation of class voting is going to be more complicated than a simple linkage between ideological polarization and class interests.

One line of development for such a conditional model is indicated by the findings in Chapters 9 and 10. For a variety of reasons, the sociological arguments supporting the class dealignment hypothesis (the 'embourgeoisement' of the working class, the rise of 'issue' voting and postmaterialist values, the decline of a traditional working class) do not hold up in post-communist countries experiencing the early stages of

[10] In their empirical analysis of the electoral dilemma of socialism, Przeworski and Sprague (1986) make considerable use of aggregate evidence but do not examine survey data on class voting.

marketization. These countries appear to be characterized by class *polarization*—both economic and political. How this might be understood in terms of the translation of voters' class-differentiated experiences of marketization into a framework for party competition is explained in Chapter 10. Even here, however, a simple 'bottom-up' model of cleavage formation is not supported. There is also an element of party manoeuvring to capitalize on such differentiated experiences. Both voters and politicans are engaged in a learning process. The initial step in this process is provided by sociological factors—the distribution of resources, the differential effects of marketization, inherited enmity between identity groups—but the ensuing steps in the process require a more iterative analysis.[11] Different models are likely to apply at different points in the evolution of the social relations of party systems.

## IN CONCLUSION

The main points of a general nature to be taken from this book can be summarized as follows.

*Method* There have been various methodological insights. Some are relatively minor but reassuring: with two-class, two-party models of electoral systems, Alford and Thomsen indexes produce similar findings. When vote is constrained to be a choice between just two options, the conclusions to be drawn using more complex class schemas do not differ dramatically from those obtained with a two-class model. The use of different techniques of loglinear analysis (that is, topological versus association modelling) is unlikely to alter our interpretation of the key features of patterns of class voting over time. Others, however, point to the costs of commonly used methodological short-cuts and indicate, for example, that the use of more or less aggregated measures of class position can change our substantive conclusions under certain conditions. Most importantly, we must conclude that when vote is standardized, it undermines the benefits of comparative analysis because it obscures important aspects of political choice and their relation to social class positions that vary cross-nationally. Given our current low levels of knowledge about the comparability of national political contexts, this indicates that intensive national case studies sharing a sufficient frame of reference for the observation of common patterns provide the most reliable, if complex, basis for inference and theory building.

[11] This argument is pursued more extensively in Evans and Whitefield (1993) and empirically evaluated in Evans and Whitefield (1995*b*, 1998*a*, 1998*b*, forthcoming) and Whitefield and Evans (1996, 1998*b*).

*Substance* The only consistent and robust evidence of declining class–vote relations is in Scandinavia: in particular, Norway, where high levels of class voting declined in the 1960s to become more like those of other West European societies. In contrast, post-communist societies appear to be contexts in which class politics and class voting are increasing in significance as classes polarize in their economic circumstances and parties signal their relevance to differing class interests. Other countries, despite displaying similar characteristics in terms of 'modernity' and 'postmodernity', display widely varying patterns of change over time. There is also evidence that the effects of class position are robust in the face of wide-ranging social-structural and value change. Controlling for over-time changes in relevant characteristics such as trade union membership, post-materialism, and a wide range of other characteristics does not alter class–vote patterns, or the centrality of class as a source of attitudes towards key issues such as inequality and redistribution.

*Theory* The patterns of constancy, dealignment, and realignment in class voting over time are such that they cannot be understood by generalized propositions about the effects of industrialism or post-industrialism. Thus generic theories of the decline of class voting and class politics in industrialized societies are empirically unsupported, as by extension are those theories which claim that all social-structural bases to politics are in decline. One message from this book is that political parties are likely to be more important than social change in shaping short-term changes in features of class politics—and most discussions of class politics focus on a relatively brief historical period. Even where such changes do occur, however, we cannot yet ascertain their cause with confidence. Top-down theories of the effects of party strategy on class-voting patterns are not supported in any consistent way by the, admittedly limited, evidence examined.

We can none the less point to possibly useful theories, hypotheses, and models that might prove fruitful in further comparative analyses. The argument that class divisions in political orientations remain relatively constant but, because of changing class sizes, parties change their strategies which *eventually* changes class–vote relations, may hold promise. However, this is only likely to be the case *if* we take into account sources of variation in the extent to which voters calculate returns to their investment rather than voting out of established allegiances. Similarly, we have seen evidence that, during periods in which alignments are first formed, voters' class-differentiated experiences in conjunction with a learning and signalling process do provide an explanation of cleavage formation—one that passes at least initial empirical testing and which could therefore repay more detailed investigation. More generally, the thesis that bottom-up and top-down influences operate under different conditions is a fruitful source of hypotheses for future analysis. This approach—in which the precise contexts that determine the relative force of sociological and political factors are specified on theoretical grounds—is a natural progression in an area of academic controversy that, although characterized by a plethora of empirical findings, has most certainly not provided the evidential basis for the highly general, not to say grandiose, claims that have captured the imaginations of both sociologists and political scientists.

In part, the discovery of 'the end of class politics' is merely an example of the well-known psychological tendency to look more closely at something when it appears to go wrong. When the pre-eminence of class politics was little questioned, it was assumed that voters in different sociological categories were formed in solid opposition over competing political interests. With the changed world of late-twentieth-century affluence and industrial restructuring this was thought surely to be no longer the case. And, of course, it *is not* the case; but it probably never was. In the absence of historical survey data rather than aggregate statistics, we might be inclined to believe in the monolithic electoral class struggle—defined as classes voting *en bloc* against other classes—but as we have seen in Chapter 5, this is probably a myth; the product of an over-fertile sociological imagination. Such fertility, while forming, as C. Wright Mills was at pains to point out, a necessary part of the social scientist's brief, is less likely to be so dramatically misleading when constrained by the sorts of evidence and analysis provided in this book.

# REFERENCES


Abbott, A. (1988). *The System of Professions: An Essay on the Division of Expert Labor*. Chicago: Chicago University Press.

Abrams, M., Rose, R., and Hinden, R. (1960). *Must Labour Lose?* Harmondsworth, Middlesex: Penguin.

Abramson, P. R., and Inglehart, R. (1995). *Value Change in Global Perspective*. Ann Arbor: University of Michigan Press.

——Aldrich, J. H., and Rhode, D. W. (1990). *Change and Continuity in the 1988 Elections*. Washington, DC: Congressional Quarterly Press.

————(1994). *Change and Continuity in the 1992 Elections*. Washington, DC: Congressional Quarterly Press.

Alber, J. (1985). 'Modernisierung, neue Spannungslinien und die politischen Chancen der Grünen'. *Politische Vierteljahresschrift*. 26 (3): 211–26.

Alford, R. (1962). 'A suggested index of the association of social class and voting'. *Public Opinion Quarterly*. 26: 417–25.

——(1963). *Party and Society: The Anglo-American Democracies*. Westport, Conn.: Greenwood Press.

——(1967). 'Class voting in Anglo-American political systems'. In Lipset and Rokkan (1967). 67–94.

Allardt, E., and Littunen, Y. (1964). *Cleavages, Ideologies and Party Systems: Contributions to Comparative Political Sociology*. Helsinki: Academic Bookstore.

——and Wesolowski, W. (1978). *Social Structure and Change: Finland and Poland in Comparative Perspective*. Warzawa: Polish Scientific Publishers.

Allum, P. A. (1979). 'Italy'. In *Political Parties in the European Community*, ed. S. Henig. London: Allen and Unwin. 135–69.

Andersen, J. G. (1984). 'Decline of class voting or change in class voting? Social classes and party choice in Denmark in the 1970s'. *European Journal of Political Research*. 12: 243–59.

Anderson, D., and Davidson P. (1943). *Ballots and the Democratic Class Struggle*. Stanford, Calif.: Stanford University Press.

Andeweg, R. B. (1982). *Dutch Voters Adrift: On Explanations of Electoral Change 1963–1977*. Ph.D. dissertation. Leiden: University of Leiden.

Bagguley, P. (1995). 'Middle-class radicalism revisited'. In *Social Change and the Middle Classes*, eds. T. Butler and M. Savage. London: UCL Press. 293–311.

Baker, K. L., Dalton, R. J., and Hillebrandt, K. (1981). *Germany Transformed: Political Culture and the New Politics*. Cambridge, Mass.: Harvard University Press.

Baldwin, P. (1990). *The Politics of Social Solidarity: Class Bases of the European Welfare State 1875–1975*. Cambridge: Cambridge University Press.

Barnes, S. H., and Kaase, M. (eds.) (1979). *Political Action: Mass Participation in Five Western Democracies.* Beverly Hills, Calif./London: Sage.

Bartolini, S., and Mair, P. (1990). *Identity, Competition and Electoral Availability: The Stabilisation of European Electorates, 1885–1985*. Cambridge: Cambridge University Press.

Bauman, Z. (1982). *Memories of Class*. London: Routledge and Kegan Paul.

Baxter, J., Emmison, M., and Western, J. (1991). *Class Analysis and Contemporary Australia*. Melbourne: Macmillan.

Beck, U. (1983). 'Jenseits von Stand und Klasse? Soziale Ungleichheiten, gesellschaftliche Individualisierungsprozesse und die Entstehung neuer sozialer Formationen und Identitäten'. In *Soziale Ungleichheiten. Soziale Welt, Sonderband 2*, ed. R. Kreckel. Göttingen: Schwartz. 35–74.

——(1992). *Risk Society: Towards a New Modernity*. London: Sage.

Bell, D. (1976). *The Cultural Contradictions of Capitalism*. New York: Basic Books.

Benson, L. (1961). *The Concept of Jacksonian Democracy.* Princeton: Princeton University Press.

Berger, M., Gibowski, W. G., Roth, D., and Schulte, W. (1983). 'Stabilität und Wechsel. Eine Analyse der Bundestagswahl 1980'. In *Wahlen und politisches System. Analysen aus Anlaß der Bundestagswahl 1980*, eds. M. Kaase and H.-D. Klingemann. Opladen: Westdeutscher Verlag. 12–57.

————————(1986). 'Legitimierung des Regierungswechsels. Eine Analyse der Bundestagswahl 1983'. In *Wahlen und politischer Prozeß. Analysen aus Anlaß der Bundestagswahl 1983*, eds. H.-D. Klingemann and M. Kaase. Opladen: Westdeutscher Verlag. 251–88.

Berglund, S. (1988). 'The 1987 eduskunta election in Finland'. *Scandinavian Political Studies*. 11: 69–76.

Biagini, E. F. (1991). 'Popular liberal, gladstonian finance, and the debate on taxation, 1860–74'. In *Currents of Radicalism*, eds. E. F. Biagini and A. J. Reid. Cambridge: Cambridge University Press. 134–62.

Bonham, J. (1952). 'The middle class elector'. *British Journal of Sociology*. 3: 222–30.

Books, J. W., and Reynolds, J. B. (1975). 'A note on class voting in Great Britain and the United States'. *Comparative Political Studies*. 8: 360–76.

Borchorst, A., and Siim, B. (1987). 'Women and the advanced welfare state—a new kind of patriarchal power?' In *Women and the State*, ed. A. Showstack Sassoon. London: Hutchinson.

Brähler, E., and Wirth, H.-J. (1995). 'Gewerkschaftsmitglieder und Nichtorganisierte im Vergleich'. In *Entsolidarisierung. Die Westdeutschen am Vorabend der Wende und danach*, eds. H.-J. Wirth and E. Brähler. Opladen: Westdeutscher Verlag. 88–108.

Brand, K.-W. (1990). 'Cyclical aspects of new social movements'. In *Challenging the Political Order*, eds. R. Dalton and M. Kuechler. New York: Oxford University Press. 34–42.

Breslauer, G. (1993). 'The roots of polarization', *Post-Soviet Affairs*. 9: 223–30.

Briggs, A. (1960). 'The language of "class" in early nineteenth-century England'. In *Essays in Labour History*, eds. A. Briggs and J. Saville. London: Macmillan. 43–73.

Brint, S. (1984). '"New-class" and cumulative trend explanations of the liberal political attitudes of professionals'. *American Journal of Sociology*. 90: 930–71.

Brooks, C., and Manza, J. (1997). 'The social and ideological bases of middle class political realignment in the United States, 1972–1992'. *American Sociological Review*. 62: 91–108.

Brown, A. (1993). 'The October crisis of 1993: context and implications'. *Post-Soviet Affairs*. 9: 183–95.

Bürklin, W. (1988). 'Wählerverhalten und Wertewandel'. Opladen: Leske and Budrich.

——(1994). 'Verändertes Wahlverhalten und der Wandel der politischen Kultur'. In *Das Superwahljahr. Deutschland vor unkalkulierbaren Regierungsmehrheiten? Köln*, eds. W. Bürklin and D. Roth. Opladen: Bund. 27–53.

Burnham, W. D. (1982). *The Current Crisis in American Politics*. New York: Oxford University Press.

Butler, D. E., and Kavanagh, D. (1980). *The British General Election of 1979*. London: Macmillan.

————(1984). *The British General Election of 1983*. London: Macmillan.

————(1992). *The British General Election of 1992*. London: Macmillan.

——and Pinto-Duschinsky, M. (1971). *The British General Election of 1970*. London: Macmillan.

——and Stokes, D. E. (1974). *Political Change in Britain: The Evolution of Electoral Choice* (2nd edn.). London: Macmillan.

Butler, T., and Savage, M. (eds.) (1995). *Social Change and the Middle Classes*. London: UCL Press.

Campbell, A., Converse, P. E., Miller, W. E., and Stokes, D. E. (1960). *The American Voter*. Chicago: University of Chicago Press.

Carmines, E. G., and Stanley, H. W. (1992). 'The transformation of the New Deal party system: social groups, political ideology, and changing partisanship among northern whites, 1972–1988'. *Political Behavior*. 14: 213–37.

Castles, F. G. (1978). *The Social Democratic Image of Society: A Study of the Achievements and Origins of Scandinavian Social Democracy in Comparative Perspective*. London: Routledge & Kegan Paul.

Chow, G. C. (1983). *Econometrics*. New York: McGraw-Hill.

Clark, T. N., and Lipset, S. M. (1991). 'Are social classes dying?' *International Sociology*. 6: 397–410.

————and Rempel, M. (1993). 'The declining political significance of social class'. *International Sociology*. 8: 293–316.

Clifford, P., and Heath, A. F. (1993). 'The political consequences of social mobility'. *Journal of the Royal Statistical Society*, series A. 156: 55–61.

Clogg, C. C., Petkova, C. E., and Haritou A. (1995). 'Statistical methods for comparing regression coefficents between models'. *American Journal of Sociology*. 100: 1261–93.

Cloward, R. A., and Piven, F. (1986). 'The welfare state in an age of industrial decline'. *Smith College Studies in Social Work*. 56: 132–55.

Converse, P. E. (1958). 'The shifting role of class in political attitudes and behavior'. In *Readings in Social Psychology*, iii, eds. E. E. Maccoby, T. M. Newcomb, and E. L. Hartley. New York: Holt. 388–99.

Converse, P. E., and Dupeux, G. (1966/1962). 'Politicization of the electorate in France and the United States'. In *Elections and the Political Order*, eds. A. Campbell, P. E. Converse, W. E. Miller, and D. E. Stokes. New York: Wiley. 269–91.

——and Pierce, R. (1986). *Political Representation in France*. Cambridge: Harvard University Press.

Coughlin, R. M. (1980). *Ideology, Public Opinion and Welfare Policy*. Berkeley, Calif.: Institute of International Studies.

Cox, D. R. (1995). 'The relation between theory and application in statistics'. *Statistics*. 4: 207–26.

Crewe, I. (1986). 'On the death and resurrection of class voting: some comments on How Britain Votes'. *Political Studies*. 34: 620–38.

——and Denver, D. (1985). *Electoral Change in Western Democracies: Patterns and Sources of Electoral Volatility*. London: Croom Helm.

——Sarlvik, B., and Alt, J. (1977). 'Partisan Dealignment in Britain 1964–1974'. *British Political Science Review*. 7: 129–90.

Crouch, C. (1980). 'Varieties of trade union weakness: organized labour and capital formation in Britain, Federal Germany and Sweden'. In *Trade Unions and Politics in Western Europe*, ed. J. Hayward. London: Frank Cass.

Dahrendorf, R. (1988). *The Modern Social Conflict*. New York: Weidenfeld and Nicolson.

——(1990). *Reflections on the Revolutions in Europe*. New York: Times Books.

Dalton, R. J. (1996). *Citizen Politics: Public Opinion and Political Parties in Advanced Industrial Democracies* (2nd edn.). Chatham, NJ: Chatham House Publishers.

——Flanagan, S. C., and Beck, P. A. (1984). *Electoral Change in Advanced Industrial Democracies*. Princeton: Princeton University Press.

——and Rohrschneider, R. (1990). 'Wählerwandel und Abschwächung der Parteineigungen von 1972 bis 1987'. In *Wahlen und Wähler. Analysen aus Anlaß der Bundestagswahl 1987*, eds. M. Kaase and H.-D. Klingemann. Opladen: Westdeutscher Verlag. 297 ff.

De Graaf, N. D. (1996). 'Politieke voorkeur en politieke participatie' (Political preference and political participation). In *Sociale Segmentatie in 2015*, eds. H. Ganzeboom and W. Ultee. Den Haag: Sdu publisher. 205–45.

——and Evans, G. (1996). 'Why are the young more postmaterialist? A cross-national analysis of individual and contextual influences on postmaterial values'. *Comparative Political Studies*. 28: 608–35.

——Nieuwbeerta, P., and Heath, A. (1995). 'Class mobility and political preference: individual and contextual effects'. *American Journal of Sociology*. 100: 997–1027.

——and Steijn, B. (1997). 'De "service" klasse in Nederland: een voorstel tot aanpassing van de EGP-klassenindeling' (The service class in the Netherlands: A proposal for adjusting the EGP class schema.) *Tijdschrift voor Sociologie*. 18: 131–54.

De Jong, J. J. (1956). *Overheid en Onderdaan*. Wageningen: Zomer and Keunings.

Dempster, A. P., Laird, N. M, and Rubin, D. B. (1977). 'Maximum Likelihood from Incomplete Data via the EM Algorithm'. *Journal of the Royal Statistical Society, series B*. 39: 1–22.

Den Uyl, J. (1951). *Verkiezingen in Nederland: De Ontwikkelingen en Verspreiding van Politieke Voorkeuren en hun Betekenis voor de Partij van de Arbeid*. Amsterdam: Dr. Wiarda Beckman Stichting.

Downs, A. (1957). *An Economic Theory of Democracy*. New York: Harper and Row.

Drexel, I. (1994). 'Alte und neue gesellschaftliche Gruppierungen jenseits der Individualisierungsthese'. In *Jenseits von Individualisierung und Angleichung*, ed. I. Drexel. Frankfurt am Main/New York: Campus. 9–32.

Dunleavy, P. (1980). 'The political implications of sectional cleavages and the growth of state employment'. *Political Studies*. 28: 364–83; 527–49.

——(1986). 'The growth of sectional cleavages and stabilization of state expenditures'. *Society and Space*. 4: 129–44.

——(1987). 'Class dealignment revisited: why odds ratios give odd results'. *West European Politics*. 10: 400–19.

——(1989). 'The United Kingdom: paradoxes of an ungrounded statism'. In *The Comparative History of Public Policy*, ed. F. G. Castles. Cambridge: Polity Press.

——and Husbands, C. T. (1985). *British Democracy at the Crossroads*. London: Allen and Unwin.

Durant, H. (1945). *Political Opinion*. London: Allen and Unwin.

——(1951). *Behind the Gallup Poll*. London: News Chronicle.

Eder, K. (1993). *The New Politics of Class*. London: Sage.

Edsall, T. (1991). *Chain Reaction*. New York: Norton.

Emmert, T., and Roth, D. (1995). 'Zur wahlsoziologischen Bedeutung eines Modells sozialstrukturell verankerter Konfliktlinien im vereinten Deutschland'. *Historical Social Research*. 20: 119–60.

Erikson, R., and Goldthorpe, J. H. (1992*a*). *The Constant Flux: A Study of Class Mobility in Industrial Societies*. Oxford: Clarendon Press.

————(1992*b*). 'Individual or family? Results from two approaches to class assignment'. *Acta Sociologica*. 35: 95–106.

————and Portocarrero, L. (1979). 'Intergenerational class mobility in three western european societies: England, France and Sweden'. *British Journal of Sociology*. 30: 415–41.

Esping-Andersen, G. (1985). *Politics against Markets: The Social Democratic Road to Power.* Princeton: Princeton University Press.

——(1990). *The Three Worlds of Welfare Capitalism*. Oxford: Polity Press.

——(1993) 'Post-industrial class structures: an analytical framework'. In *Changing Classes: Stratification and Mobility in Post-industrial Societies*, ed. G. Esping-Andersen. London: Sage.

——and Korpi, W. (1984). 'Social policy as class politics in post-war capitalism: Scandinavia, Austria and Germany'. In *Order and Conflict in Contemporary Capitalism*, ed. J. H. Goldthorpe. Oxford: Clarendon Press.

Evans, G. (1992). 'Testing the validity of the Goldthorpe class schema'. *European Sociological Review*. 8: 211–32.

——(1993*a*). 'The decline of class divisions in Britain? Class and ideological preferences in the 1960s and the 1980s'. *British Journal of Sociology.* 44: 449–71.

——(1993*b*). 'Class, prospects and the life-cycle: explaining the association between class position and political preferences'. *Acta Sociologica*. 36: 263–76.

Evans, G. (1993*c*). 'Class conflict and inequality'. In *International Social Attitudes: The 10th BSA report*, eds. R Jowell, L. Brook, and L. Dowds. Aldershot: Dartmouth. 123–42.

——(1995). 'Mass political attitudes and the development of market democracy in Eastern Europe'. *Centre for European Studies Discussion Paper no. 39*. Oxford: Nuffield College.

——(1996). 'Putting men and women into classes: an assessment of the cross-sex validity of the Goldthorpe class schema'. *Sociology*. 30: 209–34.

——(1997). 'Class inequality and the formation of political interests in Eastern Europe'. *European Journal of Sociology*. 38: 207–34.

——(1998). 'On tests of validity and social class: why Prandy and Blackburn are wrong'. *Sociology*. 32: 189–202.

——and Duffy, M. B. (1997). 'Beyond the sectarian divide: the social bases and political consequences of unionist and nationalist party competition in Northern Ireland'. *British Journal of Political Science*. 27: 47–81.

——Heath, A. F., and Lalljee, M. G. (1996). 'Measuring left-right and libertarian-authoritarian values in the British electorate'. *British Journal of Sociology*. 47: 93–112.

————and Payne, C. (1991). 'Modelling trends in the class/party relationship, 1964–87'. *Electoral Studies*. 10: 99–117.

——————(1996). 'Class and party revisited: a new model for estimating changes in levels of class voting'. In *British Elections and Parties Yearbook, 1995*, eds. C. Rallings, D. M. Farrell, D. Denver, and D. Broughton. London: Frank Cass. 157–74.

——————(1999). 'Class: Labour as a Catch-All Party?' in G. Evans and P. Norris, eds. *Critical Elections: British Parties and Voters in Long-term Perspective*. London: Sage, 87–101.

——and Mills, C. (1998*a*). 'Identifying class structure: a latent class analysis of the criterion-related and construct validity of the Goldthorpe class schema'. *European Sociological Review*. 14: 87–106.

————(1998*b*). 'Assessing the cross-sex validity of the Goldthorpe class schema using log-linear models with latent variables'. *Quality & Quantity*. 32: 275–96.

————(1999). 'Are there classes in post-communist societies? A new approach to identifying class structure'. *Sociology*. 33: 23–46.

——and Sinnott, R. (1999). 'Political development in Ireland, North and South'. In *Ireland North and South: Perspectives from Social Science*, eds. A. Heath, R. Breen, and C. Whelan. Oxford: The British Academy and Oxford University Press.

——and Whitefield, S. (1993). 'Identifying the bases of party competition in Eastern Europe'. *British Journal of Political Science*. 23: 521–48.

————(1995*a*). 'The social bases of political competition in Eastern Europe'. Presented at the 91st annual APSA meeting, Chicago, September.

————(1995*b*). 'Social and ideological cleavage formation in post-communist Hungary'. *Europe-Asia Studies*. 47: 1177–204.

————(1998*a*). 'The structuring of political cleavages in post-communist societies: the case of the Czech and Slovak Republics'. *Political Studies*. 46: 115–39.

——— (1998*b*). 'The evolution of left and right in post-Soviet Russia'. *Europe-Asia Studies*. 50: 1023–42.

——— (forthcoming). *Explaining Political Cleavage Formation in Post-Communist Democracies*. Oxford: Oxford University Press.

Featherman, D. L., Hauser, R. M., and Sewell, W. H. (1974). 'Toward comparable data on inequality and stratification: perspectives on the second generation of national mobility studies'. *Current Sociology*. 22: 383–97.

Fienberg, S. E. (1980). *The Analysis of Cross-Classified Data*. Cambridge, Mass.: MIT Press.

Fischer, C. S., Hout, M., Sánchez Jankowski, M., Lucas, S. R., Swidler, A., and Voss, K. (1996). *Inequality by Design: Cracking the Bell Curve Myth*. Princeton: Princeton University Press.

Fitzmaurice, G. (1995). 'Model selection with overdispersed data'. MS, Nuffield College, Oxford.

Forschungsgruppe Wahlen E. V. (1990). *Bundestagwahl 1990: Eine Analyse der Ersten Gesantdeutschen Bundestagwahl*. Mannheim.

Francis, B., Green, M., and Payne, C. (1993). *The GLIM System: Release 4 Manual*. Oxford: Clarendon Press.

Franklin, M. (1985*a*). *The Decline of Class Voting in Britain: Changes in the Basis of Electoral Choice, 1964–1983*. Oxford: Oxford University Press.

—— (1985*b*). 'How the decline in class voting opened the way to radical change to British politics'. *British Journal of Political Science*. 14: 483–508.

—— Mackie, T., Valen H., *et al.* (1992). *Electoral Change: Responses to Evolving Social and Attitudinal Structures in Western Countries*. Cambridge: Cambridge University Press.

Frears, J. (1991). *Parties and Voters in France*. London: Hurst.

Frognier, A. P. (1975). 'Vote, classe sociale et religion/pratique religieuse'. *Res Publica*. 17: 479–90.

Fuchs, D., and Kühnel, S. (1994). 'Wählen als rationales Handeln. Anmerkungen zum Nutzen des Rational-Choice-Ansatzes in der empirischen Wahlforschung'. In *Wahlen und Wähler. Analysen aus Anlaß der Bundestagswahl 1990*, eds. H.-D. Klingemann and M. Kaase. Opladen: Westdeutscher Verlag. 305–64.

Furre, B. (1991). *Vårt hundreår: norsk historie 1905–1990*. Oslo: Samlaget.

Ganzeboom, H. B. G., Luijkx, R., and Treiman, D. J. (1989). 'Intergenerational class mobility in comparative perspective'. *Research in Social Stratification and Mobility*. 8: 3–84.

—— Treiman, D. J., and Ultee, W. C. (1991). 'Comparative intergenerational stratification research: three generations and beyond'. *Annual Review of Sociology*. 17: 277–302.

Gilljam, M., and Holmberg, S. (eds.) (1990). *Rött, blått, grönt. En bok om 1988 års riksdagsval.* Stockholm: Bonniers.

——— (1993). *Välyarna inför 90-talet*. Stockholm: Norstedts.

Glans, I. (1993). *Det stabila klassröstandet. Utvecklingen i Danmark och Sverige.* Aarhus: Department of Political Science.

Glenn, N. D. (1973). 'Class and party support in the United States: recent and emerging trends'. *Public Opinion Quarterly*. 37: 1–20.

Goldthorpe, J. H. (with Llewellyn, C. and Payne, C.) (1980). *Social Mobility and Class Structure in Britain*. Oxford: Clarendon Press.

——(1982). 'On the service class: its formation and future'. In *Social Class and the Division of Labour*, eds. A. Giddens and G. Mackenzie. Cambridge: Cambridge University Press. 162–85.

Goldthorpe, J. H. (with Llewellyn, C. and Payne, C.) (1987). *Social Mobility and Class Structure in Modern Britain* (2nd edn.). Oxford: Clarendon Press.

——(1995). 'The service class revisited'. In *Social Change and the Middle Classes*, eds. T. Butler and M. Savage. London: UCL Press. 313–29.

——(1996*a*). 'Class and politics in advanced industrial societies'. In *Conflicts about Class: Debating Inequality in Late Industrialism*, eds. D. J Lee and B. S. Turner. London: Longman.

——(1996*b*). 'The quantitative analysis of large-scale datasets and rational action theory: for a sociological alliance'. *European Sociological Review*. 12: 109–26.

——(1997). 'Social class and the differentiation of employment contracts'. Presented at the Conference on Rational Action Theories in Social Analysis: Applications and New Developments, Stockholm, 16–18 Oct.

——(1998). 'Rational Action Theory for Sociology'. *British Journal of Sociology*. 49: 167–92.

——and Heath, A. F. (1992). 'Revised class schema 1992'. *JUSST Working Paper 13.* Nuffield College and SCPR.

——and Hope, K. (1974). *The Social Grading of Occupations: A New Approach and Scale.* Oxford: Clarendon Press.

——Lockwood, D., Bechhoffer, F., and Platt, J. (1968). *The Affluent Worker: Political Attitudes and Behaviour.* Cambridge: Cambridge University Press.

————————(1969). *The Affluent Worker in the Class Structure*. Cambridge: Cambridge University Press.

——and Marshall, G. (1992). 'The promising future of class analysis: a response to recent critiques'. *Sociology*. 27: 381–400.

Goodman, L. A. (1975). 'The relationship between modified and usual multiple-regression approaches to the analysis of dichotomous variables'. In *Sociological Methodology 1976*, ed. D. R. Reise. San Francisco: Jossey-Bass. 83–110.

——(1987). 'New methods for analyzing the intrinsic character of qualitative variables using cross-classified data'. *American Journal of Sociology*. 93: 529–83.

——(1991). 'Measures, models and graphical displays in the analysis of cross-classified data'. *Journal of the American Statistical Association*. 86: 1085–111.

Gorz, A. (1982). *Farewell to the Working Class*, trans. M. Sonenscher. Boston: South End.

Grunberg, G., and Schweisguth, E. (1993). 'Social libertarianism and economic liberalism'. In *The French Voter Decides*, eds. D. Boy and N. Mayer, trans. C. Schoch. Ann Arbor: University of Michigan Press. 45–64.

Gunther, R., Sani G., and Shabad, G. (1986). *Spain after Franco: The Making of a Competitive Party System*. Berkeley: University of California Press.

Hadenius, A. (1986). *A Crisis of the Welfare State?* Stockholm: Almqvist and Wiksell International.

Halle, D. (1984). *America's Working Man: Work, Home, and Politics Among Blue-collar Property Owners*. Chicago: University of Chicago Press.

Hancock, M. D. (1989). *West Germany: The Politics of Democratic Corporatism.* Chatham, NJ: Chatham House Publishers.

Harrop, M., and Miller, W. L. (1987). *Elections and Voters: A Comparative Introduction*. New York: New Amsterdam.

Hauser, R. M. (1978). 'A structural model for the mobility table'. *Social Forces*. 56: 919–53.

——(1979). 'Some exploratory methods for modelling mobility tables and other cross-classified data'. In *Sociological Methodology 1980*, ed. K. F. Schuessler. San Francisco: Jossey Bass.

Havelka, M. (1995). 'Recenzentovy pochybnosti o jedne tezi vyse uvedeneho clanku'. *Sociologicky Casopis*. 31: 240–2.

Hayes, B. (1995). 'The impact of class on political attitudes: a comparative study of Great Britain, West Germany, Australia and the United States'. *European Journal of Political Research*. 27: 69–91.

Heath, A. F. (1990). 'Class and political partisanship'. In *John H. Goldthorpe: Consensus and Controversy*, eds. J. Clark, C. Modgil, and S. Modgil. London: The Falmer Press. 161–70.

——Evans, G., and Martin, J. (1994). 'The measurement of core beliefs and values: the development of balanced socialist/laissez-faire and libertarian/authoritarian scales'. *British Journal of Political Science*. 24: 115–32.

————and Payne, C. (1995). 'Modelling the class party relationship in Britain: 1964–92'. *Journal of the Royal Statistical Society, series A*. 158: 563–74.

——Jowell, R., and Curtice, J. (1985). *How Britain Votes*. Oxford: Pergamon Press.

——————(1987). 'Trendless fluctuation: a reply to Crewe'. *Political Studies*. 35: 259–77.

——————(1994). *Labour's Last Chance? The 1992 Election*. Aldershot: Dartmouth.

——————Evans, G., Field, J., and Witherspoon, S. (1991). *Understanding Political Change: The British Voter, 1964–1987*. Oxford: Pergamon Press.

——and Savage, M. (1995). 'Political alignments within the middle classes, 1972–89'. In *Social Change and the Middle Classes*, eds. T. Butler and M. Savage. London: UCL Press. 275–92.

Hernes, H. M. (1987*a*). *Welfare State and Woman Power.* Oslo: Universitetsforlaget.

——(1987*b*). 'Women and the welfare state: the transition from private to public dependence'. In *Women and the State*, ed. A. Showstack Sassoon. London: Hutchinson.

Hildebrandt, K., and Dalton, R. J. (1977). 'Die neue politik'. *Politische Vierteljahresschrift*. 18: 230–56.

Hoel, M., and Knutsen, O. (1989). 'Social class, gender, and sector employment as political clevages in Scandinavia'. *Acta Sociologica*. 32: 181–201.

Holmberg, S. (1981). *Svenska väljare*. Stockholm: Liber.

——(1984). *Väljare i förändring.* Stockholm: Liber.

——(1991). 'Voters on the Loose: Trends in Swedish Voting Behavior'. Götebourg (unpublished paper).

——and Gilljam, M. (1987). *Väljare och val i Sverige*. Stockholm: Liber.

Hout, M. (1983). *Mobility Tables*. Beverly Hills, Calif.: Sage.

——Brooks, C., and Manza, J. (1993). 'The persistence of classes in post-industrial societies'. *International Sociology*. 8: 259–77.

Hout, M., Brooks, C., and Manza, J. (1995). 'The democratic class struggle in the United States'. *American Sociological Review*. 60: 805–28.

Huckfeldt, R., and Kohfeld, C. W. (1989). *Race and the Decline of Class in American Politics*. Champaign, Ill.: University of Illinois Press.

ILO (International Labour Office) (1969). *International Standard Classification of Occupations* (rev. edn.). Geneva: International Labour Office.

——(1994). *Yearbook of Labour Statistics* (53rd edn.). Geneva: International Labour Office.

Inglehart, R. (1971). 'The silent revolution in Europe'. *American Political Science Review*. 65: 991–1017.

——(1977). *The Silent Revolution: Changing Values and Political Styles among Western Publics*. Princeton: Princeton University Press.

——(1979). 'Wertewandel in den westlichen Gesellschaften. Politische Konsequenzen von materialistischen und postmaterialistischen Prioritäten'. In *Wertewandel und gesellschaftlicher Wandel*, eds. H. Klages and P. Kmieciak. Frankfurt: Campus. 279–316.

——(1984). 'The changing structure of political cleavages in western society'. In *Electoral Change in Industrial Democracies: Realignment or Dealignment?* eds. D. J. Dalton, S. C. Flanagan, and P. A. Beck. Princeton: Princeton University Press.

——(1990). *Culture Shift in Advanced Industrial Society.* Princeton: Princeton University Press.

——(1997). *Modernization and Postmodernization: Cultural, Economic, and Political Change in 43 Societies.* Princeton: Princeton University Press.

——and Rabier, J.-R. (1986). 'Political realignment in advanced industrial society: from class-based politics to quality-of-life politics'. *Government & Opposition*. 21: 457–79.

Jagodzinski, W., and Quandt, M. (1997). *Wahlverhalten und Religion im Lichte der Individualisierungsthese.* Anmerkrungen zu dem Beitrag von Schnell und Kohler.

Janos, A. C. (1994). 'Continuity and change in eastern Europe: strategies of post-communist politics'. *East European Politics and Societies*. 8: 1–31.

Johansson, S. (1994). 'Ommöblering i folkhemmet. Nytt vin i gamla läglar?' In *När gränserna flyter. En nordisk antologi om värd och omsorg*, ed. Leila Simonen. Helsingfors: Stakes.

Joppke, C. (1987). 'The crisis of the welfare state, collective consumption and the rise of new social actors'. *Berkeley Journal of Sociology*. 32: 237–60.

Kangas, O. (1991). *The Politics of Social Rights*. Stockholm: University of Stockholm.

Kelley, J., and McAllister, I. (1985). 'Class and party in Australia: comparison with Britain and the USA'. *British Journal of Sociology*. 36: 383–420.

————and Mughan, A. (1985). 'The decline of class revisited: class and party in England, 1964–79'. *American Political Science Review*. 79: 719–37.

Kemeny, J. (1981). *The Myth of Home Ownership.* London: Routledge and Kegan Paul.

Kemp, D. A. (1978). *Society and Electoral Behaviour in Australia: A Study of Three Decades.* Brisbane: University of Queensland Press.

Kerr, H. H. (1987). 'The Swiss party system: steadfast and changing'. In *Party*

*Systems in Denmark, Austria, Switzerland, the Netherlands, and Belgium*, ed. H. Daalder. London: Frances Pinter. 107–92.

Kiberg, D., and Strømsnes, K. (1992). *De norske valgundersøkelsene 1977, 1981, 1985 og 1989. Dokumentasjon. Frekvenser.* Bergen: NSD.

King, G. (1986). 'How not to lie with statistics: avoiding common mistakes in quantitative political science'. *American Journal of Political Science*. 30: 666–87.

Kis, J. (1994). 'Liberalism, democracy, and Hungarian politics'. An interview for *The Bulletin of the East and Central Europe Program of the New School for Social Research*, Dec. 1994.

Kitschelt, H. (1992). 'The formation of party systems in east central Europe'. *Politics and Society*. 20: 7–50.

——(1994). *The Transformation of European Social Democracy*. Cambridge: Cambridge University Press.

——(in collaboration with Anthony J. McGann) (1995). *The Radical Right in Western Europe: A Comparative Analysis*. Ann Arbor: Michigan University Press.

Klingemann, H.-D. (1979). 'The background of ideological conceptualization'. In Barnes and Kaase (1979). 255–78.

——(1984). 'Soziale Lagerung, Schichtbewußtsein und politisches Verhalten. Die Arbeiterschaft der Bundesrepublik im historischen und internationalen Vergleich'. In *Das Ende der Arbeiterbewegung in Deutschland? Ein Diskussionsband zum sechzigsten Geburtstag von Theo Pirker*, eds. R. Ebbighausen and F. Tiemann. Opladen: Westdeutscher Verlag. 593–621.

Kluegel, J. R., and Mateju, P. (1995). 'Principles of distributive justice in comparative perspective'. In *Social Justice and Political Change: Public Opinion in Capitalist and Post-Communist States*, eds. J. R. Kluegel, D. S. Mason, and B. Wegener. Hawthorne, NY: Walter de Gruyter.

——and Smith, E. R. (1986). *Beliefs about Inequality*. Hawthorne, NY: Aldine de Gruyter.

Knoke, D. (1973). 'Intergenerational occupational mobility and the political party preferences of American men'. *American Journal of Sociology*. 78: 1448–68.

Knutsen, O. (1995). 'Party choice'. In *The Impact of Values: Beliefs in Government*, iv, eds. J. W. Van Deth and E. Scarbrough. Oxford: Oxford University Press. 461–91.

——and Scarbrough, E. (1995). 'Cleavage politics'. In *The Impact of Values. Beliefs in Government*, iv, eds. J. W. Van Deth and E. Scarbrough. Oxford: Oxford University Press. 492–524.

Kolberg, J. E., and Pettersen, P. A. (1981). 'Om velferdsstatens politiske basis'. *Tidsskrift for samfunnsforskning*. 22: 193–222.

Korpi, W. (1972). 'Some problems in the measurement of class voting'. *American Journal of Sociology*. 78: 627–42.

——(1983). *The Democratic Class Struggle*. London: Routledge and Kegan Paul.

Kriesi, H. (1989). 'New social movements and the new class in the Netherlands'. *American Journal of Sociology*. 94: 1078–16.

——Koopmans, R., Duyvendak, J. W., and Giugni, M. G. (1995). *New Social Movements in Western Europe.* Minneapolis: Minnesota University Press.

Kühnel, S., and Terwey, M. (1990). 'Einflüsse sozialer Konfliktlinien auf das

Wahlverhalten im gegenwärtigen Vierparteiensystem der Bundesrepublik'. In *Blickpunkt Gesellschaft*, eds. W. Müller, P. Mohler, B. Erbslöh, and M. Wasmer. Opladen: Westdeutscher Verlag. 63–94.

Kurz, K., and Muller, W. (1987). 'Class mobility in the industrial world'. *Annual Review of Sociology*. 13: 417–42.

Ladd, E. C., Jr., and Lipset, S. M. (1975). *The Divided Academy*. New York: McGraw-Hill.

Lafferty, W. (1988). 'Offentlig-sektorklassen'. In *Offentlig eller privat?* eds. H. Bogen and O. Lageland. Oslo: FAFO.

Lancelot, A., and Lancelot, M.-T. (1983). *Annuaire de la France Politique, 1981–83*. Paris: Presses de la Fondation Nationale des Sciences Politiques.

Lane, J.-E., and Ersson, S. O. (1994). *Politics and Society in Western Europe* (3rd edn.). London: Sage.

Lash, S., and Urry, J. (1987). *The End of Organized Capitalism*. Madison: University of Wisconsin Press.

Laver, M., Mair, P., and Sinnott, R. (1987). *How Ireland Voted: The Irish General Election, 1987*. Dublin: Poolbeg.

Leipart, J., and Sande, T. (1981). *Valgundersøkelsen 1957. NSD rapporter no 47.* Bergen: NSD.

Lenski, G. (1970). *Human Societies: A Macrolevel Introduction to Sociology*. New York: McGraw-Hill.

——Lenski J., and Nolan, P. (1991). *Human Societies: An Introduction to Macrosociology* (6th edn.). New York: McGraw-Hill.

Lepsius, M. R. (1973). 'Wahlverhalten, Parteien und politische Spannungen'. *Politische Vierteljahresschrift.* 14: 295–313.

Levy, F. (1995). 'Incomes and income inequality'. In *State of the Union: America in the 1990's, Volume One: Economic Trends*, ed. R. Farley. New York: Russell Sage Foundation. 1–57.

Lewis-Beck, M. S. (1984). 'France: the stalled electorate'. In *Electoral Change in Advanced Industrial Democracies*, eds. R. J. Dalton, S. C. Flanagan, and P. A. Beck. Princeton: Princeton University Press. 425–48.

Lieberson, S. (1985). *Making it Count: The Improvement of Social Research and Theory.* Berkeley: University of California Press.

Lijphart, A. (1968). *The Politics of Accomodation*. Berkeley: University of California Press.

——(1971). 'Class voting and religious voting in the European democracies: a preliminary report'. *Acta Politica.* 6: 158–71.

——(1984). *Democracies: Patterns of Majoritarian and Consensus Government in Twenty-One Countries*. New Haven: Yale University Press.

Lipset, S. M. (1960). *Political Man: The Social Bases of Politics*. London: Heinemann.

——(1971). *Agrarian Socialism* (rev. edn.; orig. edn. pub. 1950). Berkeley: University of California Press.

——(1981). *Political Man: The Social Bases of Politics* (expanded and updated edn.). London: Heinemann.

——and Rokkan, S. (1967). 'Cleavage structures, party systems and voter alignments: an introduction'. In *Party Systems and Voter Alignments: Cross National*

*Perspectives*, eds. S. M. Lipset and S. Rokkan. New York: The Free Press. 1–64.

——and Schneider, W. S. (1983). *The Confidence Gap: Business, Labor, and Government in the Public Mind*. New York: Free Press.

——and Zetterberg, H. (1956). 'A theory of social mobility'. *Transactions of the Third World Congress of Sociology.* 3: 155–77.

Listhaug, O. (1989). *Citizens, Parties and Norwegian Electoral Politics 1957–1985: An Empirical Study*. Trondheim: Tapir.

——(1993). 'The decline of class voting'. In *Challenges to Political Parties: The Case of Norway*, eds. K. Strøm and L. G. Svåsand. Ann Arbor: University of Michigan Press.

——Miller, A. H., and Valen, H. (1985): 'The gender gap in Norwegian voting behaviour'. *Scandinavian Political Studies.* 8: 187–206.

Lockwood, D. (1958). *The Blackcoated Worker*. London: Allen and Unwin.

McAllister, I., and Kelley, J. (1982). 'Class, ethnicity, and voting behaviour in Australia'. *Politics*. 17: 96–107.

Macdonald, K. I. (1981). 'On the formulation of a structural model of the mobility table'. *Social Forces.* 60: 557–71.

——(1994). 'What data can say: the case of denominational switching'. *Social Science Research.* 23: 197–218.

McFaul, M. (1996). 'Russia's 1996 presidential elections'. *Post-Soviet Affairs*. 12: 318–50.

——(1997). *Russia's 1996 Presidential Election: The End of Polarized Politics.* Stanford, Calif.: Hoover Institution Press.

McKenzie, R., and Silver, A. (1968). *Angels in Marble: Working Class Conservatives in Urban England.* Chicago: University of Chicago Press.

Mackie, T. T., and Rose, R. (1991). *The International Almanac of Electoral History* (fully rev. 3rd edn.). London: Macmillan.

MacRae, D. (1967). *Parliament, Parties, and Society in France, 1946–1958*. New York: St Martin's Press.

Maddala, G. S. (1983). *Limited Dependent and Qualitative Variables in Econometrics.* Cambridge: Cambridge University Press.

Mair, P. (1993). 'Explaining the absence of class politics in Ireland'. In *The Development of Industrial Society in Ireland*, eds. J. H. Goldthorpe and C. Whelan. Oxford: Clarendon Press.

Manza, J., Hout, M., and Brooks, C. (1995). 'Class voting in capitalist democracies since world war II: dealignment, realignment or trendless fluctuation?' *Annual Review of Sociology*. 21: 137–62.

Marsh, A. (1975). '"The silent revolution", value priorities, and the quality of life in Britain'. *American Political Science Review.* 69: 21–30.

Marshall, G. (1997). *Repositioning Class*, London: Macmillan.

——Newby, H., Rose, D., and Vogler, C. (1988). *Social Class in Modern Britain.* London: Hutchinson.

——Roberts, S., Burgoyne, Swift, A., and Routh, D. (1995). 'Class, gender, and the asymmetry hypothesis'. *European Sociological Review*. 11: 1–15.

Marshall, T. H. (1964). *Class, Citizenship and Social Development*. New York: Doubleday.

Marx, K. (1967/1894). *Capital*, iii, ed. F. Engels. 1st edn.: 1894. Rev. edn.: New York: International Publishers, 1967.

Mateju, P. (1993). 'From equality to equity? The Czech Republic between two ideologies of distributive justice'. *Czech Sociological Review*. 1: 251–76.

——(1996*a*). 'Subjective mobility and perception of life-chances in Eastern Europe'. *Czech Institute of Sociology, Working papers*. 1996: 5. Prague.

——(1996*b*). 'In search of explanations for recent left-turns in post-communist countries'. *International Review of Comparative Public Policy*. 7: 43–82.

——and Rehakova, B. (1993). 'Revolution for whom? Analysis of selected patterns of intragenerational mobility 1989–1992'. *Czech Sociological Review*. 1: 73–90.

——and Vlachova, K. (1995). 'Od rovnostarstvi k zasluhovosti. Ceska republika mezi dvema ideologiemi distributivni spravedlnosti'. *Sociologicky Casopis*. 31: 215–39.

————(1997). 'The crystallization of political attitudes and the political spectrum in the Czech Republic'. Presented at the Third Berlin Conference on Elections and Democratic Consolidation: East European Research Networks, Dec.

Matheson, D. K. (1979). *Ideology, Political Action and the Finnish Working Class: A Survey Study of Political Behaviour*. Helsinki: Societas Scientiarum Fennica.

Matheson, G. (1993). 'The Decommodified in a Commodified World'. Unpublished Ph.D. Thesis, University of New England, Armidale.

Mattel, G. S. (1977). *Econometrics*. New York: McGraw-Hill.

Mayer, K. (1956). 'Recent changes in the class structure of the United States'. *Transactions of the Third World Congress of Sociology*. 3: 66–80. Amsterdam: International Sociological Association.

Meltzer, A. H., and Richard, S. F. (1981). 'A rational theory of the size of government'. *Journal of Political Economy*. 89: 914–97.

Michelat, G. (1993). 'In search of left and right'. In *The French Voter Decides*, eds. D. Boy and N. Mayer, trans. C. Schoch. Ann Arbor: University of Michigan Press. 65–90.

Mitchell, B. R. (1992). *International Historical Statistics: Europe, 1750–1988* (3rd edn.). New York: Stockton Press.

——(1993). *International Historical Statistics: The Americas, 1750–1988* (2nd edn.). New York: Stockton Press.

Mooser, J. (1983). 'Auflösung proletarischer Milieus. Klassenbildung und Individualisierung in der Arbeiterschaft vom Kaiserreich bis in die Bundesrepublik Deutschland'. *Soziale Welt*. 34: 270–306.

Müller, W. (1977). 'Klassenlagen und soziale Lagen in der Bundesrepublik'. In *Klassenlagen und Sozialstruktur*, eds. J. Handl, K. U. Mayer, and W. Müller. Frankfurt/New York: *CAMPUS*. 21–100.

——(1993). 'Social structure, perception and evaluation of social inequality and party preferences'. In *New Directions in Attitude Measurement*, eds. D. Krebs and P. Schmidt. Berlin: de Gryter/Aldine. 94–117.

——(1997). 'Sozialstruktur und Wahlverhalten. Eine Widerrede gegen die Individualisierungsthese'. *Kölner Zeitschrift für Soziologie und Sozialpsychologie*. 49: 747–60.

Müller-Rommel, F. (1990). 'New political movements and new politics parties in

Western Europe'. In *Challenging the Political Order: New Social and Political Movements in Western Democracies*, eds. R. J. Dalton and M. Kuechler. Cambridge: Polity Press. 209–31.

——(1993). *Grüne Parteien in Westeuropa*. Opladen: Westdeutscher Verlag.

Need, A. (1997). *The Kindred Vote: Individual and Family Effects of Social Class and Religion on Electoral Change in the Netherlands, 1956–1994*. Amsterdam: Thesis Publishers.

Nieuwbeerta, P. (1995). *The Democratic Class Struggle in Twenty Countries, 1945–1990*. Amsterdam: Thesis Publishers.

——and Ganzeboom, H. B. G. (1996). *International Social Mobility and Politics File: Documentation of a Dataset of National Surveys held in Sixteen Countries, 1956–1990*. Amsterdam: Steinmetz Archive.

Nisbet, R. A. (1959). 'The decline and fall of social class'. *Pacific Sociological Review*. 1959: 11–17.

NORC (National Opinion Research Center) (1948). *Opinion News Supplement*.

Offe, C. (1987). 'Democracy against the welfare state? Structural foundations of neo-conservative political opportunities'. *Political Theory*. 15: 501–37.

——(1991). 'Capitalism by democratic design? Democratic theory facing the triple transition in east central Europe'. *Social Research*. 58: 865–92.

Pakulski, J. (1993). 'The dying of class or of Marxist class theory?' *International Sociology*. 8: 279–92.

——and Waters, M. (1996). *The Death of Class*. London: Sage.

Papadakis, E., and Taylor-Gooby, P. (1987). *The Private Provision of Public Welfare: State, Market and Community*. Brighton: Wheatsheaf books.

Pappi, F. U. (1973). 'Parteiensystem und Sozialstruktur in der Bundesrepublik'. *Politische Vierteljahresschrift*. 14: 191–213.

——(1977). 'Sozialstruktur, gesellschaftliche Wertorientierungen und Wahlabsicht'. *Politische Vierteljahresschrift*. 18: 195–229.

——(1979). 'Konstanz und Wandel der Hauptspannungslinien in der Bundesrepublik'. In *Sozialer Wandel in Westeuropa. Verhandlungen des 19. Deutschen Soziologentages*, ed. J. Matthes. Berlin: Campus. 465–79.

——(1985). 'Die konfessionell-religiöse Spannungslinie in der deutschen Wählerschaft: Entstehung, Stabilität, Wandel'. In *Wirtschaftlicher Wandel, religiöser Wandel und Wertwandel. Folgen für das politische Verhalten in der Bundesrepublik Deutschland*, eds. D. Oberndörfer, H. Rattinger, and K. Schmitt. Berlin: Duncker and Humblot. 263–90.

——(1986). 'Das Wahlverhalten sozialer Gruppen bei Bundestagswahlen im Zeitvergleich'. In *Wahlen und politischer Prozeß. Analysen aus Anlaß der Bundestagswahl 1983*, eds. H.-D. Klingemann and M. Kaase. Opladen: Westdeutscher Verlag. 369–84.

——(1990). 'Klassenstruktur und Wahlverhalten im sozialen Wandel'. In *Wahlen und Wähler. Analysen aus Anlaß der Bundestagswahl 1987*, eds. M. Kaase and H.-D. Klingemann. Opladen: Westdeutscher Verlag. 15–30.

——(1994). 'Parteienwettbewerb im vereinten Deutschland'. In *Das Superwahljahr. Deutschland vor unkalkulierbaren Regierungsmehrheiten?* eds. W. Bürklin and D. Roth. Cologne: Bund. 219–48.

——and Mnich, P. (1992). 'Federal Republic of Germany'. In Franklin *et al.* (1992). 179–204.

Parkin, F. (1971). *Class, Inequality and Political Order*. New York: Praeger.
Petersson, O. (1989). *Makt i det öppna samhället.* Stockholm: Carlssons.
Petrenko, V., Mitina, O., and Brown, R. (1995). 'The semantic space of Russian parties'. *Europe-Asia Studies.* 47: 835–58.
Piven, F. F. (1985). 'Women and the state: ideology, power, and the welfare state'. In *Gender and the Life Course*, ed. A. S. Rossi. New York: Aldine.
——(ed.) (1991). *Labor Parties in Post-Industrial Societies.* Cambridge: Polity Press.
——and Cloward, R. A. (1986). *Why Americans Don't Vote*. New York: Pantheon.
Poguntke, T. (1989). 'The "new politics" dimension in European green parties'. In *New Politics in Western Europe*, ed. F. Müller-Rommel. Boulder, Colo.: Westview, 175–94.
——(1993). *Alternative Politics: The German Green Party*. Edinburgh: Edinburgh University Press.
Prokop, U. (1976). *Weibliche Lebenszusammenhang*. Frankfurt: Suhrkamp.
Przeworski, A. (1985). *Capitalism and Social Democracy.* Cambridge: Cambridge University Press.
——and Sprague, J. (1986). *Paper Stones: A History of Electoral Socialism.* Chicago: University of Chicago Press.
Raftery, A. (1986). 'Choosing models for cross-classifications: comment on Grusky and Hauser'. *American Sociological Review.* 51: 145–6.
Raschke, J. (1993). *Die Grünen. Wie sie wurden, was sie sind.* Cologne: Bund.
——and Schmitt-Beck, R. (1994). 'Die Grünen. Stabilisierung nur durch den Niedergang der Etablierten?' In *Das Superwahljahr. Deutschland vor unkalkulierbaren Regierungsmehrheiten?* eds. W. Bürklin and D. Roth. Cologne: Bund, 160–84.
Rattinger, H. (1985). 'Politisches Verhalten von Arbeitslosen: Die Bundestagswahlen von 1980 und 1983 im Vergleich'. In *Wirtschaftlicher Wandel, religiöser Wandel und Wertewandel. Folgen für das politische Verhalten in der Bundesrepublik Deutschland*, eds. D. Oberndörfer, H. Rattinger, and K. Schmitt. Berlin: Duncker and Humblot. 97–130.
Rehakova, B. (1997). 'Prijmy a spravedlnost: Tolerance ceske verejnosti k prijmovym nerovnostem v roce 1992 a 1995'. *Sociologicky Casopis*. 33: 69–86.
——and Vlachova, K. (1995). 'Subjective mobility after 1989. Do people feel a social and economic improvement or relative deprivation?' *Czech Sociological Review*. 3: 137–56.
Ringdal, K., and Hines, K. (1995). 'Patterns in class voting in Norway 1957–1989: decline or "trendless fluctuations"?' *Acta Sociologica*. 38: 33–51.
Robertson, D. (1984). *Class and the British Electorate*. Oxford: Blackwell.
Rokkan, S. (1966). 'Numerical democracy and corporate pluralism'. In *Political Oppositions in Western Democracies*, ed. R. A. Dahl. New Haven: Yale University Press. 70–115.
Rose, R. (ed.) (1974*a*). *Electoral Behavior: A Comparative Handbook*. New York: Free Press.
——(1974*b*). 'Comparability in electoral studies'. In Rose (1974*a*). 3–25.
——(1980). *Electoral Participation: A Comparative Analysis*. Beverly Hills, Calif.: Sage.

——and McAllister, I. (1986). *Voters Begin to Choose: From Closed-Class to Open Elections in Britain*. London: Sage.

——Tikhomirov, E., and Mishler, W. (1997). 'Understanding multi-party choice: the 1995 Duma election'. *Europe-Asia Studies*. 49: 799–824.

——and Urwin, D. (1969). 'Social cohesion, political parties and strains in regimes'. *Comparative Political Studies*. 2: 7–67.

————(1970). 'Persistence and change in western party systems since 1945'. *Political Studies*. 18: 287–319.

Sainsbury, D. (1987). 'Class voting and left voting in Scandinavia: the impact of different operationalizations of the working class'. *European Journal of Political Research*. 15: 507–26.

——(1990). 'Party strategies and the electoral trade-off of class-based parties'. *European Journal of Political Research*. 18: 29–50.

Sakwa, R. (1996). *Russian Politics and Society* (2nd edn.). London: Routledge.

Sarlvik, B., and Crewe, I. (1983). *A Decade of Dealignment*. Cambridge: Cambridge University Press.

Sartori, G. (1969). 'From the sociology of politics to political sociology'. In *Politics and the Social Sciences*, ed. S. M. Lipset. Oxford: Oxford University Press. 65–100.

Saunders, P. (1986). *Social Theory and the Urban Question* (2nd edn.). London: Hutchinson.

——(1990). *A Nation of Home Owners*. London: Unwin Hyman.

Saunders, P. (1994). *Welfare and Inequality: National and International Perspectives on the Australian Welfare State*. Melbourne: Cambridge University Press.

Scarbrough, E. (1995). 'Materialist-postmaterialist value orientations'. In *The Impact of Values: Beliefs in Government*, iv, eds. J. W. Van Deth and E. Scarbrough. Oxford: Oxford University Press. 123–59.

SCB (1982). *Socio-ekonomisk indelning (SEI)*. Meddelanden i samordningsfrågor 1982: 4. Stockholm: Statistics Sweden.

Schlesinger, A. M., Jr. (1946). *The Age of Jackson*. Boston: Little, Brown.

Schmidt, M. G. (1989). 'Learning from catastrophes: West Germany's public policy'. In *The Comparative History of Public Policy*, ed. F. G. Castles. Cambridge: Polity Press.

Schmitt, K. (1985). 'Religiöse Bestimmungsfaktoren des Wahlverhaltens: Entkonfessionalisierung mit Verspätung?' In *Wirtschaftlicher Wandel, religiöser Wandel und Wertwandel. Folgen für das politische Verhalten in der Bundesrepublik Deutschland*, eds. D. Oberndörfer, H. Rattinger, and K. Schmitt. Berlin: Duncker and Humblot, 291–329.

——(1988). *Konfession und politisches Verhalten in der Bundesrepublik Deutschland*. Berlin: Dunker and Humblot.

Schmitt-Beck, R., and Schrott, P. R. (1994). 'Dealignment durch Massenmedien? Zur These der Abschwächung von Parteibindungen als Folge der Medienexpansion'. In *Wahlen und Wähler. Analysen aus Anlaß der Bundestagswahl 1990*, eds. H.-D. Klingemann and M. Kaase. Opladen: Westdeutscher Verlag. 543–72.

Schnell, R., and Kohler, U. (1995). 'Empirische Untersuchung einer Individualisierungshypothese am Beispiel der Parteipräferenz von 1953–1992'. *Kölner Zeitschrift für Soziologie und Sozialpsychologie*. 47: 635–57.

Schnell, R., and Kohler, U. (1997). 'Zur Erklärungskraft sozio-demographischer Variablen im Zeitverlauf. Entgegnung auf Walter Müller sowie auf Wolfgang Jagodzinski und Markus Quandt'. *Kölner Zeitschrift für Soziologie und Sozialpsychologie.* 49: 783–95.

Schultze, R.-O. (1991*a*). 'Wählerverhalten und Parteiensystem'. In *Wahlverhalten*, ed. H.-G. Wehling. Stuttgart: Kohlhammer. 11–43.

——(1991*b*). 'Bekannte Konturen im Westen—ungewisse Zukunft im Osten'. In *Wahlverhalten*, ed. H.-G. Wehling. Stuttgart: Kohlhammer. 44–102.

Siegfried, A. (1913). *Tableau politique de la France de l'ouest sous la Troisième République*. Paris: Colin.

Sombart, W. (1976/1906). *Why is there no Socialism in the United States?* 1st edn.: 1906. Rev. edn.: New York: M. E. Sharpe, 1976.

Sorokin, P. A. (1959/1927). *Social and Cultural Mobility*. 1st edn.: 1927. Rev. edn.: New York: Free Press, 1959.

SOU (1990). *Demokrati och makt i Sverige*: Sou 1990: 44. Stockholm: Allmänna förlaget.

Stanley, H. W., Bianco, W. T., and Niemi, R. G. (1986). 'Partisanship and group support over time: a multivariate analysis'. *American Political Science Review*. 80: 969–76.

Stephens, J. D (1979). *The Transition from Capitalism to Socialism*. London: Macmillan.

——(1981). 'The changing Swedish electorate: class voting, contextual effects, and voter volatility'. *Comparative Political Studies*. 14: 163–204.

Stjernø, S. (1995). *Mellom kirke og hapital*. Oslo: Scandinavian University Press.

Streeck, W. (1987). 'Vielfalt und Interdependenz. Überlegungen zur Rolle von intermediären Organisationen in sich ändernden Umwelten'. *Kölner Zeitschrift für Soziologie und Sozialpsychologie*. 39: 471–95.

Svalastoga, K. (1979/1959). *Prestige, Class, and Mobility*. 1st edn.: 1959. Rev. edn.: New York: Arno Press, 1979.

Svallfors, S. (1989). *Vem älskar välfärdsstaten? Attityder, organiserade intressen och svensk väfärdspolitik.* Lund: Arkiv.

——(1991). 'The politics of welfare policy in Sweden: structural determinants and attitudinal cleavages'. *British Journal of Sociology*. 42: 609–34.

——(1992). *Den stabila välfärdsopinionen. Attityder till svensk väfärdspolitik 1986–92*. Working paper, Department of Sociology, University of Umeå.

——(1993*a*). 'Policy regimes and attitudes to inequality: a comparison of three European nations'. In *Scandinavia in a New Europe*, eds. T. P. Boje and S. E. Olsson. Oslo: Scandinavian University Press.

——(1993*b*). 'Dimensions of inequality: a comparison of attitudes in Sweden and Britain'. *European Sociological Review*. 9: 267–87.

——(1993*c*). *Labourism vs. Social Democracy? Attitudes to Inequality in Australia and Sweden.* SPRC Reports and Proceedings no. 107, Social Policy Research Centre, University of New South Wales, Kensington.

——(1996). *Välfärdsstatens moraliska ekonomi.* Umeå: Borea.

Swaddle, K., and Heath, A. (1989). 'Official and reported turnout in the British General Election of 1987'. *British Journal of Political Science*. 19: 537–70.

Szelenyi, I., Fodor, E., and Hanley, E. (1997). 'Left turn in post-communist politics? Bringing class back in?' *East European Politics and Society*. 11: 190–224.

Szelenyi, S., Szelenyi, I., and Poster, W. R. (1996). 'Interests and symbols in post-communist political culture: the case of Hungary'. *American Sociological Review*. 61: 466–77.

Sztompka, P. (1992). 'Dilemmas of the great transition'. *Sisyphus.* 8: 9–27.

Taylor-Gooby, P. (1991). 'Welfare state regimes and welfare citizenship'. *Journal of European Social Policy*. 1: 93–105.

Thomsen, S. R. (1987). *Danish Elections 1920–79: A Logit Approach to Ecological Analysis and Inference*. Aarhus: Politica.

Timoshenko, T. I. (1995). 'Rossiyskie partii, dvizheniya i bloki na vyborakh v gosudarstvenniyo dumu 17 dekabrya 1995: opyt, problemy, perspektivy'. *Vestnik MGU (Seriya 12), Politicheskie Nauki*. 22–30.

Tingsten, H. (1937). *Political Behavior: Studies in Election Statistics*. London: King and Son.

Ultee, W. (1993). 'Jusqu'aux troisième et quatrième générations: Questions et techniques nouvelles dans les recherches en stratification et mobilité sociales'. *Recherches Sociologiques*. 3: 5–22.

United Nations Statistical Division (1992). *Statistical Yearbook* (39th edn.). New York: United Nations.

Valen, H. (1981). *Valg og Politikk*. Oslo: NKS-forlaget.

——(1992). 'Norway'. In Franklin *et al.* (1992).

——and Aardal, B. (1983). *Et valg i perspektiv. En studie av stortingsvalget 1981*. Oslo: Statistisk Sentralbyrå.

————and Vogt, G. (1990). *Endring og kontinuitet. Stortingsvalget 1989*. Oslo: Statistics Norway.

——and Katz, D. (1967). *Political Parties in Norway*. Oslo: Universitetsforlaget.

Van der Eijk, C., Franklin, M., Mackie, T., and Valen, H. (1992). 'Cleavages, conflict resolution and democracy'. In Franklin *et al.* (1992).

Van Deth, J. W. (1995). 'Introduction: the impact of values'. In *The Impact of Values: Beliefs in Government*, iv, eds. J. W. Van Deth and E. Scarbrough. Oxford: Oxford University Press. 1–18.

Vanneman, R., and Cannon, L. W. (1987). *The American Perception of Class*. Philadelphia: Temple University Press.

Vecernik, J. (1996). *Markets and People: The Czech Reform Experience in a Comparative Perspective*. Avebury: Aldershot.

Veen, H.-J. (1984). 'Wer wählt Grün?' *Aus Politik und Zeitgeschichte.* B35–36. 3–17.

Verba, S., and Nie, N. (1972). *Participation in America*. New York: Harper and Row.

————and Kim, J. (1978). *Participation and Political Equity.* Cambridge: Cambridge University Press.

Vite, O. T. (1994). 'Tsentrizm v rossiyskoy politike (rasstonovka sil v gosudarstvennoy dume i vne ee)'. *Polis.* 1994: 29–36.

Von Beyme, K. (1985). *Political Parties in Western Democracies*. New York: St Martin's Press.

Waerness, K. (1987). 'On the rationality of caring'. In *Women and the State*, ed. A Showstack Sassoon. London: Hutchinson.

Weakliem, D. L. (1989). 'Class and party in Britain, 1964–1983'. *Sociology*. 23: 285–97.

——(1991). 'The two lefts? Occupation and party choice in France, Italy, and the Netherlands'. *American Journal of Sociology*. 96: 1327–61.

——(1995*a*). 'Two models of class voting'. *British Journal of Political Science*. 25: 254–70.

——(1999). 'A critique of the Bayesian information criterion for model selection'. *Sociological Methods and Research* 27: 359–97.

——and Heath, A. F. (1994). 'Rational choice and class voting'. *Rationality and Society*. 6: 243–70.

————(1995). 'Regional differences in class dealignment'. *Political Geography*. 14: 643–51.

Weßels, B. (1994). 'Gruppenbindung und rationale Faktoren als Determinanten der Wahlentscheidung in Ost- und Westdeutschland'. In *Wahlen und Wähler. Analysen aus Anlaß der Bundestagswahl 1990*, eds. H.-D. Klingemann and M. Kaase. Opladen: Westdeutscher Verlag. 123–57.

White, S., Rose, R., and McAllister, I. (1997*a*). *How Russia Votes.* Chatham, NJ: Chatham House.

——Wyman, M., and Oates, S. (1997*b*), 'Parties and voters in the 1995 Russian Duma election'. *Europe-Asia Studies*. 49: 767–98.

Whitefield, S., and Evans, G. (1994*a*). 'The Russian election of 1993: public opinion and the transition experience'. *Post-Soviet Affairs*. 10: 38–60.

————(1994*b*). 'The ideological bases of political competition in Eastern Europe'. Presented at the 90th annual APSA meeting, New York, Sept.

————(1996). 'Support for democracy and political opposition in Russia, 1993–95'. *Post-Soviet Affairs.* 12: 218–42.

————(1998*b*). 'The emerging structure of partisan divisions in Russian politics'. In *Elections and Voters in Post-Communist Russia*, eds. M. Wyman, S. White, and S. Oates. Cheltenham: Edward Elgar.

————(1999). 'Class, markets and partisanship in post-soviet Russia: 1993–96'. *Electoral Studies*. 18: 155–78.

Whitten, G. D., and Palmer, H. D. (1996). 'Heightening comparativists' concern for model choice: voting behaviour in Great Britain and the Netherlands'. *American Journal of Political Science*. 40: 231–60.

Wnuk-Lipinski, E. (1993). *Left Turn in Poland: A Sociological and Political Analysis.* Warsaw: Institute of Political Studies, Polish Academy of Sciences.

Wolfinger, R. E., and Rosenstone, S. J. (1980). *Who Votes?* New Haven: Yale University Press.

Wright, E. O. (1985). *Classes*. London: Verso.

Wyman, M., White, S., Miller, W. L., and Heywood, P. (1995). 'Public opinion, parties and voters in the December 1993 Russian elections'. *Europe-Asia Studies*. 47: 195–228.

Xie, Y. (1992). 'The log-multiplicative layer effect model for comparing mobility tables'. *American Sociological Review*. 57: 380–95.

Zetterberg, H. (1985). *An Electorate in the Grip of the Welfare State.* Stockholm: Swedish Institute for Opinion Polls.

# INDEX